International Cooperation on Nonproliferation Export Controls

International Cooperation on Nonproliferation Export Controls

Prospects for the 1990s and Beyond

Edited by
Gary K. Bertsch,
Richard T. Cupitt, and
Steven Elliott-Gower

Ann Arbor
THE UNIVERSITY OF MICHIGAN PRESS

Published in the United States of America by
The University of Michigan Press
Manufactured in the United States of America
♾ Printed on acid-free paper
1997 1996 1995 1994 4 3 2 1

A CIP catalogue record for this book is available from the British Library.

Library of Congress Cataloging-in-Publication Data

International cooperation on nonproliferation export controls : prospects for the 1990s and beyond / edited by Gary K. Bertsch, Richard T. Cupitt, and Steven Elliott–Gower.
p. cm.
Includes bibliographical references and index.
ISBN 0-472-10515-9 (alk. paper)
1. Nuclear nonproliferation. 2. Export controls. 3. International cooperation. I. Bertsch, Gary K. II. Cupitt, Richard T. III. Elliott-Gower, Steven.
JX1974.73.I584 1994
327.1′74—dc20 94-4256
CIP

The University of Georgia's Center for East-West Trade Policy conducts policy-relevant research on weapons-related trade and technology transfer. Its research, teaching, and service programs are supported by The University of Georgia and generous grants from the W. Alton Jones Foundation, the Robert Bosch Foundation, the Carnegie Corporation, the Ford Foundation, the German Marshall Fund of the United States, the Japan Foundation Center for Global Partnership, the Japan-U.S. Friendship Commission, the John Merck Fund, the Ploughshares Fund, the U.S. Department of Education, and the U.S. Department of Energy. The research that resulted in this book was supported by a grant from the Pew Charitable Trusts

Foreword

Martin J. Hillenbrand

Given the rapid flow of events in our time, books that deal with the analysis and solution of current problems run the risk of being dated before they appear. It is one of the merits of this collection of papers that it remains both pertinent and timely. Even after the dramatic recent changes in Eastern Europe and the former Soviet Union began to take place, few if any thought that only a few years later a major problem would be the ability of the new regimes that came into existence to establish functioning and effective export control systems.

Under the new circumstances of today, the possibility of the proliferation of nuclear and other weapons of mass destruction has become a primary concern of governments. The political declaration issued at the seven-power Economic Summit conference held July 6–7, 1992, in Munich contained, inter alia, the following language: "The end of the East-West confrontation provides a historical opportunity but also underlines the urgent need to curb the proliferation of nuclear weapons, other weapons of mass-destruction and missiles capable of delivering them."

In the past the industrialized countries of the West and Japan, united in the Coordinating Committee for Multilateral Export Controls (COCOM), withheld the shipment of many items to the countries of the former Soviet bloc on direct security grounds. They still do so now, not because the potential recipients constitute a military threat any longer but because they seemingly lack the ability to prevent the onward flow through them of proscribed items to third countries—run by so-called rogue regimes—that we do not want to see augmenting their military strength. That is particularly the case with components and technology that would enable them to develop a nuclear, chemical, or bacteriological warfare capability. The recent experience with Iraq has underlined the importance of this objective. In other words, the problem is no longer essentially related to the former East-West confrontation but has taken a North-South focus with the East, however, still very much involved, in the absence of effective export controls, as a possible source of proscribed weaponry.

Whatever one may think about the future role of COCOM—and there have admittedly been differences of view on the subject between Europeans and Americans—the organization long met a need and along with its member governments, accumulated a wealth of experience on which new and developing export control systems can draw.

How to transmit existing know-how about export control systems in the most effective manner has been a major concern of the Center for East-West Trade Policy at the University of Georgia. The center cosponsored a conference in Rynia, Poland, on September 4–5, 1992, that was attended by export control officials from East-Central Europe, including Poland, Hungary, the then Czech and Slovak Federal Republic (CSFR), Romania, and Bulgaria, along with representatives from Russia, Belarus, Lithuania, and Latvia. The conference made a useful contribution to the process of creating essential communication networks between such officials and provided a forum for the exchange of information and views. Looking ahead, the participants largely agreed that the standardization of controls across various nonproliferation regimes was desirable and likely and that their respective export control systems should prepare for that eventuality as well as adjust to policies developed by the European Community (EC) (which most hope to join). Participants discussed a number of possible courses of action to assist in this process.

Other recent developments have underlined the urgency of the problem. The emergence of what can only be described as an arms bazaar in Russia and some of the other newly independent former Soviet republics is an undeniable reality. Partly to placate the still powerful group of managers of major industrial plants providing military equipment and partly to obtain desperately needed hard currencies, most leaders of these new states have, in effect, given a green light to the maximization of arms exports. Needless to say, the example of the United States has not been helpful in this context. While the encouragement of arms exports from territories of the former Soviet Union does not apply to nuclear, chemical, or bacteriological weapons, the danger of some of these also escaping into the world black market in arms in the absence of an effective export control system is obvious.

The chapters included in this book provide both the historical background and analysis of current problems and future requirements necessary to an understanding of where we are, how we got there, and where we need to go if effective multilateral cooperation on nonproliferation export controls is to be achieved. They will contribute, we believe, to the onward process of research and discussion urgently necessary at this stage if the world is not to pass the point of no return in the proliferation of weapons of mass destruction. The ultimate outcome, as the seven heads of government recognized, will certainly determine the measure of security and stability with which the world will enter the twenty-first century.

Contents

Part 1: Introduction

Chapter

1. Introduction
Richard T. Cupitt, Gary K. Bertsch, and
Steven Elliott-Gower 3

2. Multilateral Export Control Organizations
Gary K. Bertsch, Richard T. Cupitt, and
Steven Elliott-Gower 33

Part 2: National Perspectives

3. Global Security, Democratization, and Economic
Development after the Cold War: New Goals for U.S.
Export Control Policies
William J. Long 59

4. Export Controls: The Perspective of the Czech and
Slovak Federal Republic
Richard T. Cupitt 87

5. Export Controls in the 1990s: A Polish Perspective
Andrzej Rudka 103

6. Making the Transition: A Bulgarian Perspective on
Export Controls in the 1990s and Beyond
Atanas Gotchev 129

7. The Evolution of Export Control Systems in the
Soviet Union and Russia
Elina Kirichenko 163

8. German Perspectives on Export Control Policy
Claus Hofhansel 179

9. French Export Control Policy
Marie-Hélène Labbé 201

10. The Technological Imperative: A Brazilian Perspective on Dual-Use Technologies
Clifford P. Graham 221

11. South Korea's Export Control Policy
Han S. Park 247

12. Export Controls and Proliferation: An Indian Perspective
S. Chandrashekar 261

Part 3: Conclusion

13. Synthesis and Implications: Export Controls for the 1990s and Beyond
Richard T. Cupitt 297

Contributors 319

Index 323

Part 1
Introduction

CHAPTER 1

Introduction

Richard T. Cupitt, Gary K. Bertsch, and Steven Elliott-Gower

Premise of the Study

Many policymakers, business leaders, and scholars agree that current multilateral arrangements to control the diffusion of dual-use and military technologies cannot meet the challenges of the 1990s (Bertsch, Vogel, and Zielonka 1991; Bertsch and Elliott-Gower 1992; European Round Table 1990; Heinz 1991; National Academy of Sciences 1991). Recent events in the former Soviet bloc and the Persian Gulf help illustrate an extensive list of problems that make existing export control policies ineffective and inefficient.

For example, the states of Eastern Europe were among the primary targets of Western export controls throughout the Cold War. Suddenly, as communist governments across Eastern Europe and the former Soviet Union succumbed to democratic political forces, existing Western export controls on many items, such as computers and telecommunications equipment widely available in the West, became out of date and had to be reconsidered. Western governments soon sought ways to increase support for the newly formed noncommunist governments and to promote economic growth, democracy, and stability in the region as a whole. In 1990, Western governments deleted or relaxed export controls on 55 out of 116 items on the list of dual-use industrial items maintained by COCOM ("COCOM Analysis" 1990).[1] They also agreed to treat export license requests for Poland, Hungary, and the CSFR more favorably. Negotiations to revamp the conceptual basis of the Industrial List, using a "fewer goods, higher fences" approach to create a core list, made rapid progress.[2]

Despite these changes, some problems remained. For example, decision making in COCOM in 1990–91 still focused on the impact of West to East transfers on Soviet military capabilities. Such a rationale could not easily accommodate Western interests in increasing the transfer of certain technologies, namely telecommunications systems, to some countries in Eastern

Europe (i.e., Poland, Hungary, and the CSFR) to promote democracy and economic reform, while restricting transfers or reexports to other countries, especially the former Soviet Union. Although democracy and economic reform in both Eastern Europe and the former Soviet Union directly affect Western security interests in the region, 1994 COCOM controls and decision-making rationales remain ill-suited to effectively and efficiently serve these interests.

Western political and economic interests will not be well served if delaying the transfer of controlled industrial items handicaps democratic and economic reform in Eastern Europe and the successor states of the former Soviet Union. For example, controls on telecommunication exports can slow the creation of modern banking and financial systems in the region. Retarding this activity will jeopardize the success of economic reform, which may weaken support for democratic governing coalitions. Nonetheless, calls for reform during this period, such as that of the National Academy of Sciences (1991) for a more comprehensive shift in COCOM to a more liberal "approval regime" relying on end-use safeguards rather than the traditional "denial regime," did indicate how one might better integrate, for example, the promotion of East European economic reform and democracy into the COCOM decision-making process. This problem and others led to the effort to create the COCOM Cooperation Forum (CCF) to discuss East-West cooperation on export controls in a broader fashion.

In contrast to the example of Eastern Europe, both the East and the West strove to enhance Iraqi military capabilities by supplying advanced weaponry and dual-use items through most of the 1980s.[3] This practice gave Iraq the capacity to apply significant force to regional issues, increasingly militarizing their disputes. In addition to basic violations of existing export controls, some transactions, though subject to controls, had the approval of Western governments (e.g., French Exocet missiles); some took place before the creation of a multilateral control system (e.g., German shipments of chemical precursors); some took place outside of existing export controls (e.g., biotechnology); and some simply bypassed Western controls altogether (e.g., Soviet Scuds).

Nevertheless, the transformation of Eastern Europe and the victory of the UN coalition in the Gulf War demonstrated the potential for more extensive multilateral cooperation. In Eastern Europe, the governments of Poland, Hungary, and the CSFR now work with Western governments to monitor the end use of controlled exports in their countries, and even some of the newly independent Commonwealth states have expressed an interest in making similar verification arrangements. In the Gulf, the UN coalition cut across traditional political alignments, and the support for trade sanctions against Iraq was unprecedented.[4] Furthermore, there was the potential of relaxed

COCOM controls being used to induce greater East-West cooperation on North-South proliferation issues (Elliott-Gower 1991, 222).

Are these efforts ephemeral, or can they lead to sustainable new forms of international cooperation? Is the global diffusion of military and dual-use technologies too strong a tide to be turned back? Is there a real opportunity to reshape multilateral export control arrangements to promote democracy, economic prosperity, and military security at this time, and if so, how long will the opportunity last? These and related questions now face policymakers of every country.

In this book, we propose to explore what multilateral export control arrangements in the 1990s are possible, probable, and preferred. More importantly, we ask if, how, and for whom multilateral export control arrangements can be designed to promote democracy, economic prosperity, and military security.

Our interest in efficient and effective systems that promote these three values rests on three foundations. First, these are universal values, in word if not in deed. Most governments explicitly express support for these values, and they reflect the basic triad of national interests for any state (Pearson and Rochester 1988, 148–50; Russett and Starr 1989, 190–93). Second, these values are linked to and affected by export controls (Auerbach 1990; Heinz 1991). Finally, these values are both complementary and conflictual, so real disagreement exists on if and what value trade-offs are necessary.

To explore these questions, we begin with a brief examination of three theoretical perspectives on the possibility of multilateral cooperation. From these, we develop a framework to direct the investigation of the policy-making environment, to assess the prospects for multilateral export control arrangements in the 1990s and to determine whether these arrangements can champion the cause of democracy, economic growth, and military security worldwide.

Multilateral Export Controls: Theoretical Perspectives

Broadly stated, Western theoretical literature on international relations outlines three major perspectives on the possibility of international cooperation, from which one might forecast the likely future of multilateral export control arrangements. Each perspective presents a very different view on the possibility of international cooperation, and each generates contradictory policy recommendations.

One perspective, which relies on insights from realism and neorealism, indicates that multilateral cooperation only occurs to counterbalance a perceived threat or an aggressor, as one saw in the Gulf War and the Cold War (Grieco 1988; Kaplan 1976; Morgenthau 1978). Such cooperation tends to be short lived, since long-term national interests are characterized as divergent and conflictual. On the infrequent occasions when institutionalized forms of multilateral cooperation emerge (e.g., COCOM), states use those arrangements to enhance their share of the benefits of cooperation relative to the shares of others, inside and outside of the institution.

Long-term multilateral cooperation eventually miscarries for three reasons: the dispute disappears, cooperation proves ineffective in thwarting the perceived threat, or disputes arise within the coalition over the appropriate distribution of benefits. From this realist perspective, long-term multilateral efforts to control the export of dual-use or military items will fail because governments will not be able to stop the diffusion of technology or because national governments will attempt to use export control arrangements to reap some advantage relative to the other partners in the arrangements and thereby abort cooperation.

A second, rational-functional theoretical perspective implies that long-term multilateral cooperative arrangements are not only possible but often preferred (Conybeare 1987; Keohane 1984; Oye 1986; Snidal 1985a and 1985b). Their durability and success depend on the degree to which cooperation maximizes the participants' benefit-cost ratio. Successful multilateral arrangements maximize this ratio by reducing uncertainty and the transaction costs attendant with international cooperation, as well as by permitting the exploitation of economies of scale (Conybeare 1987; Keohane 1984).

In this perspective, no single policy prescription is always appropriate since different combinations of national preferences require different forms of multilateral action to maximize net benefits (Conybeare 1987; Stein 1982).

The rational-functional perspective implies that the success of multilateral export control arrangements depends on the particular alignment of the various national sets of policy preferences for the issue. For any one government, its set of policy preferences depends on its goals, the perceived alternatives, and its assessment of the costs and benefits attached to each alternative. For any set of states, the potential for cooperation depends on how the policy preferences of these states match. Most importantly, the rational-functional perspective insists that these preferences often lead to long-term cooperative multilateral arrangements. In rational-functional analysis, game theoretic models are often used to describe sets of policy preference and explain policy choices, relying primarily on 2×2 game forms, where there are two players, each with the option of acting cooperatively or noncooperatively. Rational strategies for each player can be devised based on the payoff from each outcome.

Most research focuses on games in which cooperation is neither automatic nor lacking a stable, long-term cooperative outcome (Oye 1986). Instead, research on international cooperation emphasizes lessons drawn from an analysis of repeated plays of two other classes of games: games in which players face dilemmas of common interest and games in which the players face dilemmas of common aversion (Snidal 1985a; Stein 1990 and 1982).

Two prominent lessons emerge from the analysis of these classes of games. First, players with different interests may cooperate by using strategic rationality, whereby the "pursuit of egoistic interest requires consideration of interactions of one state's choices with other states' choices" (Snidal 1985b, 39). Second, the two classes of games require different responses to promote cooperation. For example, in common interest games, such as Prisoner's Dilemma, strategies of conditional reciprocity, including variations of Tit-for-Tat, are believed to be crucial in achieving cooperative outcomes.[5] Indeed, Axelrod (1984) indicates that a collective norm to punish players who do not enforce basic norms (a metanorm) like conditional reciprocity is a valuable means of creating and maintaining basic agreements.

However, strategies of conditional reciprocity can inhibit rather than enhance cooperation in common aversion games. Common aversion games have more than one cooperative outcome, and when the players are not indifferent to the distinct cooperative outcomes, they must agree on which outcome is fair as well as a fair way of choosing. In this game, when incentives for cheating are low, like in a common aversion game, sanctions can be redundant or counterproductive (Yarbrough and Yarbrough 1986). Under these conditions, conditional reciprocity, much less a punishment metanorm, will simply increase the losses for all players while exacerbating frictions among players who are essentially cooperative.

According to rational functionalism, creating and maintaining durable multilateral export control arrangements becomes a matter of examining the global pattern of national preferences within each separate issue area relating to export controls (though sometimes the policy response will link different issues, such as nuclear proliferation with the proliferation of other weapons of mass destruction), identifying the optimal outcome, and implementing policies designed to achieve that outcome. From this perspective, one cannot assign a probability of success for a specific multilateral export control arrangement without knowledge of the domestic and international context of factors (including the distribution of power in an issue area and the preferences of other governments) that shape national preferences regarding export controls.

The third theoretical perspective emphasizes the institutional-evolutionary setting of multilateral cooperation (Modelski 1990; Nye 1987; Young 1986). Here, consensus, even unanimity, best characterizes the style of decision making in international cooperative ventures. At the same time, these decisions are made in a highly uncertain context, so decision makers typically respond to changes (either qualitative or quantitative) in the supply of and demand for the benefits of international cooperation by building on existing international arrangements.

In many instances, governments reform existing institutions, most often incrementally. In other circumstances, new institutions emerge that rely on programs or practices transplanted, albeit in modified forms, from existing institutions. In most cases, national decision makers develop policies, on significant issues, that are considered roughly fair and satisfying rather than optimal or maximizing.

This perspective implies that multilateral export control arrangements in the 1990s are likely to look similar to existing arrangements, at least in terms of style if not in substance. Current multilateral export control institutions, especially COCOM and the International Atomic Energy Agency (IAEA), will mature or transform, taking on new responsibilities, and will breed similar institutional arrangements for other export control issues.

However, in most evolutionary processes, the exact direction of these evolutionary mutations are difficult, sometimes impossible, to forecast. Which multilateral arrangements, if any, will emerge again depends on the context of domestic and international factors (particularly the current multilateral institutional export control arrangements) that constrain the possibilities and opportunities for mutations with a high probability of survival.

Since governments are crucial ingredients in each of these three perspectives, understanding the determinants of foreign policy could generally shed light on export control policy formation. Unfortunately, research suggests that a very large array of factors may influence foreign policy formation. For example, Rosenau (1976) identified sixteen sources of foreign policy: great power structure, alliances, external situation, issue area, crises, size, geography, technology, culture and history, economic development, internal situation, social structure, moods of opinion, political accountability, governmental structure, and individual leaders. Moreover, Rosenau arranged these across a continuum of analytical aggregation from systemic to societal to governmental to idiosyncratic.

Not surprisingly, most quantitative foreign policy studies examine the impact of these determinants on international conflict rather than on cooperation (see Russett and Starr 1989; Sullivan 1976). However, two studies survey the relationship between national attributes and participation in international governmental organizations (IGOs) and so may bear on cooperation in the less formal international arrangements that mark the export control area. McCormick (1980), using the Comparative Research on the Events of Nations (CREON) project database, found that cooperation exceeded conflict as the dominant pattern of foreign policy behavior by thirty-five states for 1959 to 1968 by a large margin and that if the action took place within the context of an IGO, the margin was greater still. The study also indicated that geographic size and the level of economic development, with a few exceptions, had relatively little impact on this pattern (McCormick 1980). More recently, Jacobson, Reisinger, and Mathers (1986) found that the more years a state existed, the greater its gross national product (GNP) per capita, the larger its GNP, and the greater its degree of political party competition, the more IGO memberships it held. This suggests that economic size and the level of development may be more important as one begins to control for other factors.

Studies of export controls posit a large number of specific determinants for consideration, but most of the work is limited to understanding Western export control processes (Baldwin 1985; Bertsch 1988; Bertsch and Elliott-Gower 1992; Heinz 1991; Kemme 1991; Labbé 1990; Long 1989). Nonetheless, these studies provide a number of theoretical markers to guide the exploratory efforts of this study.

Table 1.1 lists an array of determinants or explanations of export control policy. Drawn from both the literature on foreign policy and export controls, the list is not exhaustive despite its length. Furthermore, the explanations are rarely exclusive or incompatible, and their interactive effects are not identified. The number and variety of variables alone pose theoretical hurdles of the highest degree to those trying to find a general, cross-national model of export control policies.

Multilateral Export Controls: Developing a Framework

The broad strokes of these three perspectives paint an unclear and incomplete picture of the prospects for multilateral export control arrangements in the 1990s and beyond. From these three views, it is difficult to say with certainty if any long-term multilateral cooperation is possible, much less what form of multilateral cooperation might emerge. Even if there were a theoretical consensus on the likelihood of international cooperation, the abstract nature of these perspectives, remote from contextual phenomena that dictate specific policy outcomes, limits their utility in explaining or prescribing specific policies (Lane 1990). However, the abstract focuses of these perspectives can identify key macro-level factors in the international environment that shape the set of constraints and opportunities generally facing policy makers.

From the realist or neorealist perspective, one can surmise that the key elements of the international environment involve basic political and military alignments, the amount of political and military resources, and, most importantly, the relative distribution of power, especially its military and political components. These forces play a central role in defining large-scale opportunities and constraints for multilateral action.

From the rational-functional perspective, the possibility and probability

TABLE 1.1. A Sampling of the Diversity of Export Control Policy Determinants and Explanations

Geopolitical

Changes in global and regional military balances, such as the collapse of Soviet and East European Communism or the rise of Iraqi armed forces, become important stimuli to national and multilateral export control efforts.

To the extent that export controls will reduce a military threat posed by rivals, governments will employ export controls or support strict multilateral export controls. To the extent that multilateral export controls impede one's own access to strategic military items, one will oppose such controls.

Economic, political, or military pressure can induce other countries to join in multilateral export control arrangements. For example, U.S. economic, political, or military pressure has induced other countries to harmonize their export control policies more closely to U.S. objectives.

Economic

The governments of more economically developed states are more cooperative in the international system.

Global diffusion of production capacity and supply networks limits the impact of unilateral export controls.

The increased importance of dual-use items in the global economic and security environment elevate export control issues on national and international political agendas and raises the question whether export controls will be used to promote the commercial as well as military advantage.

Societal

The closer the core values of one country are to another, the more likely their foreign policies will be cooperative.

The more publicly accountable the political system, the more likely the government will participate in multilateral arrangements.

Competition and balance between economic and military security interests shape national export control policies. The greater the political or economic influence exerted by exporters of weapons or dual-use items on a government, the less likely the government will restrict those exports or support multilateral export controls on those items.

Governmental

Efforts to assert executive flexibility or legislative prerogatives on the policy process affect the substance and consistency of export controls.

The more fragmented the bureaucratic responsibility for export controls, the less effective and efficient the policy.

The fewer the resources devoted to export licensing, intelligence, and enforcement, the greater the level of delay, error, deceit, and diversion. The fewer the resources devoted to intelligence and enforcement, the greater the opportunity for error, deceit, and diversion.

TABLE 1.1—*Continued*

International Institutional
Cooperation in other multilateral forums, including the EC, the Group of Seven, the Convention on Chemical and Biological Weapons, and the International Atomic Energy Agency, affect cooperative efforts within existing export control arrangements.

The longer the state has existed as a member of the international system, the more likely it will participate in multilateral arrangements.

Technological
Export control policies respond to changes in the nature of military strategies and technologies (though often with a significant delay).

of multilateral cooperation derives from the international combination of the various sets of national preferences. These preferences stem from assessments of both international and domestic forces relevant to issues of export controls, beyond the realist assessment of only international political alignments and military power. Since export controls directly affect the economic and technological resources of a country, the amount and distribution of economic and technological capabilities, at both the national and international levels, will be key factors in developing multilateral export control arrangements.

Finally, from the institutional-evolutionary perspective, the central elements of existing institutionalized multilateral arrangements will survive, buttressed by policy adaptation and policy adoption, to address the policy demands of the 1990s. This means that one must highlight current multilateral arrangements, especially the institutions (e.g., COCOM), as forces that shape the evolution of multilateral export controls.

Combining these factors produces a rough model of the forces determining multilateral export control arrangements (fig. 1.1). Political, military, economic, and technological forces at the international and domestic levels and the institutional setting interact to form the policy-making environment. To the extent that these vary across time and various export control issues, the consequent forms of multilateral export control arrangements will also vary.

Concepts and Assumptions

At this point, the rough model does not go far beyond the individual theoretical perspectives. Defining critical concepts and making some working assumptions will help clarify the model.

We define technology as the design and manufacturing know-how that applies scientific knowledge to produce goods (U.S. Department of Defense

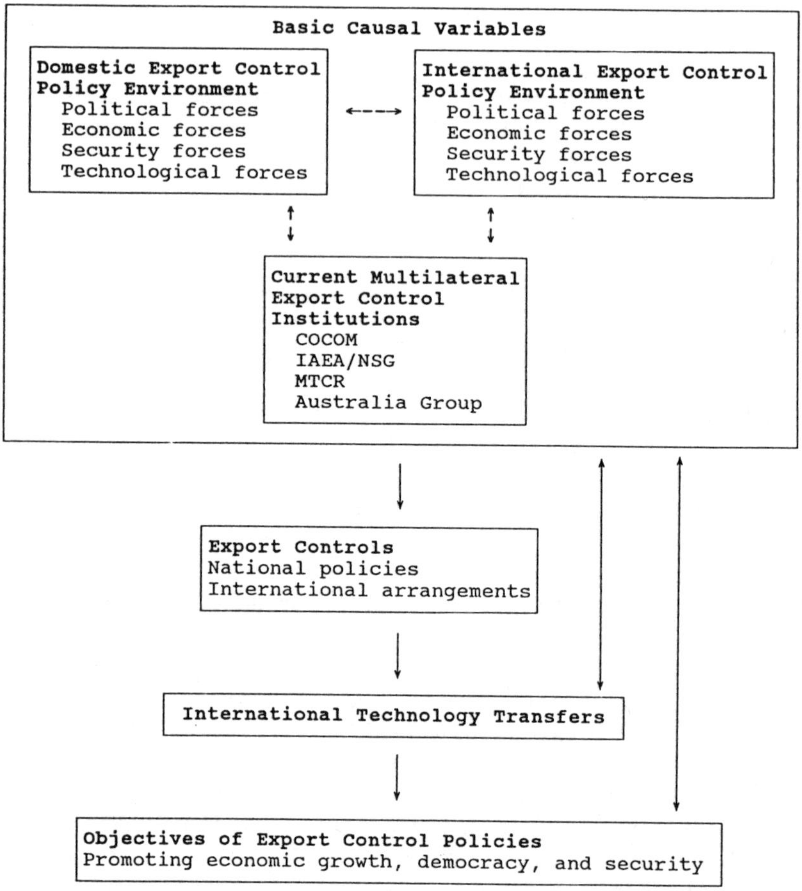

Fig. 1.1. A model of the export control policy process

1976). In this sense, technology is neither a good in and of itself nor basic, unapplied, scientific knowledge. International technology transfer includes both the direct transfer of this production-oriented knowledge from passing tangible (e.g., blueprints) or intangible (e.g., advice) technical information about the production of an item across national boundaries and the indirect transfer of technology through deductions about the production process one can derive from a product (embedded technology), usually involving reverse engineering.

Not all agents of technology transfer are equally effective. For example, turnkey plants or licensing agreements with a substantial teaching component are likely to be more effective means of technology transfer than advertising a product at a trade show or providing production documentation, particularly if it comes without consultation (U.S. Department of Defense 1976, 6). In part, that is because technology transfer entails not only the cross-border diffusion of technology but also its absorption, which requires a scientific and technological infrastructure that can make use of the know-how.[6]

Export control policy concerns the set of government actions primarily designed to prohibit or regulate exports. This book looks at export control policies devised to manage international technology transfers related to the enhancement of war-fighting capabilities. This book will not cover export control policies for other purposes (e.g., short supply) or government actions that affect international technology transfer but are not specifically meant to manage exports of dual-use or military technologies (e.g., patents). It will include so-called foreign policy export controls that are meant to restrict the flow of dual-use or military technologies.

Historically, one of the primary objectives of export control policies was to reduce and delay the cross-border diffusion of dual-use commercial and military technologies (Klitgaard 1978). Those policies have had a secondary effect of undermining the development of a general scientific and technological infrastructure, which reduces both the opportunity to absorb existing technologies or create new technologies indigenously (National Academy of Sciences 1991; Sutton 1973).

Export control policy typically results from decisions made by the officials of national governments. These choices are teleological, though the specific goals and rationales of national policies may differ. Implicit in each theoretical perspective is the assumption that national governments are likely to be key players in efforts at multilateral cooperation, so any future export control system must address the demands of national governments.[7]

In the model outlined in figure 1.1, states use export control policy for many purposes. They may modify their international environment (e.g., deny military or economic resources to another nation), change their domestic environment (e.g., symbolically oppose communism for domestic public consumption), alter the institutional context (e.g., create an international export control organization), or do all three. As with any foreign policy, one may classify national export control policies according to the scope of international cooperation involved in their execution. A unilateral policy approach involves action by one government taken without related, mutually agreed action by another government, whereas a bilateral approach requires mutually agreed action by two governments. A minilateral approach involves action by a relatively small group of governments, whereas a multilateral approach is more inclusive. National governments may use unilateral, bilateral, minilateral, and multilateral approaches simultaneously. For example, in executing its export control policy, the United States unilaterally restricts the export of some items for national security purposes, works with many non-COCOM countries on a bilateral basis, coordinates national security export controls in a minilateral fashion in COCOM, and uses a more inclusive multilateral approach in controlling nuclear proliferation through its participation in the IAEA (U.S. Department of Commerce 1988). Governments sometimes prefer unilateral export control policies over more cooperative forms of policy, since such policies afford greater independence in decision making and policy implementation; they may also better satisfy domestic demands for action, and they avoid the administrative costs of cooperation. However, mini- or multilateral export control systems can be more effective and efficient in managing the flow of exports than unilateral controls, especially if technological innovation and diffusion lie beyond the reach of unilateral controls or if a costly number of parallel international negotiations are necessary.

Export Control Objectives: Using International Technology Transfers and Export Controls to Promote Economic Growth, Democracy, and Military Security

Are there export control arrangements that can promote democracy, economic growth, and military security? Before one can answer that question, one must ask whose democracy, economic growth, and military security? To some, the existing arrangements appear to secure these values for Western states at the expenses of all others. Obviously, many export control policies, unilateral or otherwise, constrain the targets of the controls in achieving their own political, economic, or military objectives. How then can one talk about promoting military security, economic growth, or democracy on a global scale?

As the theoretical perspectives suggest, national views on export controls are an essential component in understanding multilateral cooperation. To that extent, one must explore how export control arrangements promote democracy, economic growth, and military security from the perspective of different countries, and that is the focus of most of the book. At the same time, nations exist within a global context as well. In the absence of global prosperity or global military security, it seems likely that states would have a much greater challenge in achieving national economic or military security. In this book, economic growth means sustained material progress, particularly in terms of national wealth. Such progress will be balanced across many economic sectors, so that the economy does not depend on growth in one or two economic sectors. For most countries, growth is likely to require interdependence with the global economy (rather than simple integration with the world market) and a market-oriented system with substantial private participation but with government intervention to preserve social justice and competition (Gilpin 1987).[8]

Democracy means a preference for individualism, liberty, and equality, with decision making based on majority rule coupled with minority rights. In representative democracies, democracy usually requires accountable government institutions, free and fair elections that permit the replacement of members of the government (especially the chief executive), a free press, and a competitive system of political parties (Bollen 1990; Maoz and Abdolali 1989; Vanhanen 1990).

In a broad sense, military security implies the absence of interstate military threats or punishments by one government designed to coerce another country to change its policy preferences (Small 1980). Military security must go beyond the mere absence of war to preclude governments from threatening or using military force short of war to resolve international disputes.

Are these values affected by international technology transfers and export controls? If so, how? We believe that international technology transfers and export controls do have an impact on economic growth, democracy, and military security. Most research suggests that fostering international technology transfer, both as a recipient and as a sender, is essential for economic growth in the modern world economy (Kreinin 1985; Stevens 1990; Wad 1988). For example, despite their differing views on the effects of Western policies, both Bornstein (1985) and Hanson (1981) demonstrated the historical importance of technological inputs (including the failure to absorb technologies) to the Soviet economy. Other research points out that controlling the international transfer of technologies, like most trade restrictions, is deleterious to the economic growth of both the country employing controls and the target of the controls (Ferguson 1987; Finan 1987; Hufbauer and Schott 1985). Although it is difficult to comprehend the full consequences of export controls, government policymakers implicitly adhere to similar beliefs, as is evidenced by their choice of policies. For example, during the Korean conflict, COCOM members prohibited most trade with the Soviet Union (Mastanduno 1988). By doing so, Western governments sought to deny the Soviets the opportunity to benefit from trade or to free resources for the military sector.

Others argue that for some countries to become economically competitive, international technology transfers must be strictly regulated (Stevens 1990). Governments may also try to preserve national prosperity by limiting the export of advanced technologies in the most competitive sectors of its economy and thus maintain a comparative technological advantage (Gill and Law 1988; Prestowitz 1988).

Given that export controls are, by their nature, barriers to trade, it is not obvious how export controls can promote global economic prosperity. If one starts from a presumption of free trade, clearly export controls impose an economic cost on both the target and the source of the controls to the extent that they diminish trade.[9] However, in light of historical evidence, it seems more appropriate to begin with a presumption that states permit trade and that they are inclined to manage trade in items with military applications most carefully. From this perspective, export control systems that least inhibit commercial interactions promote global economic growth.

For example, in the early 1990s COCOM countries relaxed their controls on exports to Czechoslovakia, Hungary, and Poland in return for progress on military, economic, and political reform. COCOM countries also made it a condition that the governments of the three countries create "safeguard systems" to prevent the diversion or reexport of controlled items. Without a system of controls, the countries would not have access to important dual-use technologies, including computer and telecommunication systems, making it less likely that they could become competitive in the global economy or that they could attract substantial foreign investment. Even though export controls would restrict trade flows to third parties, this restriction should be more than compensated by the increased commercial interaction between COCOM members and the three countries.

Less directly, by increasing global security, export controls may allow more investment in commercial rather than military applications of items. To the extent that commercial investment has a greater multiplier effect on the growth of the global economy than military investment, export controls also contribute to global economic growth.

By its nature, international technology transfer increases the opportunities for making choices, implying an inherently positive relationship between international technology transfer and democracy (Masciulli 1988). Modern technology permits direct mail political campaigns, better opinion polling, more representative forms of voting, and other activities that are arguably more democratic than more traditional democratic practices (McLean 1989). Global communication systems provide opportunities for individuals to become aware of conditions and ideas not native to their locality.

At the international level, modern technology permits faster, more direct, and greater volumes of communication. New transportation technologies make new forms of international diplomacy possible and preferred, including shuttle and summit diplomacy (Russett and Starr 1989, 159). It is not only easier for governments to share views with one another, government representatives overseas can be more responsive to the needs of their home country. Improvements in communication and transportation technologies have dramatically reduced the administrative costs of harmonizing or coordinating public policy, making multilateral decision making more attractive.

However, as the extensive controls imposed by all sides in the 1991 Gulf War indicated, government (or nongovernment) controls on the media can also warp the content of communication, making it a conduit for propaganda. Modern information technology allows governments to assemble an impressive (though sometimes inaccurate) array of information about individuals. These same technologies permit governments to build similar networks for their foreign policy activities and permit greater command and control over covert agents and military forces. Export controls and international technology transfers are also thought to affect peace and military security, but the exact relationships are not certain.[10]

Clearly, export controls can delay the diffusion of military or dual-use technologies (National Academy of Sciences 1991). Since maintaining superiority in military technologies was the touchstone of U.S. and North Atlantic Treaty Organization (NATO) strategic doctrine for many years, COCOM, the economic arm of the Western security network, helped the West maintain its technological lead and offset the quantitative strength of Soviet nuclear and conventional forces (National Academy of Sciences 1991, 62). Yet there were times when Western security might have been enhanced by facilitating the transfer of military technologies to the Soviet Union. For example, the Reagan administration recognized that Western implementation of the Strategic Defense Initiative (SDI) might have encouraged the Soviets to consider a first-strike or a launch-on-warning nuclear strategy. Accordingly, President Reagan proposed that SDI technology be shared with the Soviet Union (Root 1988). Sharing technology that facilitates hot-line arrangements with Russia and the Commonwealth of Independent States (CIS) is a more current example.

During the same period, little multilateral activity restricted the flow of militarily relevant technology and instruments of mass destruction to the Middle East. To the contrary, a wide array of countries in the East and West promoted the transfer of dual-use and military technologies. In the case of Iraq, the resulting level of technological sophistication of the Iraqi military forces increased its capacity to threaten its neighbors and the forces of the UN coalition.

Increased global military security, defined here as a reduction in the use of military threats or military force by countries on one another, can occur through the application of export controls. That is true even if controls restrict the security options facing a particular target country. For example, to the extent that export controls helped the West maintain an advantage in military technology over Soviet forces, controls may have reduced the chance of war or threats of war in the region as a whole. While export controls may have limited Soviet capacity to deter the West, it does not follow that this necessarily resulted in an increase in either threats of force or, more importantly, the use of force by either side.

Overall, the relative absence of agreement on these relationships probably reflects the necessity to understand better the context of specific international technology transfers and export controls. For example, Colombatto (1985, 98–99) argues that the domestic technological base and the domestic economic structure allowed the former Soviet Union to absorb "old" new technologies (mechanization technologies) fairly well but made absorbing "new" new technologies (automation technologies) not merely difficult but even harmful.

Export Control Objectives: The Indirect Effects of Export Controls and International Technology Transfers on Economic Growth, Democracy, and Military Security

Exploring the role of export control policy and the transfer of dual-use or military items and technologies becomes especially complex when one considers the interactive effects of economic growth, democracy, and military security. The potential of complementary and conflictual effects makes analyzing the direct and indirect consequences of export control policy very difficult, as well as creates serious dilemmas for policymakers. Policymakers ignore these linkages at their own peril. For example, one of the fundamental criticisms of U.S. export controls is that national security controls erode U.S. economic strength and technological leadership (National Academy of Sciences 1987). In addition, some policymakers were troubled in the late 1970s that U.S. controls on the export of oil and gas equipment to the Soviet Union were counterproductive, since an energy-hungry Soviet Union might be much more dangerous than it would be otherwise.

The first of the three basic relations to consider is whether economic growth is associated with democracy. Western experience implies that general measures of domestic economic prosperity and democracy are mutually reinforcing (Huntington and Nelson 1976). If, as some argue, economic growth in the modern economy requires limits on government intervention in the economy and accountability of public officials, then democracy may be a necessary (but not a sufficient) condition for economic competitiveness (Lewis 1990; Prybyla 1988; Scully 1988). Similarly, Dahl (1990, 80–87) argues that relative economic freedom may be a necessary (but not a sufficient) condition for democracy.

However, most research indicates that the relationship is much more complex, filled with contradictions, especially in non-Western contexts (Lichbach 1989; Midlarsky 1988; Seligson and Muller 1987; Weede 1987). The newly industrializing countries, despite continuing signs of greater democracy, indicate that export-led growth and global competitiveness can occur without fully democratic political systems. In the states of the former Soviet Union and some countries in Eastern Europe, popular opposition to some of the effects of market economics (e.g., unemployment) may well result in the maintenance of a highly protected (and uncompetitive) economy with little potential for further economic growth (Prybyla 1988; Rausser and Thomas 1990). Moreover, some of the newly independent states of the former Soviet Union may follow the Brazilian model by using repressive methods to stifle popular opposition and push ahead with economic reform, sacrificing democracy for economic growth.

Overall, the evidence is unclear. In one review of existing research, the authors conclude that democracy does not "widely and directly facilitate more rapid economic growth" nor "widely exacerbate inequality" but that one can say little else about the relationship (Sirowy and Inkeles 1990, 150–51).

Next, are economic growth and military security related? The belief that prosperous, competitive market economies breed peaceful international relations is the explicit principle on which the international economic institutions of the postwar era (particularly the IMF, the World Bank, and the General Agreement on Tariffs and Trade [GATT]) were built. Looking to the experience of the interwar years, Western policymakers at the close of the war came to believe that the economic dislocation and global depression of the 1920s and 1930s was a significant factor in the onset of World War II. Basically, if economic growth creates more mutual rather than asymmetrical interdependence, then it will promote more peaceful and secure relations among nations (Keohane and Nye 1977).

Despite these arguments, more severe interstate violence appears to occur during periods of general economic expansion, though the evidence is inconclusive (Goldstein 1985; Thompson 1988). If economic growth allows a state to purchase or produce greater relative military capacity, as was the case with Iraq, then conditions in which arms races, security dilemmas, or related phenomena arise will increase the likelihood of war (Jervis 1976; Maoz 1989).

Some evidence suggests losing a very destructive war actually stimulates rapid postwar economic growth (Olson 1982; Organski and Kugler 1980). However, in a sophisticated rebuttal of this argument, Rassler and Thompson (1985) find that positive economic effects of a very destructive class of wars (global wars) are rare, for either winners or losers, and that both the positive and the more common negative effects are temporary. Similarly, Hibbs (1973) finds no statistically significant relationship between economic growth and mass civil violence at the domestic level.

Finally, what is the relationship between democracy and military security? Fairly conclusive evidence indicates that democracies rarely threaten each other militarily or wage war against each other (Chan 1984; Lake 1992; Maoz and Abdolali 1989). Moreover, democracies are more likely to win international wars than autocratic states (Lake 1992). Ullman (1990, 117–18) suggests that, at least for the modern era, democracies are more peaceful because they have "their own self-correcting mechanisms in the form of multiple bilateral channels of access that help defuse tensions before they rise too high." Significantly, these channels of access only became possible with the innovation, diffusion, and absorption of modern communications and transportation technologies.

Finally, it is less clear that peace promotes democracy. Obviously coercive action by domestic or foreign aggressors is not democratic behavior, but many scholars also argue that effective use of military force, even in defense, requires a substantial concentration of power and secrecy, which means concentrating decision making on national security issues in the hands of a few (Gill and Law 1988). In some cases, threats to national security, either internal or external, are used to justify abuses to democratic principles, so that balancing security and democracy is one of the fundamental policy problems for Western-style governments.

The preceding discussion implies that, however murky and convoluted the relationships, promoting and managing international technology transfer—for example, between East and West—may prove more valuable to Western military, economic, and political interests than traditional policies of delay or denial. Again, it should be noted that increasing the transfer of technology depends on many factors, such as the absorptive capacity of an economy for technological innovation, something that governments may only be able to improve at the margin. Yet, to the extent that export controls affect the international transfer of technology, they will have at least an indirect effect on the spread of economic prosperity, democracy, and military security.

Though crucial to our understanding of the impact of export controls, these relationships only obliquely address the central question of this book: can governments cooperate to build durable, effective, and efficient multilateral export control arrangements that promote economic growth, democracy, and military security in the 1990s? Given the lack of specific contextual information about the domestic, international, and institutional environment, we believe that constructing well-developed hypotheses at this point would be premature and impractical. Moreover, the decidedly ambiguous implications of the theoretical discussion suggest that we also avoid making policy recommendations until we gather a great deal more contextual information. Thus, we believe that more informed prescriptions for export control policy-making must start with a better understanding of the perceptions and preferences of policymakers in countries whose cooperation will be crucial in formulating durable, effective, and efficient multilateral arrangements.

Methods and Design

As others suggest, forecasting a specific foreign policy outcome requires the integration of macro-level factors in the international environment with micro-level factors in the domestic environment, all of which affect the precise context and decision-making process in which national policy is made (Siverson and Starr 1990; Snyder, Bruck, and Sapin 1962; Sprout and Sprout 1969). This integration requires an exceptionally "concrete" methodology, one that stresses the dynamics of individual national policy processes, the interaction of multiple political and economic objectives, and the current policy-making environment (Lane 1990). Above all, a concrete approach focuses on the values, perceptions, and choices of policymakers as they function within the constraints and opportunities imposed by their perception of the environment (Lane 1990; Snyder, Bruck, and Sapin 1962; Sylvan and Chan 1984).

Given the considerations outlined in the development of the model in figure 1.1, building multilateral export control arrangements that promote democracy, economic growth, and military security depends on identifying the divergent and common (if any) elements of various national perspectives on the political, economic, security, technological, and institutional forces that influence national export control policies. Indeed, as Sylvan and Chan (1984, 11) point out, to prescribe any individual foreign policy requires "opposing systems" designs, which not only account for the beliefs and preferences of decision makers in one country but do so within the context of other, often conflicting perspectives. Taking this approach to the study of international relations, Jones (1991, xix), for example, looks at the national perceptions of the Soviet Union, the United States, America's major allies, China, and third world nations because "differences in national goals and perceptions are the origin of the two overarching conflicts of our time: the dispute between East and West and the conflict between North and South." Similarly, and almost by definition, international cooperation depends on the perceptions of the context of the international environment (George, Farley, and Dallin 1988). That is especially true for this book, because the discovery of both the possible and the potential forms of international cooperation are of interest.

If the prospects for creating or maintaining multilateral export control systems in the 1990s depend on the convergence or divergence of intra-Western and extra-Western perspectives, then the selection of perspectives should emphasize diversity, to locate common elements across the national perspectives, and similarity, to identify crucial divergent interests (Dogan and Pelassy 1984; Przeworski and Teune 1970). To diversify the sample, COCOM members or associated states, countries proscribed or recently proscribed by Western export controls, and countries largely collateral to the COCOM system were included and are addressed in the chapters that follow. We also attempted to diversify the sample by including countries of very different military and economic statures.

Given their power and their roles as producers and consumers of dual-use and military technologies, both the United States and the former Soviet Union must be included. We also chose to include other COCOM members who we believe are likely to represent the most different perspectives on export controls. We also have chosen examples of non-Western developing countries that are producers of high-technology dual-use or military items, countries that have been actively acquiring advanced military items and technologies, and countries whose policies have focused on acquiring technologies primarily for economic development. Finally, we include perspectives from countries in Eastern Europe, one from a northern tier country, where many political and economic reforms have been put in place, and one from the southern tier, where much political and economic reform may yet be done.

Identifying common and divergent interests and views of one country compared to another need not imply that a single, unified national perspective exists within one country. Indeed, differentiating between widely or deeply held views and minority or superficially held views on export controls and their relationship to technology transfer, democracy, economic growth, and military security is essential to understanding the strength of preferences for various multilateral arrangements.

Nonetheless, the question of how researchers develop national perspectives remains. For this book, using concrete theory means that the various national perspectives reveal the values, perceptions, preferences, and behavior of actual decision makers and those individuals involved in making export control policy (Lane 1990; Snyder, Bruck, and Sapin 1962). The author of each national perspective to be described in the individual chapters that follow was asked to cover five elements:

1. Perceptions in the policy-making community of the important political, military, economic, and technological environment and relevant export control institutions and policies

2. Perceptions in the policy-making community of the relationships among export controls, technology transfer, economic growth, democracy, and military security
3. Perceptions of the range of possible national and international export control systems
4. Perceived costs and benefits of these export control systems, to identify preferred export control systems
5. Perceived opportunities and constraints imposed by the environment in choosing different export control systems, to define the probabilities for various export control systems

In the chapters that follow, the authors of the national perspective papers describe the existing export control policies and the network of decision makers involved in making that policy. They do so by reviewing the public record to identify those individuals who reportedly made actual decisions or contributed to the policy debate and by asking those decision makers to identify other key decision makers. This approach can help overcome the methodological problems inherent in identifying a policy-making community or an issue network (Ricci 1970).

Next, through personal interviews of key decision makers and a review of their policy-related activities, the authors isolate crucial perceptions and preferences of the national and international settings for national export control policies and multilateral export control arrangements. By having analysts from various countries addressing a common set of questions to assess the international and domestic political, economic, security, and technological forces that determine national policies and to identify current views on the role and effectiveness of existing international export control institutions, one should be able to develop a set of analytically comparable national perspectives (the specific questions intended to guide the authors are listed in the appendix to this chapter).

Any cross-cultural research on public policy usually requires that an analyst, at a minimum, have a basic knowledge of the issue and the countries being studied (Holt and Turner 1970). Given the deeply detailed knowledge of policy and context demanded by the methodology of "concrete theory," exploring the domestic context for national export control policies, as well as eliciting the views of policymakers, requires more than a basic knowledge of the policies, the relevant countries, and the international arena. This extensive knowledge is not likely to be held by any single researcher or even a team of researchers based in a single country. Using contacts of the Center for East-West Trade Policy at the University of Georgia resulting from years of research on multilateral export controls, an international research team of scholars with expertise regarding export control issues in different countries was assembled to develop the various national perspectives and write the chapters that follow.

In a companion paper provided to all members of the research team, the three authors of this chapter outlined the institutional environment for multilateral export controls. An updated version of that paper is included as chapter 2 in this book.

Finally, developing an analytically comparable set of national perspectives increases the possibility of synthesis. Such a synthesis should reveal any patterns of international preferences conducive to the development of cooperative multilateral export control arrangements. In any case, synthesizing the national perspectives will help develop more certain knowledge about what is preferred and what is possible regarding export controls in the 1990s and beyond. With that knowledge, it may be possible to construct strategies that will maximize the probability of multilateral arrangements that promote democracy, economic growth, and peace, while minimizing the probability of less desirable alternatives. Such a synthesis represents the concluding chapter in this volume.

Appendix: Guidelines for Preparing the National Perspective Papers

I. General Instructions

What follows are suggestions for the content of each "national perspective" paper. By addressing the following issues you will help make your paper comparable to the other cases in this study. This is essential for synthesizing your case with the others.

When information on policies is requested below, please make sure to include official government positions, and your assessment of them. If current policies represent a major change from previous policies, briefly describe the nature of such change.

When information on perceptions is requested below, please respond on the basis of views explicitly expressed by members of the policy-making community (and your assessment of them). If current perceptions represent a major change from the past, briefly describe the differences.

II. Characterizing National Policies

A. Please describe *current national policies* controlling the export of dual-use or military items, if any. What are the goals of such policy? What programs or actions does the government undertake to achieve these goals?

B. Please describe the country's current participation in international export control arrangements, if any.

C. Please depict the national policy-making community for export controls.

Which government ministries, departments, agencies play a role? What kind of role does the national legislature play? Do others play an important role (e.g., enterprises, labor associations, interest groups)? If the important participants in the policy-making process have changed recently, briefly describe the changes.

D. Relative to other issues, how high a priority does the national political leadership give export controls? Are national political leaders personally committed to resolving export control issues? Please tell us who these people are and where they stand on export control issues.

III. Perceptions of the International and Domestic Policy-Making Environment for Export Controls

A. How effective and efficient are national and international export control policies according to policymakers? Why? How widely shared are these views?

B. What are the perceived linkages between export controls, international technology transfers, and economic growth? What are the perceived linkages between export controls, international technology transfers, and democracy? What are the perceived linkages between export controls, international technology transfers, and military security? What are the perceived linkages between economic growth, democracy, and military security?

C. How is the distribution of power across international military, political, economic, and technological forces perceived to affect the choices facing decision makers regarding export controls? How is the distribution of domestic military, political, economic, and technological forces perceived to affect the choices facing decision makers regarding export controls? What opportunities and constraints are perceived as most restricting the choices facing decision makers regarding export controls?

D. What is perceived as the probable future for export control policy? Are national policies and international arrangements likely to regulate exports not currently controlled? Are exports currently under controls likely to be decontrolled? How widely shared are these beliefs? What are the perceived costs and benefits associated with the probable outcome? What is the perceived effect of the probable outcome on promoting democracy, economic growth, and military security?

E. What would members of the policy-making community prefer to see regarding national and international export control policies? Why? How widely shared are these views? What are the costs and benefits associated with these views? What is the perceived effect of the preferred outcome on promoting democracy, economic growth, and military security?

NOTES

1. Five of the deleted items remain subject to other multilateral export controls ("COCOM Analysis" 1990).

2. "Fewer goods, higher fences" refers to the reform approach favoring stricter controls on fewer items. Core list refers to the 1990–91 COCOM exercise to implement this approach.

3. Dual-use items are those goods and technologies that have military and civilian application.

4. For examples of previous efforts, see Hufbauer and Schott 1985 and Baldwin 1985.

5. When a game is played repeatedly, strategies of conditional reciprocity usually require one player to take the same action that the other player took on the previous turn (i.e., cooperate if the other cooperated, defect if the other defected). This works to counter the pressure toward noncooperation inherent on any single play of the game, since unreciprocated cooperation always leaves the cooperative player worse off than if mutual cooperation took place, while the defecting player is always better off than if mutual defection occurred.

6. For example, Americans in the late eighteenth and early nineteenth centuries often attempted to acquire commercial technology from Britain. Yet two years after one such attempt in 1781, British textile machines smuggled to Philadelphia in contravention of British export controls were smuggled back into Britain because Americans could not absorb the technology ("The Edge of Ignorance" 1991).

7. Only realists presume that nation-states are the sole significant actors on the global stage.

8. For an example of this, see the International Monetary Fund (IMF) assessment of the Soviet economy (IMF 1990).

9. Countries may also use export controls to preserve an international commercial advantage or prevent a shortage of key goods or technologies in the domestic market. Particularly in the first instance, controls become a form of trade protection that most economists recognize as inimicable to global prosperity.

10. Some authors point out that technological innovations increase the incentives for preemptive or aggressive action, while other technologies increase deterrence or verification capabilities (Huntington 1958; Majeski 1986). The most insidious outcome is the security dilemma described by Jervis (1976), where governments with purely defensive intentions may still engage in an arms race. Still, systematic evidence, if anything, indicates little or no significant relationship between arms races and the onset of disputes (Diehl and Kingston 1985; Siverson and Diehl 1989). International technology transfer may also disrupt existing social structures and social balances, by changing the expectations of some domestic groups or altering their economic or political power. In such circumstances, the potential for civil violence or war may increase, though again the systematic evidence is not supportive (Hibbs 1973).

REFERENCES

Auerbach, S. 1990. "U.S. Eases Stance on Exports." *Herald Tribune,* January 20. Reprinted in *NATO Weekly Press Review Communist Economies,* 682 (January 22): 58–59.

Axelrod, R. 1984. *The Evolution of Cooperation*. New York: Basic Books.

Baldwin, D. A. 1985. *Economic Statecraft*. Princeton, N.J.: Princeton University Press.

Bertsch, G. K., H. Vogel, and J. Zielonka, eds. 1991. *After the Revolutions: East-West Trade and Technology Transfer in the 1990s*. Boulder, Colo.: Westview Press.

Bertsch, G. K., and S. J. Elliott-Gower, eds. 1992. *Export Controls in Transition: Perspectives, Problems, and Prospects*. Durham, N.C.: Duke University Press.

Bollen, K. A. 1990. "Political Democracy: Conceptual and Measurement Traps." *Studies in Comparative International Development* 25 (1): 7–24.

Bornstein, M. 1985. *East-West Technology Transfer: The Transfer of Western Technology to the USSR*. Paris: OECD.

Chan, S. 1984. "Mirror, Mirror on the Wall . . . Are Freer Countries More Pacific?" *Journal of Conflict Resolution* 28 (4): 617–48.

"COCOM Analysis: High Level Meeting Liberalizes Low Level Technology." 1990. *Export Control News* 4 (6): 2–4.

Colombatto, E. 1985. "New Technologies in the USSR." In *Adaptability to New Technologies of the USSR and East European Countries*, edited by Philip Joseph, 91–113. Brussels: NATO.

Conybeare, J. A. C. 1987. *Trade Wars*. New York: Columbia University Press.

Dahl, R. A. 1990. *After the Revolution? Authority in a Good Society*. Rev. ed. New Haven, Conn.: Yale University Press.

Diehl, P., and J. Kingston. 1985. "Messenger or Message? Military Buildups and the Initiation of Conflict." *Journal of Politics* 49 (3): 801–13.

Dogan, M., and D. Pelassy. 1984. *How to Compare Nations: Strategies in Comparative Politics*. Chatham, N.J.: Chatham House.

"The Edge of Ignorance. A Survey." 1991. *Economist* 318 (7694): 19.

Elliott-Gower, S. 1991. "Conclusion: Post-Revolutionary Thoughts." In *After the Revolutions: East-West Trade and Technology Transfer in the 1990s*, edited by G. K. Bertsch, H. Vogel, and J. Zielonka, 219–33. Boulder, Colo.: Westview Press.

European Round Table of Industrialists. 1990. *Export Regulations: European Industry and COCOM*. Brussels: European Round Table of Industrialists.

Ferguson, C. H. 1987. "High-Technology Product Life Cycles, Export Controls, and International Markets." In *Balancing the National Interest: U.S. National Security Export Controls and Global Economic Competition*, Working Papers, 60–86. Washington, D.C.: National Academy Press.

Finan, W. F. 1987. "Estimate of Direct Economic Costs Associated with U.S. National Security Controls." In *Balancing the National Interest: U.S. National Security Export Controls and Global Economic Competition*, 254–77. Washington, D.C.: National Academy Press.

George, A. L., P. J. Farley, and A. Dallin. 1988. *U.S.-Soviet Security Cooperation: Achievements, Failures, Lessons*. New York: Oxford University Press.

Gill, S., and D. Law. 1988. *The Global Political Economy: Perspectives, Problems and Policies*. New York: Harvester Wheatsheaf.

Gilpin, R. 1987. *The Political Economy of International Relations*. Princeton, N.J.: Princeton University Press.

Goldstein, J. S. 1985. "Kondratieff Waves as War Cycles." *International Studies Quarterly* 29 (4): 411–44.

Grieco, J. M. 1988. "Anarchy and the Limits of Cooperation: A Realist Critique of the Newest Liberal Institutionalism." *International Organization* 42 (3): 485–508.

Hanson, P. 1981. *Trade and Technology in Soviet-Western Relations*. New York: Columbia University Press.

Heinz, J. 1991. *U.S. Strategic Trade: An Export Control System for the 1990s*. Boulder, Colo.: Westview Press.

Hibbs, D. A. 1973. *Mass Political Violence*. New York: Wiley.

Holt, R. T., and J. E. Turner. 1970. "The Methodology of Comparative Research." In *The Methodology of Comparative Research,* edited by R. T. Holt and J. E. Turner, 1–20. New York: The Free Press.

Hufbauer, G. C., and J. J. Schott. 1985. *Economic Sanctions Reconsidered*. Washington, D.C.: Institute for International Economics.

Huntington, S. P. 1958. "Arms Races: Prerequisites and Results." *Public Policy* 18: 41–46.

Huntington, S. P., and J. Nelson. 1976. *No Easy Choice*. Cambridge, Mass.: Harvard University Press.

International Monetary Fund (IMF). 1990. *The Economy of the USSR*. Washington, D.C.: IMF.

Jacobson, H. K., W. M. Reisinger, and T. Mathers. 1986. "National Entanglements in International Governmental Organizations." *American Political Science Review* 80, no. 1 (March): 141–59.

Jervis, R. 1976. *Perception and Misperception in International Politics*. Princeton, N.J.: Princeton University Press.

Jones, W. S. 1991. *The Logic of International Relations*. New York: HarperCollins.

Kahler, M. 1990. "Organization and Cooperation: International Institutions and Policy Coordination." *Journal of Public Policy* 8 (3/4): 375–401.

Kaplan, M. S. 1976. *System and Process in International Politics*. New York: Krieger.

Keohane, R. O. 1984. *After Hegemony: Cooperation and Discord in the World Political Economy*. Princeton, N.J.: Princeton University Press.

Keohane, R., and J. S. Nye. 1977. *Power and Interdependence*. Boston: Little, Brown and Company.

Klitgaard, R. E. 1978. "A Historical Perspective on Export Controls." In *Integrating National Security and Trade Policy: The United States and the Soviet Union*, 1978 Senior Conference Final Report, 179-93. West Point, N.Y.: U.S. Military Academy.

Kreinin, M. E. 1985. "United States Trade and Possible Restrictions in High-Technology Products." *Journal of Policy Modeling* 7 (1): 69–105.

Labbé, M-H. 1990. *La politique américaine de commerce avec l'est 1969–1989*. Paris: Presses Universitaires de France.

Lake, D. A. 1992. "Powerful Pacifists: Democratic States and War." *American Political Science Review* 86, no. 1 (March): 24–37.

Lane, R. 1990. "Concrete Theory: An Emerging Political Method." *American Political Science Review* 84 (3): 927–40.

Lewis, P. G. 1990. "Democratization in Eastern Europe." *Coexistence* 27 (4): 245–67.

Lichbach, M. I. 1989. "An Evaluation of 'Does Economic Inequality Breed Political Conflict?' Studies." *World Politics* 61: 431–70.

Long, W. J. 1989. *U.S. Export Control Policy: Executive Autonomy versus Congressional Reform*. New York: Columbia University Press.

Majeski, S. J. 1986. "Technological Innovation and Cooperation in Arms Races." *International Studies Quarterly* 30 (2): 175–91.

Maoz, Z. 1989. "Power, Capabilities, and Paradoxical Conflict Outcomes." *World Politics* 41 (2): 239–66.

Maoz, Z., and N. Abdolali. 1989. "Regime Types and International Conflict 1816–1976." *Journal of Conflict Resolution* 33 (1): 3–35.

Masciulli, J. 1988. "Rousseau versus Instant Government: Democratic Participation in the Age of Telepolitics." In *Democratic Theory and Technological Society*, edited by R. B. Day, R. Beiner, and J. Masciulli, 150–64. Armonk, N.Y.: M. E. Sharpe.

Mastanduno, M. 1988. "Trade as a Strategic Weapon: American and Alliance Export Control Policy in the Early Postwar Period." *International Organization* 42 (1): 121–50.

McCormick, J. M. 1980. "International Organizations and Cooperation Among Nations." *International Studies Quarterly* 24, no. 1 (March): 75–98.

McLean, I. 1989. *Democracy and New Technology*. Cambridge, Mass.: Polity Press.

Midlarsky, M. I. 1988. "Rulers and the Ruled: Patterned Inequality and the Onset of Mass Political Violence." *American Political Science Review* 82 (2): 491–509.

Modelski, G. 1990. "Is World Politics Evolutionary Learning?" *International Organization* 44 (1): 1–24.

Morgenthau, H. J. 1978. *Politics Among Nations*. 5th ed. New York: Alfred A. Knopf.

National Academy of Sciences. 1987. *Balancing the National Interest: U.S. National Security Export Controls and Global Economic Competition*. Washington, D.C.: National Academy Press.

———. 1991. *Finding Common Ground: U.S. Export Controls in a Changed Global Environment*. Washington, D.C.: National Academy Press.

Nye, J. S. 1987. "Nuclear Learning and U.S.-Soviet Security Regimes." *International Organization* 41 (3): 371–402.

Olson, M. 1982. *The Rise and Decline of Nations*. New Haven, Conn., and London: Yale University Press.

Organski, A. F. K., and J. Kugler. 1980. *The War Ledger*. Chicago: University of Chicago Press.

Oye, K. A., ed. 1986. *Cooperation under Anarchy*. Princeton, N.J.: Princeton University Press.

Pearson, F. S., and J. M. Rochester. 1988. *International Relations: The Global Condition in the Late Twentieth Century*. 2d ed. New York: Random House.
Prestowitz, C. V., Jr. 1988. *Trading Places*. New York: Basic Books.
Prybyla, J. S. 1988. "Socialist Economic Reform, Political Freedom, and Democracy." *Comparative Strategy* 7 (4): 351–60.
Przeworski, A., and H. Teune. 1970. *The Logic of Comparative Social Inquiry*. New York: John Wiley & Sons.
Rassler, K., and W. R. Thompson. 1985. "War and the Economic Growth of Major Powers." *American Journal of Political Science* 29: 513–38.
Rausser, G., and S. Thomas. 1990. "Market Politics and Foreign Assistance." *Development Policy Review* 8 (4): 365–81.
Ricci, D. M. 1970. "Methodological Disputes in the Study of Power." In *Political Power, Community and Democracy,* edited by E. Keynes and D. M. Ricci, 155–78. Chicago: Rand McNally.
Root, W. A. 1988. "COCOM: An Appraisal of Objectives and Needed Reforms." In *Controlling East-West Trade and Technology Transfer: Power, Politics, and Policies,* edited by G. K. Bertsch, 417–41. Durham, N.C.: Duke University Press.
Rosenau, J. N. 1976. "The Study of Foreign Policy." In *World Politics,* edited by J. N. Rosenau, K. Thompson, and G. Boyd, 18. New York: The Free Press.
Russett, B., and H. Starr. 1989. *World Politics: The Menu for Choice*. 3d ed. New York: W. H. Freeman.
Scully, G. W. 1988. "The Institutional Framework and Economic Development." *Journal of Political Economy* 96: 652–62.
Seligson, M. A., and E. N. Muller. 1987. "Democratic Stability and Economic Crisis: Costa Rica, 1978–1983." *International Studies Quarterly* 31 (3): 301–26.
Sirowy, L., and A. Inkeles. 1990. "The Effects of Democracy on Economic Growth and Inequality: A Review." *Studies in Comparative International Development* 25 (1): 126–57.
Siverson, R. M., and P. Diehl. 1989. "Arms Races, the Conflict Spiral, and the Onset of War." In *Handbook of War Studies,* edited by M. Midlarsky, 195–218. Boston: Unwin Hyman.
Siverson, R., and H. Starr. 1990. "Opportunity, Willingness, and the Diffusion of War." *American Political Science Review* 84 (1): 47–67.
Small, M. 1980. *Was War Necessary: National Security and U.S. Entry into War, 1812–1950*. Beverly Hills, Calif.: Sage.
Snidal, D. 1985a. "Coordination versus Prisoners' Dilemma: Implications for International Cooperation and Regimes" *American Political Science Review* 79 (4): 923–42.
———. 1985b. "The Game Theory of International Politics." *World Politics* 37 (1): 25–57.
Snyder, R. C., H. W. Bruck, and B. Sapin, eds. 1962. *Foreign Policy Decision-Making: An Approach*. New York: The Free Press.
Sprout, H., and M. Sprout. 1969. "Environmental Factors in the Study of International Politics." In *International Politics and Foreign Policy,* edited by J. N. Rosenau, 41–56. New York: The Free Press.

Stein, A. A. 1982. "Coordination and Collaboration: Regimes in an Anarchic World." *International Organization* 36 (2): 299–324.

———. 1990. *Why Nations Cooperate: A Circumstance and Choice in International Relations*. Ithaca, N.Y.: Cornell University Press.

Stevens, C. 1990. "Technoglobalism vs. Technonationalism: The Corporate Dilemma." *Columbia Journal of World Business* 25 (3): 42–49.

Sullivan, M. P. 1976. *International Relations: Theories and Evidence*. Englewood Cliffs, N.J.: Prentice-Hall.

Sutton, A. C. 1973. *Western Technology and Soviet Economic Development 1945 to 1965*. Stanford, Calif.: Hoover Institution Publications.

Sylvan, D. A., and S. Chan. 1984. *Foreign Policy Decision Making: Perception, Cognition, and Artificial Intelligence*. New York: Praeger.

Thompson, W. R. 1988. *On Global War*. Columbia, S.C.: University of South Carolina Press.

Ullman, R. H. 1990. "European Security Organization." *Foreign Policy* 80: 102–120.

U.S. Department of Commerce. 1988. *Export Administration Annual Report*. Washington, D.C.: GPO.

U.S. Department of Defense. 1976. *An Analysis of Export Control of U.S. Technology—A DOD Perspective*. Washington, D.C.: GPO.

Vanhanen, T. 1990. *The Process of Democratization: A Comparative Study of 147 States, 1980–88*. Washington, D.C.: Crane Russak.

Wad, A., ed. 1988. *Science, Technology, and Development*. Boulder, Colo.: Westview Press.

Weede, E. 1987. "Some New Evidence on Correlates of Political Violence: Income Inequality, Regime Repressiveness and Economic Development." *European Sociological Review* 3: 97–108.

Yarbrough, B. V., and R. M. Yarbrough. 1986. "Reciprocity, Bilateralism, and Economic 'Hostages': Self-Enforcing Agreements in International Trade." *International Studies Quarterly* 30 (1): 7–21.

Young, O. R. 1986. "International Regimes: Toward a New Theory of Institutions." *World Politics* 39 (1): 104–22.

CHAPTER 2

Multilateral Export Control Organizations

Gary K. Bertsch, Richard T. Cupitt, and Steven Elliott-Gower

Introduction

From the British and Foreign Anti-Slavery Society to the International Whaling Commission, international organizations, both governmental and nongovernmental, often assist in the prohibition or limitation of trade (Nadelmann 1990).[1] Currently, there are four leading IGOs that involve controls on the international transfer of dual-use (e.g., civilian and military) items, including strategic technologies:

- COCOM for restrictions on a wide range of items that affect military capabilities
- The Australia Group (AG) for chemical and biological items
- The Nuclear (or London) Suppliers Group (NSG) for nuclear items[2]
- The Missile Technology Control Regime (MTCR) for missile systems

Other multilateral organizations and conventions affect exports of dual-use strategic technologies such as the IAEA, the NPT, and the Chemical and Biological Weapons Convention. However, only these four organizations are designed specifically to achieve a degree of international cooperation on export control policies, making them the critical components of the international institutional environment for this study.

In the abstract, international relations theories argue for very different interpretations of the importance of IGOs. By examining the origins, membership, leadership, decision-making structures, functions, and control mechanisms of these particular IGOs, we hope to illuminate the patterns of behavior that underlie multilateral export control arrangements in a more concrete fashion. By contrasting the differences among the four organizations, we hope to reveal a range of possible forms of cooperation regarding dual-use export controls. By comparing the commonalities among these four organizations, we hope to provide clues to the probable forms of cooperation in the 1990s. Finally, by examining these organizations, we describe the institutional context within which the countries (addressed in the following chapters) behave.

The Coordinating Committee for Multilateral Export Controls

Origins

As East-West relations deteriorated after World War II, the United States and some West European countries extended wartime trade controls to restrict the export of strategic goods to the Soviet bloc. From March, 1948, as part of the economic security program, the United States developed a system of national export controls and, recognizing the need for multilateral action, urged the West Europeans to adopt parallel controls (U.S. Department of State 1952). Indeed, the British and French governments had been developing national export control policies as they increasingly questioned Soviet objectives in Europe (Mastanduno 1988).[3] While there were differences of opinion over the extent of the controls, there was consensus on the need to establish a multilateral export control forum to discuss these differences and try to coordinate Western controls on exports to the Soviet Union, Eastern Europe, and, a little later, China.[4] In November, 1949, after protracted discussions in London, the allies established an informal Consultative Group (CG). In January, 1950, the allies established the working-level COCOM, which began operations that year in Paris (U.S. Department of State 1952). [COCOM members agreed to disband COCOM by March 31, 1994, and replace it with another organization.]

Members and Leadership

The Coordinating Committee for Multilateral Export Controls has seventeen members. The founding members were Belgium, France, Italy, Luxembourg, the Netherlands, the United Kingdom, and the United States. These were soon joined by Canada, Denmark, Norway, and West Germany in 1950; Japan in 1952; Greece, Portugal, and Turkey in 1953; Spain in 1985; and Australia in 1989. The governments of Austria, Finland, Hong Kong, Ireland, New Zealand, Sweden, and Switzerland have working arrangements with the United States to control exports in line with COCOM norms. All NATO members, except Iceland, belong to COCOM. Canada, France, Germany, Italy, Japan, the Netherlands, the United Kingdom, and the United States—those countries with the biggest political and economic stakes in East-West trade—are active participants in COCOM. Typically, the United States makes the majority of proposals for additions to the list of controlled items or revisions that tighten controls on existing items, and the other members propose the most deletions and liberalizations of existing controls.

Functions and Decision-Making Structure

The Coordinating Committee for Multilateral Export Controls has always been a nontreaty, nonchartered agreement. COCOM has neither the authority nor the mandate to create laws, rules, or regulations. It does not implement controls, monitor them, or enforce them. Nor does it have any independent information-gathering or distribution functions. It is a forum for governments to share threat assessments, information on foreign availability, and specifics on emerging military technologies and for monitoring technology transfers and discussing enforcement activities. It is the vehicle through which representatives of member nations convene to develop, review, and agree on lists of technologies and products that the individual nations will control in their trade with certain proscribed countries, as well as to consider appropriate rules and procedures to implement these policies. Its small secretariat of about thirty people provides translation and clerical services out of an annex of the U.S. embassy in Paris.

National delegations typically meet once a week, at a working or staff level, to consider exception requests, clarify positions on embargoed items under review, and discuss miscellaneous issues (such as budgets or staffing). Since 1982, the members have conducted semiannual high-level meetings (HLMs) at the subcabinet level to discuss broad policy issues, to establish or review the progress of COCOM's ad hoc working groups, and to approve agreements reached at the working level.[5] Though COCOM is the only authoritative decision-making body, ad hoc working groups are set up to consider issues such as intra-COCOM trade, the streamlining of the COCOM list, the harmonization of national export control systems, and, most recently, the creation of a core list.

In addition, during the Reagan administration, U.S. officials, concerned with perceived bias toward commercial interests in many COCOM members' delegations, proposed the creation of a permanent military subcommittee. Other COCOM members rejected this proposal, but as a compromise, they agreed to the creation of the Science and Technology Experts Meeting (STEM), composed of military and technology specialists from member countries. STEM is not involved in COCOM's routine activities but periodically advises COCOM on the military utility of advanced technologies. STEM meets in Paris and is organized into working groups that cover and report to COCOM on specific technologies or sets of technologies.

The review process is typically tedious, time-consuming, and often plagued by delays.[6] It usually involves a series of proposals and counterproposals "based on technical assessments colored by bureaucratic and economic interests" (Mastanduno 1990, 76). Member countries with less bureaucratic or technical resources do not actively participate in the review process but rather take their cues from others more involved in the process (National Academy of Sciences 1987).

Exceptions to COCOM prohibitions are nominally made on the basis of the extent that a particular technology, if exported, might increase the military capabilities of a proscribed communist state (for a more detailed discussion of exceptions, see the section below on "Controls"). Once an exception request is approved, it sets a precedent for the approval of similar cases. As a result, the more conservative members of COCOM may deny an exception request, not only to deny the individual export but to prevent setting a precedent for future sales. Rather than denying an exception request, a COCOM member can ask questions regarding the item under consideration. In the past, this practice could delay a decision, though recent reforms have considerably shortened the decision time.

The addition, deletion, or revision of items on the COCOM lists, the determination of exception requests, or any other business requires the unanimous consent of member states (though silence is taken as consent). Decision making within COCOM becomes something of a horse trade, with much back scratching, compromising, and bilateral dealing. Further, in the early 1980s, U.S. attempts to tighten COCOM restrictions by making demands on other member states rather than pursuing compromise did not produce a significant tightening of controls by other COCOM members and, indeed, resulted in the use of blocking legislation by some allies that reduced U.S. influence and made business with U.S. firms troublesome and uncertain.

COCOM does not publish a list of proscribed destinations for controlled exports. However, an examination of publicly available national lists indicates that COCOM-proscribed destinations at the end of 1991 included Afghanistan, Albania, Bulgaria, Czechoslovakia, Hungary, Kampuchea, Laos, Mongolia, North Korea, the PRC, Poland, Romania, the successor states of the former Soviet Union, and Vietnam. In addition, during the transition to unification, the formerly proscribed territories that constituted East Germany were subject to a "bikini" list of items.

Not all destinations are equally proscribed. Since 1985, exports that fall below a certain technological threshold (the so-called China Green Line) may be exported to China under COCOM procedures. At certain times, exports to Poland, Romania, Czechoslovakia, and Hungary have been dealt with under various exception procedures to encourage deviations from Soviet foreign or domestic policy (Root 1988, 421). By contrast, a "no exceptions" policy was applied by the U.S. on licenses reviewed within COCOM for exports to the Soviet Union between 1980 and 1989 as a result of its invasion of Afghanistan. Finally, as of 1991, contingent on the satisfactory implementation of technology safeguard systems in the CSFR, Hungary, and Poland (programs designed to prevent Western technology being diverted to the Soviet Union and other proscribed destinations), some exports to these countries qualify for favorable consideration in COCOM. If these countries (and perhaps other countries in Eastern Europe and the former Soviet Union) impose COCOM-type controls on the export of their indigenous technology and cooperate with the COCOM countries in imposing nonproliferation export controls, they may be dropped from COCOM's proscribed list. Indeed, in February, 1992, COCOM members agreed to deproscribe Hungary for this reason.

Controls

The primary control activity of COCOM is to maintain a list of items that member states include in their national export control policies.[7] The original COCOM list represented a compromise between the Anglo-French list and the U.S. 1A and 1B export control lists. Currently, COCOM embargoes items on three lists: (1) the International Munitions List (IML); (2) the International Atomic Energy List (IAEL); and (3) the often controversial International Industrial List (IL) of dual-use items. COCOM members agree that items on these lists are of strategic significance in that they contribute directly or indirectly to the military capability of their potential adversaries.

American advocacy of economic warfare through COCOM controls held sway in the earliest days of the organization, especially after the invasion of South Korea. From the broad restrictions imposed at the height of the war, periodic reviews of the COCOM lists have considerably reduced the number and scope of controlled items over the years. A comprehensive review in 1954 reduced the number of items on the embargo list from 270 to 167, and a second comprehensive review in 1958 further reduced it from approximately 167 to 150 items. While the number of items on the embargo list remained steady until the 1980s, reductions in the severity of the controls reduced its coverage by as much as 40 percent in 1968 and 30 percent in 1971 and 1972 (Klitgaard 1975, 466).

Between 1969 and 1984, COCOM members reviewed the control lists every three or four years. In 1985, to keep the lists up to date in the face of rapid technological change, members agreed to conduct a continuous, or rolling, four-year review, reviewing different segments of the lists each year. In May, 1991, COCOM members agreed to a rolling two-year review. In the list review process, officials in each member country develop proposals for list additions and deletions, which are then presented in COCOM. This process is where a large part of the coordination effort has occurred.

At the June, 1990, HLM, members agreed to delete thirty entries from the IL, and at least five items were subsequently collapsed into other categories, reducing the list to around eighty items. COCOM members also then agreed to create a core list to replace the industrial list, which, in effect, would reduce the industrial list by as much as 50 percent. Eventually, COCOM members drafted a nine-category, sixty-nine-item core list by the fall of 1991 composed of

- advanced materials,
- material processing,
- electronics,
- computers,
- telecommunications,
- sensors,
- navigation and avionics,
- marine technology, and
- propulsion systems. ("Welcome to the Core List." 1991)

The original intent was to create this list from scratch, but it was later decided to streamline the existing industrial list.

While 78 of the 80 items on the IL became part of the core list, 350 of the 600 subitems were deleted from the list or saw restrictions relaxed (Root 1991, 3). Of the remainder, 124 went unchanged, 29 were increased, and 97 had restrictions both increased and decreased (Root 1991, 3). Most of the additional or decreased coverage conformed to the items found on the U.S. Militarily Critical Technologies List (MCTL). COCOM members continued to liberalize controls after creating the core list, as when they relaxed controls on telecommunications items in June, 1992.

Because technological advances often outpace the list review process, COCOM allows exceptions to the embargo lists. The least stringent are administrative exceptions.[8] Items below a certain technological threshold in the Administrative Exception Notes may be granted an administrative exception at the national discretion of a COCOM member government, which need only report it as part of monthly statistics. At the notification level, items may be exported without COCOM approval, but COCOM must be specifically notified (this level includes only a few items).

Next, actual exception requests may require COCOM to grant "favorable consideration" exceptions case by case as long as the application meets a variety of noted conditions. Finally, general exceptions may be granted for items above a certain technological threshold, with the formal consent of other members prior to export to a proscribed destination. Because each exception request is reviewed case by case, delegates may submit only up to twenty cases per day.

Although member states may agree in principle on what should be on the COCOM lists, the practice of export controls varies among member states as a result of how the COCOM lists are interpreted in national lists and the rigor of national licensing and enforcement efforts. These differences have produced significant tensions in COCOM and have led to periodic efforts to harmonize national export control systems.

The Australia Group

Origins

By 1984, a number of Western countries had unilaterally imposed national controls on a number of chemicals, many of which were dual-use, primarily in response to Iraq's use of chemical weapons in its war with Iran. In March, 1985, the U.S. government called for a multilateral approach, and on the basis of an Australian initiative, the necessary negotiations began in June, 1985, resulting in the formation of the AG in that same year. Most members see the AG as a stop-gap measure until an international agreement (e.g., the Chemical Weapons Convention) or a broader, umbrella-type export control system can be developed. More recently, Iraqi chemical weapons capabilities in the Gulf War of 1990–91 sparked an agreement to harmonize national policies and make the controls much more restrictive.

Members and Leadership

Members of the AG are industrialized Western producers of chemicals. The initial members were Australia, Belgium, Canada, Denmark, France, Germany, Greece, Ireland, Italy, Japan, Luxembourg, the Netherlands, New Zealand, the United Kingdom, and the United States. By 1992, Austria, Finland, Norway, Portugal, Spain, Sweden, and Switzerland had also joined, and Turkey had applied to participate (the EC Commission participates as well).[9] The United States has been very active diplomatically in attempting to control the export of chemicals and dual-use chemical technology (Clarke 1991; Snidle 1990). At the same time, the government of Australia has been very influential in the AG, and others (including the United Kingdom) have made important contributions to the group.

Functions and Decision-Making Structure

The AG consults, shares information, and coordinates domestic export controls efforts related to the development and spread of chemical weapons capabilities in the world. The prospects for proliferation involving Iran, Iraq, Libya, and Syria were of special concern to the group in the late 1980s and early 1990s (Bartholomew 1989).

With no charter, treaty, or constitution, the AG is an informal association for which decision making demands consensus and unanimity. The AG is chaired by Australia and meets twice a year in Paris (Bartholomew 1989, 2). The AG allows participating states an "appreciable degree of latitude in implementing AG guidelines in their domestic export control legislation" (Wemple 1990a, 5).

The AG itself has no prohibition on chemical exports, but makes suggestions to the member countries to control chemical weapons precursors in ways that ensure their appropriate commercial use (Bartholomew 1989). The actual controls depend on the various national policies and practices of the member states. For example, the United States controls the export of chemical weapons agents through the International Traffic in Arms Regulations (ITAR) and the Export Administration Regulations (EAR). Chemical agents with strictly military applications are listed on the U.S. Munitions List of the ITAR which the State Department handles. All other chemicals, including the dual-use items on the AG list, are controlled under the Commerce Control List—known as the Commodity Control List (CCL) until 1991—of the EAR, which the Department of Commerce handles. Until recently, the controls the AG countries imposed varied widely. While Australia controlled the same fifty items the United States controlled, France controlled thirty (but included five more of its own). Austria and Denmark, on the other hand, controlled only a few of the most troublesome chemicals.

Controls

In 1989, fifty dual-use chemicals appeared on the AG warning list, with a suggestion that AG countries place controls on them. Nine of these fifty items were on an early core list to which members agreed to apply domestic export controls (Bartholomew 1989). These were methyl phosphonyl dichloride, methyl phosphonyl difluoride, dimethyl methyl phosphonate, thiodiglycol, dimethyl phosphite, trimethyl phosphite, phosphorus trichloride, phosphorus oxychloride, and thionyl chloride.[10]

These items are precursors for common commercial products, from plastics to pesticides, but are also vital components of mustard and nerve gases. In 1991, the AG agreed on additional control lists of (1) equipment related to the manufacture of chemical weapons precursors and (2) biological organisms and equipment (LeMunyon 1992, 2). The AG also prepared a document that warned the industry, the scientific community, and others against aiding the development of biological weapons (Wemple 1990a).

After being involved in a number of embarrassing export cases resulting in the proliferation of chemical weapons capabilities to such countries as Iraq and Libya, Germany studied its chemical export controls and considerably tightened them in 1990 (Najarian 1991). Concern in Australia, Japan, Luxembourg, and the Netherlands also resulted in "measures to strengthen their domestic chemical export control independently of the AG" ("Australia Group Considers Chemical Controls" 1991, 15). In its 1990 Enhanced Proliferation Control Initiative (EPCI), "the U.S. pledged to implement worldwide controls for all AG chemical weapons precursors and to control twenty-three categories of chemical and biological processing equipment" ("Australia Group Considers Chemical Controls" 1991, 15).

At the December, 1990, meeting, the members "agreed to implement more restrictive controls on AG items" ("Australia Group Considers Chemical Controls" 1991, 15) and effectively expanded domestic controls to all fifty items on the warning list.

In May, 1991, the AG accepted a U.S. plan "to adopt controls as tough as those already in effect in the United States" and reached a consensus to control all fifty precursor chemicals worldwide (U.S. General Accounting Office 1991). Since March, 1991, the U.S. unilaterally required validated licenses for the export of all fifty items on the warning list to Iran, Iraq, Syria, and Libya. The May, 1991, agreement promised the implementation of similar systems for all twenty member countries. A similar proposal for dual-use and solely military biological items was considered at the December, 1991, meeting of the group. By October, 1992, the AG members had expanded the list to control fifty-four chemical precursors (U.S. Arms Control and Disarmament Agency 1992, 9).

The Nuclear Suppliers Group

Origins

On May 18, 1974, India detonated what it called a "peaceful nuclear device" for commercial operations. Although the Indian "device" had not explicitly broken any provision of the NPT (India has not been a signatory) and India had assured the world that its newly acquired technology would be employed only as a labor-saving instrument, the explosion raised concerns among the governments of the nuclear supplier countries, particularly the United States, about the limits of the NPT approach to nonproliferation.

Even the creation in 1972 and publication in 1974 of a trigger list of exports by the Nuclear Exporters Committee (the Zangger Committee) under Article III(2)(b) of the NPT, which would require the acceptance and application of IAEA safeguards, did not satisfy these concerns (Potter 1982, 44–

45).[11] To meet the desire for a more comprehensive trigger list and more stringent safeguards, seven governments agreed to create the NSG (also known as the London Suppliers Group), which first met in London in November, 1975. After reaching an agreement on a new list, there were no formal meetings between 1977 and 1991. Though there were informal gatherings (the Bratislava Club) in the 1980s, some members opposed more formal meetings to avoid the discussion of controls on dual-use items and the appearance of a conspiracy of Northern countries against emerging industrial powers in the South.

Members and Leadership

The original members of the NSG were Canada, the Federal Republic of Germany, France, Japan, the Soviet Union, the United Kingdom, and the United States (Tate 1990, 406). Though the French insisted that the original meeting be held in secret, their participation was a major breakthrough in international cooperation since they were one of two nuclear weapons states that were not signatories of the NPT at the time (Tate 1990, 407). Twenty-one additional countries adhering to NSG guidelines are Australia, Austria, Belgium, Bulgaria, the Czech Republic, Denmark, Finland, Greece, Hungary, Ireland, Italy, Luxembourg, the Netherlands, Norway, Poland, Portugal, Romania, Slovakia, Spain, Sweden, and Switzerland (IAEA 1992, 1). The Russian Federation has replaced the Soviet Union in the meetings.

Functions and Decision-Making Structure

Broadly speaking, the purpose of the NSG is to develop internationally accepted standards of behavior for nuclear suppliers, including suppliers of nuclear technologies. The NSG is an informal association of nations, and it has no formal structure, though the United States is attempting to expand bilateral talks with the United Kingdom, the Netherlands, France, and Germany into a more formal agreement. Although the NSG is not officially associated with the IAEA, and indeed there is some evidence of tension between the two because the function of the NSG can conflict with the IAEA's assistance mandate, its address is "c/o" the IAEA in Vienna. In 1992, the Japanese government created a point of contact for NSG members in Vienna.

The NSG regulates international nuclear trade to minimize the risks of nuclear weapons proliferation. It does this by coordinating controls on exports of sensitive nuclear materials, equipment, and technology; insisting on safeguards on exported items; and providing various end-user guidelines (Potter 1982, 45).

The arrangement establishes a "uniform code of conduct" and urges "restraint" in the export of sensitive nuclear items (Potter 1982, 44–45; Müller 1990, 572). Essentially, the guidelines stipulate that recipient states pledge to not use the transferred items in the manufacture of nuclear explosives, to accept safeguards, to secure the items, and to prevent transshipment without the concurrence of the original supplier government (Fischer and Szasz 1985, 217–23).

Compliance with this code of conduct is, of course, completely voluntary. Though members generally follow the established guidelines, violations have undermined the group's nonproliferation objectives. For example, in the late 1970s, West Germany and Canada were competing to supply Argentina with controlled items. The Canadian firm offered a lower bid but required full-scope safeguards on the items. The Germans placed no safeguard conditions on the sale and won the contract (Potter 1982, 109).

Controls

The Nuclear (or London) Suppliers Group Agreement of January, 1976, included a longer version of the Zangger Committee trigger list and was further expanded in 1977 into the Nuclear (London) Suppliers Guidelines. Primarily, the NSG agreed to control the types of materials, technologies, and equipment that could be traded to non-NPT states and required recipient states to ensure that any such items would not be used in the manufacture of any nuclear explosive device. The trigger list has two parts. Part A covers material and equipment (including source or special fissionable material), reactors and equipment, and nonnuclear material for reactors. Part B covers technology defined as "technical data" (Fischer and Szasz 1985).

When consensus and agreement were achieved, these guidelines were submitted to and published through the IAEA in early 1978. While the rules of the IAEA or the Zangger Committee had no similar stipulations concerning technology and non-NPT members, the members of the NSG clearly wanted to prevent another "peaceful" nuclear explosion (Elliot and Reginald 1989, 266–67).

Unlike the Zangger list, however, which has legal standing because of its direct association with the NPT, the NSG list is not legally binding; it is an informal agreement or a "multilateral statement of national policy" designed to "minimize the proliferation risk of [nuclear] exports by imposing safeguards and government promises" (Potter 1982, 45). The participants in the NSG agree to require validated licenses for exports of controlled items to destinations in non-NSG countries.

"Although supplier states pledge to coordinate their nuclear export controls with the IAEA through the Zangger Committee and the NSG, international adherence to the safeguard requirements has been inconsistent" (Wemple 1991, 4). In recent years, exporters have disagreed about the requirement for full-scope safeguards as a precondition for the shipment of nuclear materials and equipment to nonnuclear weapons states. The full-scope requirement obligates the recipient state to place all its nuclear facilities under the inspection of the IAEA, thus giving IAEA inspectors access to all installations capable of producing nuclear explosive devices. Countries such as Brazil, Argentina, India, and Pakistan have resisted full-scope safeguards. In 1984, the Western members agreed to require full-scope safeguards of all nuclear exports to some areas.

By August, 1990, Australia, Canada, Japan, Sweden, and the United States declared their official licensing policy of approving nuclear exports only to countries that had complied with full-scope inspections. Shortly thereafter, Germany declared its adherence to this policy, closely followed by Belgium, France, the United Kingdom, Spain, and Switzerland. In March, 1992, Russia also adopted the full-scope safeguard criteria.

On the basis of a Dutch initiative, the NSG formally reconvened in March, 1991, to consider introducing controls on dual-use items. Throughout 1990–91, the United States urged NSG members to agree to a list of sixty-nine dual-use nuclear items based on the U.S. Nuclear Referral List. At an April, 1992, meeting in Warsaw, NSG members finally agreed on sixty-five dual-use items in seven categories: industrial equipment, materials, uranium isotope separating equipment and components, implosion system development equipment, explosives and related equipment, nuclear testing equipment and compounds, and other items. Most, but not all, of the items, were on the U.S. Nuclear Referral List, and one category of items strongly advocated by U.S. representatives—computers—was not placed on the NSG list.

The Missile Technology Control Regime

Origins

The successful launching of the Indian SLV-3 in 1980 spurred U.S. officials to develop an overall policy on missile proliferation leading to informal talks with the British in 1982 and formal talks with other Western governments later (Karp 1989, 13). Though an interim agreement to control the proliferation of ballistic missiles, including dual-use missile items, was reached in 1985, it was not announced until 1987 when two more years of negotiation finalized its common guidelines (U.S. Department of State 1987). However, by 1988, a variety of events (the War of the Cities, the Condor II missile program, the Jericho IIb launch by Israel, and Chinese deliveries of missiles to Saudi Arabia) resulted in an expanded agreement to conduct regular meetings and otherwise strengthen the regime (Karp 1989).[12]

Members and Leadership

Following an effort by the United States to multilateralize controls developed in the early 1980s, the United Kingdom, the United States, France, Germany, and Italy began the MTCR in 1985 and were soon joined by Canada and Japan. After the 1990–91 Gulf War and the experience with Iraqi Scuds, the MTCR took on added salience, and its membership expanded rapidly from seven to eighteen. The post-Gulf War additions were Australia, Austria, Belgium, Denmark, Finland, Luxembourg, the Netherlands, New Zealand, Norway, Spain, and Sweden (Wolfsthal 1991, 20). A number of other countries, most importantly China, Israel, and Russia, pledged to join the regime or at least abide by its guidelines. Finally, there is a series of bilateral negotiations between the United States and a number of countries that might serve to broaden participation in the regime.

Functions and Decision-Making Structure

The MTCR is an informal, nontreaty association of governments sharing intelligence information concerning missile development and proliferation. It has no secretariat, though Paris serves as a point of contact for members. Differences in the interpretation of controls are substantial. For example, the Russian government interprets some transfers of controlled items as legitimate because they were for "defensive" missiles, and the MTCR has no enforcement mechanism to ensure compliance. Wemple (1990b, 9) notes, "There are no provisions in the MTCR agreement that mandate or authorize a member government to apply sanctions against companies or other governments for shipping sensitive equipment to a country of proliferation concern."

Controls

Members of the MTCR initially sought to control the export of items for missile systems that could deliver a 500-kilogram warhead more than 300 kilometers (U.S. Department of State 1987). The focus was orginally on nuclear-capable missile delivery systems, but members later agreed in principle to include systems that could deliver all weapons of mass destruction (LeMunyon 1992, 3). Negotiations among the members produced a set of guidelines for the transfer of missile technology and a twelve-page annex that listed eighteen technologies to be controlled. There are two categories of items on the list. Category I items have a heavy presumption of control and include complete missile systems and missile subsystems. Items and technologies may be transferred if peaceful end use can be certified and an agreement prohibiting diversion is reached with the government of the recipient country (Wemple 1990b). Controls on the sixteen Category II items, such as computers and computer software, are less restrictive but still require end-use certification or verification. A November, 1991, meeting in Washington reached agreement on a revision of the control list outlining export licensing requirements and reduced discrepancies among members over which products and technologies were to be controlled ("MTCR Countries Complete Harmonization," 1991). Members also monitor states involved in missile-related trade and technology transfer and attempt to use diplomatic means to promote cooperation and compliance with the evolving export control norms.

At the June, 1992, meeting in Oslo, the members agreed to new licensing and control procedures for missiles that can deliver any payload, not just those exceeding the 500 kilograms necessary for a nuclear device. They also agreed to institute retransfer controls on restricted items.

Summary

All four of these institutions have their origins in the latter half of the twentieth century, an era of unprecedented growth in the number of IGOs (Jacobson 1984). No single event appears to have been critical to the formation of COCOM, but the members of COCOM did clearly identify the Soviet Union, and later China, as direct and specific threats to their interests. In this regard, COCOM seems much like the majority of international security arrangements, most notably military alliances, that target nonmembers for their operations. The efforts to create the CCF in 1992 are directly linked to the military, political, and economic transformation in former target states and to the specter of a large military-industrial complex no longer fully constrained by central government authority in Eastern Europe and the former Soviet Union.

One can point to specific, critical historical events that sparked the formation of the NSG (the Indian nuclear test), the MTCR (the missile war phase of the Iran-Iraq war), and the AG (the use of chemical weapons by the Iraqis), which is consistent with the observation of Young (1986) that "eye-catching" events assist in the evolution of international institutions. Curiously, none of these three institutions was formed in response to a direct and specific threat to the security of the founding members. This suggests that governments are able to agree to cooperate on export control issues, even when threats are diffuse and unspecified, such as a potential Syrian missile threat against other countries in the Middle East, despite the security dimension of the issues and policies. At the same time, the specific threat posed by the Iraqi invasion of Kuwait and Iraqi efforts (with Western assistance) to acquire weapons and technologies of mass destruction reinvigorated the three nonproliferation export control regimes.

On average, the members took less than two years to conduct the initial negotiations and then create these informal organizations. Compared to many other negotiations on arms or trade issues, this time period is remarkably short. That may result in part from the diffuse and nonspecific nature of the threats confronting the MTCR, the AG, and the NSG, which preclude exact calculations of the costs and benefits of cooperation. With little certainty about the eventual amount and distribution of the costs and benefits, the often contentious efforts to negotiate a detailed contract over the rewards, rights, and privileges of various members could be avoided.

Moreover, the specific communist threat COCOM members perceived made for greater certainty about the costs and benefits of cooperation but did not result in substantially more difficult initial negotiations. That may be explained by the economic, technological, and military dominance of the major proponent of the system, the United States, in its formative years. Since U.S. firms accounted for almost half of world trade at that time, they were most likely to be burdened by the comprehensive nature of COCOM controls (even though U.S. trade with the Soviet Union was much less than West European trade with the Soviet Union), while Western Europeans were the immediate beneficiaries of limits on Soviet war-fighting capabilities at the time.

That three organizations emerged in an era of apparently eroding U.S. relative power argues strongly against the contention of many scholars that the creation of international cooperative arrangements requires hegemonic leadership (Gilpin 1987; Keohane 1984). While the United States consistently emerges as an active participant in each group, others, particularly some West European governments, make important contributions in the decision-making process of each organization. The United States also asked for substantial economic and military assistance in its efforts to lead U.N. forces to victory over Iraq, as most saw military action in the Gulf as too great a burden to bear alone.

Nonetheless, the United States appears to play a central role in the creation or invigoration of all the multilateral export control organizations. In contrast, the country most often mentioned as the real challenger of U.S. hegemony, Japan, remained relatively inactive until the Toshiba-Konigsberg scandal of 1988.

Since the transfer of most dual-use technologies requires an array of items and services to be effective, membership in these institutions need not include all the countries with access to the technologies but only those that have the capacity to transfer these technologies. After the early years of their formation, membership in the NSG and COCOM has remained relatively stable. Like the NSG and COCOM, the AG and the MTCR are experiencing an initial increase in membership. Only one country has left an institution once it entered, and that came only with the dissolution of the German Democratic Republic on reunification. This suggests that long-term cooperation is possible, particularly among the Western nations that compose the bulk of the membership in each institution.

Though the emergence of new producers or the omission of existing producers raises questions about the utility of these institutions, membership in these institutions remains relatively small, which is thought to be an aid to cooperation (Snidal 1985). At the same time, the informal nature of the institutions and the uncertainty regarding the distribution of costs and benefits means that a larger number of nations might be accommodated around "fair" solutions (Young 1986).

Despite extensive Western participation, non-Western governments are not precluded from membership in these IGOs. The membership of the NSG spans the East-West divide, and the former Soviet Union even showed interest in participating in the AG and the MTCR. Given the significance of the East in the production of these systems, excluding the East would likely undermine the effectiveness of these organizations. That may even be true for COCOM if its targets change.

Membership says much less about the potential for North-South cooperation. So far, the southern countries remain outside the institutions though they interact with them and are affected by decisions made within the institutional context.

The proscribed destinations somewhat imprecisely mirror the members of the organizations. While the AG focuses primarily on a few Arab countries, the MTCR and the NSG include those and others in the Third World, while COCOM retained its concern with communist and postcommunist states through 1992.

Unlike typical IGOs, which have their structure and functions defined by treaty, these organizations are essentially informal agreements. At the same time, official understandings about behavior and routines and standard operating procedures have emerged over time, certainly in COCOM, which is, in this sense, the most developed of these IGOs. Like many IGOs, these organizations follow the rule of unanimity for key decisions. None of them have large administrative organizations, although national administration of the control systems may be vast (that varies across countries as well). Cooperation ranges from regular and intensive interaction between the members (e.g., COCOM in the late 1980s and early 1990s) to infrequent and low-level (e.g., NSG in the late 1970s).

A key task for all four organizations is the maintenance of a list of controlled items. Though the lists typically directly identify the item controlled, some controls are purposefully obscured within the list (e.g., in COCOM) because revealing that an item is controlled transfers some information in and of itself. While coverage of each list changes over time, the changes in the lists do not indicate that the basic problem facing each organization also changes. Rather, new organizations (and new lists) were created to meet new problems, as an organizational evolution approach would suggest (Haas 1990, 174).

The lists are all item based, though all but the AG list limit the transfer of technical data and other means of transferring a technology as well. All the lists are or have been differentiated, usually in terms of the severity of the controls.

Although there appear to be no formal sanctions to be employed against wayward member governments, sanctions against firms for violating the arrangements may be severe, including the loss of trading privileges or aid. Countries whose firms consistently violate the standards of the institution run the risk of incurring the wrath of the other members, who might impede technology transfer or impose some other punishment or metasanctions (Axelrod 1984). When the U.S. tried to impose metasanctions through extraterritorial application of its laws in the 1980s, it met great resistance by many members of COCOM. Though many states improved their export control efforts in the 1980s, it is not clear whether extraterritorial application of U.S. law provoked that behavior or served as a disruptive element in developing multilateral cooperation.

These organizations do not typically have the resources to verify end use by themselves and generally rely on information provided by the business and intelligence communities of their members. For the NSG, another IGO (e.g., the IAEA) plays a crucial role in end-use verification. Intelligence gathering and intelligence sharing in these multilateral export control organizations seems likely to be a more challenging task in the next century than in the cold war era for at least two reasons. Compared to East-West controls, nonproliferation controls affect a largely different set of countries. That means that new intelligence assets must be applied, often with great delicacy to avoid offending governments relatively friendly to the multilateral participants. Moreover, COCOM controls targeted countries, whereas controls now focus more on end users and end use, which demands a new standard of intelligence gathering and analysis.

Conclusion

So far, implementing multilateral export controls has been an exercise in coordinating mutual national interests more than bargaining to reconcile divergent national interests. The short negotiating phase prior to creating the IGO, no norm of group sanctions on members that do not enforce the rules, the unsuccessful use of hardball bargaining tactics between members, and the general appearance of consensus all indicate that common interests tend to overwhelm divergent interests in these organizations. These characteristics mark the problems facing these IGOs as ones of coordination rather than cooperation (Axelrod 1984; Stein 1990). That is not to say that no divergent interests exist within these organizations or that difficult negotiations do not occur; indeed, all these IGOs may be characterized by disagreement over the type and extent of controls. Nonetheless, the bargaining among members takes place within a shared understanding of what the problem is (e.g., the security implications of the transfer of dual-use items) and what roughly constitutes fair behavior (e.g., recognizing the need for mutual restraint in order to effectively control these transfers).

However, if these organizations come to subsume states from the East and the South, new bargains about what is considered fair must be struck. These new bargains will no longer be a matter of harmonization but will likely require significant trade-offs and side payments before meaningful agreements can be reached, if agreement can be reached at all. Negotiations between IGO members and nonmembers, such as the Third Country Initiative in COCOM whereby members seek to accommodate the policies of various third countries with COCOM controls, will become as important as negotiations within the IGOs.

More importantly, there is little evidence that members of these informal export control IGOs want to or can incorporate newly industrializing countries (NICs) or other third world states into the organizations, yet the current diffusion of dual-use technologies may already be enough to undermine the effectiveness of these IGOs without more widespread participation. In that sense, these organizations may have to learn or adapt to new definitions of both what is the problem and what is fair.

APPENDIX: PARTICIPATION IN EXPORT CONTROL REGIMES, 1992

Countries	COCOM	AG	NSG	MTCR
Americas				
Argentina				[a]
Canada	Yes	Yes	Yes	Yes
United States	Yes	Yes	Yes	Yes
Asia				
Australia	Yes	Yes	Yes	Yes
Hong Kong	[b]			
Japan	Yes	Yes	Yes	Yes
New Zealand	[b]	Yes		Yes
PRC				[a]
Europe				
Austria	[b]	Yes	Yes	Yes
Belgium	Yes	Yes	Yes	Yes
Bulgaria			Yes	
CSFR		Yes	Yes	
Denmark	Yes	Yes	Yes	Yes
Finland	[b]	Yes	Yes	Yes
France	Yes	Yes	Yes	Yes
Germany	Yes	Yes	Yes	Yes
Greece	Yes	Yes	Yes	Yes
Hungary			Yes	
Iceland				Yes
Ireland	[b]	Yes	Yes	Yes
Italy	Yes	Yes	Yes	Yes
Luxembourg	Yes	Yes	Yes	Yes
Netherlands	Yes	Yes	Yes	Yes
Norway	Yes	Yes	Yes	Yes
Poland			Yes	
Portugal	Yes	Yes	Yes	Yes
Romania			Yes	
Spain	Yes	Yes	Yes	Yes
Sweden	[b]	Yes	Yes	Yes
Switzerland	[b]	Yes	Yes	Yes
United Kingdom	Yes	Yes	Yes	Yes
Eurasia				
Russia/CIS			Yes	[a]
Turkey	Yes			
Middle East				
Israel				[a]

[a] = Agreement to abide by MTCR guidelines
[b] = 5(k) understanding with COCOM members

NOTES

The authors wish to thank research assistants Geoffrey Dillard and Peter Allen for their help on this chapter.

1. International governmental organizations are typically defined as organizations created by agreements between governments whose members are governments and whose members meet periodically, usually with the assistance of a secretariat (see Feld and Jordan 1988; Jacobson 1984; and Union of International Associations 1989).

2. In 1992, the members of COCOM agreed to create the CCF, which includes some of the former targets of COCOM controls (limited to those formerly communist governments now undergoing significant military, economic, and political reform) and Western governments (COCOM members and cooperating neutrals), to discuss export control issues. Currently, the U.S. and Japanese governments have a bilateral agreement to control exports of supercomputers, but there is some interest in expanding this into a multilateral agreement with Britain, France, Germany, Italy, and the Netherlands. The Zangger Committee, which preceded the NSG, imposes some restrictions on exports to signatories of the Nuclear Nonproliferation Treaty (NPT). Since membership in the Zangger Committee roughly parallels membership in the NSG and the NSG guidelines are more extensive, we chose to focus on the NSG.

3. An Anglo-French list of strategic exports was formulated in 1949, but it was far less restrictive than the U.S. 1A and 1B lists. List 1A consisted of items of direct military usage and items that contained advanced technology. List 1B consisted of items of general industrial significance. In 1950, there were 167 items on List 1A and about 300 on List 1B (U.S. Department of State 1952, 88–91).

4. In the early 1950s, COCOM increased controls on exports to the People's Republic of China (PRC) over and above those to the Soviet bloc as a result of the Korean War. The so-called China differential was administered by a special committee—CHINCOM—within COCOM. CHINCOM was abolished in 1957 as a result of European and particularly British pressure. In the 1980s, the PRC was granted preferential licensing treatment in COCOM, creating a reverse China differential (Root 1988, 420).

5. The CG was established in 1950 but has not met since 1958, when the French, the chairing delegation, decided not to convene it any longer.

6. For example, the core list was supposed to have been completed by December, 1990, but an agreement was not reached until May, 1991.

7. The Coordinating Committee for Multilateral Export Controls has never published a record of any of its activities, much less any lists. Apparently, the current lists have recently been released by only two governments: the United Kingdom and the United States, the latter in response to a Freedom of Information request by a private citizen.

8. Some items, in quantities of minor monetary value, may be exported without reporting to COCOM at all.

9. The membership count as of March, 1992, was twenty-three (LeMunyon 1992, 2).

10. This list can be found in Stephan, Trapp, and Weizorek 1990. Lundin (1990) notes the names of all fifty chemicals on the original warning list.

11. For example, the Zangger Committee list does not cover dual-use technologies.
12. Representatives to the group apparently meet monthly in The Hague.

REFERENCES

"Australia Group Considers Chemical Controls." 1991. *Export Control News* 5 (1): 14–17.

Axelrod, Robert. 1984. *The Evolution of Cooperation*. New York: Basic Books.

Bartholomew, Reginald. 1989. "U.S. Efforts Against the Spread of Chemical Weapons." In *Current Policy,* no. 1188. Washington, D.C.: Bureau of Public Affairs, U.S. Department of State.

Clarke, Richard A. 1991. "A Multi-faceted Approach to Non-proliferation." *Dispatch* 2 (18): 333–36.

Cupitt, Richard T. 1992. "The Future of COCOM." In *Export Controls in Transition: Perspectives, Problems, and Prospects,* edited by Gary Bertsch and Steven Elliott-Gower. Durham, N.C.: Duke University Press.

Elliot, Jeffrey M., and Robert Reginald. 1989. *The Arms Control, Disarmament, and Military Security Dictionary*. Santa Barbara, Calif.: ABC-CLIO.

Feld, Werner J., and Robert S. Jordan. 1988. *International Organizations: A Comparative Approach*. 2d ed. New York: Praeger.

Fischer, David, and Paul Szasz. 1985. *Safeguarding the Atom: A Critical Appraisal*. London: Taylor & Francis.

Gilpin, Robert. 1987. *The Political Economy of International Relations*. Princeton, N.J.: Princeton University Press.

Haas, Ernst B. 1990. *When Knowledge Is Power: Three Models of Change in International Organizations*. Berkeley, Ca.: University of California Press.

International Atomic Energy Agency (IAEA). 1992. "Communications Received from Certain Member States Regarding Guidelines for the Export of Nuclear Material, Equipment and Technology." IAEA Document INFCIRC/254/Rev.1/Part 2. Vienna: IAEA.

Jacobson, Harold K. 1984. *Networks of Interdependence: International Organizations and the Global Political System*. 2d ed. New York: Alfred A. Knopf.

Karp, Aaron. 1989. *The United States and the Soviet Union and the Control of Ballistic Missile Proliferation to the Middle East*. New York: Institute for East-West Security Studies.

Keohane, Robert O. 1984. *After Hegemony: Cooperation and Discord in the World Political Economy*. Princeton, N.J.: Princeton University Press.

Klitgaard, Robert E. 1975. "Limiting Exports on National Security Grounds." In the *Report of the Commission on the Organization of Government for the Conduct of Foreign Policy,* vol. 4, appendix K. Washington, D.C.: GPO.

LeMunyon, James M. 1992. "Statement of James M. LeMunyon, Acting Assistant Secretary for Export Administration, U.S. Department of Commerce, Before the Joint Economic Committee, U.S. Congress, Washington, D.C., March 13, 1992." Mimeo.

Lundin, S. J. 1990. "Chemical and Biological Warfare: Developments in 1989." In *SIPRI Yearbook 1990: World Armaments and Disarmaments,* 107–33. New York: Oxford University Press.

Mastanduno, Michael. 1988. "Trade as a Strategic Weapon: American and Alliance Export Control Policy in the Early Postwar Period." *International Organization* 42 (1): 121–50.

———. 1990. "What Is COCOM and How Does It Work?" In *The Post-Containment Handbook: Key Issues in U.S.-Soviet Economic Relations,* edited by Robert Cullen. Boulder, Colo.: Westview.

"MTCR Countries Complete Harmonization." 1991. *Export Control News* 5 (11): 15–16.

Müller, Harald. 1990. "Prospects for the Fourth Review of the Non-Proliferation Treaty." In *SIPRI Yearbook 1990: World Armaments and Disarmaments.* New York: Oxford University Press.

Nadelmann, Ethan A. 1990. "Global Prohibition Regimes: The Evolution of Norms in International Society." *International Organization* 44 (4): 479–526.

Najarian, Nancy. 1991. "Germany Tightens Export Curbs." *Export Control News* 5 (2): 14–15.

National Academy of Sciences. 1987. *Balancing the National Interest: U.S. National Security Controls and Global Economic Competition.* Washington, D.C.: National Academy Press.

Potter, William C. 1982. *Nuclear Power and Non-Proliferation: An Interdisciplinary Perspective.* Cambridge, Mass.: Delgeschlager, Gunn & Hain.

Root, William A. 1988. "COCOM: An Appraisal of Objectives and Needed Reforms." In *Controlling East-West Trade and Technology Transfer: Power, Politics and Policies,* edited by Gary K. Bertsch, 417–41. Durham, N.C.: Duke University Press.

———. 1991. "The Core List: Expectations vs. Reality." *Export Control News* 5, no. 7 (July 29): 2–5.

Snidal, Duncan. 1985. "Coordination versus Prisoners' Dilemma: Implications for International Cooperation and Regimes." *American Political Science Review* 79 (4): 923–42.

Snidle, Giovanni A. 1990. "United States Efforts in Curbing Chemical Weapons Proliferation." In U.S. Arms Control and Disarmament Agency, *World Military Expenditures and Arms Transfers, 1989,* 21–24. Washington, D.C.: GPO.

Stein, Arthur A. 1990. *Why Nations Cooperate: Circumstance and Choice in International Relations.* Ithaca, N.Y.: Cornell University Press.

Stephan, Ursula, Ralf Trapp, and Wolf-Diether Weizorek. 1990. "National Hazardous Chemical Legislation in the German Democratic Republic." In *National Implementation of the Future Chemical Weapons Convention,* edited by Thomas Stock and Ronald Sutherland, 85–92. New York, N.Y.: Oxford University Press.

Tate, Trevor McMorris. 1990. "Regime Building in the Non-Proliferation System." *Journal of Peace Research* 27 (4): 399–414.

Union of International Associations. 1989. *Yearbook of International Organizations, 1989/90.* Munich: KG Saur Verlag.

U.S. Arms Control and Disarmament Agency. 1992. *Annual Report on the Proliferation of Missiles and Essential Components of Nuclear, Biological, and Chemical Weapons.* Washington, D.C.: U.S. Arms Control and Disarmament Agency.

U.S. Department of State. 1952. *Foreign Relations of the United States, IV.* Washington, D.C.: GPO.

———. 1987. *American Foreign Policy Current Documents.* Document 31. Washington, D.C.: GPO.

U.S. General Accounting Office. 1991. *U.S. and International Efforts to Ban Chemical Weapons.* Washington, D.C.: U.S. General Accounting Office.

"Welcome to the Core List!" 1991. *Export Control News* 5, no. 8 (August 25): 2–5.

Wemple, Erik. 1990a. "Chemical Weapons Controls: Old Problems, New Solutions?" *Export Control News,* Special Report.

———. 1990b. "Fighting an Uphill Battle: Missile Technology Export Controls." *Export Control News,* Special Report.

———. 1991. "Preventing the Proliferation of Nuclear Weapons: Multilateral Efforts and US Attempts." *Export Control News,* Special Report.

Wolfsthal, Jon. 1991. "Israel Accepts MTCR Guidelines." *Arms Control Today* 21, no. 9 (November): 20.

Young, Oran R. 1986. "International Regimes: Toward a New Theory of Institutions." *World Politics* 39 (1): 104–22.

Part 2
National Perspectives

CHAPTER 3

Global Security, Democratization, and Economic Development after the Cold War: New Goals for U.S. Export Control Policies

William J. Long

Background on U.S. Export Control Policy

The United States has long controlled the export of dual-use goods and technologies, that is, civilian technologies with potential military applications such as computers or avionics, to further its national security interests. To further a broader set of foreign policy interests, the United States has limited the export of dual-use items and purely civilian items as well. Since the early days of the Cold War, U.S. policy has primarily revolved around implementing a strategic embargo against communist countries—strengthening the economic arm to containment.

Beginning with the Export Control Act of 1949, Congress gave peacetime statutory authority to the president to develop a list of controlled products and proscribed destinations to prevent the transfer of technology that would contribute to the military capability of a real or potential adversary.[1] Section 5 of the Export Administration Act (EAA) (the 1949 act's successor) maintains this authority. The president, through his designee, the Commerce Department, draws up a list of controlled dual-use products—the Commerce Control List (formerly the Commodity Control List)—and identifies countries as proscribed destinations. The Commerce Department administers the system through licensing dual-use exports with the advice of other agencies, primarily the Departments of Defense and State.

In addition to devising a system of unilateral restraints, the United States has sought to promote multilateral cooperation in implementing national security export controls. To this end, the United States organized COCOM in 1949. Although similar to the U.S. controls, in one notable respect COCOM's mandate has always been narrower than that of the U.S. export control regime: COCOM restricts only exports that have potential military utility and, in contrast to the United States, does not impose foreign policy export controls.

During the early years of the Cold War, the West maintained extensive unilateral and multilateral export controls toward the communist East. Initial COCOM security strategy sought to prohibit the export of virtually all equipment and technology that would assist the military or economic capabilities of the East by licensing the export or reexport of technology within the West and between East and West. This comprehensive approach was not without its costs.

By the late 1960s, growing allied and U.S. business dissatisfaction with the economic consequences of an expansive embargo of the East led to congressional reforms. Congress stipulated that export controls should govern only products and technologies that *significantly* contribute to a potential enemy's military capability, and then only if a comparable product could not be obtained from foreign suppliers.[2] Preserving the West's superiority over the East in defense-related technologies, rather than economic warfare itself, became the statutory goal of U.S. and COCOM policy and the scope of the U.S. and COCOM lists were reduced somewhat.

Still, during the 1970s and 1980s the strategy of containment remained the guiding principle of dual-use export control policy, albeit with limited recognition of the importance of expanding nonstrategic trade. Offsetting the quantitative superiority of the Warsaw Treaty Organization's forces by maintaining NATO's qualitative, technological superiority was the premise of export control policy.

In addition to national security export controls, the U.S. Congress has authorized the president to use export controls to further the foreign policy of the United States or to fulfill its international obligations.[3] Section 6 of the EAA currently provides this authority. Foreign policy export controls have been directed against certain communist and noncommunist countries for reasons ranging from human rights to terrorism and regional stability.[4] Controls on chemical and biological weapons precursors, missiles, and missile-related technologies, for example, have been maintained under the foreign policy provisions of the EAA. Authority for controls over nuclear-related dual-use items is contained in section 17 of the EAA.

Unlike most national security controls, the U.S. carries out most foreign policy controls unilaterally. Foreign policy controls generally lacked a mechanism such as COCOM to coordinate their restrictions with the practices of U.S. allies or other nations. This important difference has been the source of protracted and heated domestic debate with regard to the costs and effectiveness of foreign policy export controls and diplomatic imbroglios with allies that have resisted the extraterritorial application of U.S. foreign policy controls.

More recently, the United States has entered into organizations whose jurisdiction includes certain foreign policy controls. These include the MTCR and the AG. The MTCR generates a common export control list for certain technologies useful in making ballistic missiles. The MTCR is designed to restrict the export of goods or technologies used in the assembly of missiles capable of carrying a nuclear payload. The controls apply to missiles with ranges greater than 190 miles and payloads of more than 1,100 pounds. The MTCR establishes policy guidelines for its members and prepares two annexes of controlled items: one for munitions and the other for dual-use items. Exports of listed munitions are to be denied to nonmembers; dual-use items may be exported if appropriate safeguard assurances are received from the government of the importing country. All members agree to coordinate their policies and share information on projects of concern.[5] National authorities implement the controls without formal review or consensus by other MTCR members, however.

The AG controls certain substances useful as chemical weapon precursors and related production equipment. The AG is designed to serve as an interim arrangement until the ratification and implementation of the Chemical Weapons Convention negotiated in 1991 as part of the Conference on Disarmament in Geneva. An informal organization whose recommendations are not binding on its members, the AG identifies chemical weapons precursors and production technology of concern and shares intelligence about states that are potentially developing chemical weapons.

In contrast to dual-use items, the United States controls the trade or transfer of purely military articles and services, that is, articles without a civilian end use, under the Arms Export Control Act of 1976, as amended.[6] The Office of Defense Trade Controls (previously the Office of Munitions Controls) at the Department of State, in consultation with the Department of Defense, administers controls specified by the act and its corresponding International Traffic in Arms Regulations. The regulations contain a separate itemization of military equipment subject to export licensing known as the Munitions List.

Those items that could be used to produce nuclear weapons fall under yet another statutory and regulatory regime. The Atomic Energy Act of 1954 and the Nuclear Nonproliferation Act of 1978 authorize controls over the export of such items.[7] Generally, the United States only licenses exports of sensitive nuclear materials to an atomic energy facility that is protected by IAEA safeguards. The purpose of the IAEA safeguards is to ensure that nuclear materials and technologies are not diverted from peaceful energy uses to weapons production. The U.S. Nuclear Regulatory Commission licenses the export of goods and services that are wholly nuclear energy related, whereas the Commerce Department, in consultation with the Department of Energy and others, licenses dual use nuclear-related technologies and products. The Subgroup on Nuclear Export Controls (SNEC), an interagency body, is the principal review group for nuclear-related license applications.[8]

To improve international cooperation in the prevention of nuclear weapons proliferation, the United States joined the so-called Zangger Committee in 1974, pledging not to export certain items to nonweapon states without a pledge of "no explosive use" and the acceptance of IAEA safeguards by the recipient. In 1978, it committed to a more comprehensive set of international guidelines in support of nonproliferation goals that added technology and technical assistance to the Zangger Committee list of goods. This latter group, the NSG, has been relatively dormant until recently.

The National Policy-Making Community

Perhaps the most striking feature of U.S. export control policy-making is the diffusion of authority across executive bureaus. Currently over a dozen agencies administer U.S. technology controls of one kind or another. A recent study by the Congressional Research Service was unable to find any analogous area of government with a comparable number of bureaucracies.[9] Moreover, these agencies hold distinctive and often diverse policy positions that reflect their historical mission and current constituencies. For example, the key players in administering dual-use export controls—Commerce, Defense, and State—have vied for control over policy for over forty years, each believing (perhaps correctly) that it brings a unique commercial, security, or diplomatic understanding to the problem. Equally true, however, is that these multiple perspectives make it difficult to coordinate the economic, military, and foreign policy dimensions of technology transfer policy.

The diffusion of policy-making authority within the executive branch ensures that the development of the various domestic control lists and the export licensing process is a complex interagency dynamic that often makes coordination with industry and allies problematic. The preparation of the national security controls on the CCL, for instance, begins with Defense Department generation of a Militarily Critical Technologies List that is adapted through interactions with the Commerce, State, and Energy Departments and the intelligence community along with advice from industry. Inevitable disputes arising from list-making exercises are aired in an ascending series of interagency review groups beginning at the senior civil service level, through the assistant secretary level, and ending at the National Security Council in the White House, if the dispute cannot be resolved at a lower level.

The licensing of exports is equally complex. Three principal agencies administer most export licenses: the Bureau of Export Administration at the Department of Commerce is charged with licensing items on the CCL; the

State Department's Center for Defense Trade, Office of Defense Trade Controls issues licenses for items on the Munitions List; and the Defense Department's Defense Technology Security Administration serves in an advisory and review capacity to both agencies. The areas of jurisdiction among these agencies are often unclear and overlapping. Disputes over whether an item is properly classified as a Munitions List good under State Department purview or is better viewed as a dual-use good under the CCL subject to Commerce Department control are not uncommon, and disputes over the proper scope and effect of Defense Department licensing review authority have raged for more than a decade.

As a consequence of the multiple agencies and numerous statutory and regulatory regimes governing dual-use and military technologies, the exporting community, Congress, and independent auditors have often criticized U.S. technology transfer policy as confusing, unnecessarily complex, inherently inefficient, slow to change, unable to resolve internal disputes, lacking clear lines of jurisdiction, and generally impenetrable to those societal groups most affected by controls. The system, many allege, puts at risk the values they were charged to serve—U.S. national security and U.S. economic competitiveness.[10]

Arguably, White House involvement or regular, effective congressional oversight could overcome some of these problems, but the administration of U.S. export control policy has not been the subject of sustained and systematic attention from either branch of government. Congress has intermittently attempted to streamline the system with only mixed success. For example, in a major reform of export control laws in 1969, Congress attempted to (1) limit the number of commodities subject to export controls for national security purposes; (2) instill a recognition within the executive that the foreign availability of a controlled commodity should be an important factor weighed by the bureaucracy in granting or denying export licenses; (3) make the export licensing process more open and accountable to the business community; and (4) harmonize the export practices of the United States with those of its allies through COCOM. For reasons touched on below, Congress was unable to achieve these reforms. Likewise, Congress's efforts to reduce costly delays in export licensing throughout the 1970s and 1980s achieved only grudging progress. The explanation, in short, is that broad congressional initiatives for reform have often been blunted by executive opposition or inertia, and Congress's efforts to micromanage export control administration have proven beyond its expertise, interest, or oversight capabilities.

White House leadership can have, and on occasion has had, a salutary effect in overcoming some of the problems associated with the diffusion of authority in export control administration. For example, President Bush's interest and involvement in export control policy added substantial impetus to U.S. leadership in COCOM list reform in 1990. By the same token, the lack of White House leadership in the 1980s contributed to executive departmental infighting (particularly between Commerce and Defense) and thereby complicated export control policy-making.

As is apparent, authority for the direction of U.S. export control policy is also shared somewhat unevenly between the executive and legislative branches. Under the U.S. Constitution, Congress is given plenary power over foreign commerce, and executive authority comes from legislative delegation. In practice, however, Congress reigns over export control policy while the executive rules. Despite meaningful differences between agencies and within Congress over the proper direction of policy, over the past two decades the executive has successfully retained authority to use export controls in serving its conception of the nation's security needs and in promoting diverse foreign policy interests. Executive branch autonomy has been the norm despite Congress's repeated efforts to control executive discretion in the use of foreign policy controls and ensure that national security controls be administered more efficiently, narrowly, and with greater bureaucratic accountability.[11]

There are many reasons for de facto executive autonomy in export control policy. The origins of broad executive authority can be traced to the emergency powers over exports it garnered during World War II that were retained and significantly expanded during two decades of unquestioned U.S. hegemony, cold war rivalry, and executive-congressional interest group congruence on the purposes to be served by U.S. export controls. This extensive and unchallenged delegation of authority led to the establishment of an elaborate and insulated export control apparatus that has preserved many of its prerogatives from congressionally mandated reforms and societal pressures. In maintaining substantial authority over export control law and policy, the executive has drawn on partisan influence, a historic role in protecting and promoting U.S. security and foreign policy interests, and superior expertise and experience in export control administration. Throughout the 1970s and 1980s, executive prerogatives continued to dominate export control policy despite the resurgence of congressional authority in foreign policy in the 1970s, the erosion of cold war norms, and the growing dissatisfaction of the U.S. business community with the burdens of the export control system.[12]

Thus, by extension, as the president and the executive branch have dominated Congress in export control policy-making, so too have they dominated societal groups whose primary channel of influence into the policy-making process is their elected representatives in Congress. During the first two decades of U.S. export control policy—the height of the Cold War—the American exporting community remained generally quiescent over the widespread American-led embargo of the East. To do otherwise would have been perceived as un-American. Moreover, American industries were focused on the domestic market and more familiar foreign markets in Western Europe and the Americas.

In the thaw of détente and with the rapid deterioration in America's balance of payments position in the late 1960s and 1970s, the business community became less reticent about speaking out over the impact of the export control bureaucracy on its ability to reach potential markets in the East and, more importantly, to do business in the West. Business efforts were translated into statutory provisions calling on the executive to streamline the licensing process, reduce the list of controlled dual-use goods, and restrain the resort to foreign policy controls. Many of these reform initiatives proved to be of limited consequence. In foreign policy export controls, for example, the foreign policy prerogatives of the president have predominated over business demands that considerations of domestic economic costs and the effectiveness of the proposed controls be given greater weight. For example, in the 1979 EAA, Congress established criteria to be considered before the implementation of foreign policy export controls and required consultation with allies and affected businesses before their use. Congress also mandated executive branch reports after the implementation of such controls, with an eye toward removing ineffective controls. In practice, these procedural hurdles did little to dissuade the president from extending existing foreign policy controls and imposing new foreign policy controls in unprecedented numbers when that choice appeared expedient during the 1980s.[13]

In sum, a historical overview of the U.S. policy-making community reveals three important features. First, numerous executive branch institutions with varying mandates and vested interests regulate the existing system. These structures historically limited the system's ability to undertake significant reform. Any institutional change needed to affect policy reform will result in bureaucratic winners and losers and will create bitter opposition in one quarter or another.

Second, although the bureaucracies are powerful determinants of U.S. export control policy, that does not mean that the president is wholly unable to articulate or implement policy reform because of the inertia of self-serving procedures of permanent government. The president has in fact demonstrated a great deal of authority and efficacy in articulating policy change through the heads of the relevant bureaucracies and, when motivated, has moved with alacrity in marshaling his powers to serve, via foreign policy controls, particular ideological interests. The White House is not necessarily the hostage of the bureaucracy.

Third, societal groups—the U.S. exporting community—and Congress are important players in agitating and articulating demands for reform. When they act in opposition to executive interests, however, their effectiveness is limited.

Contemporary Perceptions of the International and Domestic Policy-Making Environment for Export Controls

Looking back over the end of the cold war era, government officials responsible for the administration of U.S. export controls generally believe that national export controls, along with other post–World War II economic policies, contributed to the West's substantial qualitative, and often quantitative, lead times in essential defense-related technologies.[14] With the fall of communism—first in Central and Eastern Europe and then in the Soviet Union—a case can be made that containment policies, including export control policy, played a role in the downfall of America's chief ideological and military rivals. The argument is simple: denying militarily relevant technology to the East forced the Soviets to divert resources into efforts to develop such technology indigenously or to procure it through illegal means and thus contributed to policies that would ultimately cripple their internal economic strength and political legitimacy. The inability of the communist system to compete economically and technologically with the West ultimately loosened its grip on its internal and external empires. Because no one can know what the course of communism would have been absent such policies, this argument is also ultimately unprovable.

Despite this general consensus, the U.S. policy-making community does not agree on how much export control policy contributed to this end. Some, primarily those in the defense establishment, are inclined to view export controls as an important pillar of American and Western strategy. Those in the public or private sector more intimately aware of the economic consequences of export controls on America's own technological advancement are more inclined to doubt the success of the policy or to note that export control policy tended to retard the advancement of technology and economic development of both the sender and the target.[15]

Today, there is also a degree of consensus in the policy-making community that, whatever the security accomplishments of U.S. and multilateral export controls, the accomplishments have come with economic and political costs.[16] American policymakers have not always appreciated the economic costs of export control policy. During the first two decades of export control policy, the cold war imperatives and America's unchallenged economic supremacy made any economic costs associated with the embargo of the East of little consequence to most policymakers. Even in the 1970s and early

1980s, the economic costs of export controls were seldom fully appreciated, in part because it was easy to assume that the restrictions applied only to the relatively insignificant amount of U.S. trade with the East bloc.

By the 1980s, America's changed economic circumstances made policymakers more aware that the economic consequences of the U.S. export control regime lay not in denying the United States access to Eastern markets but in burdening so-called West-West trade—that is, U.S. transactions with its allies and neutrals.[17] Studies undertaken by the National Academy of Sciences and others highlighted that the comprehensive and complicated U.S. export control system was a competitive drag on American business and a threat to the nation's long-term security. In 1987 alone, the Department of Commerce reviewed over 100,000 license applications involving more than $80 billion worth of goods. Nearly 90 percent of these involved trade with other market economies—so-called West-West transactions.[18] The direct cost of the system to the U.S. economy was estimated to be $7 to $10 billion per year (with total direct and indirect costs roughly twice that figure).[19] The policy-making community became increasingly aware that the broad system of U.S. controls (most U.S. allies maintained far fewer controls through a narrow reading of the COCOM restrictions and by eschewing unilateral controls) led to lost sales from licensing delays, a shift among Western companies to non-U.S. suppliers, and reduced participation by U.S. companies in international joint ventures and alliances—the source of technology and profitability critical to future innovation.[20] Ironically, the burden of West-West controls fell most heavily on the U.S. high-technology sector, damaging not only U.S. economic interests but the military security controls supposedly safeguarded.

By the late 1980s, the U.S. policy community also recognized that the costs of the U.S. export control system could also be measured in growing tensions between the United States and the other COCOM members. This perception also evolved slowly and gathered momentum by the late 1980s. When COCOM was founded in the immediate postwar period, U.S. economic hegemony and cold war tensions made an extensive regime both logical and affordable. As the West's unchallenged economic and technological leader, the United States could be expected to dictate the terms to COCOM allies without encountering serious resistance. But U.S. decline relative to a rebuilt Europe and the drastic changes in the East during the late 1980s and 1990s have made it virtually impossible for the United States to impose its export control policies on its allies.

Differences within COCOM have always existed, of course. Throughout the cold war era, the United States pursued a more restrictive export control policy, controlling a larger number of product categories than any of its COCOM allies. The United States maintains a list of controlled items that goes beyond the COCOM list, pursues independent foreign policy controls, and insists on reexport authorization for U.S. goods and technologies to destinations outside of COCOM. The other COCOM members have historically defined the scope of the COCOM list more narrowly and have had a greater interest than the United States in expanding East-West commercial contacts. But in the early years of COCOM, the United States had two important levers of influence to prod other members into following its lead. The Battle Act authorized the United States to deny Marshall Plan assistance to countries that undercut COCOM controls. More important, the United States was able to use access to coveted U.S. technology and the U.S. market as an incentive for allied participation in COCOM.

As U.S. influence waned, the other COCOM members felt freer to vent their opinions and to challenge U.S. leadership. With the far-reaching reforms initiated by Soviet leader Mikhail Gorbachev in the 1980s, a serious rift developed between the United States and its COCOM allies over the scope of COCOM restrictions. For example, in the mid-1980s, COCOM allies began to take issue with (and later circumvent) the U.S. no-exceptions policy adopted following the Soviet invasion of Afghanistan. Under this policy, the United States refused to approve any general-exceptions licenses within COCOM. The effect of the no-exceptions policy was to give the United States a veto over the export of all advanced Western technology to the East bloc, regardless of whether or not it had a potential military application.

Allied hostility to U.S. policy peaked in late 1989 over American intransigence toward reforming the list of controlled items. At a COCOM HLM in October of that year, European COCOM members—particularly Germany and Italy—advocated a rapid relaxation of strategic controls to allow Western firms to take advantage of growing trade opportunities with Eastern Europe and the Soviet Union. The United States was the sole dissenter in several key votes to update the controls and drew the wrath of many COCOM members. The tensions within COCOM were not diffused until a few months later when the United States finally agreed to work with COCOM to undertake a fundamental reform of East-West controls.

Taking stock of cold war national security export controls, most in the U.S. policy-making community conclude that they have been a qualified success in serving a broader East-West security strategy but that the economic and political costs have increased substantially and their future must come to grips with a fundamentally different security environment. In addition, the concept of national security itself, policymakers note, may need to be reconfigured and expanded to encompass new, nontraditional security threats such as the proliferation of weapons of mass destruction, environmental threats, terrorism, and other threats that have traditionally been treated as special cases or unique foreign policy control issues ancillary to the principal threat from the East.

With regard to foreign policy export controls, there has been less consensus that such controls have been successful. Congress and Congress's policy auditors, the General Accounting Office, as well as exporters, academics, and allies have often criticized foreign policy export controls as ineffective if not counterproductive policy instruments. As noted, most foreign policy controls are unilateral, as America's allies do not see them as related to their own security interests. Because they are unilateral, they seldom succeed in inflicting meaningful economic damage on the target or even in denying the target state the embargoed goods. Instead, the economic impact is felt largely by U.S. exporters, who lose sales to other Western suppliers. Moreover, some COCOM allies believe these unilateral actions undermine multilateral cooperation in other areas. This negative effect is most evident when the United States has applied foreign policy controls extraterritorially, thereby directly challenging the sovereign prerogatives of COCOM members. One important example was the aborted U.S. attempt to force its allies to comply with a ban on exporting equipment for a massive Soviet oil and gas pipeline construction project in the early 1980s.

The major defender of foreign policy controls has been the executive branch, in particular recent presidents, who have viewed these controls as an important policy option in those instances when they needed to go beyond rhetoric in demonstrating American resolve but military options were too dangerous or impractical. Beginning in the 1970s, presidents have increasingly resorted to foreign policy export controls and, as noted, have retained considerable flexibility in the use of foreign policy export controls despite repeated congressional efforts to restrain presidential power. Forced to justify the effectiveness of such controls to Congress, the executive has argued that, while foreign policy controls seldom alter the policies of the target state, such controls demonstrate America's resolve, distance us from unpopular regimes, and should be maintained so that we do not send the wrong signals to our opponents.[21]

A Changed Global Environment

The end of the Cold War and America's involvement in a hot war in the Persian Gulf present policymakers with a dramatically different security and foreign policy environment. As the editors have discussed in chapters 1 and 2, several political and economic events of the late 1980s and early 1990s call for an appraisal of the effectiveness of export control policy in meeting past exigencies and a realignment of policy to meet future challenges. The foremost change facing policymakers is the end of the Cold War and the unrelenting East-West ideological and geopolitical hostility of the past forty years. The original security premise for Western technology controls has all but vanished. The fundamental Western security concern of a sudden Soviet attack on Western Europe or the more diffuse concern of a Soviet policy of radical activism in the Third World has dissolved. In its place are concerns over centrifugal tendencies and economic decay and, in the countries that the Soviet Union once comprised, the possible export of dangerous technologies from these states to unstable regimes in the developing world.

Revolutions in Central Europe and the dissolution of the Soviet empire require Western economic and technological assistance to replace command economies with market systems. Certain technologies, for example telecommunications and personal computers, are particularly important in promoting democratic pluralism and contributing to the creation of modern financial markets. Today, the greatest potential security threat from Central Europe or in the successor states to the Soviet Union would be the failure of their economic and political reforms and the regional instability that would ensue.

Second, U.S. policymakers increasingly recognize the importance of economic and technological competitiveness to national security. Today civilian applications, not defense procurement, drive technological progress essential to both national security and economic health. Therefore, before controlling technology, policymakers are considering the importance of a healthy commercial sector to U.S. security. Increasingly, this means eliminating restrictions and allowing domestic firms to compete on an even footing in international markets and to enter into cooperative arrangements that advance Western technology.

Finally, nuclear, chemical, and biological weapons and missile technology have proliferated throughout the developing world. Countries acquiring these weapons include several in unstable regions or known terrorist states. As many as twenty nations have or are developing chemical weapons capabilities, ten nations (including five in the Middle East) are suspected of developing biological weapons, and missile delivery systems development is currently underway in as many as a dozen countries.[22]

In this changed environment, the effectiveness of strategic technology policy will be measured by how well it addresses several different goals. First, restrictions impeding the competitiveness of U.S. industries must demonstrate that the economic costs of controls are outweighed by the security benefits. Second, while continuing to control certain sensitive technologies to the former Soviet republics in the near-term, technology transfer must simultaneously encourage cooperative problem-solving and pluralistic, democratic, and market-oriented reforms there and in Eastern Europe. Third, export control policy must address new security threats posed by the proliferation of dangerous weapons to certain states in the developing world while recognizing the limits of export control policy and balancing U.S. control interests with legitimate development needs.

How have U.S. policymakers and interest groups responded to these challenges and changed realities? There are several important initiatives underway that point toward new directions in export control policy in the 1990s and several unanswered questions as well. Below is an initial assessment.

Meeting the Competitiveness Challenge: Higher Fences around Fewer Products at Last?

In response to the escalating costs and declining security benefits of expansive national security controls, the United States concluded an agreement with its principal allies and trading partners in COCOM that streamlined the list of items controlled in East-West trade and eliminated much of the West-West licensing burden. As part of this reform, COCOM established a new core list of goods and technologies to be controlled to the East.[23]

This reform is part of a related effort to create a license-free zone for West-West intra-COCOM trade. The key to this reform is establishing consistent enforcement mechanisms for exports of core-list items from any COCOM member. Now that this reform is in place, COCOM members are dropping most licensing requirements for high-technology exports among themselves.

These two reforms are creating "higher fences around fewer items"—a goal first articulated in the 1950s.[24] When COCOM members fully implement these changes, they will significantly reduce the licensing burden of U.S. and Western exporters and contribute to meeting the dual needs of competitiveness and security. Under new U.S. regulations, exporters can ship without government review up to 95 percent of the items previously licensed for export to COCOM members and cooperating countries. In the United States, the effect of this change could be a two-thirds reduction in overall licensing. President Bush remarked, "We have relaxed trade restrictions on exports that served us well during the Cold War but are no longer necessary in our New World."[25]

The U.S. exporting community is not wholly satisfied with the core list reforms. Initially, the U.S. government's insistence on stricter telecommunications controls in the core list hurt U.S. companies when a German firm used a loophole in the COCOM regulations to ship a fiber-optic system to Russia that a U.S. firm had earlier been denied the right to export. Although the United States has since agreed to liberalize telecommunications controls in COCOM, other dissatisfactions remain. Surveys of American exporters suggest that many continue to experience regulatory difficulties with high-technology exports despite U.S. and COCOM steps to relax licensing burdens. Some report that President Bush's unilateral controls directed at prohibiting the proliferation of dangerous technologies offsets the beneficial effects of COCOM's streamlining exercise. On the other hand, U.S. government officials are quick to point out that American exporters were the first to benefit from the streamlined core list of controls because of their timely work in translating the multilateral agreement into national regulations.

Other U.S. government initiatives appear to recognize the need to weigh the importance of Western trade flows to U.S. security and prosperity. For example, in late 1990 President Bush called for creating a multilateral regime governing the export of supercomputers—high-powered machines useful for everything from weather forecasting to nuclear weapons production.[26] Several months later, the United States and Japan formally agreed to the formation of the new regime to prevent unauthorized access to, or the transshipment of, supercomputers.[27] The regime effectively eliminates licensing for supplier countries (Japan) and limits safeguard and licensing burdens for exports to other COCOM nations while it tightens restrictions for exports to nations of proliferation concern. The approach reflects U.S. worries that supercomputers could be transferred to proliferants and its belief that U.S. high-technology firms must be permitted to compete in Western markets if they are to survive and remain viable elements of the nation's industrial base. One unnamed administration source explained, "We don't want supercomputer exports to go unencumbered from those [supplier] countries. Secondly, we want to make sure that a level playing field is maintained between the United States and Japanese manufacturers."[28]

Nonetheless, regulations issued in May, 1992, to implement the new agreement did not fully satisfy U.S. industry. The regulations define supercomputers as machines with a Composite Theoretical Performance Rate of 195 million operations per second or more. Industry believes that the U.S. government set the level defining supercomputers too low, reflecting performance standards of early 1991. They believe rapid developments in the industry will require the two governments to adjust the threshold upward in the annual review of the agreement. Industry remains concerned that the government will not aggressively monitor policy to keep pace with the technological advancement.

Fostering Democratic, Market-Oriented Reform: Focusing on the End Use

United States policy is also adapting to serve security strategies that recognize the altered political and economic conditions in Eastern Europe and the former Soviet Union. U.S. technology transfer policy has begun to recognize the possibility of a more constructive relationship with the East without ignoring the remaining security threats posed by potential instability in the region and the possibility for the diversion of Western technology from the East. U.S. policy now reflects a linkage between technology transfer and democratic market-oriented reform and political stability.

Beginning in the late 1980s, U.S. policy moved haltingly toward a new relationship with cold war adversaries. Despite clinging to highly restrictive technology controls to the Soviet Union throughout the 1980s, dramatic events in the East and the possible rupture of COCOM led the administration to adopt a new approach in 1989. The administration lifted its veto over high-technology sales by COCOM that year and shortly thereafter called for a restructuring of East-West controls embodied in the core list exercise. Even before agreeing on the core list, the United States and its COCOM partners dropped one-third of existing controls[29] and partially decontrolled computers, telecommunication equipment, and machine tools—sectors that account for a large number of license applications and are relevant to the infrastructure improvements underway in Eastern Europe. Finally, the United States agreed to more favorable licensing treatment for those Eastern European countries that adopt COCOM-approved safeguards against the diversion of controlled goods to unauthorized destinations or end users.

Beginning in June, 1990, Hungary, Poland, and the CSFR embarked on programs to meet the requirements COCOM set for favorable licensing treatment. In May, 1992, Hungary became the first country removed from the COCOM list of proscribed destinations for high-technology exports, and COCOM dropped virtually all controls for Poland and the CSFR in recognition of the radical political and economic changes of the past few years. COCOM's decision followed Hungary's creation of its own technology control system to safeguard imported Western technology and improvements in the Polish and the Czech and Slovak systems. By all accounts, COCOM has demonstrated considerable ability to adapt to the new international environment.

United States policies toward the Soviet Union also began to change by the late 1980s. U.S. policymakers began to grapple with inevitable security tradeoffs in their export control–technology exchange policy toward the Soviets. Two cases from this period illustrate the point. In one instance, the U.S. government prohibited US West from constructing a $500 million fiber-optics telephone link across the Soviet Union when the intelligence community raised the possibility that the Soviet military could use the technology to secure military communication. The government issued the denial despite the commercial returns and the potential benefits of democratization through the freer flow of information created by the deal.[30] Yet in a second case, U.S. government officials concluded that the strategic value of technology came not from controlling its transfer but in sharing it. In that case, Control

Data Corporation (CDC) proposed exporting six relatively sophisticated CYBER 960 mainframe computers to the Soviet Union to improve its civilian nuclear power plant safety. The proposal presented American officials with another vexing security trade-off. The Soviet civilian nuclear power program was one of the world's largest with approximately fifty plants in operation. The safety of the program—as Chernobyl demonstrated—was not only a Soviet issue but a global one. Yet the United States historically opposed the sale of computers far less powerful than the CYBER 960 on national security grounds. As one observer noted, "On the one hand [the CYBER computer] can be used for nuclear safety, to make the world more safe, and on the other hand it might handle [the question] 'How do you bomb the United States?' "[31] CDC alleviated the government's concerns by negotiating end-user safeguards in the computer contract, including on-site monitoring by U.S. personnel and government-to-government assurances that the mainframes would be dedicated to safety analysis of civilian nuclear reactors, and the U.S. government approved the export.

New approaches to technology transfer to the East continue to characterize U.S. and Western policy in the post–cold war period. In June, 1992, for example, COCOM approved a dramatic decontrol of telecommunications equipment and technology for export and installation in the republics of the former Soviet Union. The removal of these controls eliminated one of the impediments to the economic restructuring of the former Soviet economy. As noted, in the past the U.S. government, led by the National Security Agency and the Defense Department, had staunchly opposed such decontrols when Germany and other COCOM members originally proposed them. They argued that Soviet acquisition of fiber-optics technology would frustrate U.S. intelligence gathering and improve Soviet military control, command, and communication capabilities. After the dissolution of the Soviet Union, these arguments gave way to the belief that such technology could improve the process of democratization and economic reform under way in the former republics and link them more closely to the West.

United States technology policy toward its former cold war adversary recognizes that American security is no longer enhanced by containing certain nations and impeding their technological progress. Rather, U.S. and COCOM technology policy now engages its former adversaries in a constructive dialogue that encourages their adoption of Western values or their participation in addressing regional or global security matters such as the environment or weapons proliferation.

Since the breakup of the Soviet Union, the outlines of a very different East-West technology policy have taken shape. The United States has encouraged certain former Soviet republics to participate in emerging regimes dedicated to preventing the spread of technologies of mass destruction. Russia, for example, recently joined the NSG. Russia has also agreed to abide by the provisions of the MTCR, which includes the major industrialized states. Perhaps most startling in this regard was COCOM's invitation to the former Soviet republics to join the organization in an advisory capacity. Former U.S. Secretary of State James Baker launched this initiative at the June, 1992, COCOM HLM. Under the proposal, COCOM will create a new cooperation council that includes the countries of Eastern Europe and the former Soviet Union. The council will serve as a forum for realizing three goals: (1) facilitating access by these states to COCOM-controlled items, (2) providing technical assistance to them to establish export control systems comparable to COCOM, and (3) collectively addressing new strategic threats. COCOM members are presently defining the precise structure and function of the council. At this point, the council will serve in an advisory capacity to COCOM rather than becoming fully integrated into the organization. The proposal, however, presents the possibility for a radically different membership and mission for COCOM in the years ahead.

In a related initiative, the United States has encouraged and assisted former Soviet republics (particularly Russia, Ukraine, Belarus, and Kazakhstan) in developing laws, regulations, and institutions essential to creating their own export control systems.[32] Russia, in fact, has responded with its own initiative. On April 11, 1992, Russian president Boris Yeltsin issued a decree authorizing the creation of Russia's own export control system.[33] The system will be patterned on the COCOM list and licensing procedures. According to the decree, a new Russian Federation Export Control Commission was constituted at the end of 1992 with particular attention to fulfilling the international obligations of the Russian Federation on the nonproliferation of weapons of mass destruction. The Yeltsin decree also authorizes the Russian Ministry of Foreign Affairs and the Export Control Commission to conduct negotiations with other members of the CIS to coordinate export control policy. The decree stands as a clear sign of Russia's willingness to move toward adopting Western technology transfer standards and to contain the spread of dangerous technologies. Successful implementation of the policy is far from certain, however. Perhaps the greatest strain on its good intentions will be the dire need for foreign exchange and the temptation to sell military-useful technologies to obtain it. The sale of powerful rocket engines by the Russian firm Glavkosmos to the Indian Space Research Organization in apparent violation of the control guidelines set by the MTCR illustrates this point.

Nonetheless, as domestic export control systems take shape in Russia and other Commonwealth countries, the United States and COCOM may eventually relax the remaining high-technology controls applied against these nations. It is hoped that increased access to Western technology will improve the economic conditions in these countries, help them in the process of defense conversion, and encourage democratization.

The United States is pursuing this relaxation process in conjunction with other forms of technological and economic assistance. One innovative approach in this regard was the decision by the U.S. Congress to allocate $400 million to help destroy Soviet nuclear weapons and create a science center to employ Soviet nuclear scientists who might otherwise seek employment in Tripoli, Tehran, or Baghdad. Likewise, the decision of the Bush administration to expand purchases of Russian weapons-quality uranium for cash and dilute the material for American nuclear energy applications suggests that the flow of technology from East to West may also contribute to mutually beneficial economic and political conditions in the future. Unfortunately, disputes between Congress and the president and America's ballooning budget deficit have severely constrained overall U.S. assistance levels.

In sum, U.S. technology strategy has increasingly focused on ways to transfer technology where it bolsters appropriate political and economic reform or enhances global security. If the Soviet Union's successor states maintain a level of political stability and make progress in setting up internal technology control systems to ensure against diversion to dangerous recipients, the pace of change in West-East technology exchange could quicken. Under this new approach the United States is increasingly directing its efforts toward monitoring the use of technology rather than prohibiting its transfer. The questions for U.S. policymakers in the 1990s will revolve around safeguards against diversion or misuse, the verification of end use, and the level of intrusion into national sovereignty permissible in a technologically independent world.

Many challenges lie ahead. Thus far, U.S. policy toward the Eastern European reformers should help meet the technological needs of these countries and recognizes their efforts to establish modern economies including a viable export control apparatus that prevents the diversion of Western high technology. The recent experiences of these Eastern European states have become models for other former communist countries, including Soviet successor states that wish to reestablish technology ties to the West.

The Challenge of Proliferation

As COCOM has removed controls affecting East-West and West-West trade, U.S. authorities have directed their attention toward North-South issues, a shorthand expression for concerns about the proliferation of chemical, biological, and nuclear weapons and missile technology to certain countries in the Third World. The Gulf War turned up the heat on long-simmering security concerns over the spread of weapons of mass destruction. As noted, at present three independent multilateral regimes—the NSG, the MTCR, and the AG—address the question of regulating dual-use technology for nuclear, missile, and chemical weapons, respectively.

Recent U.S. efforts have helped expand the membership of these regimes. They now include most COCOM and several non-COCOM members. Nonetheless, policymakers generally acknowledge that the proliferation regimes face significant challenges and must build consensus among their members over targets and methods. The widespread availability in the Third World of some of the technologies at issue, the divergent interests among regime members over what should be controlled to whom, the absence of certain key players, and the lack of harmonized licensing or enforcement standards present vexing challenges to U.S. policymakers.

Whereas the Soviets lacked the technologies subject to COCOM controls, proliferation technologies are available in the Third World in some cases. Developing countries already have large amounts of missile technology (particularly short-range missiles), and some programs (Israel's, for example) appear largely independent of foreign technology.[34] The foreign availability of chemical weapons also is widespread. And, as Iraq's use of low-level calutron equipment to manufacture weapons-grade nuclear material demonstrates, some nuclear facilities do not have to rely on imported high technology for their development.

Unlike the basic COCOM consensus surrounding national security controls, not all U.S. allies share America's enthusiasm for export controls over commercially significant proliferation items. Some NSG members reject controls on computers, arguing that a crude nuclear device can be made without a computer and that the widespread availability of computers makes controls impossible. The United States reluctantly agreed with this position in exchange for the creation of an expanded nuclear control list in the NSG. Some MTCR members, such as France and Germany, reject the need for controls on launch and guidance systems technology to legitimate civilian space programs. Key AG countries—Switzerland, France, Australia, and Denmark—initially indicated they did not intend to regulate production equipment that can be useful in developing chemical weapons, although they later reversed their positions.

More importantly, these new regimes will have difficulty agreeing on the targets for controls because of members' varying foreign policy interests and commitments in regions of concern and their differing perceptions of the threats posed by proliferation. Incorporating key supplier countries such as China or India into the regimes could exacerbate these disagreements. In short, the proliferation regimes are caught in a dilemma: to be truly effective they may need to expand membership to include supplier countries that will make agreements very difficult or impossible to obtain.

The groups are also informal organizations. They have not agreed to a uniform system of referring license applications for decision making, nor have they obliged themselves to common enforcement standards. Institutional weakness is part of the problem here. At present these regimes lack the routines and institutional arrangements that could facilitate coordinated action.

Two overall conclusions flow from a recognition of these problems. First, the United States and other nations will need to apply certain lessons of the COCOM experience to strengthen the nonproliferation regimes. Second, supplier regimes alone are not the answer to the problem of proliferation. Although the proliferation problem differs from East-West national security export controls, COCOM and forty years of experience in East-West export controls provide important policy guidance on how to proceed toward more effective proliferation controls. First, considering widespread foreign availability of proliferation items, effectiveness requires multilateral controls. Multilateral in this context will mean more than merely Western cooperation. Second, because of the important commercial uses of many of these technologies, the regimes should focus their efforts on the most critical and most controllable items. The U.S. policy-making community has debated whether unilateral U.S. actions can break ground for later multilateral accession or whether they are self-defeating. Third, although COCOM is unlikely to assume responsibility for proliferation controls because of its cold war origins and mission, COCOM institutions and methods—licensing and enforcement mechanisms, documentation procedures, and information exchanges—are solid models for the proliferation regimes to emulate.

Thus far, U.S. proliferation policies have partially incorporated these lessons into policy. In November, 1990, President Bush declared his intention to develop controls over products that would help a country in acquiring the capability to develop, produce, stockpile, deliver, or use chemical or biological weapons and authorized sanctions against foreign companies and governments that trade or produce chemical weapons.

One month later, the White House announced the EPCI. The EPCI is series of measures expanding existing foreign policy controls to encompass civilian goods and technology used to make chemical, biological, and missile weapons systems and related production equipment. The key provision of the initiative commits the United States to adopting worldwide controls on fifty precursors for chemical weapons[35] (most with widespread commercial use and availability) and to requiring export licenses for a wide variety of items potentially useful to chemical weapons-related industrial facilities.[36] The controls were unilateral, although the White House pledged to urge all nations to adopt equivalent controls. The Commerce Department implemented the controls the following spring.

The EPCI permitted the administration to "take the moral high ground," as one Commerce official put it.[37] The executive branch argued that someone must step up and lead on this issue and that the United States, drawing on renewed authority following the Gulf War, must show its willingness to absorb the costs of new controls before others will follow. In fact, subsequent developments at AG meetings suggest that the regime has gravitated toward U.S. positions. The AG adopted a U.S.-sponsored list of controls on processing and manufacturing equipment useful in the production of chemical and biological weapons. The AG members have also agreed to tell other members of licensing denials—the first step toward harmonizing licensing practices. These developments represented a considerable victory for the Bush administration and a fulfillment of its pledge to eventually achieve multilateral support for stronger controls. The implementation of the agreement by member states still remains a question, and U.S. industry remains concerned that others will not rigorously enforce the new nonproliferation controls. Should the controls not become fully multilateral, they argue, U.S. enforcement will only succeed in harming legitimate U.S. business through the costs and delays of licensing while adding little to national or global security. There is some basis for this concern. As one U.S. Commerce Department official conceded, at present the controls are only "semilateral."

The NSG has made similar strides in strengthening its controls and improving multilateral participation. In April, 1992, the twenty-seven members of the NSG (including several former Soviet bloc countries) reached final agreement on a common list of about sixty products and common control guidelines for regulating trade in commercial technologies with application in the development of nuclear weapons. The control list closely parallels the controls maintained by the U.S. Department of Commerce. The agreement marked the culmination of a yearlong negotiation begun in the aftermath of the Gulf War. Under the guidelines established, all NSG member countries were to implement licensing requirements for the export of all listed items to all destinations except NSG member countries by January 1, 1993. The agreement was a significant step forward but fell short of U.S. government aspirations—particularly in the critical area of enforcement. Contrary to U.S. wishes, the agreement only encouraged member countries to share information with other members on license application denials of controlled items. Absent stronger language on this point or a provision binding members to share information on license application approvals, a situation where one member country denies a sensitive export while another approves a similar shipment, remains a distinct possibility. The U.S. efforts to create an NSG secretariat also proved unsuccessful. The United States believes that a secretariat would improve intelligence gathering, information sharing, and the full harmonization of members' procedures.

Although committed to strengthening the proliferation regimes, U.S. policymakers generally recognize that technology controls aimed at developing nations cannot, acting alone, do more than slow the proliferation of dangerous technology. Technology policy must be combined with other measures, positive and negative: intelligence gathering, regime building, regional conflict resolution, and even the threat of force. Moreover, policymakers realize that the demand for weapons of mass destruction grows out of underdevelopment, regional antagonism, and inadequate protection of human rights. U.S. policymakers acknowledge that they must do more to address the demand side of the proliferation problem. Despite this acknowledgement, some developing nations see recent U.S. nonproliferation efforts as essentially dictating a policy of technology denial while doing little to meet their legitimate economic and technological needs or to diffuse the root causes of regional tensions. Critics of U.S. policy also note that the United States continues to export sophisticated arms to certain regional belligerents in unstable areas such as the Middle East while demanding that other countries follow America's lead in restricting commercial technology exports to countries in the same region. This contradiction, they claim, undercuts U.S. nonproliferation efforts.[38]

In the near term, however, it appears that the United States will continue to make the strengthening of multilateral institutions the centerpiece of its policy. In July, 1992, President Bush stated that "the United States is committed to taking a leading role in the international effort to thwart the spread of technologies and weapons that cast a cloud over our future."[39] Several options have circulated in the U.S. policy-making community about the form multilateral cooperation might ultimately take. Some favor a single multilateral regime to coordinate technology transfer, while most believe that such a regime is unlikely or unwise. Most U.S. policymakers believe that creating an institution under U.N. auspices would reduce policy to rhetoric or the lowest common denominator of control. Likewise, the United States has shown limited enthusiasm for a German initiative to transfer policy guidance to the G-7 organization. Expanding COCOM to encompass proliferation problems is doubtful since COCOM's cold war mission is rapidly vanishing. However, the creation of a cooperation council within COCOM to discuss proliferation concerns with former adversaries suggests that a broader role for COCOM in the years ahead is not out of the question.

Most likely, U.S. and Western efforts to strengthen the individual proliferation regimes—expanding membership among supplier nations; agreeing to core controls; exploring the possibility for parallel control efforts with the former Soviet republics, China, and other nations; and encouraging countries to improve their licensing and enforcement mechanisms—will continue. While less than ideal, these piecemeal steps are exercises in the art of the possible. If the United States and other nations work to resolve the problems of multilateral cooperation—harmonizing preferences, reducing transaction costs, and developing collective enforcement—most believe that each nonproliferation regime will become stronger and more effective.

In the meantime, many point to the need for the United States to get its house in order. Domestically, there is periodic interest in creating a superagency for strategic technology controls. Legislation calling for the creation of a single Office of Strategic Trade and Technology that would incorporate the implementation of all controls (dual-use and military) in a single agency resurfaces occasionally on Capitol Hill. The National Academy of Sciences has recommended the creation of a new interagency coordinating body at the National Security Council to set more coherent interagency policy with all administrative functions consolidated in the Department of Commerce. The Committee on Government Operations in the House of Representatives recommended the creation of an independent Agency for Export Administration, which would administer a single consolidated statute and a single consolidated list of controlled items. Until the Agency for Export Administration is up and running, the committee recommended that the Department of Defense be given oversight responsibility for all controls.

As a group, these proposals tend to win support as good ideas in theory but not in practice from the majority of the policy-making community. Few believe that the complex and entrenched system can be so transformed without a tremendous expenditure of effort that would be better placed in reforming the substance of policy rather than organizational flow charts.[40] Moreover, the specifics of any of these proposals would create winners and losers within the executive branch and, as a result, generate visceral opposition from the agency or agencies that would be slighted in the proposed reorganization.

Others in the policy-making community believe that the deeply entrenched interagency process of technology transfer policy-making cannot be willed away. As a result, some suggest more modest reforms. For example, breaking down barriers within the key institutions to help create strategic technology policy with a nonproliferation dimension is a favored possibility. At present the National Security Council, the State Department, and the Department of Defense formulate proliferation policy and national security technology policy in separate bureaus or groups, and the linkages between them are ad hoc. Currently, three State Department groups share jurisdiction over proliferation policy alone! Several U.S. government officials have noted in discussions that it seems both logical and feasible to unify technology transfer policy within agencies to give policy greater coherence and to give equal priority to the security challenge of the South.[41]

Conclusion

United States technology transfer policy is evolving to play a cautious but constructive role in East-West relations. More reforms may be in store, including paring the core list; removing Central European reformers from the target destinations of COCOM; creating a special status for Romania, Bulgaria, and the Baltic states; and developing greater technology ties to many of the Soviet Union's successor states. U.S. policymakers should also be given credit for reducing barriers that have traditionally impeded the ability of U.S. exporters to do business in the West. U.S. policy more realistically incorporates the economic dimension of national security and the importance of fostering national economic competitiveness through technology transfer. In the near future the United States will direct its efforts toward expediting the licensing process and creating a license-free COCOM. In addressing the challenge of proliferation, U.S. policymakers may face their greatest challenges. U.S. efforts to stay the flow of many proliferation technologies will try to apply fully the lessons of cold war technology restrictions: effective controls must be multilateral, focused, and supported by strong institutions. The first steps toward more effective policy will involve strengthening the new nonproliferation regimes. In the long term, meeting the threat posed by the proliferation of weapons of mass destruction may involve the United States in new initiatives designed to help resolve the problems of unstable regions (the current Middle East peace process may be a case in point) and closer coordination of U.S. technology policy with its arms, aid, and diplomatic initiatives.

NOTES

1. The president has the authority to control exports during wartime or other emergencies under the Trading with the Enemy Act of 1917, as amended by the International Emergency Economic Powers Act of 1977 (IEEPA). Controlling exports under IEEPA requires a presidential determination of national emergency or an "unusual or extraordinary threat." Presidents have frequently invoked the IEEPA to impose export embargoes against particular nations, including Iran, Iraq, Libya, and Nicaragua. IEEPA has also been used as statutory authority for all dual-use export controls during those periods when authority under the Export Administration Act had lapsed and its reauthorization was pending in Congress.

2. Export Administration Act of 1969, Pub. L. No. 91-184 (emphasis supplied).

3. Pub. L. No. 96-72, §6, as amended by Pub. L. No. 96-538, Pub. L. No. 97-145, Pub. L. No. 98-108, Pub. L. No. 98-222, Pub. L. No. 99-64, Pub. L. No. 99-399, Pub. L. No. 99-633 and Pub. L. No. 100-418.

4. Foreign policy controls have been targeted at countries such as Cambodia,

Cuba, Iran, Iraq, Libya, North Korea, South Africa, the Soviet Union, Syria, Vietnam, and PDR Yemen.

5. Committee on Science, Engineering, and Public Policy, U.S. National Academy of Sciences, *Finding Common Ground: U.S. Export Controls in a Changed Global Environment* (Washington, D.C.: National Academy Press, 1991), 71 [hereinafter, *Finding Common Ground*].

6. Pub. L. No. 90-629.

7. Pub. L. No. 54-703, and Pub. L. No. 95-242.

8. SNEC members include the Departments of Commerce, Defense, Energy, and State; the Arms Control and Disarmament Agency; and the intelligence community.

9. *Finding Common Ground,* 87.

10. Interviews with U.S. government officials, 1983–1992. For a recent example, see U.S. Congress, House, Committee on Government Operations, *Strengthening the Export Licensing System,* 102d Cong., 1st Sess., July 2, 1991, H. Rept. 137.

11. See generally William J. Long, *U.S. Export Control Policy: Executive Autonomy versus Congressional Reform* (New York: Columbia University Press, 1989).

12. Ibid.

13. Ibid., chap. 5.

14. Interviews with U.S. government officials, 1990–91. For a similar conclusion, see *Global Trends in Computer Technology and Their Impact on Export Controls* (Washington, D.C.: National Academy Press, 1988), 1, which concluded that the United States and other COCOM countries have maintained a lead of five to ten years in computer technology.

15. Interviews with U.S. government officials and American exporting associations, 1990–92.

16. Ibid.

17. Because of the potential for diversion to East bloc countries, all commercial exports, including those to noncommunist countries, are licensed. There are two kinds of licenses: general licenses that permit export without explicit permission and validated licenses that require formal application and government approval.

18. National Academy of Sciences, *Balancing the National Interest: U.S. National Security Export Controls and Global Economic Competition* (Washington, D.C.: National Academy Press, 1987), 21.

19. Ibid.

20. Interviews with American exporters and exporter associations, 1988–92.

21. See, for example, U.S. Department of Commerce, Office of Export Administration, *Foreign Policy Report to Congress,* January 18, 1985.

22. Janne E. Nolan, "Ballistic Missiles in the Third World—The Limits of Nonproliferation," *Arms Control Today,* November 1989, 9–14.

23. The core list is divided into eight categories: electronics design, development, and production; materials and material processing; computers; sensors, sensor systems, and lasers; navigation and avionic systems; marine technology; telecommunications; and aerospace and propulsion equipment.

24. Although not expressed as such, the United States agreed to some COCOM decontrols in 1954 because "there was some satisfaction to be derived from the fact

that the reduced list would be more strictly policed and enforced." "Economic Defense: Report of the Tripartite and COCOM Review of International Lists (NSC 152/3)," *FRUS,* 1952–54, vol. 1, 1160.

25. "U.S. Ease Controls on High-Tech Exports to Western Europe, Other Allied Countries," *International Trade Reporter* 9 (April 29, 1992): 749.

26. White House press release, November 16, 1990.

27. In 1993, the United States was continuing to negotiate with several European countries whose parallel processing techniques enable them to reach supercomputer performance capabilities to encourage their cooperation in a multilateral regime.

28. John Markoff, "U.S. Seeks Broad Ban on Computers," *New York Times,* March 11, 1991, C1.

29. Specifically, the administration proposed that most goods and technologies be decontrolled to all destinations up to the "China Green Line" (i.e., a level at which export controls are imposed on the PRC). Goods at this level are generally more sophisticated than those that could be exported to the Soviet Union.

30. As noted, ironically, a former East German company capitalized on a loophole in the COCOM regulations and made a similar sale in 1991.

31. Samuel Perry, "Cold War's End Revives Debate on Computer Exports to the East," *Reuters,* December 18, 1989.

32. The U.S. initiative began in January, 1992, when Richard Bartholomew, Undersecretary of State for Security Assistance, Science, and Technology, led a U.S. delegation to these four countries.

33. The Russian export control system is to include government administrative agencies, "whose activities must be directed toward the prevention of harm to the state interests of the Russian Federation arising from the export to foreign countries of particular types of raw and other materials, equipment, technologies, and services which have peaceful purposes, but could be used in the creation of the missile, nuclear, chemical and other forms of weaponry of mass destruction."

34. Aaron Karp, *The United States and the Soviet Union and the Control of Ballistic Missile Proliferation to the Middle East* (New York: Institute for East-West Security Studies, 1990), 21.

35. In final regulations, the nations of the AG were exempt from the licensing requirement.

36. The White House, Office of the Press Secretary, "Fact Sheet on Enhanced Proliferation Control Initiative," December 13, 1990.

37. Statement of Michael P. Galvin, Assistant Secretary of Commerce for Export Adminstration, as reported in "U.S. Plans New Export Controls to Stem Spread of Chemical, Biological Weapons," *International Trade Reporter,* January 16, 1991, 76.

38. See, for example, William D. Hartung, "Relighting the Mideast Fire," *The New York Times,* September 20, 1991, A17. The article notes that less than a month after Secretary of State Baker acknowledged the need to curtail arms shipments in the Middle East in view of the Gulf War, the president announced a $20 billion arms deal to Saudi Arabia. Although Congress cut the proposal to $7.5 billion, "The Administration's pattern had been set: lofty rhetoric on curbing arms trading would be immediately and decisively contradicted by a flurry of military sales."

39. "President Bush Promises Broadened Effort to Halt Spread of Nuclear, Other Weapons," *International Trade Reporter* 9 (July 15, 1992): 1208.

40. Interviews with U.S. government officials, 1991–92.

41. Ibid.

CHAPTER 4

Export Controls: The Perspective of the Czech and Slovak Federal Republic

Richard T. Cupitt

Introduction

In ten days, the policies of forty years came undone. In late 1989, the communist government of Czechoslovakia collapsed before a spontaneous groundswell of opposition. Without a large and experienced opposition movement as in Poland or reform-minded party leaders as in Hungary, the rapid success of the "velvet revolution" felled a government with little more than a simple cry for change.

The new government adopted a few broad objectives: (1) the deregulation of a highly centralized economic and social system, (2) the currency convertibility, (3) the privatization and restitution of property, and (4) joining the Western community of nations. After forty years of denouncing Western institutions, of being a target of Western sanctions, of maintaining an economic and political system incompatible with the West, the new government sought to integrate politically and economically with the West.

Becoming part of the West held tremendous promise for the CSFR. Access to Western markets, goods, and technologies could revive a moribund economy. Support for Western principles of democracy and human rights were thought to be the basis for a spiritual awakening and the creation of a civic society. However, just as being a member of a civic society engenders the individual to fulfill civic obligations, joining the West required the CSFR to accept obligations and duties as well, many of which demanded bitter social changes.

After the new government under President Vaclav Havel made clear its commitment to democratization and market reform, delegations from the United States and the CSFR met in the summer of 1990 to discuss the possible relaxation of restrictions on dual-use (military and commercial) Western exports to the CSFR. These items (both goods and technologies) were controlled through COCOM, which restricted trade between its members and Czechoslovakia for over forty years. In November, 1990, through a memorandum of understanding, the United States endeavored to decontrol, in phases, exports to the CSFR. In return, the new government of the CSFR was to create and implement its own system of export controls that would meet prerequisites set by COCOM.

This process has proved very difficult. Curiously, the very political and economic reforms that the CSFR underwent to become part of the West also made it difficult to meet the conditions necessary for a complete relaxation of Western controls.

This chapter examines the prospects for export control policy for whatever political arrangement emerges from the disintegration of the CSFR. When Czechoslovakia was under communist rule, the sensitive nature of the items and policies in question made interviews or correspondence with officials of dubious value, if not generally impossible. Under the atmosphere of openness in the new government, the author had constructive interviews with a dozen CSFR officials or researchers involved in export controls or technology transfer policy. The interviews were conducted in Prague in July, 1991, and supplemented by interviews after the election in the summer of 1992. In addition, political freedom quickly invigorated the print and broadcast media, creating a lively forum for the exchange of views and information on almost every public policy, including export controls. From information garnered from these and other sources, the author proposes to illustrate recent developments in CSFR export control policy and the prospects for the CSFR cooperating with the West in a variety of multilateral export control arrangements (MXCAs), particularly COCOM.

Why focus on the CSFR? Though trailing Western standards in many technologies, enterprises in the republics of the CSFR have the capacity to produce an array of heavy weapons, weapons of mass destruction, and dual-use items controlled by existing multilateral export control arrangements. Noncooperative behavior by the CSFR or its constituent republics would undermine the effectiveness of a host of MXCAs, including COCOM, the AG, the NSG, and the MTCR. The problems facing CSFR policymakers in accepting the duties and obligations of the Western community regarding export controls may also provide insights on similar efforts by other postcommunist states.

Incentives for Cooperation

After its brief flirtation with reform in the spring of 1968, the communist government of Czechoslovakia reverted to one of the most conformist, Soviet-style systems in Eastern Europe. Highly centralized, with virtually no private sector, the economy of Czechoslovakia remained immune to the experimentation of the Gorbachev era. Strict political controls effectively negated the domestic impact of potential opponents, such as Charter 77, and stunted the growth of any large-scale opposition movement.

In many instances, the collapse of communism meant that a small core of dissidents and young people became government officials almost overnight. These new officials, and many of those that had served the old regime, swiftly recognized the advantages of cooperating with the West on export control issues.

In the later years of communist rule, national economic growth rates had begun to stagnate, including a contraction in the national economy in 1981 (Brown 1991, 153). Aware of the prosperity of the Federal Republic of Germany (FRG) and the EC, the inadequacies of the economic system became increasingly apparent, undermining the central claim of the communist party to political legitimacy. Moreover, the implications of glasnost and perestroika in the Soviet Union and elsewhere in Eastern Europe meant that without change, Czechoslovakia would be increasingly isolated, risking even greater marginalization, dependence, and poverty.

Most clearly, the postcommunist government saw access to Western technology as essential for the CSFR economy. Without a host of modern technologies then subject to COCOM controls, including telecommunications systems, computers, and machine tools, enterprises in the CSFR would be unable to compete effectively in the global economy. Inefficient or uncompetitive industries could not attract foreign investment, placing the burden of conversion squarely on the government and a small coterie of domestic entrepreneurs. There was widespread recognition that modernizing the economy required greater access to Western technology. The first action in unlocking the door to this technological bounty necessitated cooperation between the CSFR and the West on export controls.

In addition to the economic benefits, cooperation with the West bore considerable symbolic significance. As the principal economic weapon of the Cold War, export controls, no matter how ineffective in restricting the transfer of technology, signified that business as usual did not apply in East-West relations. Removing these controls would be a concrete expression of the end of the Cold War and a symbol of acceptance by the West.

Finally, by the imposition of its own export controls, the government would discharge a moral duty as well. In one of its first actions, the new government promised to end arms exports. As one report put it, the decision to end arms exports would "raise our moral credit, which the new Czechoslovak government sees as its top priority" (Suchanek 1990, 13).

Creating an Export Control System

Members of COCOM, primarily through U.S. contacts, made it explicit that exports of controlled items to Hungary, Poland, and the CSFR would receive "favorable consideration" status if each country implemented an acceptable program of safeguards against diversion to unacceptable end users. As each country harmonized its export control system with the full range of COCOM controls, it would be deproscribed (removed from the list of countries to which exports of controlled items are proscribed) and attain treatment by COCOM members similar to that accorded countries now eligible for the 501(k) procedure under U.S. export control law.

To achieve this, the CSFR had to create an entirely new export control system, rather than redirect an existing bureaucratic mechanism. In a command economy, decisions to export military or dual-use items were at the discretion of the central planners of the communist party. Western-style systems of licensing based on a legal framework were unnecessary. At most, permission to export occasionally had to be obtained from Moscow because many military items were made under Soviet license. The continued existence of many communist laws and regulations on the economy after the revolution granted the Ministry of Foreign Trade time to formulate an appropriate export control policy while using older practices to restrict the flow of dangerous items. For example, the Ministry of Foreign Trade simply put a stop to the sale of SEMTEX by the VCHZ (East Bohemia Chemical Works) Synthesia-Semtin in 1989 (*Pravda* 1990).[1]

After the initial phase of policy formulation in the fall of 1990, the Federal Assembly of the CSFR adopted Law 547/1990 on December 5, 1990. Entitled "On Dealing With Certain Kinds of Goods and Technologies and Control Thereof," it came into force on February 1, 1991. This law made the import and export of controlled goods subject to license by the Federal Ministry of Foreign Trade, gave the authority for inspection to the Customs Office of the CSFR (whose officials could be accompanied by authorities from the state of the supplier of a controlled good), and identified penalties for the violation of the statute. This law was supplemented by Law 545/1990, which amended the criminal code to create the legal basis for penalties, sanctions, and punishments for violating the export control law. These two laws provided the initial framework for the CSFR to show that it would become a good partner with COCOM countries.

Besides cooperation with COCOM, the capabilities of its chemical industry made CSFR participation crucial for an effective multilateral program to stop the proliferation of chemical weapons. Responsive to these concerns, the proposed list of chemical exports to be controlled by the CSFR encompassed those items controlled by the AG. More importantly, in November, 1990, the CSFR made clear that it no longer objected to the ban on chemical weapons in the proposed Convention on Chemical and Biological Weapons ("No Objections to Total Ban on Chemical Weapons" 1990). In 1991, the CSFR became the first country to pass a list of chemical production facilities for inspection to the international community ("List of Chemical Warfare Agent Producers Reported" 1991).

In the nuclear field, Czechoslovakia had for many years exported uranium ore to the Soviet Union for processing, with some returning as fuel for the Czechoslovak nuclear power industry. The new government moved to stop this trade, largely because it was heavily subsidized and the Soviets no longer wanted any ("Exports of Uranium to USSR Discontinued" 1990). The postcommunist government also maintained the historical commitment to the relatively strict guidelines of the NSG, which the CSFR joined in 1978.

In early 1991, the government also organized an interdepartmental commission as a consultative and supervisory body for exports of military and related dual-use items. By decree 174/1991, this commission would have representatives from the Ministries of Foreign Trade, Foreign Affairs, Defense, Interior, and Economics; the State Defense Council; and the Economic and Industry Ministries at the Republic level ("Calfa Interviewed on Arms Trade, Policy" 1992; Lamper and Mlynar 1992, 12; "Spokesman Notes Arms Trade Control Problems" 1992). Under Act 560/1991, the CSFR restricted arms exports, based on the U.S. ITARs.

This nascent framework was sufficient to convince COCOM members of the sincerity of the new approach of the government of the CSFR. Consequently, at their June, 1991, HLM, COCOM members agreed to grant favorable consideration for exports to the CSFR (along with Hungary and Poland). This status considerably reduced or removed controls from a number of high-technology goods, in many ways paralleling the status enjoyed by the PRC.

A draft decree detailing the licensing procedures was outlined by the summer of 1991, but officials decided not to complete the proposed decree until after September, when COCOM members would release the results of its core list exercise.[2] CSFR officials intended to use the core list to identify most of the items to be controlled by their new export controls.

The complex bureaucratic mechanics of creating a licensing system makes rapid implementation difficult. In the Ministry of Foreign Trade, the COCOM department handles the licensing of all dual-use items, including chemicals. Another department, KOVAM, directed by a deputy in the Federal Assembly who also serves on the Defense and Security Affairs Committee of the assembly, issues export licenses for arms. Another department has responsibility for licensing trade in nuclear materials. Given the technical and secretive nature of the issue, the production and control of nuclear materials also falls under the charge of the Atomic Commission of the CSFR.

The COCOM office, with less than a handful of officers, tends to review licenses case by case and generally has to approve or deny licenses for trade in controlled items within thirty days. From February, 1991, to February, 1992, the office issued about 1,100 import licenses and only 2 export licenses. The paucity of export licenses results from the relatively low level of technological sophistication of CSFR exports and the lack of more detailed regulations on the broad system of export controls rather than safeguards against the diversion or reexport of imports from COCOM countries.

The CSFR created an import certification/delivery verification license system, similar to that used by COCOM countries. There were a number of practical hurdles to overcome. For example, an early version of the license application form had no space for an end-user declaration, even though such a declaration was required by law. Another delay emerged when some officials insisted that each item have a tariff number, even though the various multilateral export control lists are not based on tariff classifications.

As in many other countries, export control enforcement falls to another bureaucracy, customs. Customs officials had to learn largely new skills and procedures. For example, a system had to be created to inform customs officials prior to the arrival of a controlled item. As a first step in a long-term assistance program, customs officials from the U.S. trained CSFR customs officials in Prague during the fall of 1990 on export control enforcement.

By the end of 1991, compliance with Western export control criteria became more and more problematic. Part of the problem has stemmed from interdepartmental differences. Typically, the Ministry of Foreign Trade vigorously supports export applications, along with the Ministry of Defense (which has an interest in maintaining the defense industry of the CSFR through exports). These views are often contested by the Ministry of Foreign Affairs, which argues for a tighter rein on arms and dual-use items.

No single agency in the interdepartmental commission on arms has a veto. This lack of a veto troubles the Minister of Foreign Affairs, whose ministry maintains a list of proscribed destinations and raises some controversy in his dealings with the Federal Ministry of Foreign Trade, which has the general responsibility for supervising exports and administering trade licenses ("Dienstbier Discusses German Ties, Arms Exports" 1992). Nonetheless, if the Ministry of Foreign Affairs disagrees with a decision by the commission, it can still raise the issue at a higher level of government, either at the State Defense Council or at a cabinet meeting. The interdepartmental commission on arms or the State Defense Council makes the authoritative decisions on export licenses on military material, whereas the Federal Ministry of Foreign Trade has authority to decide other export licenses.

The decision-making process not only depends on whether the CSFR controls an item but on its country of destination. Generally, the CSFR maintains a fourfold classification: (1) exports to some countries, essentially the COCOM and associated Western countries, are not subject to licensing restrictions; (2) exports of controlled items to some countries are strictly prohibited (though the name and number of these countries are secret, the list is based on controls imposed through commitments the CSFR made to the UN and other international bodies); (3) exports to countries in regions at risk, such as the Middle East, are reviewed by the interdepartmental commission; and (4) exports to all other countries are done case by case (requiring license approval by the Ministry of Foreign Trade, including an end-user certificate and a ban on reexports) ("Foreign Trade Minister Baksay on Arms Export Rule" 1992). In the absence of new legislation on arms export controls, the State Defense Council moved in the spring of 1992 to ban the export of arms and related spare parts to ten countries and the successor states of the former Yugoslavia and to restrict exports to twenty-seven other countries.

After failing to reach an agreement on a number of substantive policy issues, the CSFR also created an interdepartmental commission in February, 1992, to consult on exports of dual-use items controlled by COCOM and other multilateral bodies, with membership parallel to the commission overseeing arms exports. However, agreement on many dual-use export controls remains elusive. For example, the CSFR supports broadening the NSG guidelines to encompass recent changes in the Trigger List of the Zangger Committee and tighten restrictions on the supply of nuclear materials to dubious countries, all of which has recently been the subject of negotiations. The CSFR also advocates expanding the membership of the NSG. However, efforts to amend national legislation in light of the agreement by NSG members to adopt controls on dual use were still being debated in the fall of 1992.

The Costs of Implementing Export Controls

The delays in adopting and implementing a new export control policy stemmed from the larger dispute about the jurisdiction of the federal and republic levels of government. In its effort to deregulate and move away from the straitjacket of central planning, the federal government granted greater authority over the economic sphere to the governments of the Czech and Slovak republics. One immediate result of this dispersion of power was the decision by the government of the Slovak Republic to slow the pace of the federal government's radical defense conversion plans in 1991.

Under communist rule, Czechoslovakia usually devoted more than one-third of its investment in manufacturing to building its defense industry (Leitenberg 1991a, 109). Most of this investment went to enterprises in Slovakia, especially heavy machine works (tank and armored vehicle production) in and around Martin. At its peak in the mid-1980s, Czechoslovakia was the fifth leading arms exporter in the world, with as many as 150,000 employed directly in defense production.

The collapse of communism had a devastating impact on the market for CSFR defense products. The demise of the Warsaw Treaty Organization and the political and economic changes that swept the region sharply diminished the demand for CSFR arms in its traditional markets. Moreover, the end of the Cold War found neither the East nor the West very amenable to supporting arms buildups elsewhere, an attitude only heightened by events surrounding the Gulf War. Coupled with the moral opposition to arms exports by the leaders of the new federal government, the drop in demand reduced CSFR arms exports from $1.4 billion in 1987 to $186 million in 1991 (*New York Times,* February 19, 1992).

Representatives of the rapidly collapsing coalition of opposition groups in Slovakia, the Public Against Violence (VPN), that replaced the communist government, soon found themselves defending defense conversion and export control policies that could result in the immediate loss of more than 100,000 jobs in the republic. In the spring of 1991, Slovak Prime Minister Vladimir Meciar traveled to the Soviet Union to get assurances from the Soviets that they would continue to purchase Slovakian goods, including arms. Claims and counterclaims regarding this visit helped precipitate Meciar's dismissal. Already rife with dissension, the VPN splintered. As arguably the most popular political figure in Slovakia, Meciar formed a new political party, the Movement for an Independent Slovakia, which captured the lead in the polls (though no single party had close to majority support).

In launching his campaign for the general election of June, 1992, Meciar stated two objectives relevant to export controls. Above all, Meciar argued for a new, confederal relationship between the two republics, which would enhance the power of the republican governments. Despite polls showing that a substantial majority of the electorate in both the Czech and Slovak Republics would like to maintain a single state structure with authority over many policies such as defense and foreign affairs, no agreement was reached during negotiations prior to the election on a referendum for a new constitutional arrangement (negotiations were suspended because no constitutional referendum can be submitted so soon before an election according to the CSFR law). Election victories by Meciar in Slovakia and Vaclav Klaus in the Czech Republic pushed the CSFR toward disintegration into two sovereign states. In 1993, the two republics developed separate export control systems, similar to that of the CSFR. One immediate consequence of this dispute was that COCOM chose to delay deproscribing the CSFR.[3]

Meciar also promised continued support for defense production. He argued that federal government limits on arms sales were irresponsible. Specifically, he believed that there were sufficient orders to keep the enterprises running for seven years and, though weapons should not be transferred to politically sensitive regions, other countries would make a sale if Slovakian enterprises did not (*New York Times,* February 19, 1992). Nonetheless, after the election, Julius Toth, the new Slovak Finance Minister, announced that arms production would continue but that it would be reduced by 5 to 10 percent each year ("Minister Says Slovak Arms Production to Continue" 1992).

Oddly, the democratic devolution of political power may jeopardize cooperation between the CSFR and the West on export controls. Given the jobs at stake, there appears to be profound support for continuing defense production and arms exports among the Slovakian electorate. Moreover, the relatively small size and large number of constituencies for the federal and republican legislature, a relic of communist government, mean many candidates must respond to very narrow interests to win election. Greater independence for Slovakia, coupled with great local interest in maintaining arms exports, constrains the negotiating position of the CSFR in its dealing with the West on export controls overall.

The incentive of greater access to Western technology has also waned. With favorable consideration status, enterprises in the CSFR gained access to all but the most technologically sophisticated items. Most enterprises could neither afford nor absorb these high technologies, so access to these items became less important in the short run.

The burgeoning number of new companies delving into arms trade further complicates the issue. Under communist rule, only the foreign trade organization Omnipol (with a deputy minister of foreign trade as its director) had the right to trade in arms. In contrast, twenty-eight firms now have a permit to engage in arms trade (Lamper and Mlynar 1992, 11). The promulgation of the new Commercial Code on January 1, 1992, made administering export controls even more complex. Essentially, the code permits any legal entity the opportunity to negotiate export sales, including sales of controlled goods ("Calfa Interviewed on Arms Trade, Policy" 1992, 12). Though government officials deny that this abrogates the need to get a license and approval from the Ministry of Foreign Trade, it has resulted in reports of arms deals involving companies of questionable status to suspect destinations.[4]

Balancing Interests: The Sale of T-72s to Syria

No other incident illustrates the delicate balancing of republic, federal, and international forces, along with the traditional mix of economic, political, and military security factors, at work in export control policy-making in the CSFR than the recent decision to sell tanks to Syria. Just as the demand for CSFR arms underwent a cataclysmic decline, Omnipol, the old state arms foreign trade organization, completed negotiations for the sale of 252 T-72m tanks, produced at ZTS-Martin. In April, 1991, Jiri Dienstbier, the Foreign Minister of the CSFR, announced that the government approved the sale (Foreign Broadcast Information Service 1991b; Prague CSTK 1991a).

Many governments harshly criticized this decision. The United States issued an official note of protest, arguing that the sale violated the recently concluded negotiations on force reductions under the Conventional Forces in Europe (CFE) Treaty (Urban 1991). Not surprisingly, the most vociferous outcry against the sale came from Israel (Prague CSTK 1991b).

At first, the CSFR responded without compromise. CSFR officials dismissed the note of protest on two grounds. One, the contract was settled before the CSFR signed the CFE treaty. Two, the contract specified new production rather than a transfer of existing weapons, which would have violated the treaty. Justifying the sale itself, the CSFR position was that this would be a one-time sale to pay for defense conversion. Indeed, officials indicated that if the United States or Israel wished to pay for converting the plants producing the tanks, no sale need be made (Foreign Broadcast Information Service 1991a).[5]

Many observers saw objections to the sale as hypocritical. They mentioned that many Western nations were much more active than the CSFR in selling arms to Middle Eastern countries, including Iraq (Cibula 1991; Foreign Broadcast Information Service 1991a and 1991b).

Nonetheless, domestic support for the sale was mixed, and press commentary divided (Foreign Broadcast Information Service 1991b). Political parties also had mixed views, some saw it as a desperation sale or a deplorable but temporary necessity, while the ex-communist and Slovakian parties were much more supportive of this and future sales (Foreign Broadcast Information Service 1991a).

Eventually, the CSFR softened its position. On the occasion of a state visit by President Herzog of Israel in October, 1991, the CSFR suspended delivery of the T-72s and related materials. Officials of the CSFR took note of the initiative of the five permanent members of the UN Security Council to limit arms transfers to the Middle East during the peace talks, which deflated one of the basic arguments made by proponents of the sale.

In January, 1992, economic and political pressures obliged the federal government to resume the delivery of the tanks. As the fortunes of the defense industry continued to decline, this production would help keep thousands employed for many weeks. Since the tanks were produced in Slovakia, with unemployment levels double that of the Czech lands, continuing production and delivery had significant economic and political appeal, which opponents of the government were putting to good use in campaigning for the general election.

As shipments of the tanks left the Polish port of Szczecin, the story turned melodramatic. One transport ran aground and was briefly detained in Denmark. The German navy intercepted and turned back a shipment of sixteen T-72s and related materials on board a German vessel in the eastern end of the Mediterranean. While German maritime law does not permit the use of ships of German registry for such purposes, the vessel and its cargo harbored in Hamburg for some time without incident. Since the interception took place at the same time the CSFR was hosting the CFE conference and signing a treaty on compiling an arms transfer registry, the timing of the interception may not have been coincidental. Those tanks eventually joined another shipment of fifteen T-72s on a Polish ship bound for Syria in March, 1992 (Prague CSTK 1992).

Conclusion

In a democracy, the political and economic interests of the electorate matter, especially as an election approaches. Consideration of these interests created the incongruous mix of President Havel saying he hoped the sale of T-72s to Syria would be the last of its kind, while the federal minister of economics, Vladimir Dlouhy, on a visit to Slovakian arms enterprises in Martin, "pledged a pragmatic new arms sales policy," as long as it fit the overall foreign policy aims of the CSFR (*New York Times*, February 19, 1992). In the case of the T-72s, domestic economic pressures, exacerbated by a political dispute about the disposition of authority in the federal system, the approach of an election, and constituencies of a size that enhances the influence of narrow local interests, outweighed foreign policy aims.

Generally, the transition from a defense-based to a commercial-based economy magnifies the enormity of the transition from a command to a market economy in the CSFR. In the early months after the revolution, there was some optimism that defense plants would soon convert to civilian production, especially since defense enterprises in communist systems usually maintained some civilian production at the same time. That optimism has long faded.

Despite the resumption of deliveries of tanks to Syria, there is little concrete evidence to question the underlying commitment of the current government to cooperating with the West on export controls. In a number of other cases, the CSFR has not approved the sale of heavy assault technology in accordance with its general objective of reducing arms exports. At least three forces should keep the CSFR on the path of cooperation with the West.

First, there is no market comparable to that lost with the collapse of the Warsaw Treaty Organization. While the West may purchase some defense items from the CSFR, Western governments are also reducing their military forces and have their own defense conversion problems. The CSFR has sold in other markets in the past, but even oil-producing states have not proven to be reliable customers. For example, the CSFR stopped arms sales to Iraq in 1988 because of Iraqi failure to make payments. The Syrians may have only gotten the tanks after making a commitment to repay substantial sums already owed CSFR defense enterprises (Economist Intelligence Unit 1991). Though it was common practice under the communist government to supply arms for ideological purposes in lieu of payment, the fiscal restraints facing the postcommunist government make such debts impossible to ignore. For example, Slovak Finance Minister Toth recently indicated that arms would no longer be exported on credit as they had been in the past ("Minister Says Slovak Arms Production to Continue" 1992).

Second, as real prices emerge for raw materials, labor, and other inputs into defense production, many defense enterprises will be discovered to be inefficient and unprofitable. For example, one recent estimate puts the sale price of T-72s produced in the CSFR at less than the cost of production (Lamper and Mlynar 1992). As it is, Slovak T-72s are not technologically competitive with the latest Western tanks or price competitive with T-72s produced in Russia. Since the Slovak government lost the subsidies it received from Prague when the federation split in two, T-72 sales will become extremely difficult to maintain. Indeed, under the fiscal restraints facing most postcommunist governments, subsidizing unprofitable enterprises may be less defensible than broader programs to ensure social welfare, such as maintaining unemployment benefits.

Third, in the wake of the Gulf War, the international community, especially the Western powers, have become increasingly concerned about the proliferation of weapons and technologies of mass destruction. Since many of the items controlled by these arrangements, as well as those controlled by COCOM, are critical for the competitive survival of industries in the global economy and for attracting investment capital, the costs of noncooperation are high.

The very existence of multilateral agreements regarding export controls makes it easier for the CSFR to enact its own system. Officials often referenced the international obligations of the CSFR, including adherence to multilateral export control arrangements, when discussing the rationale behind export control and arms trade policy. Not only are international standards and rules useful in harmonizing administrative export control practices, they are also a political tool in building a domestic consensus in support of export controls.

To enhance this possibility, Western governments must avoid even the appearance of hypocrisy in their own export control policies. Observers in the CSFR quickly pointed out the extensive participation by Western firms in the arming of Iraq as an example of why the CSFR needed a more realistic policy. Worse, in 1991 the United States asked the CSFR to block the sale of 500 T-72s to Egypt, only to approve the sale for U.S. manufacturers (Leitenberg 1991b, 16). Though the decision to join a cooperative arrangement may be different than a decision to violate or cheat on an agreement, in both cases it makes sense for Western governments to demonstrate common restraint to achieve a common purpose.

NOTES

The author wishes to thank Olga Fantova, a graduate research assistant, who helped the author update this chapter for publication.

1. A ban on sales to some countries, possibly including Libya, had been put into effect as early as 1982 (Prague Domestic Service 1990). The producer is set to resume exports since it has created a new explosive that is relatively easy to detect by standard methods (Prague CSTK 1991c).

2. By the summer of 1991, COCOM members had agreed to streamline (or at least restructure) the existing list of dual-use items, to focus multilateral controls on groups of crucial (core) goods and technologies. Though the outcome of this exercise remains controversial, there was some effort to follow the credo of "higher fences, fewer goods" in the creation of the new list.

3. Members of COCOM did agree to make exports to the CSFR under favorable consideration eligible for consideration under national discretion, meaning that the licenses for these exports will not be subject to individual review by COCOM or, in the case of U.S. exports, by the U.S. Department of Defense ("COCOM Deproscribes Hungary " 1992, 3).

4. For example, arms sales to Croatia, Iran, Nigeria, Pakistan, Peru, and Slovenia are rumored.

5. Soon after this announcement, U.S. Defense Department officials took a team of U.S. business leaders on a tour of five defense enterprises in Slovakia and one near Prague for precisely this purpose (Prague CSTK 1991c).

REFERENCES

Brown, J. F. 1991. *Surge To Freedom: The End of Communist Rule in Eastern Europe*. Durham, N.C.: Duke University Press.

"Calfa Interviewed on Arms Trade, Policy." 1992. *Mlada Fronta Dnes* (Prague), March 5, 7. Translated in *East Europe*, FBIS-EEU-92-047, March 10, 11-14.

Cibula, Igor. 1991. "Are They Looking for Pretexts?; [sic] Objections to the Decision to Halt Conversion." *Narodna Obroda* (Bratislava), January 11, 3. Translated in *East Europe*, FBIS-EEU-91-012, January 17, 1991, 21.

"COCOM De-Proscribes Hungary, Loosens Poland and Czechoslovakia Controls." 1992. *Export Control News* 6, no. 2 (February): 3.

"Dienstbier Discusses German Ties, Arms Exports." 1992. *Mlada Fronta Dnes* (Prague), February 6, 3. Translated in *East Europe*, FBIS-EEU-92-029, February 12, 8–9.

Economist Intelligence Unit. 1991. *Czechoslovakia* 3 (July): 19.

"Exports of Uranium to USSR Discontinued." 1990. *Lidova Demokracie*, October 23, 2. Translated in *East Europe*, FBIS-EEU-90-208, October 26, 22–23.

Foreign Broadcast Information Service. 1991a. "Commentaries View Tank Deal with Syria." Editorial report, in *East Europe*, FBIS-EEU-91-093, May 14, 18–19.

———. 1991b. "Havel, Dienstbier on Exporting Tanks to Syria." Editorial report, in *East Europe*, FBIS-EEU-91-088, May 7, 8.

"Foreign Trade Minister Baksay on Arms Export Rule." 1992. *Verejnost* (Bratislava), February 1, 1. Translated in *East Europe*, FBIS-EEU-92-023, February 4, 10.

Lamper, Ivan, and Vladimir Mlynar. 1992. "Klondike: Czechoslovak Trade in Arms." *Respekt* (Prague), 4 (27 January–2 February): 5–7. Translated in *East Europe*, FBIS-EEU-92-023, February 4, 10–16.

Leitenberg, Milton. 1991a. "Defense-Industry Conversion and Czechoslovakia." In "Trade in Conventional Weapons: The International Arms Bazaar," for the U.S. Senate Permanent Subcommittee on Investigations, Committee on Governmental Affairs, 99–119. Washington, D.C.: GPO.

———. 1991b. "Defense Industry Conversion—The Case of Czechoslovakia." Occasional paper. College Park: The Center for International Security Studies, University of Maryland.

"List of Chemical Warfare Agent Producers Reported." 1991. *Mlada Fronta Dnes* (Prague), February 21, 2. Translated in *East Europe*, FBIS-EEU-91-039, February 27, 22.

"Minister Says Slovak Arms Production to Continue." 1992. *Salzburger Nachrichten*, August 24, 10. Translated in *East Europe*, FBIS-EEU-92-165, August 25, 16.

"No Objections to Total Ban on Chemical Weapons." 1990. *Svobodne Slovo*, October 25, 2. Translated in *East Europe*, FBIS-EEU-90-212, November 1, 18.

Prague CSTK. 1991a. "Havel on Arms Industry Conversion." May 15. Reprinted in *East Europe*, FBIS-EEU-91-096, May 17, 9.

———. 1991b. "Israel Asks Arms Sales to Syria Be Reconsidered." June 12. Reprinted in *East Europe*, FBIS-EEU-91-114, June 13, 18.

———. 1991c. "Semtex Enterprise Creates Detectable Explosive." January 24. Reprinted in *East Europe,* FBIS-EEU-91-143, July 25, 24.

———. 1991d. "U.S. Delegation Ends Tour of Arms Factories." January 19. Reprinted in *East Europe,* FBIS-EEU-91-141, July 23, 12.

———. 1992. "31 T-72 Tanks Leave Szczecin Port for Syria." March 2. Reprinted in *East Europe,* FBIS-EEU-92-042, March 3, 5.

Prague Domestic Service. 1990. "News Conference Reviews Semtex Production Plans." April 5. Translated in *East Europe,* FBIS-EEU-90-067, April 6, 11.

"SEMTEX Exports Officially Halted in 1989." 1990. *Pravda* (Bratislava), February 24, 1. Translated in *East Europe,* FBIS-EEU-90-044, March 6, 21.

"Spokesman Notes Arms Trade Control Problems." 1992. *Lidove Noviny* (Prague), February 8, 3. Translated in *East Europe,* FBIS-EEU-92-028, February 14, 4.

Suchanek, Milan. 1990. "Nations Urged to Heed Example, End Arms Exports." Prague International Service in English, January 26. Reprinted in *East Europe,* FBIS-EEU-90-025, February 6, 12–13.

Urban, Jan. 1991. "Concerning Tangos with Shirley." *Lidove Noviny* (Prague), May 8, 3. Translated in *East Europe,* FBIS-EEU-91-093, May 14, 1991, 19–20.

CHAPTER 5

Export Controls in the 1990s: A Polish Perspective

Andrzej Rudka

In the autumn of 1989, the first Polish postcommunist government faced the enormous task of quickly evaluating the entire domestic and foreign economic policy and changing it along the lines of a new economic program that was being worked out at that time. It was not only a huge administrative task but also a big political challenge.

The Polish government did accomplish the task, and by the end of 1989 a broad package of economic reform laws was introduced and subsequently passed by the parliament. It went into effect on January 1, 1990, and created a solid foundation for a long, very difficult, and painful, but so far fairly successful transition period from a command to a market-oriented economy.

Since the very beginning, the Polish authorities viewed the economic opening to the world as a prerequisite of any success of their new economic policy. The issue of technology transfer from the West, in particular changing Western policy on export controls towards Poland, was an intrinsic element of that opening strategy.

Thinking the Unthinkable

The new Polish government treated the issue of export controls as a priority in its relations with Western counterparts. There were quite a few political reasons for that emphasis.

First, the Polish government was eager to get rid of the past (communist era) image of the West as an enemy and at the same time prompt the West to similarly change its view of Poland.

Second, the government wanted to score a quick and relatively easy success in an issue-area that the Communist regime had long exploited for its anti-Western value. This success was important from the point of view of both internal and external politics.

Third, it was very important for the new authorities to show the Polish people a quick reversal of Solidarity's risky policy of the early 1980s when—fighting with the communist regime—it supported Western economic sanctions, including stricter technology export controls, against Poland.

Fourth, the government wanted to collect on earlier Western promises that economic support for Polish reforms would be forthcoming immediately after political changes were introduced in Poland.

Finally, there was a strong desire on the side of the authorities to distance and distinguish Poland from the Soviet Union and quickly end long-lasting Western identification of Poland's foreign policy with that of the Soviet Union.

These political reasons, however, were not more important than the economic factors. Since the early days of the first postcommunist government, there was no doubt that Polish economic (and political) reforms could succeed only with significant economic assistance from the West. Poland's access to Western technology was to be one of the most important elements of that assistance. The Polish government considered numerous arguments supporting that view in its approach to that issue.

First, the vast modernization of existing and new sectors of industry, services (including financial ones), and especially telecommunications demanded the influx of modern—until then largely restricted—Western technology. It would have been unwise, inefficient, and very risky to undertake such a gigantic effort by spending huge sums of money (most of it new Western credits) on outdated low- or medium-level technology.

Second, as Polish reforms were planned in the form of a shock therapy (i.e., were to be introduced in a quick and massive way), the authorities wanted to create the most favorable conditions possible for that operation to ensure the best chances for success. It was argued that lifting or at least significantly reducing most of the controls would essentially contribute to that end. The government wanted to take at least this burden from the shoulders of already hard-pressed enterprises, create a more competitive environment for them, and allow them to make economic choices based predominantly on the economic factors (including technical performance of the new technology).

Third, in projecting future economic changes, the authorities counted on foreign capital increasingly coming to Poland, also in the form of direct investments. After finally eliminating most of the administrative and other restrictions for such investments in Poland, rigid Western export controls could become the critical stumbling block in the success of that policy. It would be difficult to imagine serious Western investors ready to commit themselves to longer-term projects in the East if they were not allowed to use modern technology.

Fourth, it was extremely important to use the modern imported technology to increase exports to the West. These new exports were to become the prime driving force of Poland's reforming economy.

All these political and economic factors combined stood behind the government's decision in the fall of 1989 to approach the government of the United States and propose negotiations on changing Poland's status within the Western export controls system, to do something that for more than forty years—and even a few months earlier, in the spring of 1989—seemed almost incomprehensible.

On December 1, 1991, during the visit of the U.S. presidential delegation to Poland, a letter of intent from the Polish minister of foreign economic relations, Marcin Swiecicki, was delivered to the secretary of commerce of the United States, Robert Mosbacher.[1] It stated the willingness of the Polish government to enter into negotiations and sign an agreement with the U.S. government on the reduction of restrictions on exports of U.S. (Western) technology to Poland. It also included the Polish government's readiness to abide by the Western rules and standards, governing the home end use and retransfer of imported Western technology to other countries (proscribed destinations).

It is worth noting that Czechoslovakia and Hungary approached the U.S. government about the same time with similar offers (Hungary simultaneously approached a few other members of COCOM, at least officially informing them about starting negotiations with the United States). As a result of these offers and as a follow-up of the revolutionary changes that took place in East-Central Europe in the fall of 1989, the United States undertook in early 1990 a strategic review of the U.S. export controls policies to assess the changing nature of the strategic threat posed by the Soviet Union and especially its Warsaw Pact allies.

A Way to Negotiations

The initial response of the U.S. administration to the Polish initiative was very encouraging. On January 11, 1990, Secretary Mosbacher sent a letter to Minister Swiecicki confirming the U.S. readiness to start negotiations and designated the under secretary for export administration, Dennis Kloske, as a chief negotiator. Soon after that, additional materials and information on the structure and functioning of the U.S. export controls system were sent to Poland. They were updated and supplemented later in the spring of 1990 by detailed materials from the Departments of Commerce and State, including expected provisions of the future agreement and necessary elements of a safeguards regime that Poland was expected to introduce after signing an agreement.

As mentioned above, the main thrust to change the Polish status within the Western export controls system came from the Ministry of Foreign Economic Relations. In March, 1990, a Polish task force to prepare for negotiations with the U.S. government was established. It was chaired by the deputy minister of the Ministry of Foreign Economic Relations, Andrzej Wojcik, and consisted of fifteen to twenty members (its membership fluctuated a bit over time) from the Ministries of Foreign Affairs, Internal Affairs, National Defense, Finance, Industry, and Home Trade and Services; the Committee of Science of the Council of Ministers; and the research community.[2]

The team met four times before the official round of negotiations took place in June, 1990, discussing all the relevant issues of negotiation and the agreement. One of the meetings included Lionel H. Olmer, former under secretary for export administration, and Richard S. Elliott, a representative of the U.S. law firm Paul, Weiss, Rifkind, Wharton & Garrison, hired in early 1990 to assist Poland in its negotiations with the U.S. government. In April, 1990, a delegation visited the United States to hold talks on export controls issues (organization, functioning of the system, etc.) with U.S. experts in the Departments of Commerce, State, Defense, and Treasury (Customs).

In the meantime, the debate intensified in the United States on the future scope and character of its export controls, especially in relation to most reform-minded East-Central European countries. On February 8, 1990, Senator J. Heinz introduced the Central and Eastern Europe Investment and Enhancement Act (S. 2113), later referred to the Committee on Banking, Housing, and Urban Affairs. It was introduced "to promote and assist in the development of the private sector, including small and medium-sized businesses in Central and Eastern Europe through an export enhancement regime that will encourage direct private investment in such countries."[3] The bill proposed to establish an export enhancement regime to facilitate private direct investment by offering to extend full and immediate China "green line" treatment to countries in Central and Eastern Europe that met, at a minimum, the following criteria: replaced communist governments with democratically elected ones; took concrete measures to lessen and ultimately eliminate the military threat to the West; developed free market mechanisms; and demonstrated the political willingness to negotiate technology security regimes based on conditions established by the United States and COCOM. It was then largely understood that Poland, Hungary, and Czechoslovakia were well on their way toward meeting these criteria. Though in the end the bill did not become a law, it represented the attitude of many members of the U.S. Congress.

On May 2, 1990, the U.S. administration announced that it had completed its evaluation process and, based on its findings, made a number of recommendations to its COCOM partners for essential reforms of that organization and the entire system of export controls. These recommendations constituted the basis of discussions held during the June 6–7, 1990, COCOM HLM in Paris, which ended in agreement on the most sweeping reforms ever made by that organization. It was decided there, among other things, to delete completely 38 items (out of 120) from the COCOM Industrial List; to relax licensing requirements on the export of most computers, telecommunications equipment, and machine tools; and to raise the technological levels of export controls (i.e., to limit their scope) to all the proscribed destinations to those of the PRC. Exception level requests were to receive COCOM's favorable consideration (i.e., with the presumption of approval) for countries that organization determined to represent a lesser strategic risk, provided they adopted COCOM-approved safeguard regimes to protect imported technology against unauthorized use or reexport.

That Paris meeting also cleared the way for the United States (or any other COCOM member country) to represent interests in that forum of any third country willing to change its status within that organization. This decision stemmed from the earlier controversy involving Poland negotiating only with the United States and, early in the process, practically neglecting other COCOM members. In the spring of 1990, Japan and France strongly resented being left out and demanded (especially France) direct negotiations with Poland on that issue.

Negotiations and Agreements

The first and final round of negotiations between the Polish and the U.S. delegations took place in Warsaw on June 18–19, 1990. Both sides were well prepared, the negotiations went very smoothly and quickly ended in a full agreement. It was decided that the final arrangement would take the form of a memorandum of understanding sent by the Polish government to the U.S. administration in which the former accepted certain obligations on its side in exchange for the easing of U.S. controls and its support for further liberalization of COCOM controls toward Poland. Such a form was preferred over the strategic trade agreements the United States had signed before with a group of neutral or third (non-COCOM) countries, because Poland was still on the list of proscribed destinations.

The Polish national legislature accepted the concept and the approach to the United States in the first place as well as the resulting negotiations, but it was not directly involved in that process. The final decisions accepting the negotiated agreement and concerning the implementation of the safeguards system were made at the Council of Ministers level. It officially endorsed the negotiated agreement at its session on July 23, 1991.[4]

On July 27, 1990, the Polish minister of foreign economic relations, Swiecicki, sent a letter—a memorandum of understanding—to the U.S. secretary of state Baker. On behalf of the Polish government, he expressed its intentions with respect to the adoption of a technology safeguards system (i.e., to implement measures designed to prevent the illegal acquisition or diversion of U.S.-origin controlled strategic goods or technology contrary to COCOM restrictions, whether such a diversion involved a transfer within Poland or a reexport from Poland). Comparable protection was assured in relation to strategic goods and technology originating in other COCOM member countries and in COCOM cooperating countries. The Polish government also agreed to refrain from being involved in any unauthorized acquisitions of controlled technology and from intelligence cooperation related to unauthorized acquisitions of controlled technology. To implement the system in question, the Polish government agreed to introduce an import certificate and delivery verification program already used for many years in technology trade among the Western countries. A commitment was made to enforce the elaborate system requirements under the current Polish law with assurances of subjecting would-be violators to criminal penalties.

On the other hand, the Polish government expected that the United States would support within COCOM an increase in the level of controlled strategic technology available to Poland and consider further liberalization of our licensing status in that organization in the future to the level no less favorable than that received by any other COCOM proscribed country that adopted comparable export control measures, with the eventual goal being the removal of Poland from the list of proscribed destinations. Poland's deproscription was to be conditioned on the adoption by Poland of a second stage of export control measures beyond those described above. The additional measures would include the protection of strategic goods and technology originating in countries that are neither COCOM member nor COCOM cooperating countries, including Polish indigenous strategic goods and technology.[5]

During the Warsaw negotiations, the U.S. delegation promised to provide technical assistance, especially for the Polish Customs Offices, in organizing and implementing the safeguards system. Similar provisions, though in a more general form, were included in the Polish-U.S. customs-to-customs agreement signed on August 8, 1990.

The conclusion of the other agreement constituted an important additional factor in the process of the creation of the safeguards system in Poland. It allowed American customs officers to directly participate in on-the-spot verifications and inspections, fact-finding inquiries, and inquiries into an offense of concern to them. It also provided, among others things, for the organization of special training programs for Polish officers. In fact, such programs took place at least twice in the autumn of 1990 when Polish representatives participated in a special program organized for them in September, 1990, in Washington, D.C., and in a conference organized in Vienna for East European participants in November, 1990.[6]

Implementation

Pursuant to these developments, the Polish Ministry of Foreign Economic Relations, together with the Central Board of Customs, prepared a set of documents necessary for the implementation of the safeguards system. After further consultations with the U.S. Departments of Commerce and State and final corrections to those documents, on September 26, 1990, the Ministry of Foreign Economic Relations issued a "communiqué governing the importation of goods and technologies on the COCOM list from COCOM member states and states operating with COCOM and the re-exportation of these goods and technologies."[7]

This communiqué included all the necessary samples of documentation (import certificate, delivery verification certificate, application for an export permit, etc.) and pronounced the establishment in the Ministry of Foreign Economic Relations of an office handling all matters concerning the transfer of goods and technologies. So the main responsibility for implementing and managing the safeguards system was vested in the Ministry of Foreign Economic Relations and the Customs Office. There is also some involvement, on the practical level, of the Ministry of Foreign Affairs, the Ministry of Industry, and the Ministry of National Defense.[8] Their participation in the export controls process generally depends on the character of the imported technology involved as well as the destination of Polish exports.

On October 1, 1990, Poland's safeguards system officially went into force. For the next few months, COCOM member countries to which the Polish system was presented inquired about its details and asked for clarifications of different aspects of its organization and functioning. A few other COCOM member states, particularly France, Japan, and the United Kingdom (presumably also Canada and Belgium), demanded that Poland sign agreements similar to—or even more formal than—the agreement with the United States. To ease the burden of negotiations, the United Kingdom even distributed a unified text of a proposed agreement. Such agreements, as well as customs-to-customs agreements allowing for participation of foreign customs officers in on-site inspections and verifications, were reportedly signed with these countries.

Japan was the most critical of the Polish reforms. In response to a Polish oral message of December 28, 1990, Japan raised criticisms in its note of January 22, 1991. In January, 1991, during the COCOM meeting in Paris, still a few countries questioned the wisdom of granting Poland a "favorable consideration" status, citing inconsistencies in its safeguards system. All the doubts were cleared up by mid-February 1991. That fact and the positive results of the first two U.S. Department of Commerce's missions to Poland, held in November, 1990, and January, 1991, contributed to clearing the way for final acceptance by COCOM of the Polish safeguards system.[9]

The acceptance decision was made on February 28, 1991, and since then Poland has been eligible for COCOM's favorable consideration status.[10] This status means that licenses for import realized under that formula are issued within twenty-eight days, and there is a presumption of approval at the "national discretion" level (at the "general exceptions" level, with a presumption of denial, it takes up to eight weeks to get a license, and the clock may be stopped any time if any COCOM member country raises questions). That status was later formalized by individual countries' executive regulations—on April 25, 1991, the U.S. Department of Commerce announced revised export licensing procedures for most shipments of sophisticated technology to Poland (as well as Czechoslovakia and Hungary).[11]

In May, 1991, representatives of the U.S. Department of State's COCOM Office confirmed, in a discussion with the author of this chapter, that the United States had thus far been fully satisfied with measures undertaken by Poland, stating that "everything that had been promised was delivered."[12]

At a May 23–24, 1991, COCOM HLM in Paris, members approved a new industrial list of controlled technology—a core list—which was officially published by the United States (as the first COCOM country) just before the set deadline of September 1, 1991. The existing scope of export controls was reduced by about 50 percent, on top of the 33 percent reduction made in June, 1990.[13] It is worth stressing that practically all the equipment (except cryptographic technology) falling into the most controversial area of telecommunications was released for exports to Poland (as well as to Czechoslovakia and Hungary). According to the newly accepted procedures, the core list is to be reviewed biennially with the first review starting on September 1, 1992.

During the May meeting, all COCOM member countries, on the insistence of the United States, also agreed to formulate preliminary conditions for final removal of Poland, Czechoslovakia, and Hungary from the list of proscribed destinations in the foreseeable future.[14] The list of conditions included (1) the creation of a legal basis for export controls systems in these countries;[15] (2) the introduction of controls on their indigenous technologies; and (3) successful implementation of the first stage of their safeguards systems.[16] COCOM members will discuss the issue in more detail in the near future, but the fact that even preliminary conditions were formulated was regarded as a success of the U.S. diplomatic efforts. For the time being, Poland, Czechoslovakia, and Hungary are subject to a special procedure that establishes a presumption of approval for all but the most sensitive equipment to these three countries.[17]

It is worth mentioning that, besides participating in the Western system of technology export controls, Poland also abides by the rules of the international community not to sell military items to countries that are recognized as endangering international security. This policy was invoked without any exceptions in 1990 after Iraq invaded Kuwait and Poland joined the international embargo on exports of arms to that and other regions of the world involved in military conflicts. Poland took this action with full understanding of the extent of economic costs of that move born by a country struggling with the difficult process of its political and economic transformation.

Poland is also a member of the IAEA in Vienna and adheres to its rules in exporting technology and equipment related to the production of nuclear energy. It also cooperates very closely with the MTCR on exports of missile technology. At the time of this writing, Poland has not had much direct cooperation with the AG on exports of strategic chemical technology, but Poland's internal controls on exports of chemical products and technology are very tough and reportedly meet international standards. In fact, since the liberalization of Poland's foreign trade in the late 1980s, the export and import of products in these categories have been the only ones requiring the permission of the minister of foreign economic relations.[18]

Effectiveness of Controls

So far, there have been no problems with the functioning of the safeguards system in Poland. The controls have been apparently fairly effective,[19] though it is still difficult to fully assume their efficiency. There are definitely still not enough well-trained specialists to manage the system and not enough technology installed to organize it in the most efficient way, especially at the factory level. Nevertheless, it looks effective enough to get praise even from Western auditors (representatives of the U.S. Department of Commerce).[20] It seems that there are quite a few reasons contributing to these early successes.

First of all, there is a firm commitment on the Polish side to prove that the Western confidence in its ability to control imported technology was justified. There is also a fairly enthusiastic attitude toward opening the economy to the West among managers of Polish enterprises, and they do not want to spoil the current positive and economically favorable climate after so many years of waiting. Polish compliance with export controls is especially important in view of Polish efforts to negotiate an association agreement with the EC, with a final goal of fully joining it somewhere by the end of the 1990s. In this context, the introduction of Western standards in technology trade is only one of many elements of adjusting the Polish economic system to the requirements of that existing in Western Europe.

Everyone understands, however, that what Poland started on October

1, 1990, is only the first stage of introduction of the system—of gaining experience in managing controls and protecting imported Western technology from unauthorized use. So, the present lack of any serious difficulties in the implementation of export controls does not mean that there are no future risks in that respect. Surprisingly enough, they may even multiply as an indirect outcome of some aspects of current economic reforms in Poland, in particular of the nearly total liberalization of foreign trade and progressive privatization of the state-owned enterprises.

Paradoxically, one may say that the prereform foreign trade regime was—at least in principle—much more secure from the point of view of export controls than the present one. Under the system of state monopoly of foreign trade, all export and import transactions were conducted by a relatively small group of licensed companies (foreign trade organizations) that specialized in dealing with different categories of products. So quite often there was an actual monopoly of one company on trade in individual products. On top of that, each transaction (later on, only a series of similar consecutive deliveries or purchases) had to be individually licensed by the entitled representatives of the Ministry of Foreign Economic Relations. Since economic reforms have eliminated the state monopoly of foreign trade, foreign trade is now open to a practically unlimited number of fully independent actors (also individuals), though most industrial enterprises that can directly enter foreign transactions are still state owned.

But, if the process of their privatization, which is the goal of the efforts aimed at restructuring the economy, continues—and according to the government's plans, in two to three years half of those enterprises will be private—even more serious enforcement problems may arise. Logically, it seems relatively easy (at least in theory) for the authorities to control the behavior of firms of which more than 90 percent are still state owned. However, it may become much more difficult to control those privatized and mushrooming new private firms when their number and share in the economy grow. The greed for additional profits may, in some cases, prevail over obeying the rules of the game, especially in the early stages of building young, immature capitalist enterprises. To avoid that risk, or at least to limit it significantly, Poland must build a comprehensive, effective, and efficient system of safeguards before the transformation is complete.

Perspectives

Recently, internal economic reform issues have clearly dominated Polish political and management circles, and there has not been much talk about export controls. That stems, first of all, from the piling up of problems connected with the successful transition of the economy from a centrally managed to a market system. On the other hand, there is a widespread perception that the most important obstacles to our freer access to modern Western technology have been removed. However, any future problems may be resolved as high up as the Council of Ministers. The postcommunist Polish government is clearly committed to continuing close economic (and political) cooperation with the West and to maximizing the free flow of Western technology to Poland, and it is ready to remove quickly all obstacles to that end.

It is too early, however, to judge the real distribution of power in Poland influencing its export controls policy, since the Polish political arena is still very fragmented and far from stable. Nevertheless, as far as the issue of export controls is concerned, there has been in fact practically full agreement among all major political forces in favor of close economic cooperation with the West and gaining a privileged position within the system of Western export controls.

There is no doubt, however, that there are still factions in the country that are not entirely happy with the quickly growing dependence of Poland's industry and economy on imported technology. In the still volatile world affairs, there are people who remember very well the enormous costs of relatively high dependence on Western technology and credits paid by Poland—though in a completely different political environment—in the 1970s and early 1980s.

So even in the entirely changed political and strategic orientation of today's Poland, the issue of economic security has not yet fully disappeared. The constraints or reservations that can exist on the Polish side usually have a form of some fear that a sudden change in the Western policy on export controls may be possible if something (politically) unfavorable happens in Poland or in East-Central Europe in general.[21] That fear still exists, even though it is now difficult to imagine anything specific that could directly affect that sphere of our relations with the West. However, the experience of the past showed how quickly its policy can change, especially since there is a history of export controls shifting toward the tightening of restrictions much more quickly than they relax.

As was mentioned above, the present Polish safeguards system concerns only dual-use items imported from COCOM member countries. It does not yet cover technology imported from non-COCOM countries that do not cooperate with that organization or indigenous Polish technologies. They will be covered in the second phase of building the safeguards system in Poland. This phase must be preceded by the introduction of a new comprehensive law on technology trade. There were plans to enact it by the end of 1991, but Poland's preoccupation with the extremely difficult processes of economic reform and the apparently inadequate—to the existing needs—legislative efficiency of the parliament delayed that effort. Thus, the expected start of the second phase of building the safeguards system in Poland (January, 1992) was also delayed. Nevertheless, it is expected that the required law will be in place in the fall of 1993 and that the building of the comprehensive safeguards system will soon proceed further.

As was already mentioned, Poland's ultimate goal in the area of export controls is to be removed from the list of proscribed destinations. Consequently, it will become—if not a COCOM member country—at least a COCOM cooperating country as most other Western non-COCOM countries are. Polish authorities have pursued this goal since the early days of negotiations with the United States and COCOM. It is well understood that the timing of that removal depends to a large extent on the positive experience gathered during earlier stages of the implementation of the controls and the successful introduction of the second phase of the safeguards system.

There are, however, certain economic costs associated with involvement in the system (for example, the costs of establishing an effective and efficient safeguards system), but there is little hesitation concerning the need to pursue that goal. Most experts have no doubt that the benefits of such a policy outweigh its costs and that such a trend should continue in the future—both in the area of economic growth and the democratization of the internal politics in Poland, as well as in the sphere of military security of the country.

On top of that, there is also widespread understanding within the policymaking community that the Polish (as well as Czechoslovakian and Hungarian) example of exactly such an outcome of that policy should serve as an encouragement to other countries, including the newly emerging states of the former Soviet Union. And that, in turn, should promote economic growth and democracy in that region as well as increase the level of military security for Europe and the entire world.

In the case of Poland, as well as practically all other East European countries, there is a direct connection—in the understanding of their authorities—between export controls and a relative freedom of technology transfer on one side and the economic growth of those countries on the other. As all these countries struggle at the same time not only with their difficult economic plight but also with the internal political consequences of the long communist era, a direct connection between economic growth and chances for building more democratic societies is generally perceived. Without economic progress there may be a strong tendency toward political chaos and some other form of political dictatorship.[22] Of course, that does not mean that easing Western export controls is a sufficient condition for avoiding those dangers, but it is definitely perceived as a significant factor in facilitating economic growth in Eastern Europe.

There is also a broad understanding in Poland's political circles that international cooperation on controls of weapons and dual-use technology transfer is a necessary and useful tool for protecting the military security of the international community. The Iraqi adventure in Kuwait is a good example of what can happen without such cooperation. Up until Iraq invaded Kuwait on August 2, 1990, Poland was one of the main suppliers of military hardware to Iraq.

On the other hand, the predominant view in Poland is that countries that are better off economically (to which the free transfer of technology contributes) and have a more democratic political system generally pose a smaller military threat to others. This view is especially well proved in postwar Europe where the economic success (among other things) of its Western part essentially ensures the overcoming of earlier long-lasting grievances and animosities between nations (France and Germany, for example). Thus, it is generally believed that the well-being of a country positively contributes to a more secure international environment. The critical question is how to address all three issues in question at the same time, i.e., how, through more liberal technology transfer, to support economic growth and democratization processes and—at the same time—not to compromise international security.

There is no doubt whatsoever that the need for certain kinds of export controls will continue in the foreseeable future and that there has to be a kind of international arrangement or organization to serve that purpose. It may be COCOM, evolved in a certain way; it may also be another—more official—international organization, structured along the lines of already existing examples with similar purposes (for example, the IAEA) or an institution with an entirely new structure.[23] However, there is a growing need to create a more comprehensive system in the near future. It is also possible to imagine one international export control system, covering all existing regimes (including those concerning conventional and nonconventional weapons). This new system should be less oriented to individual countries and primarily stress the prevention of the diversion of technology to unauthorized use.

This new system will have to accommodate new, emerging countries in Eastern Europe—the Baltic states and at least a few of the now independent former Soviet republics (for example, Ukraine). Depending on the evolution of events in other parts of the former Soviet Union, it will also probably have to cooperate with Russia, which officially declared its friendship with the West and now constitutes a much smaller military threat to the West than the former Soviet Union. One can even argue that leaving those newly emerging state entities outside the system, in fact keeping it turned against them, could become extremely dangerous in the new political environment arising in Eastern Europe (especially in view of the creation of a number of independent, nationalist-driven and militant states in the place of the former Soviet Union).

In view of those developments, one can also expect a growing need for the coordination of the safeguards activity among newcomers to the COCOM system—Poland, Czechoslovakia, and Hungary as well as possibly other countries of that region that will be gradually involved in the system of export controls. This coordination should increase its effectiveness and facilitate those countries' full integration within the system. It should also work in favor of dissuading those dangerous tendencies recently developing in Eastern Europe.

APPENDIX 1: CALENDAR OF EVENTS

December 1, 1989
Polish Minister of Foreign Economic Relations Marcin Swiecicki sends a letter of intent to Secretary of Commerce of the United States Robert Mosbacher. Hungary and Czechoslovakia approach the U.S. government about the same time with similar offers concerning their countries.

January, 1990
Poland receives a positive initial response from the U.S. administration—Secretary Mosbacher's letter of January 11 to Minister Swiecicki and the designation of Under Secretary for Export Administration Dennis Kloske to take the lead for Commerce.
A strategic review of U.S. export control policies is started to assess the changing nature of the strategic threat posed by the Soviet Union and its Warsaw Pact allies.

Early 1990
Poland hires of the U.S. law firm Paul, Weiss, Rifkind, Wharton & Garrison (former Under Secretary for Export Administration Lionel H. Olmer and Richard S. Elliott) to assist in its negotiations with the U.S. government.
A COCOM mid-level meeting in February, 1990, identifies three sectors as priorities for revised controls: machine tools, telecommunications, and computers.
On February 8, Senator John Heinz introduces S. 2113—Central and Eastern Europe Investment and Enhancement Act, later referred to the Committee on Banking, Housing, and Urban Affairs (S. 1125).

February–May, 1990
Representatives from other COCOM countries seek contact with Polish officials, apparently willing to discuss the issue of export controls directly with them and disappointed that Poland approached only the U.S. (especially Japan and France).

March, 1990
The Polish multiinstitutional team is created to prepare for negotiations with the U.S. government.

March–April, 1990
The Departments of Commerce and State give Poland more detailed materials (revised in April) on an expected agreement and all the necessary elements of a safeguards regime that Poland should introduce.

April, 1990
The Polish fact-finding mission visits Washington, D.C.

May, 1990
On May 2, the U.S. administration announces that it has completed its evaluation of export controls policies.
U.S. advocates visit Poland and have discussions with the Polish authorities and the Polish negotiating team.

June, 1990
June 6–7, a COCOM HLM in Paris makes crucial decisions on changes of policy.
June 18–19, the first and final round of negotiations between the Polish and the U.S. delegations in Warsaw are held.
The Warsaw meeting is followed by visits of the same U.S. delegation to Czechoslovakia and Hungary to conduct similar negotiations, apparently with similar results.

July 16, 1990
Wojcik sends a letter to Secretary Mosbacher asking for the technical assistance the U.S. delegation promised during negotiations in Warsaw; Kloske sends a positive answer on August 17, 1990.

July 23, 1990
The Polish government accepts the negotiated agreement with the United States.

July 27, 1990
A memorandum of understanding, signed by Minister Swiecicki, is sent to U.S. Secretary of State Baker; the United States later presents it to other COCOM member countries.

August 8, 1990
Poland and the United States negotiate and sign a customs-to-customs agreement.

September 9–15, 1990
A seven-member delegation of Polish specialists from the Ministry of Foreign Economic Relations, the Defense Department, and the Main Customs Office, responsible for the implementation of the Polish safeguards system, pays a working visit to the United States.

September, 1990
The U.S. Departments of Commerce and State suggest corrections to the proposed Polish safeguard documents, which Polish authorities subsequently consider and mostly accept.

September 26, 1990
The Ministry of Foreign Economic Relations issues a communiqué governing the importation of goods and technologies on the COCOM list from COCOM member states and states operating with COCOM and the reexportation of these goods and technologies.

October 1, 1990
Poland's safeguards regime goes into effect. Hungary's does the same on the very same day. Czechoslovakia starts its own system on February 1, 1991 (it also introduces a specific law on technology trade, including indigenous technology).

October 8, 1990
Swiecicki sends a letter to Secretary Baker informing the United States about the introduction of the Polish safeguards system on October 1, 1990.

October, 1990–February, 1991
Poland has bilateral contacts with different COCOM member countries, answering questions and clarifying doubts concerning details of its safeguards system.

December 28, 1990
A Polish oral message is sent to other COCOM member-countries; Japan responds with remarks on January 22, 1991.

End of October–early November, 1990, and January, 1991
The first two U.S. Department of Commerce's missions concerning the implementation of safeguards and the postshipment verification program come to Poland.
In January, 1991, during a COCOM meeting in Paris, a few countries question granting Poland "favorable consideration" status.

February, 1991
A U.S.-COCOM mission visits Poland to evaluate progress in establishing and implementing the safeguards regime and to analyze the handling of the first fifteen cases of controlled technology imports to Poland.

February 28, 1991
After resolving all the remaining questions, COCOM approves Poland's safeguards regime; since that moment Poland has been eligible for the favorable treatment (favorable consideration) envisioned in COCOM's June, 1990, decisions. COCOM had approved Hungary's safeguards on December 11, 1990, and Czechoslovakia's on February 7, 1991.

April 25, 1991
The U.S. Department of Commerce announces revised U.S. export licensing procedures for most shipments of sophisticated technology to Poland, Hungary, and Czechoslovakia (favorable consideration licensing procedures, i.e., the implementation of favorable consideration status).

May, 1991
The U.S. Department of State (COCOM Office) presents the view (to the author) that the U.S. was satisfied with measures undertaken by Poland (as well as Czechoslovakia and Hungary).

May 23–24, 1991
An HLM approves a new COCOM core list, to be published by September 1, 1991.

June 28, 1991
The Warsaw Pact is dissolved, removing that obstacle on the road of Poland and other East-Central European countries toward freer access to Western technology.

December, 1991
Poland signs an agreement with the Soviet Union on the withdrawal of all Soviet battle units from Poland by the end of 1992 (i.e., the next step in removing obstacles to Poland's freer access to Western technology).

End of 1991
Poland gathers experience, assesses the workability of the safeguards regime, and drafts a comprehensive law on technology transfer (waiting in the parliament for approval in early 1992).

APPENDIX 2: TEXT OF THE AGREEMENT

A letter to His Excellency James Baker, Secretary of State
Minister of Foreign Economic Relations Warsaw, July 27, 1990

Dear Mr. Secretary,
As an outcome of recent discussions between our two governments, I am writing to express the intentions of the Government of the Republic of Poland with respect to the adoption of a technology safeguards system and to seek confirmation concerning the intentions of the Government of the United States of America with respect to technology transfer to Poland.
The Government of the Republic of Poland understands the importance that the United States and other COCOM governments attach to strategic trade controls. The Government of the Republic of Poland is fully prepared to implement measures designed to prevent the illegal acquisition or diversion of U.S.-origin controlled strategic goods or technology contrary to COCOM restrictions, whether such diversion involves a

transfer within Poland or a reexport from Poland. My Government is, moreover, fully prepared to extend comparable protection to controlled strategic goods and technology originating in other COCOM member countries and in COCOM cooperating countries.
The Government of the Republic of Poland will refrain from government involvement in unauthorized acquisitions of controlled technology and from intelligence cooperation related to unauthorized acquisitions of controlled technology.
The Government of the Republic of Poland intends to implement an import certificate/delivery verification program. Import certificate and delivery verification forms would be provided to Polish importers of controlled items whenever these documents are required in support of an export of controlled goods or technologies to Poland.
The import certificate will indicate the end-user of controlled items and shall contain commitments by the importer:

a) to import controlled items directly into Poland as specified in the certificate;
b) not to divert or otherwise transfer the controlled items to another destination or end use without prior consent of the Ministry of Foreign Economic Relations;
c) to notify the Ministry of Foreign Economic Relations of any changes in the information presented in the certificate;
d) to allow pre-license and post-shipment checks to verify that the installation and use of controlled items conform to export license requirements. These checks will be performed on the importer's premises by Polish customs officers assisted by appropriate exporting government officials.

The Government of the Republic of Poland will also require an export license for the export of controlled items from a COCOM or COCOM cooperating country that enter Poland subject to an import certificate. In reviewing applications for such export licenses, the prospective exporter will be required to furnish one of the following from the appropriate government:

a) a reexport authorization;
b) evidence that the reexport was authorized under the original export license;
c) evidence that the reexport is otherwise authorized, for example, under a general authorization.

As appropriate, the Government of the Republic of Poland will consult with the exporting government concerning such an application for an export license. The statements made in connection with the issuance of import certificate and delivery verification forms, as well as export license requirements, could be enforced under current Polish law. Parties in Poland who violate end-use assurances or export restrictions will be subject to criminal penalties. The Government of Poland is prepared to dedicate personnel and resources to the administration and enforcement of controls, to ensure that the exporting country can obtain adequate information regarding the export of controlled goods and technology before and after licensing and to cooperate and exchange information on violations or suspected illegal activities in order to prevent unauthorized acquisitions.

The conclusion of a Customs-to-Customs agreement between the Republic of Poland and the United States of America, the text of which has already been agreed, will constitute an important additional factor strengthening the practical implementation of the safeguards.

Based upon Poland's adoption of these measures, it is the understanding of the Government of the Republic of Poland that the Government of the United States of America will support within COCOM an increase in the level of controlled strategic technology available to Poland. In addition to the immediately applicable special treatment for Poland in telecommunications, my Government understands that it will receive preferential treatment to include presumption of approval for all remaining goods on the COCOM Industrial List except for a small number of items that will remain subject to COCOM General Exceptions treatment. It is my understanding that, in light of the evolving strategic situation, COCOM members will consider in January, 1991 the possibility of upgrading the degree of liberalization afforded to qualifying countries. I further understand that Poland will qualify for such liberalization.

It is the understanding of my Government that the Government of the United States of America intends that Poland will receive technology liberalization benefits which are no less favorable than those received by any other COCOM proscribed country adopting comparable export control measures.

My Government agrees that progress on export control issues should be reviewed periodically by our two governments, and that either government should be sympathetic to requests from the other government to consider on an expeditious basis any problems or concerns that may arise.

Based on the discussion between our two governments, the Government of the United States of America has noted the intention of the Government of the Republic of Poland to implement a safeguards regime by October 1, 1990.

It is the understanding of my Government that the Government of the United States of America will discuss in detail the issue of the possible removal of Poland from the proscribed destinations list. My Government understands that in the consideration of this issue, experience with the Polish safeguards regime will be an important factor. In the context of such discussions, I can confirm that my Government will be prepared to consider the adoption of a second stage of export controls that extends beyond the one described above, including protection of strategic goods and technology originating in countries that are neither COCOM member nor COCOM cooperating countries.

I would be honored if your Government would inform the other COCOM members of the intentions of the Polish Government and seek appropriate preferential treatment for controlled exports to Poland. The actions described in this letter will constitute a major step toward the modernization of Poland and its revival as a stable democratic member of the modern world economy.

With assurances of my highest personal regards,

Marcin Swiecicki

APPENDIX 3: AGREEMENT BETWEEN THE GOVERNMENT OF THE UNITED STATES AND THE GOVERNMENT OF THE REPUBLIC OF POLAND REGARDING MUTUAL ASSISTANCE BETWEEN THEIR CUSTOMS SERVICES

The Government of the United States of America and the Government of the Republic of Poland;

Considering that offenses against customs laws are prejudicial to the economic, fiscal, and commercial interests of their respective countries;
Considering the importance of assuring the accurate assessment of customs duties and other taxes;
Recognizing the need for international cooperation in matters related to the administration and enforcement of the customs laws;
Convinced that action against customs offenses can be made more effective by cooperation between their Customs Services;
Having regard to the Recommendation of the Customs Cooperation Council on Mutual Administrative Assistance of December 5, 1953;
HAVE AGREED as follows:

ARTICLE 1
Definitions

For the purpose of the present Agreement,

1. "Customs laws" shall mean such laws and regulations enforced by the Customs Services concerning the importation, exportation, and transit of goods, as they relate to Customs duties and other taxes, or to prohibitions, restrictions and other similar controls respecting the movement of goods and other controlled items across national boundaries.
2. "Customs Administrations or Services" shall mean, in the United States of America, the United States Customs Service, Department of the Treasury, and in the Republic of Poland, the Central Board of Customs.
3. "Provisional measures" include:
   a. "seizure" or "freezing" which means temporarily prohibiting the transfer, conversion, disposition or movement of property or temporarily assuming custody or control of property on the basis of an order issued by a court or competent authority; and
   b. "forfeiture" which includes confiscation where applicable, and means the deprivation of property by order of a court or other competent authority.
4. "Offense" shall mean any violation of the Customs laws as well as attempted violation of such laws.
5. "Property" means assets of every kind, whether corporeal or incorporeal, movable or immovable, tangible or intangible, and legal documents or instruments evidencing title to or an interest in such assets.
6. "Parties" to this Agreement are:
   a. the United States of America; and
   b. the Republic of Poland.

ARTICLE 2

Scope of Assistance

1. The Parties agreed to assist each other through their Customs Services to prevent, investigate and repress any offense, in accordance with the provisions of the present Agreement.
2. Assistance, as provided in this Agreement, shall also include, upon request, all information apt to ensure the accurate assessment of customs duties and other taxes by the Customs Services.
3. The Parties agree, in accordance with their respective domestic law, to assist each other in proceedings involving the use of provisional measures directed at property, proceeds and instrumentalities involved in offenses related to the Customs laws.
4. Assistance as provided in paragraphs 1, 2 and 3 shall be provided for use in all proceedings, whether judicial, administrative or investigative and shall include, but not be limited to, proceedings on classification, value and other characteristics relevant to the enforcement of the Customs laws and proceedings of fines, penalties, forfeitures and liquidated damages.
5. The Parties shall, if not contrary to their domestic law, also seek to cooperate in:
   a. initiating, developing or improving specific training programs for their personnel;
   b. establishing and maintaining channels of communication between their administrations to facilitate the secure and rapid exchange of information;
   c. facilitating effective coordination between their Customs Services, including the exchange of personnel, experts and the posting of liaison officers;
   d. considering and testing of new equipment or procedures; and
   e. any other general administrative matters that may from time to time require their joint action.
6. All assistance under the present Agreement by either Party will be performed in accordance with its domestic law. Where, pursuant to Article 5, the requesting Party is permitted to act in the territory of the requested Party, such actions shall be subject to the law of the requested Party.
7. This Agreement is intended to enhance and supplement mutual assistance practices presently in effect between the Parties. No provision in this Agreement may be interpreted in a manner that would restrict agreements and practices relating to mutual assistance and cooperation that are already in effect between the Parties.

ARTICLE 3

Confidentiality of Information and Documents

1 Information, documents and other communications received in the course of mutual assistance may only be used for the purposes specified in the present Agreement, including the use in judicial or administrative proceedings. Such information, documents and other communications may be used for other purposes only when the supplying Party has given its express consent.
2. Inquiries, information, documents and other communications received by either Party shall, upon request of the supplying Party, be treated as confidential. The reasons for such a request shall be stated

3. Any intelligence, documents or other information communicated or obtained under this Agreement shall be afforded, in the receiving country, the same protection in respect of confidentiality and official secrecy as applies in that country to the same kind of intelligence, documents and other information obtained in its own territory.

ARTICLE 4

Communication of Requests

A. Form and Substance of Requests for Assistance

1. Requests pursuant to the present Agreement shall be made in writing. Documents necessary for the execution of such requests shall accompany the request. When required because of the urgency of the situation, oral requests may also be accepted but shall be promptly confirmed in writing.
2. Requests pursuant to paragraph 1 of this article shall include the following information:
    a. the authority making the request;
    b. the nature of the proceedings;
    c. the object of and the reason for the request;
    d. the names and addresses of the parties concerned in the proceedings, if known; and
    e. a brief description of the matter under consideration and the legal elements involved.

B. Channel of Communication

1. Assistance shall be carried out by direct communication between officials designated by the Heads of the respective Customs Services.
2. In case the Customs Services of the requested Party is not the appropriate agency to comply with a request, it shall promptly transmit the request to the appropriate agency, and so advise the requesting Party.

ARTICLE 5

Execution of Requests

1. The requested Customs Service shall take all reasonable measures to execute the request, and if required, will endeavor to seek any official or judicial measure necessary to carry out the request.
2. The Customs Service of either Party shall, upon the request of the Customs Service of the other Party, conduct or permit the requesting Party to conduct any necessary investigation, including the questioning of persons suspected of having committed an offense, as well as of experts and witnesses.
3. The Customs Service of either Party shall, upon the request of the Customs Service of the other Party, undertake, or permit the requesting Party to undertake verifications, inspections, and fact-finding inquiries in connection with the matters referred to in the present Agreement.
4. Upon request, the requested Party shall, to the fullest extent possible, authorize officials of the requesting Party to be present in the territory of the requested Party to participate in inquiries into, or the official report of, an offense of concern to the requesting Party.

5. A request by a Party that a certain procedure be followed shall be complied with, subject to the domestic law of the requested Party.
6. The requesting Party shall, if it so requests, be advised of the time and place of the action to be taken in response to the request, so that such actions may be coordinated.

ARTICLE 6
Exemptions from Assistance

1. In cases where the requested Party is of the opinion that compliance with a request would infringe upon its sovereignty, security, public policy or other substantive national interest, assistance can be refused or compliance may be made subject to the satisfaction of certain conditions or requirements.
2. In the event that the request cannot be complied with, the requesting Party shall be promptly notified of that fact, and provided a statement of the reasons and circumstances which might be of importance for the further pursuit of the matter.
3. Assistance may be postponed by the requested Party on the grounds that it will interfere with an ongoing investigation, prosecution or proceeding. In such a case, the requested Party shall consult with the requesting Party to determine if assistance can be given subject to such terms or conditions as the requested Party may require.

ARTICLE 7
Files, Documents and Witnesses

1. Originals of files, documents and other materials shall be requested only in cases where copies would be insufficient. Upon specific request, copies of such files, documents and other materials shall be appropriately authenticated.
2. Originals of files, documents and other materials which have been transmitted shall be returned at the earliest opportunity; rights of the requested Party or of third parties relating thereto shall remain unaffected.
3. The Customs Service of one Party shall authorize its employees, upon the request of the Customs Service of the other Party, to appear as witnesses in judicial or administrative proceedings in the territory of the other Party and to produce such files, documents or other materials or authenticated copies thereof, as may be considered essential for the proceedings.
4. With the agreement of the requested Party, authorization may be given for officials specially designated by the requesting Party to consult, in the offices of the requested Party, the relevant books, registers and other documents or data media held in those offices, take copies thereof, or extract any information or particulars relating to the offense.

ARTICLE 8
Costs

1. The Parties shall normally waive all claims for reimbursement of costs incurred in the execution of the present Agreement, with the exception of expenses for witnesses, fees of experts, and costs of interpreters other than government employees.

2. If expenses of a substantial and extraordinary nature are or will be required to execute the request, the Parties shall consult to determine the terms and conditions under which the request will be executed as well as the manner in which the costs shall be borne.

ARTICLE 9

Special Instances of Assistance

1. Upon request, the Customs Services shall inform each other whether goods exported from the territory of one Party have been lawfully imported into the territory of the other Party. The information shall, upon request, contain the Customs procedure used for clearing the goods.
2. The Customs Service of one Party, upon request of the Customs Service of the other Party, shall, to the extent of its ability, exercise special surveillance of:
   a. means of transport suspected of being used in offenses within the territory of the requesting Party;
   b. goods designated by the requesting Party as the object of an extensive clandestine trade of which it is the country of destination;
   c. particular persons known or suspected by the requesting Party of being engaged in an offense.
3. The Customs Services of the Parties shall, upon request, furnish each other all available information regarding activities which may result in offenses within the territory of the other Party. In serious cases which could involve substantial damage to the economy, public health, public security, or any other vital interest of the other Party, such information shall be supplied without being requested.
4. The Customs Services of the Parties shall, upon request, provide documentation relating to transportation and shipment of goods showing value, disposition and destination of those goods.
5. Subject to their domestic law, the Parties agree:
   a. to assist each other with respect to the execution of provisional measures and proceedings.
   b. to dispose of property, proceeds or instrumentalities forfeited as a result of the assistance provided for under this Agreement, in accordance with the legislation of the Party in control of the property, proceeds or instrumentalities.
   c. that either Party may transfer, without regard to the requirement of reciprocity, forfeited property or instrumentalities, or the proceeds of their sale to the other Party, to the extent permitted by their respective domestic law, upon such terms as may be agreed.

ARTICLE 10

Implementation of the Agreement

The United States Customs Service, Department of the Treasury of the United States of America and the Central Board of Customs of the Republic of Poland agree that they shall:

a. communicate directly for the purpose of dealing with matters arising out of the present Agreement;

b. after consultation, issue any administrative directives for the implementation of the present Agreement; and
c. endeavor by mutual accord to resolve problems or doubts arising from the interpretation or application of the Agreement.

ARTICLE 11
Entry into Force and Termination

1. This Agreement shall enter into force on the ninetieth day following the date on which the Parties notify one another by an exchange of diplomatic notes that they have accepted its terms, and that all necessary national legal requirements for entry into force have been fulfilled.
2. The Parties agree to meet in order to review this Agreement at the end of five years from the date of its entry into force, unless they notify one another in writing that no review is necessary.
3. This Agreement may be terminated by either Party:
   a. upon receipt by the other Party of written notice through diplomatic channels;
   b. in which case, it shall cease to be in force six months after such notice has been given.

IN WITNESS WHEREOF, the undersigned, being duly authorized by their respective governments, have signed this Agreement.
DONE at *Warsaw,* on *August 8, 1990* in English and Polish languages, both texts being equally authentic.

FOR THE GOVERNMENT OF THE THE UNITED STATES OF AMERICA	FOR THE GOVERNMENT OF THE REPUBLIC OF POLAND

NOTES

1. A calender of the events described in this chapter is provided in appendix 1.

2. The author of this chapter was a direct witness and participant of the work as a member of the team, and many of his direct observations come from this experience.

3. S. 1125.

4. See A. Zielinski, "COCOM blizej Polski" ["COCOM is Closer to Poland"], *Rzeczpospolita,* July 25, 1991.

5. The full text of the agreement is in appendix 2.

6. For the full text of the agreement, see appendix 3.

7. *Dziennik Urzedowy [Official Journal*], no. 8, item 20, September 28, 1991.

8. That their representatives took part in the training programs organized in 1990 by the United States in Washington, D.C., and Vienna implies some say in the process of export controls. It is very probable that the Ministries of Defense and of Foreign Affairs are involved in controls of weapons sales, but this issue should be further investigated.

9. The first mission visited five foreign trade enterprises importing Western technology: Elektrim, Eximpol, Mundial, Varimex, and Unitra-Cemi. The second one,

concerning prelicense investigation and postshipment verification, visited enterprises that already were end users of imported technology: Comp Ltd., LB Impex, Pewex, the Warsaw Institute of Elektron Technology, and LOT Polish Airlines in Warsaw and Elwro in Wroclaw. More missions have visited Poland since then.

10. Hungary's safeguards system was accepted on December 11, 1990, and Czechoslovakia's on February 7, 1991.

11. *Federal Register* (April 25, 1991).

12. According to the COCOM office director, Robert Price.

13. The Department of Commerce estimates that the new list represents a 65 percent reduction in the number of controlled goods over the pre-June, 1990, control list.

14. Allen Wendt, "U.S. Export Controls in a Changing Global Environment," U.S. Department of State Dispatch, July 1, 1991.

15. Czechoslovakia passed the necessary legislation in February, 1991.

16. However, my interlocutors in the Department of State have stressed that this condition does not necessarily mean no violations. Violations also occur in Western countries, members of COCOM. Rather, the success of implementation will be judged by how responsible authorities handle violations.

17. Wendt, "U.S. Export Controls."

18. The Directive of the Minister of Foreign Economic Relations of December 21, 1989, listing goods and services the turnover of which require permission, *The Journal of Law,* no. 72, item 432.

19. So far there have apparently been no violations of controls, but this assumption was made mainly on the basis of the first fifteen cases of the export of U.S. technology to Poland in the first few months of the functioning of the system.

20. On the basis of information given to the author by R. Rice from the Bureau of Enforcement of the Department of Commerce. See also L. Peters, "Krzemowy Hit Pod Wawelem" ["Silicon Chips a Hit at Wawel Palace"], *Rzeczpospolita,* June 23, 1991.

21. For example, a successful antidemocratic coup in the Soviet Union.

22. The August, 1991, events in the Soviet Union prove how ineffective is the policy of democratization without economic progress.

23. See, for example, M. R. Lucas, "The Abolition of COCOM and the Establishment of a Technology Disarmament and Transfer Agency in the CSCE," *Bulletin of Peace Proposals,* 21, no. 2 (1990): 219–25; and D. Hobbs, "Technology Policies in a New Strategic Environment," in *Jane's NATO Handbook 1990–1991,* edited by B. G. Coulson, (Surrey, U.K.: Jane's Information Group, 1990).

CHAPTER 6

Making the Transition: A Bulgarian Perspective on Export Controls in the 1990s and Beyond

Atanas Gotchev

Introduction: Nature and Scope of the Problem

In this chapter, the main determinants that are likely to affect Bulgaria's potential attitudes and actual policies in multilateral export control cooperation in the 1990s are reviewed and assessed. The main emphasis is on how and in what way domestic change affects all the elements connected to the national stance on export control issues. The chapter begins with a brief examination of the domestic and international developments that influence the national export control policies. From this perspective, the current developments in legislation and policy are examined.

The issue of strategic export controls has always been the subject of a lot of debate. The events of 1989 changed Eastern Europe and the world and gave new impetus to this debate. Old political and economic structures and ideological dogmas were scrapped. At the beginning of the 1990s, new trends increasingly dominate the system of international relations. Among them, one can point to the emerging pluralism and diversity in Eastern Europe, the unification of Germany, the economic integration of Europe, the spread of regional conflicts, the rising Islamic fundamentalism, and the like.

In Eastern Europe, these entirely new developments include the disintegration of the Warsaw Pact alliance and the Council for Mutual Economic Assistance (CMEA) structures. One could also add here the Soviet and Yugoslavian domestic developments and the enormous problems that the nations in Eastern Europe are facing. Most of the countries have severe economic problems and in certain instances the scope of the crisis could overwhelm the reform efforts.

Prospects for military confrontation between East and West have diminished. Strategic thinking has been affected by the unprecedented discussion of domestic social, economic, and political problems of Eastern Europe. Undoubtedly all these create new dimensions in international relations, and a new type of East-West interdependence is emerging. As a result, the nature of national security threats is rapidly changing. Both from the Western and from the Eastern perspectives, the spread of high-technology weapons and the proliferation of nuclear, chemical, and biological weapons and missile capabilities change the nature of national security perceptions.

These developments create pressures and provide opportunities to redefine the entire spectrum of East-West relations, the prerequisites for security, and, last but not least, the export control regulations and challenges for Eastern and Western policies. However, as was noted in the study of the National Academy of Sciences, policymakers and the public in the West, especially in the United States, view these changes very differently and suggest widely divergent policy responses.[1] There has recently been a series of arguments over a variety of East-West issues, including arms and commodity control issues. These clashes result from different views about precisely what Soviet and East European reform efforts mean and what should be the appropriate response to them. The conflict was rooted in the fundamentally different perceptions about the significance of recent East European developments.

Taking the view that changes in Eastern Europe are irreversible and that the proliferation of dual-use high technology could be a factor in expanding local and global conflicts, the main issue is how to change the basis of technology transfer relationships with Eastern Europe and move from the denial regime into an approval regime based on mutually agreed and verifiable end-use conditions. Moreover, the development of a nonproliferation regime is not feasible without the participation of at least some of the former East European countries.

Simultaneously, it is very important to examine what type of modus operandi is appropriate for Eastern Europe in the emerging international system. This issue is tremendous in its scope and can hardly be investigated here. However, one can explicitly put forward some of the main problems: Do changes in Eastern Europe create a new form of East-West interdependence? In what way do these changes affect the security perceptions and the policy responses of the individual East-European countries? What is the balance between national economic and military interests and what type of East-West cooperation will emerge? What are the possibilities for multilateral export control cooperation?

Broadly stated, East European, and particularly Bulgarian, attitudes toward cooperation in the field of export controls will depend on the old and the emerging new interdependencies. The interdependence perceptions will determine, from the point of view of Eastern Europe, the possibilities for international cooperation and will influence future policy actions.

As has been pointed out, interdependence could be perceived as threatening dependence on the external environment.[2] In this understanding, interdependence perceived either as sensitivity (dependence threat) or actual vulnerability has a wide range of security implications, reflected in domestic and foreign policy behavior.

The sources of dependence also widely vary. They may derive from features of the state's external environment (which the state may or may not be able to affect or change), they may derive from the inadequacy of resources at the state's disposal, or they may derive from inadequate internal support for a regime.[3] The three sources of dependence are frequently related, but in all cases they limit the freedom of the state's decision makers to maneuver and are reflected in their domestic and foreign policy decisions.

The problem that Eastern Europe is confronting is that interdependence tends to be asymmetrical dependence. The international economic system reduces the extent of autonomy for national economic policy. The decline of autonomy is the price that the less developed countries in Eastern Europe have to pay for the access to the world markets and the gains in efficiency from foreign trade.

Thus, democratization, modernization, restructuring, and market reform in Eastern Europe are conducive not only to domestic developments but also to the new structures in the system of international relations and to the new forms of East-West interdependence. Perhaps, it is in the interest of the West to sustain these developments since the reintegration of Eastern Europe into the world system is important for the whole community of democratic nations.

Apart from that, there are some moral arguments rooted in recent East European history that the West should be more active and financially more involved in the peaceful democratization of the former socialist countries. The international response to the transformation of Eastern Europe into a state socialist society was not adequate, and for forty-five years in Eastern Europe millions of people were forced to comply with the new social rules of the game. The image of the Soviet Union as a superpower capable of destroying the other party perhaps limited the Western response to criticism, containment, and other policy actions that could not prevent these developments.

Furthermore, the integration of the reforming former socialist economies into the world economic system is the main method to support their democratic change. However, this integration implies the acceptance of at least two basic ideas. The first is that former socialist countries have to be legitimate partners in the changing international political economy. This partnership includes creating an appropriate export control regime that favors economic growth and democracy in Eastern Europe, thus promoting international security. The second is that nation-states in the East and the West have shared, although not necessarily equal, responsibility in adjusting national policies and priorities to the international political and economic processes.

Bulgaria in the 1990s: Old Dependencies, New Dependencies

When analyzing the current state of Eastern Europe and its future role in world society, one cannot overlook its historic roots. The post–World War II system of international relations emerged as a bipolar system with two contrasting pillars: the Soviet (socialist) dimension and the Western (democratic) one.

Moreover, for various reasons, the Soviet Union was the sole master of its own sphere of influence. That meant that nations in Eastern Europe were reformed on the basis of the Soviet model: industrialization with an emphasis on heavy industries, based on energy- and resource-consuming technologies, without any pollution considerations. In addition, what the comparative advantages of the individual nations were was not a prime concern. It was more important to create a dependency model, which was called an international community of brotherly nations. This type of industrialization affected the individual East European countries differently, but among the most crippled were the less developed ones such as Bulgaria and Romania. Thus, countries with strong agricultural traditions and lacking a substantial raw material base were turned into a backyard of the Soviet industry, dependent for its imports and exports on the Soviet Union.

As Detlef Lorenz correctly observes, after 1945 the political division of Europe forced it to develop in an economically irrational way.[4] The East European countries that were in the gravitational field of the West European industrial countries were forced by political means into the Soviet orbit, developing a kind of core-periphery relationship. The Soviet Union became the center of this politico-economic gravity. However, this core was increasingly unable to supply the peripheral countries with an adequate flow of goods and financial and technological resources.

These economic changes coincided with the suppression of civil rights and criticism and the suppression of intellectuals, creating mute and conforming societies where everyone was supposed to be happy and proud because of the mythical social equality. However, the events of 1989 showed not only the crisis of communism but its end. Much to the satisfaction of the West, those who believed that the Great October Revolution was the gate to the future of world history have been provided with a lot of evidence that they were wrong.

Therefore, at the beginning of the 1990s, the starting position for profound economic, and hence, political reforms in Bulgaria is very unfavorable. The supply-constrained economic environment with shortages of production factors (raw materials, energy, machinery, technological and financial resources), labor, and consumer goods, compounded by additional elements, such as unforeseen slumps in world markets, the Gulf War and the like, has created adverse initial conditions for any reform efforts.[5]

The existing macroeconomic tensions create different but strongly related threat perceptions, which will influence future policy-making in Bulgaria. In nation-states, national interests dominate national policies and the choices of policy instruments. But problems arise when the choice of these policy instruments is limited or when they lose their policy effectiveness. Then countries find themselves unable to achieve their objectives satisfactorily. That is what has happened with some of the East European countries, Bulgaria in particular.

The one-sided orientation of the economic relations of some of the East European countries, based on historical reasons and relative benefits in the past, proved at the beginning of the 1990s to be a destabilizing factor, decreasing the level of economic security of these countries. This created an external economic security issue with a different importance for the individual East European nations.

Taking Bulgaria, one could note that the traditional socialist approach to maintaining external economic security had turned the nation's economy into a kind semiautarky, dependent largely on the CMEA partners. CMEA countries accounted for about 80 percent of Bulgarian foreign trade and the Soviet Union had a share of 60 percent.

The destruction of the CMEA puts at stake the former stable market for agricultural and technologically nonintensive manufactured goods. This market is vanishing because of the changing commercial policies of the Central European countries and the former Soviet Union and the introduction of accounting based on U.S. dollars in the economic relations of the former CMEA partners. In 1991 overall Bulgarian exports shrunk by 57 percent to $2.56 billion from $5.83 billion in 1990. Exports fell most steeply to the former Soviet Union (59.7 percent) and the countries of Central and Eastern Europe (69.6 percent). These decreases contrast with the decline of exports to the EC (26.5 percent) and to other industrialized countries (15.3 percent). The decline of imports from the former Soviet Union was 70.7 percent from January to September, 1990, and 86.7 percent from Central and Eastern Europe. These figures indicate that traditional markets have shrunk and the share of industrialized countries slightly increased. Nevertheless, the former Soviet Union is still the main market of Bulgarian goods, accounting for 53 percent of total exports, down from 57 percent in 1990.[6]

After the breakup of the CMEA, Bulgaria tried to negotiate new trade arrangements with its former CMEA partners in 1991. In fact, a trade protocol between Bulgaria and the Soviet Union was signed within the framework of a clearing arrangement. However, there were severe difficulties in the implementation of these arrangements. For instance, a significant part of traditional Bulgarian manufactured exports were not included in the so-called indicative lists of the protocol, leaving out telecommunications equipment, electronic components, agricultural machinery, and others. As a result, in the middle of 1991 there were substantial stocks of Bulgarian goods ready for export but deprived of the traditional markets. Price factors (the indicative lists were valued at world market prices) and the unrealistic rate of exchange used by the Soviet Union in its trade with Bulgaria (R 1.8 to $1) also contributed to the sharp contraction of bilateral trade.

The matter was further complicated by the breakup of the Soviet Union. Currently, trade protocols have to be signed with the individual republics of the former Soviet Union, and it is expected that Russia and Ukraine will account for nearly 90 percent of the trade with Bulgaria. The lack of such trade agreements with the former Soviet republics had already created difficulties. Ukraine, through whose territory electric power lines pass, twice at the end of 1991 nearly blacked out Bulgaria. The electricity supply from Russia was stopped because its transmission was not negotiated with Ukraine earlier in the year.

Bulgarian trade with other former CMEA partners was also affected by the negative outstanding transferable ruble balances at the end of 1991. Hungary, Czechoslovakia, and Poland demanded a settlement of the deficit and made it a precondition for the normalization of trade relationships with Bulgaria.

The difficulties in trade relations with former CMEA countries have led to severe shrinkage in production, and according to some reports, nearly half of the gross domestic product (GDP) drop in the first quarter of 1991 is due to the closing of the Soviet market.[7]

Another economic threat perception is Bulgaria's relative backwardness in the high-technology field. Competence in high technology is perceived to be a crucial determinant of national economic performance. In a highly competitive international environment, the quality of national economic performance affects not just the nation's balance of payments and the standard of living of its population. It affects the nation's international standing and capabilities. Therefore, the ability to induce technological change could be related to the nation's capacity to maintain its overall economic competitiveness, to sustain international commitments, to maintain its security, and to counteract dependencies on the policies of other countries.[8]

System-specific features of the Bulgarian economy and the former CMEA regime did not create enough incentives for technological innovation.

Exports of manufactured goods were guaranteed under the umbrella of bilateral treaties, which did not provide market signals for Bulgarian enterprises to upgrade products, incorporate technological innovations, and improve the quality of the manufacturing process. That also contributed to the economic self-sufficiency doctrine that was imposed on the country. Thus, Bulgaria finds itself increasingly unable to match Western standards of equipment and technology. As the former minister of finance, Ivan Kostov, notes, foreign debt growth could largely be attributed to the incompetent technological policies of previous regimes and hence to poor technological performance.[9]

The mastering of new technologies requires a substantial amount of resources. This characteristic of the present technological development favors big nations, particularly those that can quickly mobilize financial, scientific, and technological resources. It creates an international environment where the existing technological gap and the technological lead of developed Western countries will acquire even greater importance. The inability to move swiftly and efficiently into an intensive, information technology–based economic system will hamper the performance of the less technologically developed East European nations, Bulgaria in particular.

The lack of sufficient technological resources on the one hand and the availability of these technologies in the West on the other elevates the significance of East-West economic and technological cooperation for the democratic reforms in Bulgaria and Eastern Europe. Economic contacts with the West are thus an important factor at the present stage of economic reform in Bulgaria. The West can play an important role in the creation of new infrastructure and communication systems in Bulgaria. Western countries can provide significant assistance for updating Bulgarian technical standards such as the elimination of the existing differences, which is an important prerequisite for the development of the future international economic system.

Technological backwardness is perceived to create an external economic security issue with a different importance for individual East European nations. Data on East-West technology trade indicate a broadening of the technological gap in the last fifteen years.[10] Economic reform in Bulgaria more than anything requires substantial increases of appropriate technology flows from the West. However, technology transfer is a multidimensional phenomenon and depends on a variety of factors, one of them being Western export control policies. The relaxation of export control policies might in the short run substantially contribute to the progress of structural reforms in Bulgaria.

A different but strongly connected economic dependency threat perception is related to the debt problem. The economic capacity of Eastern Europe to service its foreign debt tends to be one of the main constraints for the reintegration of Eastern Europe into the international economic system. Economic modernization and the promotion of export capabilities require new technologies, modern information and communication facilities, different infrastructure, and so on—all of which need new credits—and last but not least, a relaxation of Western export controls. However, new credits presuppose financial reliability and the clearing of previous obligations. It is more than certain that countries like Bulgaria cannot simultaneously pursue the two objectives.

Bulgarian foreign debt rose from $4 billion in 1985 to $11.2 billion in 1990, mainly due to purchases of capital goods, often inadequate secondhand technologies. Currently, debt servicing runs into several major difficulties: First is the sharp decline of export earnings of hard currency. In 1990 the debt-to-exports ratio was nearly 300 to 1. Second, short-term borrowing takes up an unprecedentedly large proportion of the debt. Third, the Gulf War and the switch to dollar accounting with the former CMEA countries from the beginning of 1991 plunged production and exports into grave crisis.[11]

Both the debt problem of Eastern Europe and Western export control policies require a new approach on the part of Western policymakers. Having in mind the adjustments in the strategic and foreign policy of Central and East European countries and the destruction of the military structure of the Warsaw Treaty Organization, one cannot overlook that the disparity in the levels of economic development of the East and the West is a greater potential threat to international security and the emerging new international regimes than an imaginary military threat. Any successful reintegration of Eastern Europe in the world economy will require a more stable international export control environment than the current regimes could provide. To create this environment, the West has to develop a comprehensive long-term policy directed at diminishing the impact of military considerations and trade barriers on economic relations. The long-term perspective should be targeted toward new institutional frameworks and new international export control regimes.

Furthermore, it is clear that the goodwill of the West has to be met by the efforts of the indebted East to undertake reasonable domestic policies in the area of export controls, targeted toward restoring the confidence of the West. However, the endeavor of Eastern Europe will be in vain if it is not combined with sufficient Western assistance for overcoming the problems, thus contributing to new opportunities for capital investment that will allow their economies to pull out of the hopeless economic situation with some reasonable adjustment programs.

However, even if one takes the view that the participation of Eastern Europe in the new system of international economic relations depends predominantly on its ability to be a reliable partner, the importance of Western economic assistance must not be overlooked. The West has to reassess its economic interest in Eastern Europe. At this stage, at least for the sake of stability and common security, the West should be more involved in the economic modernization of Eastern Europe.

The reintegration of Eastern Europe into the world economy is in the long-term interest of Western governments and firms. To facilitate this process, they have to make an effort to create favorable international economic and political conditions under which the conversion to a market-based economy and modernization in Eastern Europe could be easily pursued. That means lifting the remaining unnecessary barriers for Eastern European participation in world trade and implies the revision of export control procedures.

Reform in Eastern Europe requires a certain period of time. Transition from a centrally planned economy to a market economy lacks historical precedent. What is certain is that this process will take many years. After World War II, the introduction of the centrally planned system took ten to fifteen years, so one should not expect the reverse process to take substantially less time.

The time factor is even more important when one considers the expectations of the different players in this process. The East European governments need instant international recognition for their intentions to guarantee the people a democratic society based on a market system. That makes favorable export control regulations politically highly desirable for the newly elected democratic governments.

Western partners would probably like to see much quicker economic improvement of Eastern Europe so that these countries will be reliable partners in a future system of multilateral export controls. However, it has to be recognized that neither of these expectations can be achieved in a short period of time. Nevertheless, it is very important to achieve some progress in the area of export controls and visible economic growth in a politically acceptable period of time.

The existing political and economic conditions in Eastern Europe require realistic mechanisms that can sustain the process and can guarantee the irreversibility of the reforms. All that elevates the importance of international institutions and international cooperation and the responsibility of both Western and Eastern countries for the new multilateral export control regime in a new international economy.

Determinants of National Export Control Policies

Bulgarian export control policy is being substantially adjusted to reflect the major political, economic, and social changes in the country and in the international community. This process has its own history and development, which in a way influences the current reform.

After 1985 there was a dramatic increase of East European academic and official publications dealing with East-West technology transfer and the consequences of the Western strategic embargo. A lot of attention was paid to the very substance of the embargo policy: its history, its rationale, and its objectives. Gorbachev addressed this issue quite often. He dedicated considerable attention to it in his book on the new political thinking and did not fail to raise the issue at the press conference after the 1991 summit with President Bush. The main points that were made on this issue are that the embargo is a potential source of mistrust and that it prevents mutually beneficial economic cooperation between the East and the West.

The post-1980 development of the COCOM list was generally regarded in East European official statements as the beginning of a new technological war against the socialist community. It was believed that it was aimed at isolating the socialist countries from the world market of new technologies. In academic writings this was described as an attempt to divert the new technological wave away from Eastern Europe. Some even went so far as to say that if the present trends were sustained, Eastern Europe might become a technological desert by the end of this century. For example, according to Bauer, due to the growing technological gap between West and East, the East European countries cannot do without Western imports of modern technologies.[12] The revival of COCOM was perceived as an attempt on the part of the technologically more developed countries to retard the economic development of their adversaries and hence destroy strategic military parity. The embargo was considered to be consistent with the increased military technological effort—in other words, an attempt on the part of the United States to achieve military superiority in space via the SDI project.

To counteract this strategy, East European policymakers tried to devise adjustment policies. CMEA devised several programs for scientific and technological development. Simultaneously, strong efforts to evade the embargo were undertaken. For instance, in 1987 in Bulgaria at a top political level, a memorandum was issued to develop a second market for the machinery and equipment that were subject to COCOM export control regulations. The memorandum envisaged the creation of consortia that could finance in the West Bulgarian participation in Western companies and in risk ventures of breakthrough areas of technology. For this purpose a government fund of $100 million was set up, which was later increased. To facilitate transactions with Western counterparts, several special Bulgarian companies and a special department in the Ministry of Foreign Economic Relations were created.[13]

Simultaneously, after 1985, there was a new, quite different development in assessments of the significance of East-West economic relations. In academic writing and, though not so openly, in public discussions, the feasibility of the policy of technology purchases from the West was questioned.

Should one hold COCOM solely responsible for all of the East European technological misfortunes, or are there other reasons? Apparently there were other reasons, which can be called the consequences of economic romanticism. This was the policy based on a series of assumptions about the importance and role of borrowing Western technologies.

Proponents initially thought that the introduction of Western technologies on a large scale might substitute for major economic, and hence, political reforms. They believed that the advanced technologies acquired from the West would make the economic system more efficient and promote the export capabilities of the CMEA countries. In this way, these technologies would help to sustain relatively rapid economic growth and a steady rise in the living standards of the population. On the whole, the successful borrowing of technologies and their subsequent introduction into the economic systems of the socialist countries was considered one of the important ways for securing the functioning of the socioeconomic system. The only trouble was that this paradigm did not work. Economic efficiency was stumbling, technological and structural changes failed to be achieved, and foreign debt was soaring. By the beginning of the 1980s, the beneficial outcomes hoped for had not been accomplished. There were many domestic reasons for the limited success of the technology borrowing policy.

The Domestic Domain

The main domestic factors that determine the import policies of dual-use technologies could be linked with the changes in the economic policy as a result of the transition from the administrative bureaucratic system to democracy and a market economy. The general export-import regime and the regulations concerning the regime of dual-use technologies and military-related items are affected by the economic reform in several important ways.

In early 1991 a stabilization policy was applied, and the country gradually moved from a supply-constrained economy into a demand-constrained one. Stabilization policy is determined by a strong and uncritical faith in the forces of the free market, the state believing intervention to be harmful. The measures are confined to balancing the budget, to sustaining a restrictive monetary policy, and to achieving a positive real interest rate, even in the face of very high rates of inflation and achieving convertibility at the same time.

However, because Bulgaria has not become a microeconomically functional market economy of a Western type because of a lack of flexibility in supply, economic development in Bulgaria is characterized by recessive tendencies, failure to achieve desired structural change, and high inflation expectations. It is to be feared that from this failure, social and political instabilities may arise, undermining the social consensus, a sine qua non for the transition to a market economy.[14]

One of the consequences of reform is increased economic insecurity and instability. The main economic actors are not very confident under the new rules of the game. Besides, rising unemployment figures and the swift disappearance of small but certain past social benefits of the totalitarian state preserving the minimum living standard as pensions, free education, and health care cause a lot of concerns among some social groups. Radical economic reform based on market mechanisms presupposes considerable inequalities of income, as well as price changes and the transformation of social structures in a way that is not compatible with traditional ideology and values incorporated in the socialist ideas for distributional justice. This change has resulted in a substantial strata of society, particularly the less skilled and qualified and people in the process of retiring, forming a conservative social group with a vested interest in maintaining the basic features of the rigid administrative and centralized economic system.[15] It also means a nostalgia for the security of the past and perhaps a drift toward the social values of the previous system and some pressures not to abandon entirely the Soviet type of economic, political, and social development. Taken together, economic insecurity and instability could bring a return of the profitable old export-import practices and grounds to sustain these practices and an advocacy of the old methods among certain social groups.

The other important component in the domestic domain is that the legal framework of economic reform either is late or has gaps and possibilities for inconsistent and ambiguous treatment of different procedures. The privatization process also does not have a legal base but is carried on in some instances in a covert manner. Under these circumstances some social groups try to make use of the legal chaos for quick and easy profits.

For instance, according to reports of the former Ministry of Foreign Economic Relations, some 15,000 private companies handle a quarter of Bulgarian exports. The government itself cannot determine the exact share of private companies taking part in Bulgarian foreign trade because they are not obliged to submit accounts and because it also does not have reliable information on incoming and outgoing goods because customs information is not centralized.[16] In addition, the government does not have adequate information about investments Bulgarian companies have made abroad and about foreign investment in the country.[17] Finance Minister Kostov pointed out that 260 foreign-based joint ventures owe the public 1.14 billion lev for a period from January 1, 1980, until April 30, 1990. Moreover, foreign-based Bulgarian companies have not supplied information on their operations since December, 1990.[18]

Another example of the lack of appropriate rules and enforcement procedures are the reports on tax evasion cases. It has been impossible to determine the precise number of taxable companies and persons, and from January, 1991, until September, 1991, privately owned companies evaded taxes worth 348 million lev. In October, 1991, tax evasion was in the range of 52 million lev.[19] In this environment one could speculate that that could be the case with dual-use technologies exported or reexported to undesirable destinations. Some of the old structures, with personnel with experience and connections in these areas, still exit. It is hypothetically possible to use them under somewhat different conditions for similar purposes. In an address to the nation, Prime Minister Philip Dimitrov admitted that there are huge money laundering operations and exports of capital as well as large development of illegal exports and imports of arms and strategic raw materials.[20]

There are reports about investigations of reexports and other special operations conducted by the former Ministry of Foreign Economic Relations. However, official reports released on the matter have indicated that no diversion of funds or embezzlement has been detected. Nevertheless, Finance Minister Kostov was quoted as saying that "there was some lack of clarity about the operation of Bulgarian foreign trade companies."[21] That was one of the major reasons for closing down the Ministry of Foreign Economic Relations in November, 1991.

The conversion of the military-industrial complex to civilian use is in a very preliminary state. Ad hoc conversion began without a comprehensive plan or concept, not taking into account all the circumstances and the balance of the different national interests. Conversion requires a lot of investments, imported raw materials, and new technologies. However, Bulgaria currently is a country with severe financial and currency constraints. In addition, the devaluation of the local currency means very expensive imports, which makes the prices of the civilian output of the military complex unacceptable for the majority of the population as incomes grow at a substantially lower rate.

The destruction of the CMEA also contributed to the worsening state of military industry. Customers in the former Soviet Union alone owe the Bulgarian arms industry some $380 million.[22] Facing the current lack of a stable market for their civilian production and the financial constraints (the industry owes 2 billion lev and has recently borrowed another 100 million lev from the National Bank to stay in business), to survive and to avoid layoffs, the national military-industrial complex has two basic options. One is civilian production not related to its technologies, know-how, and experience (e.g., clothing, simple household utensils, and the like), and there are some examples of that option. For instance, at Metalchim Holding Inc. and the Electron consortium, civilian production (food processing machines, medical engineering, farm machinery, bicycles, and coffee mills) takes up to 70 percent of the output.[23] The other option is to continue with its usual production programs and maintain the established markets and trade relationships.

These circumstances led to drastically diverging perceptions and policy responses. 1990 to 1992 brought increasingly negative feelings about the former practices and methods of arms and technology trade of the previous regime. Moreover, this attitude has spread to the activity of the military-industrial complex. All these circumstances have led to demands for virtually liquidating the military industry, to different ideas of how it should be reorganized on a democratic basis compatible with the common practices in the world.

The prevailing attitude is that the military-industrial complex should be reformed. The main arguments supporting this approach are based on the fact that due to past dependencies, there are a lot of specialized investments in heavy machine building, electronics, and the like. According to international experts, these industries have adequate equipment, and qualified personnel and their technological base can meet international standards. At a meeting of chief executive officers of the military equipment manufacturers, President Zhelev pointed out that U.S., Japanese, and NATO experts assess highly some of the products of the military industries (antiaircraft guided missile systems, optronics, and fuses). At this meeting he also mentioned that he will agree with NATO countries on special production orders to stabilize these industries.[24]

Last but not least, the output of these industries supplied nearly half of the demands of the Bulgarian army. The rest played a very important role in the currency earnings of the country, mainly in trade with the Arab world.

Another argument is that the appearance of Bulgaria in the international arms bazaar nowadays could be facilitated by the lack of political or ideological restrictions and preferences.[25] Furthermore, Bulgarian arms are traditionally bought by countries in the Middle East, Africa, and Asia. In an interview, Anton Saldjiiski, director-general of Kintex (Bulgaria's biggest arms dealer), said that his company makes a lot of profit and has been Bulgaria's number one exporter for many years.[26] According to him, this is the only business that does not need state subsidies. On the contrary, the state needs it since it provides a lot of revenue to the budget.[27]

The production and trade of military-related items is a fact for many industrially developed countries. What makes a difference is the ethics of dealing with these items. The current Bulgarian administration is strongly committed to avoiding any forms of gunrunning. In his program address,

Prime Minister Dimitrov emphasized that there will be tough controls and regulations on deals with arms and strategic materials.[28] There also are statements that places of regional conflict (e.g., Iraq and Yugoslavia) were tacitly embargoed by official Bulgarian arms dealers.[29]

On these grounds, the issue how the country shall economically compensate for its new ethics in the trade of military-related items is raised. Some point to the fact that Bulgaria's stance in the embargo against Iraq was an economic disaster that the international community did not adequately compensate. Iraq owed Bulgaria $1.2 billion in oil deliveries, which were not received because, unlike some Western companies, Bulgaria was effectively participating in the embargo against Iraq. The only form of compensation was the IMF credit of $86 million extended to compensate the rise in oil prices resulting from the Gulf crises.[30] Altogether, the external shock (the Gulf War and the disintegration of the CMEA) is assessed as a 13 percent drop of GNP and 15 percent drop of real industrial output.[31] The new ethics in the trade with the Arab countries also contributed to the loss in traditional markets. In 1991, the exports to the Arab world declined by 63 percent.[32]

The point is that similar developments in the process of converting the military-industrial complex would be highly undesirable. This argument has been most strongly expressed by Valentin Tserovski, deputy chairman of the Bulgarian Democratic Center.[33] According to him, there are mainly foreign interests (U.S., Russian, Serbian, Turkish, and even Albanian) in the rapid conversion of the Bulgarian military industry. The Western intentions are perceived as directed at the elimination of a possible competitor in world arms markets. The objectives of former CMEA and Warsaw Pact partners are similarly perceived. As Tserovski pointed out, former Bulgarian partners mainly aim at the conversion of the industries where Bulgaria has some specialization and competitive advantage. The basic argument is that the military-industrial complex has to be preserved to sustain national economic interests.[34]

On these grounds, the basic assumption is that the national economic and strategic interests of the country require the maintenance of least 50 percent of the existing military-industrial base. What has to be changed is how the country and its companies deal with military and dual-use technologies. Here the problem is much more related to private and state exporting companies than to the actual producer. Besides, destroying the state foreign trade monopoly could aggravate this problem since instead of the few state trading companies dealing with these commodities, one might expect the emergence of many other actors in this field (e.g., Armtech is a new 1991 licensed Bulgarian arms dealer).

Another important area for the future of export control practices is the outcome of the more general discussion for the future socioeconomic development of Bulgaria and its relationships and interdependence with other countries and international economic, political, and military organizations.

However, the struggle of divergent political ideas and concepts leads to consensus on only a few issues. No one denies that the democratic traditions in the country were curbed for forty-five years. It is also widely accepted that a lot of stereotypes from the totalitarian era, such as egalitarianism, social justice, the need for strong central power to take care of the individual, and the like, remain. In the area of foreign relations, the uniting concepts are that the East-West rift and confrontation have ceased to affect international relations and that Bulgaria has to participate in a dialogue with every nation based on international law, the acceptance of democratic values, and the consideration of national economic interests of the country as the starting point for any form of mutual cooperation.

Simultaneously, the various political forces have an incongruous view of foreign policy and national security. Here one can point to at least three distinct perceptions that are related to the platforms of the various political parties and that will be part of contemporary Bulgarian politics. These perceptions will be the basis for future national policies and are of significance for the development of the national stance on export control issues.

The first broad concept for the development of foreign relations is that of the Bulgarian Socialist (formerly Communist) Party and of some of the small nationalist parties and organizations. The core of the concept is that the country should be politically independent and at the same time should maintain the policies established and verified during a long period of good relationships with traditional partners, namely the Slavic countries, thus implying the nations of the former Soviet Union.

The radical opposition that struggles for drastic change has quite a different view. It is promoting as a priority political cooperation with the EC, the United States, and Germany, the latter being Bulgaria's closest economic, political, and military partner before World War II.

The third broad concept belongs to the moderate opposition. It is also accepted by the so-called radicals in the Bulgarian Socialist Party. Its essence is to compromise and to adjust the other extreme views, arguing that political and economic independence could be achieved through cooperation with all democratic countries and the EC in particular. These three broad concepts clash on the issue how national security is to be interpreted and how it can be sustained.

The outcome of the parliamentary elections in October, 1991, and the presidential elections in January, 1992, seem to guarantee the progress of democratic reforms. The newly elected government and the president will pursue stability in the country, stabilizing policies on the Balkans, and generally pro-European foreign policy. However, it seems that foreign relations will require a mosaic approach. The new Foreign Minister Stoyan Ganev undertook several initiatives, and among them one could not miss the efforts to normalize relations with traditional partners in the Middle East, Iran being one such partner.

However, the Bulgarian Socialist Party, which is the second major political power, still believes in liaison with traditional partners, namely the Slavic republics of the former Soviet Union. It emphasizes economic relations with Russia as a base for future political partnership. This idea is articulated in a variety of arguments. Here one can list the traditional connections, old economic partnerships, and the like. Nonetheless, it is undisputable that a number of Bulgarian companies that have produced and still produce mainly for the former Soviet market do not have an alternative, both in terms of raw material supplies and markets.

Undoubtedly, if one tries to sum up the factors in the domestic domain, it is evident that general foreign policy orientations and concepts for economic reform and national security are a function of the political cycle in the country and depend on a variety of factors. The cycle in its turn is very unsteady, and it is very difficult to predict its direction. Some of the attitudes and perceptions bear a lot of the heritage of the past. At the same time, some of the new perceptions are based on unrealistic assumptions. Taken together, the components of the domestic domain do not contribute to a uniform trend in economic and foreign policy and national security, including export controls.

The International Domain

In the past Bulgarian export control policy was dominated by the notion of technological independence (mainly from the West). Here one can point to several main assumptions. Technological independence was perceived as reducing or avoiding imports of investment commodities and raw materials from particular Western countries, thus trying to maintain a low level of import dependency. The imports from the West were linked to exports on Western markets, which had to secure a certain level of foreign exchange for crucial imports from the West. Until the mid-1980s, there were also a limited amount of credits used to support the Western imports. From this point onwards, imports from the developed countries had the function of supporting the market equilibrium and preventing supply bottlenecks.

The Soviet Union regarded technological independence as a national priority and mainly handled this problem on a national basis. The smaller East European countries took a kind of two-track approach. On one side was the bilateral cooperation of every East European country with the Soviet

Union and on the other was multilateral CMEA cooperation, which had to integrate the industrial and technological cycles of these countries.

The priority was to link each of the small East and Central European countries with the industrial complex of the Soviet Union. Thus, trying hard to be independent from the West, these countries were pushed into heavy production, technological, and trade dependence on the Soviet Union. For Bulgaria in particular, the dependence on the Soviet Union has several dimensions.

First, there are import dependencies on Soviet investment commodities, raw materials, and semi-manufactured products for nearly all the main industries. For example, during the 1980s Bulgaria annually imported 13 million tons of crude oil from the Soviet Union. In comparison, in 1991 there were contracts for only 5 million tons of oil imports from the Soviet Union. In addition, until 1990 imports from the Soviet Union were paid in transferable rubles, usually underpriced under the CMEA system of contract prices in comparison to the prevailing world market prices (the average price of Soviet crude imports in the 1980s was about $8). These price structures encouraged high energy and raw materials consumption in the East European industries, which reinforced import dependence on the Soviet Union.

Second, the predominant imports of raw materials from the Soviet Union created technological dependencies based on equipment capable of reprocessing mainly Soviet industrial inputs. That is the case in the Bulgarian petrochemical industry. It is extremely difficult to diversify imports, even if there are credit facilities for imports from other sources, since the equipment cannot use different types of inputs.

Third, other forms of dependence arise from the export dependence of Eastern Europe on the Soviet market. More than 80 percent of the CMEA countries' exports were for the Soviet market. Whole industries and enterprises in Eastern Europe ranging from clothing, food, and beverages to electronics produce entirely for the Soviet market. Moreover, some of the recently developed industries such as electronics were established to serve the Soviet market.

Because of the COCOM export control regulations, Bulgaria had to play an important role as an intermediary between the Western high technologies and the Soviet market. This was not done directly (i.e., reexports of Western military and dual-use technologies to the Soviet Union) but through more subtle and indirect methods. The basic scheme was to develop production facilities based on Western materials and relatively high technologies and then export the bulk of the output to the Soviet Union. Perhaps the best example is the electronics industry in Bulgaria.

Fourth, another type of dependence is technologically related financial dependence. In this case, a small East European country was involved in a big investment project in the Soviet Union, usually the production of resources (oil, iron ore, and other mineral concentrates; asbestos; cellulose; timber; and the like). The participation of the small East European country in this type of project was to credit the Soviet Union by providing imports of Western equipment, which at a later stage were paid back by the output of the production facility. This method of providing credit to the Soviet Union was developed because of the possibly incorrect perception that Western export controls in some cases were favoring certain smaller East European countries.

This type of credit arrangement created a dual dependence for the Central and East European countries. First, the country providing the equipment to the Soviet Union had to pay back its currency expenses to the Western supplier. However, this type of indebtness to the West did not modernize the existing production facilities in the country or create new ones. In turn, that was reflected as a failure in the expansion of the export potential of the country as a source of foreign currency earnings. Second, the economy of the supplier of the equipment became even more dependent on imports of Soviet resources and energy.

Bulgaria and the other countries of Eastern Europe were simultaneously receiving credits from the Soviet Union for purchases of Soviet machinery and equipment. The bulk of the technological base of the economy was developed almost entirely on Soviet equipment, technology, and technical standards; and that made the economies of Eastern Europe even more dependent on the Soviet Union.

If one comes back to the dependence-interdependence discussion, it might be incomprehensible why these one-sided dependencies on the Soviet Union were developed. The prevailing theories and perceptions were that the technological links and dependencies in the CMEA framework had an entirely different economic and social nature. It was believed that between socialist countries there could not be any form of exploitation or one-sided advantages detrimental to some of the partners. The relationships were supposedly based on equality and mutual economic assistance that was assumed to be to everyone's advantage. In reality the economic interest was of secondary importance. The utopian character of this framework was revealed when the Soviet Union demanded payments in convertible currencies based on current international prices.

The National Legal Framework and Participation in International Export Control Arrangements

Prior to analyzing current developments in Bulgarian export control regulations, it is worthwhile to describe briefly the previous system. Under the conditions of state monopoly of foreign trade, virtually every transaction was subject to export-import regulations. The exporter or importer had to obtain export or import licenses. In addition, foreign trade was concentrated in state trading enterprises, which were specialized by branches of industry. Thus, the trade in military-related items and dual-use technologies subject to COCOM regulations was the exclusive right of two or three state trading enterprises. However, their activity was considered to be a state priority, and no information was released about it.

Furthermore, legislation prohibited trade in chemical weapons, nuclear materials, drugs, and the like since Bulgaria had signed the respective nonproliferation agreements and was taking part in the international nonproliferation regime. Trade in other military-related items and dual-use technologies was subject to strict control and monitoring on the part of the Ministry of Foreign Trade.

The state monopoly on foreign trade was eroded by Decree No. 56 on economic activity in April, 1989, and was entirely destroyed by subsequent economic reforms. There was concern that the existing export control regime would not work under these circumstances.

Reflecting these concerns and taking into consideration the negative reputation of Bulgaria in import controls, several interest groups and individuals suggested a wide range of initiatives to update the national system of export control regulations to meet the requirements for future multilateral export control cooperation.

In 1991, the government issued several acts concerning the export control regime. The first was Ordinance No. 13 of February 12, 1991, which introduced a temporary regime for export-import restrictions.[35] According to Article 3.4, exports of military equipment and other military-related items, military technologies, and know-how, as well as engineering activities for production and exports abroad, are not allowed. The government may grant exceptions. Article 3.5 introduces the same regime for nuclear materials.

This ordinance was in force until June 24, 1991, when the government issued Ordinance No. 119 for the export-import regime in 1991, subsequently extended by Ordinance No. 247 until the end of 1992.[36] The ordinance indicated the items subject to export and import controls and the government agencies authorized to give clearance for export licenses in these cases.

Article 2.a of the ordinance required export or import licenses for military equipment and for military-related technologies, know-how, and engineering activities, cleared by the standing Government Regulation Committee for the control of the production and trade of military-related items and special equipment (see below).

Article 2.b of the ordinance required clearance by the committee for the export and import of nuclear materials for civil use of atomic energy.

Articles 2.c and 2.d required similar clearance by the Ministry of Health or by the Ministry of Industry and Trade for some pharmaceuticals and chemicals.

According to Article 3 of the ordinance, the export or import license was to be issued by the Ministry of Foreign Economic Relations in 1991 and by the Ministry of Industry and Trade in 1992, if the respective specialized government agencies gave clearance.

As can be seen, in 1991 legal and administrative provisions were created for a framework of export and import controls. Commodity control was mainly based on military-related items and nuclear materials. Dual-use technologies were neglected or dropped out of the main discussion, probably as a result of a misperception that the West was interested primarily in the export control of nuclear and military-related items. However, according to Article 4.6 of Ordinance No. 249 of December 12, 1991, the Ministry of Industry and Trade and the Ministry of Defense have the responsibility to draft rules and establish controls on trade both with military-related items and dual-use technologies.[37]

The rules for trade with military items were published in February, 1992. There was no document referring to trade with dual-use technologies until the end of June, 1992. At that time the Bulgarian government issued Ordinance No. 114 of June 30, 1992, on the export-import regime.[38]

The main part of the ordinance covers conventional foreign trade. However, the ordinance refers to military items and technologies and also to dual-use and nonproliferation items and technologies as reasons for enforcing national export controls. Article 1 of Ordinance No. 114 states that exports and imports in the Republic of Bulgaria shall be executed freely, except in the case of the export, import, and reexport of military and special equipment and the export, import, and reexport of goods, services, technologies, materials, and equipment with possible dual use for nuclear, chemical, or biological mass destruction weapons; their carriers; and other internationally controlled goods and technologies. Thus, in mid-1992 the Bulgarian government explicitly stated that trade with dual-use and nonproliferation goods and technologies was subject to special licensing procedures.

After intensive consultations with COCOM member states, and particularly with the United States, the Bulgarian government proceeded to develop its national export control system. The main idea was to establish a system that conforms to all international standards and incorporates the existing nonproliferation and dual-use export control regimes. As a result, Ordinance No. 114 of 1992 was amended by Ordinance No. 224 of November 10, 1992.[39]

The amendment is in fact a new legal document creating regulations for trade in items and technologies with possible dual-use applications.

According to this ordinance, all types of transactions with dual-use and nonproliferation items and technologies, including indigenous materials, are subject to licensing procedures. An intergovernmental commission has the responsibility to create and amend the commodity lists and to appoint experts who have to deal on the level of the government with nonproliferation export controls. The licensing of the transaction is the responsibility of the Department of Foreign Trade Regime of the Ministry of Trade. For exports, the Ministry of Trade issues a license after clearance from the Ministry of Foreign Affairs. The enforcement of the regulations is the responsibility of the Customs Department of the Ministry of Finance.

As can be seen from this brief account, the process of change in the Bulgarian national export control regulations has been rather slow and painful. There were several major reasons for this.

The work on the proposed nonproliferation export control regulations has been delayed largely as a result of the political competition between different groups. The main problem was who would be in control of the institutions dealing with the export controls, particularly of those dealing with the arms trade. This issue was reflected in coordination problems between the interested government agencies—the Ministry of Foreign Economic Relations (Ministry of Trade since 1992), the Ministry of Industry and Trade (Ministry of Industry since 1992), the Ministry of Foreign Affairs, the Ministry of Defense, the Ministry of the Interior, and the Ministry of Finance. From a technical point of view, the problem was further complicated in November, 1991, when the new government closed down the Ministry of Foreign Economic Relations. At the end of December, 1991, responsibility for the development of the export-import regime was transferred to the Ministry of Industry and Trade. According to Ordinance No. 241 of December 23, 1991, the Ministry of Industry and Trade and the Ministry of Finance are to develop and implement the legal and economic mechanisms of foreign economic activity and trade, including the export control regime.[40] Simultaneously, the ordinance refers to trade with special and military-related equipment as the joint responsibility of the Ministry of Industry and Trade and the Ministry of Defense. Production and trade in these items, according to the ordinance, is licensed by the Government Regulation Committee.[41] In May, 1992, the Ministry of Industry and Trade was transformed into two separate ministries: of industry and of trade.

The other issue is rather more political and economic in its essence than technical and organizational. In the early discussion the suggested regulations envisaged legal and administrative procedures that third countries might have perceived as discriminatory. It was also believed that they could lead to market losses and an undesirable deterioration of relations with some third world countries and possibly with the former republics of the Soviet Union and other former East European socialist countries.

The economic side of the problem is that it is believed that Bulgaria has a few technological islands, mainly in machine-building and electronics.[42] It was understandable that any legal changes and adherence to an international export control regime had to be compatible with national economic interests. That is quite obvious from the analysis above of the discussion concerning the future of the Bulgarian military-industrial complex.

In spite of the problems, in early 1992 the Bulgarian decision makers were inclined to join all international agreements for monitoring exports and reexports of conventional arms and related materials since this action was perceived to be in the national interest of Bulgaria. Neighboring countries are larger dealers in arms than Bulgaria, so European or Balkan monitoring procedures would be a kind of national security safeguard for Bulgaria.

It has to be noted that the favorable developments in the Bulgarian nonproliferation export control policy were stimulated by the growing international multilateral export control cooperation. For instance, in early 1990 the Vienna Council COCOM working group approached the Ministry of Foreign Economic Affairs. Thus for the first time an international group working on multilateral export control cooperation drew the attention of Bulgarian officials to such problems as the simplification and speeding up of the review processes of and the transparency of the rules of internationally controlled commodities; the methods of verification and end use; the study of the economic effects of the past and future export controls; and the development of a new international export control regime. The latter was perceived to be a very important development as some case studies for Bulgaria demonstrated that the nonproliferation export controls were not very effective.[43] This ineffectiveness indicated the necessity to participate in future negotiations leading either to the relaxation of the current export control regulations or to the creation of a new international export control regime.

Furthermore, Bulgarian officials of the Ministry of Foreign Affairs participated in the December 13–14, 1990, London meeting of the AG. The Bulgarian delegation informed the meeting about legal and institutional changes concerning export control of chemicals and expressed a positive attitude toward participating in a coordinated multilateral export control regime of chemical weapons and dual-use chemical technology. Until December 1, 1992, Bulgaria unilaterally controlled ten chemicals produced in the country out of the list of fifty chemicals of the AG. To avoid reexports or the transit of internationally controlled chemicals, at the end of 1992 the Bulgarian government expanded the list and included all the chemicals controlled by the AG.

In 1990 to 1991 the attitude of the Ministry of Foreign Affairs (namely the United Nations and Disarmament Department of the ministry) was that Bulgaria should also participate in the activities of the NSG and in the MTCR. Any activities in the former group are perceived to be of great importance because of the safety problems encountered with the Kozloduyi nuclear power plant. Some believe that this participation will allow easier access to safety equipment for this power station.

As for the MTCR, with a few minor exceptions, Bulgaria does not have any significant dual-use missile technologies. Nevertheless, to gain international recognition as a country abiding by all export control regulations, Bulgaria is prepared to participate in the activities of the MTCR, particularly if it is a case of dual-use missile technologies. As a result of this attitude a memorandum of understanding was signed, and in late 1991 Bulgaria joined the NSG. With Decision No. 107 of March, 1992, the Bulgarian government adopted the NSG guidelines and participated in the NSG meeting in Warsaw in April, 1992.

Finally, apart from the multilateral negotiations, Bulgaria began bilateral export control discussions with the United States in the summer of 1990. The discussions brought U.S. expertise, technical assistance, and information and stimulated the Bulgarian export control reform efforts. After several rounds of discussions, in September, 1992, the Bulgarian government submitted a letter of intent expressing its intentions to comply with COCOM regulations. This letter was followed, as mentioned above, by the introduction of new legal regulations that closely follow COCOM export control practices.

National Institutional Framework

The reform of the national export control system affected the institutional framework and enforcement regime. As mentioned above, until the end of 1991, the export control regime was administered by the Ministry of Foreign Economic Relations and enforced by the Customs Department of the Ministry of Finance. At the time of this writing, the export control system is administered by the Government Regulation Committee (the production and trade of military-related items, technologies, munitions, and special equipment) and the Department of Foreign Trade Regime of the Ministry of Trade. Exports require a clearance from the Ministry of Foreign Affairs. The Customs Department has to enforce the export controls. The Ministry of Foreign Affairs, the Ministry of Industry, the Ministry of Defense, the Committee for Civil Use of Atomic Energy, the Ministry of Interior, and the National Security Council in the Office of the President consult the government and the other specialized agencies about the export control procedures (see the appendix for the structure of the Bulgarian export control community).

The Government Regulation Committee plays a major role in the national export control system for the control of the production and trade of military-related items and special equipment. The committee was established in 1991 as a body of the Council of Ministers with Ordinance No. 115, and its competence and functions were later developed by several complementary government acts in January 1992.[44] The committee was initially chaired by the Minister of defense, but in mid-1992 the prime minister became the chair.[45] The committee has an interdepartmental representation. The members of the committee include representatives of the government and of the Office of the President. On the government side, there are representatives of the Ministry of Industry, the Ministry of Trade, the Ministry of Transport, the Ministry of Defense, the Ministry of Foreign Affairs, the Ministry of Interior, and the government adviser on the legal acts of the Council of Ministers. The national security adviser to the president represents the Office of the President.

The primary function of the Regulation Committee is to regulate the production and trade of military-related items. It drafts the proposals for intergovernmental cooperation in military industry, determines the basic principles of the national control policy on the trade of military equipment, and supervises these activities.[46] The committee has a permanent organizational structure that comprises a chairperson, a secretary, and members. The committee has at least two meetings every month. The day-to-day activity of the committee is conducted through a standing secretariat based in the Ministry of Defense.

The committee issues annual renewable licenses to trading companies to deal with military-related items based on information of the financial sources of the companies, ownership of the company, and personnel data. For an existing company, the application should comprise a report of the previous activities of the company in question.

Another task of the committee is to issue export, import, or reexport licenses for single transactions. The committee has to review, verify, and approve all applications for trade in military-related items. Thus, through the committee a permanent regime to control the trade of military related items is established.

The items subject to the regulations of the committee are armaments, military equipment, munitions, military-related equipment, and spare parts; materials and equipment with application in the arms industry; explosives, arms, and munitions for the police force; technologies for the defense industry; and repairs of military equipment. The controls established with the regulations of the committee are applied to exports, imports, reexports, and transit through Bulgaria and in the existing free trade zones in Bulgaria.

The procedures concerning military-related items resemble those of Western countries, and in some instances the requirements are compatible with Western regulations. The trader has to apply for a one-year or a single license to deal with the items subject to regulations. The trader must complete a special customs clearance form, which is valid only if the trader has a license issued by the Government Regulation Committee. The regulations require the submission of an end-user certificate, a certificate of origin, and technical information. The committee may also require the provision of other information related to the particular transaction.

The Regulation Committee provides the forms. They contain data on the quantities and a detailed description of the exported commodities. The Regulation Committee and Customs verify whether the trader has a license to trade in these commodities, check the lists, verify whether the commodity or the destination are not subject to restrictions by the national control regime, and check the end-user certificates. If the results of the checks are positive, the committee grants clearance for an export license.

To enforce the procedures, the Regulation Committee directly inspects the production and trade of military-related items. It may cancel or refuse to issue licenses. It may also check and seal production sites and issue related documents verifying that the dispatch is in accordance with the national control regime. Bulgarian exporters are also obliged to submit a statement that they have a written agreement with their foreign counterpart that excludes the reexport of the delivered items. The committee also verifies and confirms end-user certificates for equipment imported in Bulgaria.

As noted above, Ordinance No. 18 of January, 1992, broadly describes the military-related commodities subject to regulations. Experts in the permanent secretariat of the Regulation Committee will have to develop further the commodity lists. This process may also include the differentiation of the destinations on the basis of national policies and multilateral and bilateral commitments, also taking into account the type of the commodity.

The second major institutional change in 1992 was the establishment of the Intergovernmental Commission on the trade of dual-use and nonproliferation goods and technologies.[47] The Minister of Trade chairs the commission. The deputy minister of the Ministry of Foreign Affairs, the deputy minister of the Ministry of Trade, the deputy minister of defense, the deputy minister of the Interior Affairs, the head of the Department of Foreign Trade Regime of the Ministry of Trade, the head of the Customs Department of the Ministry of Finance, the president of the Committee for Civil Use of Atomic Energy, a representative of the National Intelligence Service, and an adviser to the president are members of the commission.

Taking into account the national interests and the international commitments of the Republic of Bulgaria, the commission is empowered to develop four different lists: an atomic energy list; an industrial list; a chemical and biological weapons nonproliferation list; and a missile technology control list.

The licensing procedures related to these lists are carried out by the Department of Foreign Trade Regime of the Ministry of Trade. The department licenses imports subject to control by the issue of an International Import Certificate. The application for the import certificate has to be accompanied by an end-user statement and an import and delivery verification certificate. All these documents are filled in both Bulgarian and English and contain all the necessary data for the particular transaction. The decision for the denial or approval of the license has to be made within thirty days.

On the export side, the Department of Foreign Trade Regime of the Ministry of Trade issues an international export certificate. The export certificate has to be accompanied by an end-user statement. This statement indicates the purpose and the site of the application of the acquired controlled item or technology. The statement is valid only if it is legalized by a representative of Bulgarian authorities in the importing country. The other required document is a statement by the import licensing agency of the recipient country that the item or technology will not be reexported without the permission of the Bulgarian authorities. In cases of reexports, the Department of Foreign Trade Regime requires permission from the export licensing authorities of the exporting country. The decision for the denial or approval of the export license has to be made within thirty days.

The current state of the Bulgarian export control regime effective since December 1, 1992, could be summarized as follows:

Nuclear Referral List: Bulgaria has signed the NPT and complies with its regulations. All nuclear facilities in the country are under the supervision of the IAEA. The country follows the guidelines of the NSG. Since December 1, 1992, the country has adopted a list identical to the COCOM International Atomic Energy List. The licensing procedures are carried out by the Ministry of Trade, and enforcement is the responsibility of the Customs Department of the Ministry of Finance. The amendment of the list is the responsibility of the intergovernmental commission, where the Committee of Atomic Energy is represented by its president.[48]

Munitions List: The production and trade of munitions is subject to licensing procedures by the Government Regulation Committee. The application is on a special form, and the license regime applies both to the commodities that are traded and to the permission for this activity. The regime requires the submission of an end-user certificate, verified by the Ministry of Defense of the recipient country (or other government agency), certifying that the commodities will be used in the respective country. The Bulgarian supplier has to include a guarantee clause in the contract that the shipment will not be reexported by his or her counterpart. In Bulgaria, local inspections are not a problem since there are only a few licensed arms dealers and several state arms manufacturers.

Commodity Control List: Since December 1, 1992, the country has adopted a list identical to the COCOM IL. Licensing procedures are conducted by the Ministry of Trade, enforced by the Customs Department.

In addition to these lists, the country has adopted the chemical weapons nonproliferation list and the MTCR controls.

Thus, since December 1, 1992, the full range of nonproliferation export controls is in place and is a legal requirement for all exporters and importers operating in Bulgaria.

Conclusions

It is clear that national policies have substantially changed compared to previous practices. There is strong political commitment to provide a safeguard nonproliferation regime for military-related items and dual-use technologies. The recommendations of export control experts favor further development of a national export control system and legislation and cooperation with relevant international institutions.

However, due to the transition to a market economy, the number of possible actors has dramatically increased and the implementation of the national export control regime will therefore require additional funding and training of professionals.

Because of the unstable political and economic environment, the implementation of a national export control system is bound to be a difficult task. The main difficulties stem from the unstable domestic structures. It is very difficult to enforce export controls in a country where governments frequently change and where immediate priorities are not directly related to nonproliferation export controls.

Here one can add purely technical problems. The Customs Department is not well equipped with facilities for monitoring these types of transactions. Besides, since the banking system is not computerized, it is impossible to monitor the financial course of these transactions.

International developments also complicate the problem. The breakups of the Soviet Union and Yugoslavia have led to the appearance of a number of actors with similar severe political and economic problems. In spite of the strong political commitment for multilateral export control cooperation, existing mutual dependencies between the former East European countries and immediate economic interests could be a deterrent for effective collaboration in this area.

Another problem is the need for greater coordination of the various government agencies. The traditional institution in the development of the export control regime with the appropriate experience and personnel is the Ministry of Trade. Its principal efforts are directed toward the implementation of the nonproliferation licensing regime developed by the intergovernmental commission established in December, 1992. Also, the Ministry of Trade has the difficult task of building the organizational structures of a working export control regime. However, military technologies, armaments, and munitions are licensed by the Regulation Committee of the Council of Ministers. The two main bodies dealing with export controls must cooperate and coordinate their efforts.

To avoid reciprocal actions, country lists are not published. However, the desirability of particular destinations is determined on a working level by the Ministry of Foreign Affairs and Ministry of Defense. This procedure could also pose some coordination and communication problems.

Thus, further change in national policies will require better national coordination and subsequent developments in national legislation. In 1992 the bulk of the legislation in this area was introduced as government ordinances that defined the national export control regime. However, future international cooperation will require unified legislation in this area. The new legislation must also have strong enforcement and legal responsibility procedures. So far, the amendments to the penal code have been proposed and a strong enforcement administration has been established. The positive change in 1992 was that these developments are becoming less dependent on the domestic political cycle.

Summarizing the change of Bulgaria's attitude and policy in the area of export controls, one could come to the conclusion that the government will try to abide with the regulations of all multilateral export control regimes, become a member of all of them, and on these grounds will seek the lifting of COCOM barriers. A strong effort will also be made for bilateral and regional cooperation with the Balkans in the area of export controls.

Finally, Western countries have to facilitate changes in East European export control policies by creating better international conditions, thus softening some of the economic security threat perceptions in Eastern Europe. The reform of the national export control systems also requires technical, organizational, and financial support from the West.

APPENDIX: EXPORT CONTROLS IN BULGARIA: INSTITUTIONAL STRUCTURE

National Assembly
  Committee on Foreign Policy
  Committee on National Security
  (Legislation and policy formulation)
Office of the President
  Participation in the government
  Regulation Committee and the intergovernmental commission on the trade of dual-use technologies
  National security adviser
  (Policy formulation)
Council of Ministers
  Government Regulation Committee
  (Policy-making and implementation: trade in military items; the issuing of export-import licenses)
Ministry of Defense
  Department of Military Economy
  (Policy-making and implementation: production and trade targets for the state companies in the military-industrial complex; the control of state enterprises; participation in the development of the Munitions List and in the MTCR)
  Departments of Military Strategy
  (Determines the desirability of destinations of exports if necessary)
Ministry of Trade
  Chairing the intergovernmental commission on the trade of dual-use technologies
  (Policy-making and implementation: trade of dual-use items and technologies; participation in the development of the industrial list and chemical and biological nonproliferation list, the Atomic Energy List, and the MTCR; the control of state and private enterprises by issuing export-import licenses)
Ministry of Industry
  Participating in the intergovernmental commission on the trade of dual-use technologies (Participating in the development of the industrial list and the MTCR)
Committee for Civil Use of Atomic Energy
  (Participation in the development of the Atomic Energy List)
Ministry of Foreign Affairs
  Determination of the desirability of destinations in the Government Regulation Committee and in the intergovernmental commission on the trade of dual-use technologies
  Department of International Organizations, Division One, Security Arms Control and Disarmament (negotiation, policy-making, and implementation)
Ministry of Finance
  Customs Department (enforcement)
Ministry of Interior
  (Intelligence, monitoring)

Bulgarian Chamber of Commerce
(Coordination and possibly recommendations in the area of export controls)

NOTES

The research is based primarily on a review of the national literature and interviews with officials from different Bulgarian institutions relevant to export control issues. No reference to the interviews is made since that was the precondition for conducting the interviews. From this point of view, the paper represents solely the views of the author and should in no way be considered an official Bulgarian position.

The article represents Bulgarian developments until December 1, 1992.

1. National Academy of Sciences, *Finding Common Ground: U.S. Export Controls in a Changing Global Environment,* Executive Summary (Washington, D.C.: National Academy Press, 1991), x.

2. Robert O. Keohance and Joseph S. Nye, *Power and Interdependence: World Politics in Transition* (Boston: Little, Brown, 1977), 12–19.

3. Philip A. Reynolds and Robert D. McKinlay, "The Concept of Interdependence; Its Uses and Misuses," in *Power, Capabilities, Interdependence: Problems in the Study of International Influence,* edited by Kjell Goldman and Gunar Sjosted (London: Sage, 1979), 142.

4. Detlef Lorenz, "Regionalization versus Regionalism: Problems of Change in the World Economy," *Intereconomics* 26, no. 1 (1991): 8.

5. For an account of the macroeconomic tensions in the initial stages of reform, see Rumen Avramov, "Makroikonomitcheskata Dinamika Prez 1991" ["Macroeconomic Dynamics in 1991"], *Bankov Pregled* [*Bank Review*] 1, no. 1 (1991): 8–15.

6. "Trade Deficit Declines," *Bulgarian Business News: 168 Hours BBN* 1, no. 15 (1991): 5.

7. Economic Programming and Development Agency, *Report on the Course of the Economic Reform and the Objectives of the Economic Policy to the End of 1991* (Sofia: Economic Programming and Development Agency, July 10, 1991), 5.

8. Eugene Skolnikoff, "The Technological Factors Shaping East-West Relations," in *Technology and Change in East-West Relations,* edited by F. Stephen Larrabee (New York: Institute for East-West Security Studies, and Boulder, Colo.: Westview Press, 1988), 23.

9. Ivan Kostov, "Debt between Two Systems," *Bulgarian Economic Review* 1, no. 1 (1992). 5.

10. Atanas Gotchev, "Economic Modernization in Eastern Europe: The 1973–1985 Experience of Borrowing Technologies from the West," paper presented at the Annual Meeting of the International Studies Association, London, 1989.

11. Kostov, "Debt Between Two Systems," 5.

12. Tamas Bauer, "Deceleration, Dependency and 'Depaternalization': Some Considerations concerning the Changes of the Soviet Union and Eastern Europe in the Coming Decades," *Acta Oeconomica* 39, nos. 1–2 (1988): 164.

13. See Grigor Lilov, "Nasite Taini Sluzbi Polzvali Uslugite na Maxwell" ["Our Secret Police Used the Services of Maxwell"], *168 Chasa* [*168 Hours*] 2, no. 52 (1991): 20.

14. See Hubert Garbish, "System Transformation under Severe External and Internal Shocks," in *Forshungsberichte* (Vienna: Vienna Institute of Comparative Economic Studies), 11.

15. Jiri Kosta, "Can Socialist Systems be Reformed?" in *Economic Reforms in Eastern Europe and the Soviet Union,* edited by Hubert Garbish (Boulder, Colo.: Westview Press), 12–19.

16. "Private Companies Handle a Quarter of Exports," *Bulgarian Business News: 168 Hours BBN* 1, no. 11 (1991): 6.

17. Ibid.

18. "Foreign Economic Relations Ministry Audited," *Bulgarian Business News: 168 Hours BBN* 1, no. 10 (1991): 7.

19. "Tax Control Should Be Tightened," *Bulgarian Business News: 168 Hours BBN* 1, no. 15 (1991): 9; "Tax Reform Ahead," *Bulgarian Business News: 168 Hours BBN* 1, no. 17 (1991): 9.

20. Philip Dimitrov, "Programno Obrastenie na Ministar Predsedatlia Philip Dimitrov" ["Program Address of Prime Minister Philip Dimitrov"], *Demokratsia,* January 7, 1992.

21. "Foreign Economic Relations Ministry Audited," 7.

22. "Conversion Produces Many Problems," *Bulgarian Business News: 168 Hours BBN* 1, no. 18 (1991): 8.

23. Ibid.

24. Ibid.

25. "Arms Mean Easy Money, So Why Not?" *Bulgarian Business News: 168 Hours BBN* 1, no. 15 (1991): 13.

26. "Who Trades in Arms in Bulgaria," *Bulgarian Business News: 168 Hours BBN* 1, no. 18 (1991): 8.

27. Ibid.

28. Dimitrov, "Programno Obrastenie."

29. "Who Trades in Arms in Bulgaria."

30. "Semi-Annual Report," in *News Bulletin,* no. 5 (Sofia: Bulgarian National Bank, September 1, 1991), 11.

31. Avramov, "Makroikonomitcheskata Dinamika," 9 and 12.

32. "Trade Deficit Declines."

33. See Mariana Svetoslavova, "Voennite Zavodi se Zadushavat ot Stari Natrapeni Dalgove" ["Military Industry is Strangled by Bad Debts"], *168 Chasa* 3, no. 3 (1992): 4.

34. Ibid.

35. *Darzaven Vestnik* [*State Gazette*], no. 12 (Sofia: Bulgarian Government Publication, 1991).

36. Ibid., no. 52 (1991), and no. 3 (1992).

37. Ibid., no. 4 (1992).

38. Ibid., no. 53 (1992).

39. Ibid., no. 92 (1992).
40. Ibid., no. 2 (1992).
41. Ibid., nos. 60 and 96 (1991), no. 3 (1992).
42. Richard Rahn, *Bulgarian Economic Growth and Transition Project* (Washington, D.C.: U.S. Chamber of Commerce, 1990).
43. Gotchev, "Economic Modernization in Eastern Europe."
44. *Darzaven Vestnik,* nos. 60 and 96 (1991), nos. 2, 11, and 50 (1992).
45. Ibid., no. 50 (1992).
46. See Chapter 2 of the Rules of the Regulation Committee, ibid., no. 11 (1992).
47. Ibid., no. 92 (1992).
48. Ibid.

CHAPTER 7

The Evolution of Export Control Systems in the Soviet Union and Russia

Elina Kirichenko

Introduction

Soviet export control policies during the communist era were never exposed to public scrutiny. Addressing this topic was then, and remains now, a great challenge since it encounters three basic obstacles.

First, a lack of transparency or openness is an obstacle one encounters when studying export control policies and proliferation issues in the former Soviet Union and its successor states. Certainly, glasnost and the collapse of communism lifted the veil of secrecy from certain aspects of these issues, but much more information is necessary for full and complete analysis. Detailed and specialized information on export regulations is not available. Official publications like the U.S. *Federal Register* or periodicals like *Export Control News, Jane's Defense Weekly,* and *Defense News* did not exist in the former Soviet Union and do not exist in Russia today.[1]

Second, the political and economic situation of the former Soviet Union is in a state of incredible flux. The attempted coup and velvet revolution of August, 1991, ruined the federal structures formed during the perestroika period and tilted the power from the center to the republics and now to independent states. The collapse of the central Soviet authorities and the federal government accelerated the adoption of foreign trade regulations by the former republics. But these regulations became obsolete before their implementation. The formal agreement establishing the CIS left key questions of export controls unresolved. It is clear, however, that export administration authority has been transferred to the independent states.

Third, export controls were historically integrated into the command system and, like a mirror, reflected all the authoritarian characteristics of the latter. There were no publicly observable laws but many different classified regulations and several guidelines of the Council of Ministers of the USSR. There were no proscribed countries. The export control regime was comprehensive, which was in keeping with the traditions of the Communist Party's desire to put any and all social and economic activity under its control.

Characteristics of the Soviet Export Control Mechanism and Policy

The Soviet command system did not require export control legislation. The Soviet export administration mechanism was part of the classical system of the state monopoly of foreign trade under which all transactions with foreign partners were approved by a few authorized government bodies, for example, commodity deals by the Ministry of Foreign Trade, license sales by Licensintorg, and disembodied technology exports by the State Committee for Science and Technology. In addition, the decisions about munitions exports were handled by the Military Industrial Commission (VPK) of the Presidium of the Council of Ministers and approved by the Council of Ministers of the USSR.[2] Since the decision-making process was hidden from the public, it is difficult to judge whether the Soviet Union had an analogue to the U.S. Munitions List or the U.S. Commodity Control List before the 1980s. In reality, one was not required because Soviet foreign trade activity was limited, and any transaction was approved case by case on the basis of the state plan of foreign economic turnover. The lack of transparency served the interests of the state bodies that monopolized foreign trade operations. For them, it was easy to control all exports according to any criteria the authorities wished to apply, including national security, foreign policy, or others.

In the early 1980s, foreign policy concerns—for example, considerations surrounding Soviet participation in international nuclear nonproliferation arrangements—required the Soviet Union to develop more appropriate rules for the export of nuclear items. The USSR Council of Ministers approved the first set of so-called guidelines in 1982.[3] The Office of Export Controls (OEC) of Gosplan (later the Ministry of Economics and Forecasting) was one of the institutions of the mighty VPK. For more than ten years, it was headed by Vladimir Sementsov.[4] Under the aegis of the OEC, scholars and other nongovernmental experts conducted studies on Western export controls.

With the dismantling of the state monopoly on foreign trade in the late 1980s and early 1990s, the decentralization of foreign economic activity among thousands of state-owned enterprises and privately owned cooperatives, and the establishment of joint ventures with foreign partners on Soviet territory, it became clear that a new regulatory export control mechanism was required.

Soviet society took its first steps to move from a command system to a market-oriented economy in the late 1980s. The former Soviet government tried to begin the economic reorganization in the foreign trade sector, and this decision influenced the export control mechanism. The Soviet Union created a licensing system based on Order No. 203 of March 7, 1989, entitled "On Measures of State Regulation of External Economic Activity." According to this order, the State Foreign Economic Commission of the Council of Ministers of the Soviet Union had the authority to restrict exports and imports for the purposes of balancing internal supply and demand, fulfilling international obligations of the Soviet Union, reaching mutually beneficial agreements on international trade negotiations, and undertaking retaliatory measures. The provisions of Order No. 203 were valid until the end of 1991. A list of products subject to licensing was established in 1989 and 1990.

There were two types of export licenses—General and Single Deal Licenses—and neither was granted for more than one year. At first, the right to grant export licenses was given to fifty-eight bodies, including the Ministry of Foreign Economic Relations of the USSR, the State Committee for Science and Technology of the USSR (GKNT), and many all-union branch ministries and republic-level councils of ministers.

Initially the export control list included only twenty-seven entries, but in late 1989 it was expanded to include other major Soviet Union exports. The reason this list grew was commodity shortages in the Soviet Union and imbalances in foreign trade and not, it should be noted, nonproliferation export control. The only high-technology item on the list was "Soviet inventions and findings of scientific and technical activities."

License applications were reviewed by GKNT. As Soviet expert Igor Artemiev said,

> the inclusion of disembodied technology on the list of regulated export items is puzzling if one considers the nation-wide effort to expand exports and upgrade technological quality. It is very doubtful whether the regulation of disembodied technology exports administered by the State Committee for Science and Technology is capable of motivating industry to speed up the implementation of inventions by Soviet production enterprises and to facilitate foreign marketing of resultant products. The modest magnitude of the Soviet technology exports precludes any opportunity to use them as a tool of foreign policy.[5]

GKNT representatives held that the licensing of inventions was necessary for conducting patent infringement research and checking their potential military significance.

The list did not include machinery and equipment; however, that did not mean that the Soviet state had given up regulating exports of these items. An addendum to the list stated,

> Enterprises, associations, production cooperatives, and other Soviet organizations cannot export armament, ammunition, military equipment and parts for their production, explosives, nuclear material, technology equipment, installations, special non-nuclear materials and services applied, the sources of ionizing radiation; precious metals . . . ; precious stones . . . ; individual types of products and technology, which are used or can be used in armaments or in military technique production . . . ; poisons; drugs . . . ; pieces of art and antiquity . . . .[6]

Indeed, these notes prove that there were export controls of armaments, nuclear materials, and dual-use commodities and technologies. Thus, although Order No. 203 officially did not govern export controls imposed for national security reasons, further analysis reveals that Soviet regulations were also implicitly targeted at the administration of dual-use and militarily significant goods and technologies.

The year 1991 brought new changes for the export administration regulations of civil, military, and dual-use items. The main factor behind these changes was the increasing sovereignty of the Soviet republics. The licensing approval responsibilities were divided between the USSR Ministry of Foreign Economic Relations and republican bodies, while the number of departments that had such rights had been reduced.

The State Foreign Economic Commission (GVK) was abolished in 1991. A new commodity control list was discussed at Union-Republican Monetary Committee meetings, in which only eleven republics took part. A new list published under the title "1991 Commodity List and Export Quota of the USSR and Republics" came into effect on July 1, 1991. It included only sixteen entries of "all-Union importance" (involving mainly raw materials and agricultural goods) and did not contain manufactured goods or disembodied technology at all.[7] But the republics began to develop their own more comprehensive commodity control lists, some of which contained machinery, equipment, and disembodied technology. For example, a new commodity control list was adopted in Russia on August 27, 1991.[8]

Export controls of dual-use or military items were subject to a small revision. As before, a list of dual-use machinery and equipment controls was imposed on state enterprises according "to due order." The Presidential Decree of April 5, 1991, and Decision of the Cabinet of Ministers No. 428 of July 3, 1991, imposed controls on the export of commodities, materials, and technology considered important to the military. The decree also restructured existing nonproliferation regimes, addressing export controls on items in all areas of weapons proliferation (nuclear, chemical, biological weapons, and missile delivery systems). The Commission on State Export Controls of the USSR was redesigned. Its activity was declassified. The commission was supposed to develop national policies controlling exports for national security and foreign policy purposes. Vladimir Scherbakov, the deputy prime minister of the USSR, was nominated as the head of this commission. After the aborted coup of August, 1991, he retired along with the whole Cabinet of Ministers.

The commission was to include representatives of all Soviet republics (that wished to take part in its activity) at the level of deputy prime minister and act as a union-republican agency. As a coordinating agency, it was supposed to include all interested state departments, representatives of the military-industrial complex, the Soviet Ministry of Defense, the Ministry of Foreign Affairs, and the Ministry of Foreign Economic Relations. This commission was intended to meet regularly to develop the security strategy in foreign economic relations. The OEC of the Ministry of Economics and Forecasting was to be incorporated as a working group of the commission.

With the growing political turmoil in the Soviet Union in 1991, the commission's activity remained ink on paper, but the OEC continued its work. Among other activities, it identified critical items for potential control. These items were sorted into groups. First, a list of strategic raw materials, equipment, and technology was developed. It was subdivided into five categories: (1) materials and their production and processing; (2) chemicals and petrochemical products; (3) drugs, biological preparations, and biotechnology; (4) apparatus and instruments; and (5) power and transport equipment. Controls were applied to commodities and technology that were militarily critical and that were of the very highest technology. The resulting export control list was supposed to be valid for 1991 and 1992.

Several lists were developed for nonproliferation export controls. Two lists involved the production of missiles. Items falling under List 1 were subject to embargo; items of List 2 were subject to licensing. Three lists covered dual-use chemicals. The first list included fourteen of the most dangerous precursors, which could not be exported unless end-use safeguards were provided. The export of these items could be carried out only by Soyuzkhimexport in consultation with the Soviet Union Ministry of Foreign Economic Relations and the Soviet Union Ministry of Foreign Affairs. The second list included nineteen dual-use entries. They could be exported by all legal entities after obtaining a license issued by the Soviet Union Ministry of Chemical and Oil Refining Industry (according to the Soviet Union Council of Ministers Order No. 203). The third list contained twelve technologies that could be used in the production of dual-use chemicals. They were subject to the Soviet Union State Committee on Science and Technology Licensing (in accordance with the Order No. 203).

A nuclear list was constructed in accordance with the Soviet Union Council of Ministers Order No. 28 of 1982. It was originally wider in scope, but experts decided to adhere to the regulation that was to be adopted by the NSG during a March, 1992, meeting in Poland. Finally, a biological list was developed covering virus, rickettsieae, bacteria, microscopic fungi, agents of food-poisoning, and agents of plant and animal diseases.

However, the Soviet Union Council of Ministers approved only the nuclear and chemical lists. That approval was followed by President Gorbachev's Special Decree on April 5, 1991, which was not completely implemented into the framework of the Soviet Union because of the internal political turmoil that followed.

The Soviet export control mechanism was not explicitly oriented toward nonproliferation. Before the political reforms began, the power of governmental agencies was based on their right to distribute resources and to approve (or disapprove) any deal or activity. The closed and highly bureaucratized Soviet system often helped to hide governmental actions, including incompetence. Despite pressure on agencies to prevent the leakage of any strategic information, they failed to create a special enforcement mechanism. As a result, there were many examples of exports of sensitive technology to the West.[9]

During the period of perestroika, a paradoxical situation emerged. On the one hand, the former mechanism of secrecy and rigid controls on military and dual-use technology export was maintained. On the other hand, with the increasing devaluation of the ruble and the growing attractiveness of hard currency for all Soviet consumers, enterprises were trying to earn hard currency and increasingly paid little if any attention to nonproliferation export control and national security issues in their foreign economic activity. Exporters were not keen to protect their industrial technologies and know-how. For example, one innovator from a military-industrial enterprise under the Ministry of Aviation Industry (Minaviaprom) attempted to create a joint venture with a Western foreign partner on the basis of his laboratory's invention. The invention could be used in modern military hardware and technology. The innovator's decision reflected his despair because the attempts to apply his invention to industrial production at his plant had failed.[10] There was also evidence of barter deals in which modern jet fighters had been exchanged for rice.[11]

From time to time, the press published sensational exposés about the export of a military or strategic commodity. A notable case was that of the state-cooperative ANT in 1990. ANT was given an exclusive right to export a wide range of goods and to buy consumer goods and technology abroad without a license. Then a scandal broke out over the export of several tanks. It was unclear how the tanks could leave the plant under the system of comprehensive and rigid control. The ANT affair put much pressure on the Ryzhkov government. The communist and conservative press began a campaign against cooperatives that "were ready to sell Russia." ANT foreign economic operations were stopped, and all its documents and bank accounts were confiscated. After several years of investigation, corpus delicti was not found in ANT activity. As was disclosed later, it was the Party Control Commission of the Central Committee of the Communist Party of the Soviet Union (CPSU) that ordered the case opened. So behind the declaration about national security interests were ideological and political motives. Conservative hardliners had attempted to discredit nonstate entrepreneurs and the liberal Ryzhkov, and this was not an isolated case.[12]

There were also some striking examples indicating the vigilance of Soviet decision makers. In one case, collective farmers discovered a tank, sunk in a lake during World War II. After great efforts, they were able to drag it out. It turned out to be of Canadian origin. The Canadian firm, now the producer of diesel locomotives, offered to give the farmers two miniplants for cheese and sausage production in exchange for the tank, which they wanted to install in their firm's museum. But the head of the collective farm could not get an export license for a year. The competent organizations did not want to approve the export of "military technology." Only after journalists intervened was this barter deal permitted.[13]

Soviet export controls during the communist years were a combination of super vigilance, mismanagement, favoritism, and corruption. The Soviet press occasionally published vivid examples calling attention to such things. For example, a young Soviet doctor made unsuccessful (and tragic) attempts to stop the illegal barter of Soviet drugs for consumer goods between the Chegdomin military district leaders and North Korean representatives. This attempt was in vain because it would have undermined the career of a number of Far East generals, including future Soviet Minister of Defense Yazov. In another example, Mikhail Gorbachev demanded an investigation after the plundering of an abandoned supersecret military research facility krug (circle). In another case, twenty Strela rockets (Soviet Stingers) were stolen from the Baltic fleet store of weapons in Tallinn, and nobody knows where they went.[14]

Security policy was generally of great national interest, but the country faced so many problems during the perestroika period that export control policy was generally ignored. Indeed, export controls did not reach the Supreme Soviet agenda at all during Gorbachev's rule. In an environment where there was no true market economy, the economy was not integrated into the global community, and the interests of the military-industrial complex prevailed over the interests of other groups. It was impossible to develop an open, legal, and balanced export control strategy.

For example, U.S. nuclear export control policy was based on the Atomic Energy Act of 1954, the Nuclear Nonproliferation Act of 1978, the Foreign Assistance Act of 1961 as amended, the Export Administration Act, which authorizes the Department of Commerce to regulate dual-use nuclear exports, and more than a dozen other laws. But the Soviet Union did not adopt similar national legislation. Nevertheless, nuclear export control and nonproliferation policy was a subject of special consideration in the Soviet Union. After Stalin's reign, the Soviet Union began to cooperate with the United States in the development of a nuclear multilateral nonproliferation mechanism. The Soviet Union played an active role in developing norms of behavior in this nuclear sphere of international affairs. On July 1, 1968, the Soviet Union signed the NPT and ratified it on March 5, 1970. The United States and Soviet Union decided it was in the interests of both to freeze the number of nuclear weapons states at five. The Soviet Union, Canada, the Federal Republic of Germany, France, Japan, the United Kingdom, and the United States are the original members of the NSG, created in 1975. In the 1980s the Soviet Union continued its cooperation with the United States in international nonproliferation arrangements. Twenty-four nations, including the Soviet Union, ratified the Convention on the Physical Protection of Nuclear Material in 1987, which codified international legal norms for the safeguarding of nuclear commerce. The convention stipulates international security requirements for the protection of nuclear materials against terrorism and provides punishment for violators of international rules.

The changes in the international security environment had a great impact on both Western and Eastern export control policy. A major element of the new environment concerned expanded cooperation to control the proliferation of weapons of mass destruction. On the threshold of the demise of the Soviet Union, Soviet authorities began to be more committed to cooperation with all international nonproliferation organizations, including the MTCR and the AG. On September 27, 1988, Soviet Minister of Foreign Affairs Shevarnadze called for a multilateral agreement limiting the proliferation of military missile technology. In 1989, the Soviet Union agreed to adhere to MTCR export guidelines, as reaffirmed in the bilateral statement of June 1, 1990. However, the Soviet Union withdrew support when it was not allowed to join the MTCR on equal terms with other nations. However, the USSR remained in touch with the MTCR and the AG, and sent representatives to the Chemical Weapons Nonproliferation Seminar held in London in December, 1990.

Export Control Policy of Russia

Russia's export control policy in the 1990s has evolved through several stages. Russia began to create its export controls infrastructure on November 15, 1991, when President Boris Yeltsin issued Decree No. 213, "On Liberalization of Foreign Economic Activity on RSFSR Territory." One of its articles charged the Russian government with providing a new list of commodities and services subject to licensing and quotas, taking into consideration the necessity of reducing the size of the control list. It also charged the government with issuing guidelines on the system of licensing exports and imports for 1992.[15]

The months following the breakup of the Soviet Union marked a new stage in Russian export control policy. The disintegration of the USSR posed two challenges for export controls. One of them concerned export controls on advanced or sensitive technology as a whole. The second challenge concerned nonproliferation issues. The collapse of the military superpower raised several problems: (1) the control of strategic nuclear forces; (2) the threat resulting from the proliferation of weapons of mass destruction; (3) the possible dissemination of sensitive technology through brain drain, illicit sales, and so forth; and (4) the participation of all former republics in international nonproliferation arrangements.

To deal with these challenges and problems, Russia developed a mechanism for export licensing. On December 30, 1991, the Russian government adopted Order No. 90, "On Quotation and Licensing of Export and Import Commodities (Works and Services) on the Russian Territory in 1992," with some supplements and guidelines for setting up a new licensing regime in Russia. The list of products subject to quotas (Supplement 1) and licensing (Supplements 2 and 3 for export deals and Supplement 4 for import deals) was established. The first commodity list was targeted at short supply problems (first of all, it concerned shortages of raw materials in Russia) and some fulfillment of international obligations (such as textile export quotas to the EC). The export of items included in this list was subject to licensing within the existing quota. The Ministry of Economics determined quotas. The second list included several strategic and sensitive entries subject to licensing.

The Ministry of Foreign Economic Relations was given the right to grant licenses for the export of all commodities. Appropriate ministries were charged with developing lists of dual-use items used in the production of weapons of mass destruction. During this period the nuclear nonproliferation factor stood out as very important for development affecting export controls. The global community was particularly sensitive to nuclear arms control and controls on the materials, technology, and expertise used in the production of nuclear weapons.

After the demise of the Soviet Union, Russia succeeded the USSR as a nuclear weapons state assuming its obligations and rights. But Russia also inherited economic disaster, a large budget deficit, and foreign debts coupled with ethnic turmoil, uncertain economic and political relations with other former republics, and potential rivalry with them. Thus, the first months of 1992 found Russian authorities attempting to bring the situation under control. Russia also tried to respond to the concerns of the West in the nuclear nonproliferation sphere. Moscow agreed to create an international nuclear center with the help of the United States and other Western countries to employ nuclear specialists and to prevent them from emigrating and aiding dangerous regimes in the Third World.

A new stage in the evolution of the Russian nuclear export controls can be conditionally identified following Presidential Decree No. 312 of March 27, 1992. An overview of the provisions of this decree reveals that Russia intends to follow the policy of insisting on full-scope safeguards as a condition of nuclear export to any nonnuclear state. This is a direct response to the concerns of the West.

On April 11, 1992, Yeltsin signed Decree No. 388, providing the legal basis for nonproliferation export controls. This decree established controls on the export of a number of specific categories of raw and other materials, equipment, technologies, and scientific and technical information and services that are used or can be used in the creation of weapons and military equipment. It also prohibited the export of dual-use materials, equipment, technology, and services that have a peaceful purpose but could be used in the production of weapons of mass destruction. To ensure a unified state policy in export controls, as well as to coordinate and provide organizational and methodological support for export control activity, an intergovernmental commission on export controls was established under the authority of the first deputy prime minister. The commission includes deputy chiefs of the Ministry of Economics; the Ministry of Foreign Affairs; the Ministry of Defense; the Ministry of Science, Higher Education and Technical Policy; the Ministry of Industry; the Ministry of Foreign Economic Relations; the State Customs Committee; the Ministry of Security; the Committee on Protection of Economic Interests of Russian Federation; the State Committee on Nuclear and Radiation Security Supervision; and the Russian Academy of Sciences. Prime Minister Gaidar first became chairman of this commission. He was replaced by Deputy Prime Minister Khizha, the head of the Military-Industrial Commission, who was also later replaced. President Yeltsin charged the commission with drafting a list of items that are used or can be used in the production of weapons or military equipment and technology.

The Ministry of Foreign Affairs and the Export Control Commission were authorized to begin negotiations with the governments of the other

Soviet successor states on the issue of multilateral coordination of nonproliferation export controls. On July 26, 1992, the heads of the governments of the CIS signed an agreement on the coordination of activities concerning export control of raw materials, equipment, technologies, and services that could be used for the production of weapons of mass destruction.

Despite a somewhat inconclusive meeting in September, 1992, there were positive steps in 1993 when Ukraine, Belarus, and Kazakhstan developed national licensing procedures for nuclear trade. Among other things, they agreed to adopt mandatory licensing requirements for nuclear-related items. At another meeting on May 31, 1993, CIS foreign ministers agreed to establish the CIS Export Control Council—an export control coordinating mechanism. Then at a June 3-4, 1993, meeting, CIS representatives agreed to complete their work on their national export control systems and to bring these systems into line with existing international regimes.

The Russian Ministry of Justice drafted proposals on measures of administrative and criminal responsibility for nonproliferation export control violations. An appropriate act on additional provisions was incorporated into the criminal code by the Supreme Soviet in 1993. These provisions stipulate the imposition of fines and imprisonment for violators of Russian export control laws.

Yeltsin's April, 1992, decree providing for nonproliferation export controls was very timely. The Russian government urgently needed a coordinating interagency body like the Export Control Commission. This body is intended to help Russia balance the competing foreign, economic, and security interests involved in export licensing issues. It may also help avoid controversial decisions like that involving the 1992 Glavkosmos export to India. The Ministry of Foreign Affairs warned of negative Western reactions to the Russian-Indian missile engine deal because the decision had been made without intergovernmental discussion and expertise.[16]

The April, 1992, presidential decree authorized the Export Control Office of the Ministry of Economics to function as a working group of the Export Control Commission. In cooperation with other interested governmental bodies and experts, it has constructed five control lists.

The first list was adopted by an order of the president of Russia on July 30, 1992. It includes items of raw and other materials and equipment. It also includes items of technology and scientific research findings that are considered militarily critical or technologically significant. This list was to be fully harmonized with its COCOM equivalent by the end of 1993. The second list covers dual-use equipment, materials, and related technologies used for nuclear purposes. This list was constructed in compliance with the NSG guidelines. The third list contains two sections covering dual-use chemicals and technologies. The fourth list includes pathogenic organisms, fragments of their genetic materials, genetically engineered organisms, and equipment that can be used in the production of bacteriological weapons. This list was developed in accordance with the AG recommendations. The fifth list contains items used in missile production. It is divided into two categories.

The Governmental Order N1005 of December 21, 1992, "On the Order of Export and Import of Nuclear Materials, Technology, Equipment, Installations, Special Non-Nuclear Materials, Radioactive Sources of Ionizing Radiation and Isotopes" and the associated guidelines provide the licensing mechanism for Russia's nuclear trade. These guidelines codified definitions of nuclear exports, nuclear imports, nuclear materials, nuclear technology, nuclear equipment, installations, special nonnuclear materials, and so on. The guidelines also established mandatory licensing procedures under which the Ministry of Foreign Economic Relations would grant licenses in consultation with Minatom. Licenses would only be granted to legal entities that have the permission of Gosatomnadzor to engage in certain types of nuclear-related activities, such as production, transportation, and storage.

Russia has also pledged to export nuclear items in accordance with its international obligations. For example, exports to nonnuclear weapons states would only be authorized if such states verified that the nuclear items would: (1) not be used to produce nuclear weapons or other nuclear explosives or for any military purpose; (2) be placed under IAEA control and safeguards; (3) be protected at IAEA-recommended levels; and (4) be subject to IAEA reexport conditions.

On May 12, 1992, Presidential Decree No. 507, "On Military and Technological Cooperation Between the Russian Federation and Foreign Countries," was enacted.[17] Together with the new law on the conversion of the defense industry adopted on March 20, 1992, this decree provides a legal basis for the national system of export administration on arms and military technology.

Therefore, Russia has two export control systems. One is targeted at economic (e.g., short supply and hard currency deficit) problems. Russia also has a system for national security and nonproliferation export controls. The first of the systems is more unstable. Governmental Order No. 90 was revised and amended during 1992. Presidential Decree No. 628 changed the system for exporting strategically important raw materials. The government published a new list of such materials subject to mandatory licensing.[18] The right to sell these items abroad is given to a number of registered enterprises and organizations that the Ministry of Foreign Economic Relations has approved. These measures are contradictory. No doubt there have been too many cases of illicit export of nonferrous metals, especially through the open borders between Russia and the Baltic states. The Baltic states have been reexporting such materials for hard currency. For this and other reasons, Russia felt it needed more rigid export controls on raw materials. On the other hand, these new rules of registration for export organizations and licensing can revive monopolization in the foreign economic sphere. Governmental Order No. 854 of November 6, 1992, sets up the rules of quotation and licensing for exports and imports in 1993.

Although the outlines of a Russian nonproliferation policy exist, much remains to be done. In the early 1990s, economic rather than national security and nonproliferation considerations will play a leading role in licensing. The dominance of the military-industrial complex and its economic needs in the current period poses a challenge to the Russian export control system. The influence of representatives of the military-industrial complex in the present export control community of Russia is significant.

Russia's Export Control Community in Transition

Although the decision-making community for export control in Russia is only now being shaped, a few observations are in order. Up until now, the legislature did not play an active role in the national policy-making community on export control and nonproliferation issues. For example, legislative proposals have not been brought before, and export control laws have not been passed by the Supreme Soviet of the Russian Federation.

At the time of this writing, the executive branch dominates the export control system. But decisions are not easily reached, and interagency conflict characterizes the executive's handling of export control policy. All the executive branch actors agree that Russia needs an effective export control system. However, the implementation of nonproliferation policy and the integration of a national export control system into an international one arouse fierce debates. For example, there is some strong opposition to Russia's joining the MTCR and the CCF. The Ministry of Foreign Affairs adheres to a more balanced opinion aimed at the integration of Russia into the global community. But at first the Minister of Foreign Affairs was not even included in a new and very influential body—the Security Council—that is making important policy decisions.

The hardliners include the top echelon of the military complex, representatives of "patriotic" parties, and various groups who question participation in international nonproliferation.

Many new business and social organizations, associations, and parties have emerged in contemporary Russia. They reflect views of various social strata and groups. One of them is the Civic Union, reflecting the positions of the directorate (directors of state enterprises). Its initiator was A. Volsky, the head of the Russian Union of Industrialists and Entrepreneurs. Volsky has long suggested an alternative to Gaidar's program of economic reforms in Russia.[19]

With the conversion process and the opening of the Russian economy, many directors of defense industry enterprises have perceived the advantages of a market economy. The interests of defense enterprises began to differ from the interests of the military community. But with their natural desire to survive in a new environment, the directors of these state enterprises are responding slowly to market incentives and rely instead on state subsidies.

In the public sector, the Association for Nonproliferation was created in 1992 in Moscow. The objectives of the association are to promote research programs on nonproliferation problems, to open educational establishments on corresponding issues, to develop alternative versions of new export control legislation, and to prepare materials for the 1995 conference on the extension of the NPT.

The Soviet Greens are also taking an active part in the ongoing discussion of nonproliferation problems. This movement has strong social support in the regions of ecological disaster and nuclear tests, for example, in Ukraine, Belarus, Northern Russia, the Urals, and Semipalatinsk (Kazakhstan). Their interest in the ecological problems, the proliferation of weapons of mass destruction, and international export control cooperation is very timely. Some experts argue that the global community must expand the framework of international nonproliferation arrangements, placing tectonic, geophysical, and bioelectronic weapons under international controls.[20]

It is important to note that the export control policy-making community is expanding. The involvement of representatives of various groups in the policy-making process may allow for the creation of a more rational Russian export control system balancing the interests of different national groups and agencies, including national security, foreign policy, and national competitiveness interests. However, several factors may impede this process in Russia. First, economic and financial problems are compounded by corruption, mismanagement, and threats of regionalization. Second, export control reform may yet be derailed by the results of various constitutional referendums and political elections. Third, 70 percent of the military-industrial capabilities of the former Soviet Union is located in Russia. This group is strong enough to impede progress in establishing meaningful export controls. The economic hardships of the early 1990s can even strengthen their position. Moreover, the legislative body is a weak actor in the decision-making community of Russia, and is still in a formative state.

The transformation of executive structures, the reorganization of the KGB, the elimination of classified normative rules and instructions within the framework of the ministries, the removal of the Communist Party from governmental bodies and state enterprises, and the opening of society will unavoidably affect the future development of export control policies and mechanisms. New structures of responsibility and authority will undoubtedly affect the administration of export control policy.

The international security environment has changed and has had a great impact on export control policy in both West and East. A major element of the new security environment is the threat of proliferation. Most Russian authorities recognize this threat and are ready to cooperate with international nonproliferation organizations, including the NSG, the CCF, the MTCR, and the AG. Such cooperation, however, will require further development of Russian export control mechanisms.

NOTES

1. Divulging state secrets was a criminal offense under Soviet law. A new Bill of State Secrets was under consideration for two years in the USSR Supreme Soviet during the Gorbachev period but was not adopted by the time of the collapse of the USSR (December, 1991). As popular daily newspaper *Komsomolskaya Pravda* commented in 1991, "Glavlit (censorship) died a year ago giving birth to the Main Office on the Protection of State Secrets in the Press attached to the Council of Ministers. The latter died the other day giving birth to the Agency on Protection of State Secrets in mass media attached to the USSR Ministry of Information. In the meantime we have to investigate what these 'state secrets' are." "Secrets of the First Office," *Komsomolskaya Pravda,* August 13, 1991. For the first time, this daily newspaper slightly lifted the veil on the issue of state and departmental secrets. *Nezavisimaya Gazeta* [*Independent Newspaper*] on August 1, 1992, published an article under the title "Authorities Struggle with Leakage of 'state secrets.' The case of chemical scientist V. Mitzojanov shows the urgent need for the adoption of the new legislation on state secrets. See *New Times,* No. 46 (1992): 46–47. Adopting a new law on mass media at the end of 1991, the Supreme Soviet of Russia revised Article 57 providing for the protection of journalists from governmental authorities' arbitrariness concerning the divulgence of state secrets. *Rossiikaya Gazetta,* December 31, 1991, 2. No clear legal distinctions exist between commercial confidentiality and state secrets or between intellectual property and nonproprietary information of public bodies. Russia and the other successor states of the CIS have yet to develop appropriate legislation. Suffice it to say that it was not possible until 1991 to publish analytical studies on the issue of Western export controls policies, to say nothing of Soviet export controls. E. Kirichenko, "Politika eksportnogo regulirovania Ameriki" [U.S. Export Regulation Policy], *IMEMO,* 1991, was the first open publication on the topic.

2. P. Felgengayer examined the army export mechanism of the late 1980s in *Nezavisimaya Gazeta* [*Independent Newspaper*], February 19, 1992, 1–2.

3. For guidelines on the export of nuclear materials, technology, equipment, and

installations, special nonnuclear materials and services, see *Vneshniya Torgovlia* [*Foreign Trade*], 1982, N4.

4. *Izvestia,* November 26, 1991.

5. Igor Artemiev, "Global Technology Markets and Security Issues," in *Technology Markets and Export Controls in the 1990s,* edited by David Kemme (New York: New York University Press, 1991), 92–93.

6. "Pamiatka po voprosam priamih proizvodstvennih i nauchno—technicheskih sviazei obiedinenii, predpriatii i organizatzii USSR s partnerami iz sotzialistischeskih stran," in *Vneshtorgizdat* (Moscow: 1989), 66; Igor Faminski, ed. *Osnovi Vneshneeconomicheskih Sviazei* (Moscow: Vysshaia Shkola, 1990), 511–16.

7. *Commersant,* no. 28 (July 8–15, 1991): 7.

8. *Rinok* [*Market*], no. 19 (October, 1991).

9. See *The Journal of Commerce,* December 31, 1986.

10. *Economica i Zhizn,* no. 37 (1990).

11. *Nezavisimaya Gazetta* [*Independent Newspaper*], August 6, 1991.

12. Journalists from the daily *Izvestia* investigated the ANT case. They published a series of articles. *Izvestia,* November 1, 4, 5, 11, 15, and 21, 1991, N261, 268, 272.

13. *Komsomolskaya Pravda,* September 4, 1991.

14. *Nezavisimaya Gazetta,* November 5, 1991, 6; *Izvestia,* October 24, 1991; *Megapolis-Express,* no. 43 (1991).

15. *Commersant,* no. 3 (January 13–20, 1992): 22, no. 4 (January 20–27, 1992): 25.

16. *Izvestia,* May 19, 1992, 5.

17. *Vneshniya Torgovlia,* no. 6 (1992): 52–53.

18. *Vneshniya Torgovlia,* no. 8 (1992): 55.

19. *Rabochaya Tribuna,* September 29, 1992.

20. Interview with Dr. Ivan Anureev, one of the Soviet creators of strategic offensive weapons, in *Megapolis-Express,* April 25, 1991, 14; *Tryd* [*Labour*], December 27, 1991.

CHAPTER 8

German Perspectives on Export Control Policy

Claus Hofhansel

Until the late 1980s, export control policy was a rather esoteric subject in West German politics. To some extent, German policy mirrored the physical setting of the now (in)famous *Bundesamt für Wirtschaft* (Federal Economic Agency), a dark, nondescript office building in a suburb of Frankfurt. Largely as a result of the Rabta affair and other scandals, since 1989 German export control policy has become a hotly debated issue, and one legislative or organizational change followed another. Despite all the recent changes, however, German policy retains distinct features, both in terms of content and policy-making process.

Statutes and Their Implementation

The legal basis for German export controls comprises three acts: the *Aussenwirtschaftsgesetz* (AWG) (Foreign Trade Act), the *Gesetz über die Kontrolle von Kriegswaffen* (War Weapons Control Act), and the *Atomgesetz* (Atomic Energy Act). Overall, the Foreign Trade Act is the most important of the three since it covers the whole range of West German exports and imports. The AWG states that foreign trade is mostly unrestricted; export controls are the exception.[1] In contrast, the United States regards "the freedom to export . . . [as] a privilege and not a right."[2] In practical terms, however, more significant than the AWG, which sets out the basic principles of German foreign trade law, are the implementing provisions in the *Aussenwirtschaftsverordnung* (AWV) (Foreign Trade Decree) and one of its appendices, the export list. Since the Libya (Rabta) affair, the German government has repeatedly amended the AWV to close loopholes or to counteract potential new embarrassments. For example, the fourth amendment to the AWV made the export of goods for an aerial refueling project in Libya illegal. The seventh amendment dealt with the transit of goods for a long-range cannon in Iraq, while the eighth amendment responded to the involvement of German citizens in missile projects in Egypt, Argentina, and Iraq.

One of the most significant changes of the Foreign Trade Decree took place in 1991 with the fourteenth amendment to the AWV. A new section, 5(c), specifies that the export of goods and technical documents requires a license if the destination is included in the newly created country group H and if the exporter knows that the intended use is an arms project. The goods themselves may not be listed on Germany's export control list, but they will be subject to export controls in any case if used for arms projects.[3] Among the numerous changes in German export control regulations, representatives of the German business community regarded section 5(c) and the rather long country list H as particularly onerous. On January 22, 1992, the German cabinet decided to cut the list from fifty-four to thirty-four states, eliminating such countries as Singapore and South Korea. Furthermore, the German government created a new country list I, which includes nine countries that have not signed the NPT but that are not judged to be high proliferation risks, such as Chile, Niger, and Tanzania.[4]

In the area of arms exports, the *Kriegswaffenkontrollgesetz* (KWKG) regulates the export of war weapons. The KWKG is an act implementing article 26, section 2 of the constitution, which states that the production, transportation, and sale of war weapons require governmental approval. While the KWKG only covers war weapons, such as tanks or combat aircraft, the scope of the AWG includes other armaments, such as armored but unarmed vehicles. Generally, the provisions of the foreign trade act are less stringent than those of the KWKG. In 1982 the German government also issued a revised set of "political principles for the export of war weapons and other armaments" to guide the licensing process.[5] Regarding nuclear energy equipment, export controls are based primarily on the AWG, while the *Atomgesetz* regulates the export and import of nuclear fuel.[6]

On the basis of this legislation the German government constructed export control lists that enumerate the goods and technologies subject to export controls. The most important list is the *Ausfuhrliste* (export list), an appendix to the foreign trade decree. For our purposes only part I of the *Ausfuhrliste* is relevant; other parts deal, for example, with steel exports to the United States, which are subject to voluntary export restraints. Part I is divided into five sections. Section A covers weapons, munitions, and other armaments, section B goods for the generation of nuclear energy, and section C other goods and technologies of strategic importance, while sections D and E list goods for the production of chemical and biological weapons. The *Ausfuhrliste* changes frequently, largely to bring it into line with revisions of the COCOM lists, but other changes reflect unilateral German decisions. After the series of recent scandals, the German government occasionally overreacted, which led to ridicule. For example, Germany now restricts the export and transshipment of hang gliders to Lebanon, Libya, and Syria. Germany also maintains a separate war weapons list that is considerably shorter than the *Ausfuhrliste*. While the *Ausfuhrliste* takes up over 150 pages, the war weapons list is only 5 pages long.

To determine the economic significance of German export controls in any precise fashion is difficult, partly because the German government in the past pursued a rather restrictive information policy in this regard, although that has begun to change. Virtually the only publicly available information on export control statistics consists of scattered government responses to inquiries by members of the Bundestag. During the late 1980s, West Germany and the United States alternated in the position of the world's largest exporting nation. For the specific areas of trade considered here, in the 1980s West Germany consistently was the largest Western exporter to the Soviet Union. Furthermore, West Germany also held the top rank in the worldwide export of chemicals. Not all trade with the former Soviet Union or chemical exports are subject to export controls, however. In 1987 the *Bundesamt für Wirtschaft* (BAW) issued licenses for the export of armaments valued at DM 6.3 billion. Export licenses for goods listed in the nuclear energy section came to DM 2.7 billion, while licenses for section C products reached a level of DM 19.4 billion.[7] As shown in table 8.1, exports subject to licensing requirements represent a significant but still relatively small proportion of Germany's overall exports. Table 8.2 shows the value of German war weapons exports during the 1980s. Again, although the absolute figures go beyond the billion deutsche mark level, their relative importance is marginal.

In the past, Eastern Europe and the former Soviet Union constituted the primary target of export controls. To illustrate the value of German export licenses for these destinations, table 8.3 provides more detailed licensing statistics than previously available. Table 8.4 presents data on export license denials to Eastern bloc destinations. The unusually high figure for 1984 reflects the value of a telecommunications project for Hungary that did not receive approval.[8] Broken down by industry, the electrotechnical and electronics industry accounted for 84 percent of all denials.[9]

Politically even more sensitive than East-West trade has been the involvement of German companies in Iraqi weapons programs. In 1991 the German government presented more detailed figures on this trade than in the past, which are presented in table 8.5. As these data show, throughout the Iran-Iraq war, West Germany supplied Iraq with goods for the Iraqi military, although the West German government did not issue licenses for war weapons according to the war weapons control act.[10] With all these figures, it is important to realize, though, that they represent licenses and not actual exports. Typically, exports are lower than the value of export licenses.

TABLE 8.1. Summary of German Export Licensing Statistics (in Billion Deutsche Marks)

Year	Total Exports	Value of Export Licenses[b]	Export Licenses as Percentage of Total Exports
1988	568	32	5.6
1989	641	46	7.2
1990	643[a]	21	3.3

Source: Germany, Deutscher Bundestag, *Drucksache,* 12/1140.
[a] Does not include the five new (former East German) states.
[b] Does not include bulk licenses.

TABLE 8.2. German War Weapons Exports (in Billion Deutsche Marks)

Year	Total German Exports	Export of War Weapons Licensed According to KWKG	Percentage
1982	427.7	1.03	0.24
1983	432.3	3.20	0.74
1984	488.2	3.38	0.69
1985	537.1	1.46	0.27
1986	526.4	1.60	0.30
1987	528.3	2.43	0.46
1988	567.8	0.97	0.18
1989	641.3	1.49	0.23
1990	642.7[a]	1.50	0.23

Source: Germany, Deutscher Bundestag, *Drucksache,* 12/1140.
[a] Does not include the five new (former East German) states.

TABLE 8.3. Value of Export Licenses to Eastern Bloc Destinations in 1989 (in Deutsche Marks)

	Sections of the Export List (Ausfuhrliste)			
Country	A	B	C	D
Bulgaria	483,657	[a]	28,172,981	290,378
Czechoslovakia	652,877	[a]	110,452,222	2,741,313
Hungary	388,384	[a]	51,144,303	89,003,078
Poland	552,235	[a]	63,111,940	1,926,680
Romania	10,537	0	2,740,807	182,286
Soviet Union	30,982	[a]	279,125,722	75,941,467

Source: Germany, Deutscher Bundestag, *Drucksache,* 12/1140.
[a] For legal reasons, the German Federal government does not provide information if there are less than three licensees.

Participation in International Export Control Arrangements

Besides maintaining national export controls, Germany also participates in all major multilateral export control regimes. The Federal Republic of Germany (FRG) was a member of COCOM almost from the beginning. Furthermore, the FRG ratified the NPT and has been an active member of the Zangger Committee and the NSG. However, the signing and ratification of the NPT generated considerable controversy within the FRG. On July 1, 1968, sixty-two countries signed the NPT, but the West German federal government did not sign until November 28, 1969, under a new government led by the Social Democrat Willy Brandt. Furthermore, the FRG did not ratify the treaty until 1975, five years after the treaty had become effective.[11]

TABLE 8.4. Value of Export License Denials to Eastern Bloc Destinations

Year	Value
1982	15,861,404 DM
1983	3,062,878 DM
1984	183,249,030 DM
1985	21,018,198 DM
1986	25,198,313 DM
1987	19,858,766 DM

Source: West Germany, Deutscher Bundestag, *Drucksache* 11/3726, p. 3.

TABLE 8.5. Value of Export Licenses to Iraq (in Million Deutsche Marks)

	Sections				
Year	A	B	C	D	E
1981	1.4	0[a]	256.1	NA	NA
1982	237.5	1.0	97.9	NA	NA
1983	45.9	0[a]	46.3	NA	NA
1984	5.0	0[a]	59.7	NA	NA
1985	64.9	0[a]	138.2	0[a]	NA
1986	4.4	0[a]	59.6	NA	NA
1987	0.1	NA	53.4	NA	NA
1988	0.0[a]	NA	93.2	NA	NA
1989	0.1	0[a]	95.5	0.5	NA
1990	0.0[a]	NA	24.7	3.9	NA

Source: Germany, Deutscher Bundestag, *Drucksache* 12/487, p. 2.

Note: Sections A through E refer to Sections A through E of Part I of the German export list.

[a] Less than 50,000 DM.

In the 1970s West Germany developed a distinctive approach to nuclear nonproliferation and nuclear export policy that frequently brought it into conflict with the United States and other countries that favored more restrictive policies. While the United States sought to deny nuclear technology to proliferation-risk countries in the Third World, West Germany countered this approach with a policy of cooperation. A recurring theme in West German nuclear policy statements in the 1970s was that any attempts to strengthen the nonproliferation regime had to be based on the participation of as many countries as possible, including countries of the so-called Third World. Attempts by a single country or a small group of nations, such as the United States or a nuclear exporter cartel, to unilaterally change the rules of the game would prove to be counterproductive. Any nonproliferation agreements had to be "multinational, nondiscriminatory and universally binding."[12] West Germany denied that there was any inherent conflict between nuclear exports and nonproliferation. Instead, nuclear exports, even to countries that had not signed the NPT, could in the long run advance nonproliferation goals more than shortsighted technology denials because export contracts and nuclear cooperation between supplier and customer countries helped to integrate the recipients of nuclear technology into the existing international safeguards system to control the spread of nuclear weapons. Walker and Lönnroth call this the spider's web argument.[13]

These fundamental differences led to disagreements at the NSG meetings in the mid-1970s. At these meetings Canada and the United States pushed for restrictive nuclear export guidelines, while France and West Germany opposed such attempts. Edward Wonder argued that "the German position had been the least common denominator upon which agreement could be reached."[14] One specific point of contention in the 1970s and 1980s was the refusal of the FRG to require "full-scope safeguards" as a condition of nuclear exports. As late as 1985, during the third NPT review conference, West Germany, Switzerland, and Belgium actively resisted the inclusion of a provision in the conference's final declaration that would have urged all nuclear suppliers to require full-scope safeguards for their exports.[15]

When West German and U.S. nuclear export policies diverged in the 1970s, West Germany frequently let France take the lead and on a couple of occasions explicitly adopted French initiatives. Thus, West Germany's establishment of a nuclear council and a nuclear cabinet committee in the 1970s were partly modeled on France's nuclear export council, and after France had declared a moratorium on the export of reprocessing facilities and technology, Germany followed suit with a similar declaration in 1977.[16] For the future, it would appear reasonable to expect that Germany will not follow French leads as often as in the past. However, the proliferation of weapons of mass destruction is a rather sensitive issue, and Germany, more than other countries, is particularly vulnerable to the "merchants of death" label, which will result in German caution.

In the 1980s West Germany participated in the MTCR and the AG, which seeks to contain the spread of chemical weapons capabilities. Paralleling changes in German national export control policy, the German government has advocated a reform of COCOM and a drastic reduction of COCOM lists, but at the same time, it recently supported a tightening of proliferation controls. Within COCOM, an important source of German irritation has been the restrictions on telecommunication equipment exports to the former Soviet Union.[17] While Germany has pushed for the elimination of telecommunications equipment from COCOM lists, the United States and Great Britain resist such a move. Regarding proliferation controls, at the end of 1990 Germany was one of the few countries that had placed export controls on all fifty chemicals on the AG's warning list.[18] Furthermore, in 1990 the West German government also reversed a long-standing policy and decided to require full-scope safeguards as a condition for future German nuclear exports. This policy will require a renegotiation of the notorious German-Brazilian nuclear cooperation agreement as well.[19] In the following section, the major actors in German export control policy are discussed.

The Policy-Making Community

Within the German executive branch, a number of ministries participate in export control policy-making, including the Economics Ministry, the Foreign Office, and, less frequently, the Defense Ministry and the Ministry for Research and Technology. The importance of the individual ministries has varied by issue area. Although relevant legislation designates the Economics Ministry as the lead agency, in the area of arms exports, the Foreign Office in the past dominated the decision-making process.[20] In the area of nuclear exports, on the other hand, the Foreign Office typically lost in bureaucratic struggles with the Ministries for the Economy and for Research and Technology.[21] Within the Economics Ministry, different sections handle COCOM matters and arms exports. As of summer 1990, section V B8 dealt with export control policy in COCOM, while the implementation of the war weapons control act fell within the responsibility of division IV, specifically section C6. From an American perspective, a very significant contrast to U.S. policy-making is the fact that the Ministry of Defense plays only a minor role in this policy area. This holds true, to some extent, even for arms exports. After the Social Democratic party came to power in 1969, then Defense Minister Helmut Schmidt advocated a very restrictive arms transfer policy and attempted to remove the Defense Ministry from the arms export decision-making process.[22]

In the area of arms exports, there is also a coordination mechanism at the cabinet level in the form of the *Bundessicherheitsrat,* a cabinet committee. Its permanent members include the chancellor, the foreign minister, and the ministers for defense, interior, finances, and economics. In contrast to other cabinet committees, the *Bundessicherheitsrat* meets fairly frequently, on the average thirty to forty times per legislative period. Its primary areas of concern have changed over the years; in the 1970s arms exports became one of the major points on its agenda.[23] In the wake of the Rabta affair, policymakers realized the need for better coordination efforts and created a working group to investigate suspicious export activities. This working group includes representatives of all relevant federal agencies, such as the Ministry of Economics, the Foreign Office, the *Bundesnachrichtendienst* (intelligence agency), etc.[24]

Essentially, the Ministry of Economics, the Foreign Office, and, on occasion, other ministries make export control policy and leave the day-to-day administrative tasks to a detached agency subordinate to the Ministry of Economics. This mode of operation is characteristic of German administrative practice in general and builds on a tradition that predates the establishment of the FRG, and even the Weimar Republic for that matter.[25] The BAW is the agency in Germany that issues export licenses and thus implements export control policy. It has had a checkered history, which is reflected in the functions that it performs.[26] Besides reviewing export applications, it also regulates imports. Functions not related to trade include economic assistance to depressed regions and small businesses. In the area of energy policy, the BAW administers funds supporting the German coal industry and plays a role in energy crisis management. Finally, the BAW has a few limited responsibilities in regard to environmental protection.

Since 1986 the BAW has been composed of six divisions. Important for our purposes are divisions V and VI, which deal with imports and exports, respectively. Until the mid-1980s, there had not been a separate export control division. As part of the reforms of 1989-90, the BAW's export control division has been expanded from six to twenty-two sections, including a special group on missile technology. Staffing of the division increased from around 70 employees in 1988 to 171 by September 1990.[27] In the late 1980s, the BAW came under intense scrutiny, which brought to light inadequate working conditions within the agency and a number of rather questionable bureaucratic practices. For example, after 1985, BAW's section VI 5 assumed responsibility for a large number of product groups, including chemicals, rubber, asbestos, nonferrous and precious metals, ferrous alloys, and radioactive materials. Besides the section head, seven staff members worked in the section, including two clerical workers and two secretaries. According to Manfred Ruck, a former section head, the caseload reached such proportions that a thorough treatment of individual license applications was for the most part impossible.[28]

Even if the volume of license applications overwhelmed the BAW in the 1980s, on occasion, foreign intelligence services tipped off German authorities about suspicious activities of German companies. Foreign intelligence services, most often the United States and Britain, provided this information in the form of so-called nonpapers. There is evidence, however, that at least some German bureaucrats processed nonpapers rather sloppily. A former BAW section head wrote in 1984 that anonymous papers of that sort usually ended up in his wastebasket.[29] Richard Perle charged that German agencies treated nonpapers as "démarche-mellows."[30]

As if the Rabta affair and other export control scandals had not been enough, the agency continued to face uncertain times, most recently because of ramifications of the unification process. In August, 1991, the German cabinet debated legislation to transform the BAW's export control division into a separate agency entitled *Bundesausfuhramt* (BAA). At that time, one of the unresolved questions about this agency was whether it would continue to operate out of its predecessor's offices at Eschborn or move to Bonn as part of an overall effort to compensate Bonn for the loss of its capital status.[31] On January 23, 1992, the Bundestag passed the bill creating the BAA.[32] To attract qualified personnel for the new agency, the act authorized special bonuses above the regular federal pay scale.[33] One of the problems that the BAW had faced in the past was its low status and pay. Typically, engineers and natural scientists who actually had some knowledge of chemical or nuclear technology could find much more lucrative jobs in the private sector. But even ambitious lawyers, who tend to dominate the German civil service, would not necessarily have wanted to work for the BAW since they would have been classified at a lower pay grade than in a ministry and promotions within the BAW tended to be very slow. The new act represents an attempt to overcome some of these problems. The BAA officially began its work on April 1, 1992. It currently has 300 employees, but the agency is expected to grow to almost 400 employees. In its recruitment efforts, the new agency has placed particular emphasis on the hiring of engineers and natural scientists to expand its base of technical expertise.[34]

On the enforcement side of German export controls, the *Zollkriminalinstitut* (ZKI) plays a crucial role. Although the ZKI was established as early as 1952, its existence did not receive a statutory basis until the mid-1980s. Similar to the BAW, export controls and their enforcement constituted only one of the responsibilities of the ZKI, but as a consequence of the Rabta affair, this area has now become the agency's most significant function. In June, 1991, the German cabinet approved draft legislation that would change the status of the ZKI to that of a higher federal agency and its name to

Zollkriminalamt.[35] Substantively, one of the most significant recent tasks of German customs agencies has been to set up a data bank named KOBRA (*Kontrolle bei der Ausfuhr*), which would make it easier for customs officials to access information on suspicious export activities. Although the ZKI's reputation did not suffer as much as that of the BAW, it has become an object of controversy as well. In the latest round of amendments to Germany's export control laws, the Christian Democratic–led government wanted to give the ZKI the authority to tap phones. The Social Democrats, as the main opposition party, opposed this proposal on civil liberties grounds and used its majority in the upper chamber, the Bundesrat, to block this legislation until the Christian Democrats found a way to overcome this legislative hurdle.[36] Parallel to changes in the BAW, the ZKI has undergone considerable expansion, from 94 employees in 1988 to 300 in 1992. Furthermore, the number of investigations conducted by the ZKI has substantially risen.[37]

Turning to the role of the legislature, we have to distinguish between the formal powers of parliament and their actual use. Furthermore, in the German parliamentary system of government, opportunities for the majority to influence policy differ from those available to the opposition. A major comparative study of the U.S. Congress and the German Bundestag concluded, on the basis of developments in the 1970s and 1980s, that the legislature had gained ground in the United States but lost terrain in West Germany.[38]

In contrast to the situation in the United States, the German parliament does not have the power to interfere directly in specific export control decisions. However, there are two exceptions to this general rule. The first exception is based on section 27, part 2 of the AWG which states that foreign trade regulations have to be submitted to the Bundestag, which can cancel them within three months of their promulgation. This led Baker and Bohlig to the conclusion that "[c]learly the German Parliament has been more restrained than the legislatures of the other three countries [the United States, Canada, and Japan] in delegating responsibility for formulating a system of export controls."[39] However, in actual practice, this provision played a significant role in only one documented case. It involved a regulation that the federal government had passed on December 14, 1962, requiring export permits for large-diameter pipe.[40] Thus, this case was part of the famous pipe embargo of 1962–63.[41] There was considerable domestic opposition to the embargo, and the government only narrowly avoided the defeat of the regulation through a parliamentary maneuver. The other exception to the lack of legislative involvement concerns military assistance agreements. Since 1966 the annual budget statutes include provisions that require the approval of military assistance agreements by the Bundestag committees for foreign affairs and for the budget.[42] Initially, the Social Democrats had pressed for these provisions.[43]

Thus, on the whole, the German legislature did not become heavily involved in the setting of export control policy. More recently, however, there have been exceptions to the pattern just described. After the scandal over the Libya affair, the West German government came under heavy pressure, particularly from the United States, to tighten West German controls. In response, the government introduced a number of bills to stiffen criminal sanctions against export control violations, to upgrade the information basis of export control agencies, and to provide for a better coordination of control and enforcement efforts. These bills were drawn up fairly quickly and introduced in the Bundestag without prior consultation of members of the Christian Democratic party in parliament. On top of that, these legislative proposals affected five ministries, four of which are led by Free Democrats, the junior coalition partner. As a result, a kind of "backbench revolt," to use British terminology, ensued, and Christian Democratic deputies forced a number of amendments that weakened some of the criminal sanctions provisions. Thus, observers witnessed a rather curious situation in which the opposition Social Democrats defended the original government proposals, while the ruling majority was busy watering down those same proposals.[44] In this particular case, a number of special factors had to come together to produce this outcome, such as inadequate prior consultation of parliament, combined with tensions among the coalition partners.

As a general rule, in the German parliamentary system, only the majority parties, which by definition also fill the top executive positions, have a real chance of making a significant impact on policy. The situation gets more complicated, though, when, like at the time of this writing, the opposition party in the Bundestag controls the second chamber, the Bundesrat. In the episode described above, on May 30, 1989, the federal government led by Christian Democratic Chancellor Kohl introduced a bill to tighten the War Weapons Control Act.[45] The bill specified that anybody who developed, manufactured, or traded nuclear, chemical, or biological weapons would receive a minimum jail sentence of two years. Opposition within the governing party led to the passage of a weakened bill on June 1, 1990.[46] This version lowered the minimum jail sentence to one year and included a clause that limited the criminal liability of scientists, a provision that science organizations had lobbied for. On June 22, 1990, the Bundesrat, where the Social Democrats enjoyed a majority at the time, approved two bills to amend the foreign trade act but rejected amendments to the war weapons control act and referred the bill to the conference committee (*Vermittlungsausschuss*).[47] The Bundesrat objected specifically to the one-year minimum jail sentence and the science clause.[48] When the act finally went into effect in November, 1990, its provisions followed the recommendations of the Bundesrat. Thus, the final result followed a general pattern in which the Bundestag gives in more frequently than the Bundesrat.[49] In 1991, the Social Democrats again used their majority in the Bundesrat to block export control legislation.[50] This time, though, the government reacted differently and decided to change the bill in such a way that approval by the Bundesrat was no longer necessary.[51] On January 23, 1992, the Bundestag passed the revised bill.[52]

Besides its involvement in passing legislation, the Bundestag may also use various instruments of legislative oversight, such as questioning cabinet members. Following press reports that German companies had sold blueprints for submarines to South Africa and had allegedly shipped nuclear fuel to Pakistan, the Bundestag set up two fact-finding committees in 1987 and 1988.[53] Particularly the committee that investigated the activities of the West German company Transnuklear brought to light much embarrassing information on West German export controls.[54] On the whole, though, the effectiveness of such tools is limited. Among individual legislators, the Social Democrat Norbert Gansel built his reputation by uncovering questionable arms export practices, most notably the illegal export of blueprints for German submarines to South Africa. Another Social Democrat, Wolfgang Roth, the party's economics expert, achieved some notoriety through some rather blunt statements, such as his recommendation to German companies to simply ignore COCOM rules.[55]

Regarding interest group participation in export control policy-making, industry is the primary client of export control policy. On October 23, 1989, the Bundestag committee on economic affairs held a public hearing, which, in contrast to the U.S. Congress, is still a relatively rare occasion in Germany.[56] The hearing dealt with amendments to the Foreign Trade Act and the War Weapons Control Act, and the list of invited associations, other organizations, and individual experts provides a fairly clear picture of interest group participation in this policy area. The committee had invited representatives of six industry associations, including the powerful association of German industry (BDI), the chemical industry association, the association of the electrotechnical and electronics industry, the German machinery and industrial equipment association, the association of the German precision mechanics and optical industry, and the German chamber of commerce (DIHT). Other experts included two trade union representatives, two merchant associations, representatives of three major research organizations, including the Max Planck Society, the ZKI, a prosecutor, and finally four academics, including three law professors and one political scientist. As a result of the numerous recent scandals involving German industry participation in Iraqi and Libyan nuclear and chemical weapons programs, industry representatives have become more cautious, however, when they take public positions on export control issues. At a November, 1991, hearing on the bill that gave the ZKI the right to tap phones, industry representatives avoided stating anything that would have suggested that they did not support strict enforcement of controls and the prosecution of violators of export control laws.[57] In contrast to the situation in the United States, in Germany, ethnic groups have not lobbied in favor of or against trade with the Soviet Union.

While East-West trade does not carry the same kind of "trading with the enemy" overtones as it does for some groups in the United States, the issue of arms exports is a different matter. While the arms industry has lobbied for a relaxation of arms export restrictions, its opponents in this controversy include the trade unions, church groups, peace movement organizations, and groups active on third world issues.[58] Unions were caught in an uncomfortable position. On the one hand, their ideological position pushed them toward opposing arms exports. On the other hand, unions are active in the arms industry, and they have to represent the interests of workers employed by arms manufacturers. The metalworkers' union (IG Metall), under which most workers in the arms industry are organized, favors a restrictive approach. But the union had problems in dealing with workers and union representatives who had bypassed official union channels and argued for increased arms exports.[59] In 1989, the German trade union federation wrote in its statement for the hearing on October 23 that it supported a tightening of German export control laws.[60]

Salience of Export Control Issues

A discussion of the attention that German politicians pay to export control issues has to distinguish between East-West controls and proliferation or North-South concerns. As Jacobsen has argued for German East-West controls,

> There is a basic consensus in the FRG on the desirability of non-strategic trade with the East. This consensus includes the business and banking communities, the labor unions, and all of the major political parties. There is virtually no opposition to improving economic ties with the East. Indeed, there has been no domestic public debate about the necessity or desirability of export control vis-à-vis the East for decades.[61]

In its 1988 report, the BDI claimed that German industry always supported the primary role of security concerns in this area.[62]

The situation looks rather different in the area of proliferation controls. In the past, export controls were a low-priority item for the political leadership in charge of the Economics Ministry and other agencies. The head of the foreign trade division in the Economics Ministry testified at a Bundestag hearing that the responsible politicians had always expressed the wish to administer German export controls as quickly and smoothly as possible. There had been no interest in strict controls.[63] Count Lambsdorff, a former economics minister, concurred and noted that during his tenure, the prevention of illegal exports was not an acute issue that ended up on the desk of the minister.[64]

After the Libya affair and other scandals, this pattern changed. Since 1989, one reform proposal followed another, and there are signs that some of the recent changes have now affected the traditionally close cooperation between industry and government. In August, 1991, several peak associations of the German business community, including the BDI and DIHT, wrote coordinated letters to the ministers for the economy and finance in which they expressed grave concern about the recent tightening of German export control laws and delays in the export licensing process. They received political support from the Bavarian finance minister, Georg von Waldenfels, who also warned that the overly strict implementation of the foreign trade act hurt the ability of German companies to compete in international markets.[65]

As is the case in German politics in general, political controversies over export control policy inevitably involve partisan differences. At the risk of some oversimplification, parties of the left (Greens, Social Democrats, and now also the Democratic Socialists) have favored relatively strict guidelines for arms exports, while conservatives in the Christian Democratic Union/Christian Social Union (CDU/CSU) parties in the past advocated fewer restrictions. This division applies to dual-use exports, such as nuclear technology transfers, as well. However, in the area of arms exports, we need to distinguish between "a level of publicly proclaimed restrictions, a level of bureaucratic policy and a level of actual licensing arms exports."[66] Brzoska asserts that throughout the 1970s and 1980s, the basis for a restrictive arms export policy eroded more and more, and "[t]he change of power from the SPD to a conservative government in 1982 speeded the erosion process somewhat, but did not change its structure or dynamics."[67]

We also have to distinguish between the stance political parties take while in opposition and their behavior in government. In the case of nuclear export policy, the Social Democratic Party supported the government line of not requiring full-scope safeguards during its years in government until 1982, but it changed its position as an opposition party later in the 1980s.[68] In the area of East-West controls, the German government has followed a quite consistent policy, which has been supported by all parties that participated in government coalitions during the last two decades, although the Social Democrats have been more critical of COCOM than the Christian Democrats.

Perceptions of the International and Domestic Policy-Making Environment for Export Controls

Any discussion of German perceptions on the effectiveness and efficiency of export control policies again needs to distinguish between the positions of government and opposition politicians. While government officials naturally tend to defend their own policies, opposition politicians have criticized German export control policy rather harshly in recent years. There have been significant areas of agreement as well, however. In interviews conducted by the author in 1990 with officials in the Economics Ministry, an industry representative, members of parliament, and a customs official, all interview partners expressed a rather low opinion of the BAW and its handling of export licensing requests.

Regarding perceived linkages between export controls and the goals of economic growth, democracy, and military security, it is difficult to find policy statements that directly address this issue. In a speech to the German foreign policy society in June, 1990, Foreign Minister Genscher advocated a broad definition of security. According to Genscher,

> Stability and security can less than ever be defined in military terms under current conditions. All areas of cooperation, including political, economic, technological and ecological issues should be included. The comprehensive definition of stability and security is the central characteristic of the new cooperative stability structure which we seek to achieve. Therefore, the Soviet Union has to be integrated economically into this comprehensive cooperation.[69]

Although Genscher made these comments in the context of the dramatic changes in Eastern Europe and the former Soviet Union, such differences between broad definitions of security in Germany and more narrow perceptions in terms of military security in the United States are not new. In fact, as Spaulding pointed out in an article in 1991, "[n]o aspect of the German presence in Eastern Europe has been more enduring than the economic connections between Germany and its Eastern neighbors. The persistent pattern of German–East European trade is one of the few areas of German economic history, German–East European relations, and German foreign policy in which we can connect the activities of 1990 to those of the 1950s, to those of the 1920s, to those of the 1890s."[70] Essentially, the German position appears to be that increased technology transfer to Eastern Europe and the former Soviet Union will facilitate the modernization of their economies and thus contribute to economic growth. Economic growth in Eastern Europe not only is important for its own sake but also will provide a much more favorable environment for democratic institutions and values to take root than continued economic decline and hardship. In turn, stable and prosperous democracies in Eastern Europe will pose much less of a security threat to Germany, and Western Europe as a whole, than authoritarian regimes on the brink of economic collapse. Thus, from a German perspective, the indirect links between technology transfer, economic growth, democracy, and secu urity call for a relaxation of COCOM controls.

The extent to which German decision makers have openly pursued export control policies at variance with those of the United States has changed along with changes in the distribution of power. To use the example of East-West energy trade, in the case of the pipe embargo of 1962–63, the FRG followed the leadership of the United States rather than defying American demands as the British did. In the early 1980s, West Germany joined France and the United Kingdom in their opposition to President Reagan's attempt to block the Urengoi natural gas pipeline project. At the end of the decade, West Germany strongly pushed for a relaxation of COCOM controls against continuing resistance by the United States. Nevertheless, despite the way these controversies have often been portrayed in the media, intra-alliance struggles over export control policy often involve more than a simple division between control-oriented Americans and more trade-dependent Europeans and Japanese. In an interview conducted in the summer of 1990, a German Economics Ministry official characterized the British position in COCOM as surprisingly restrictive, and the same applied to Japan at that time. France had become much more cooperative and no longer played a capricious special role as in earlier periods. Nevertheless, from a German perspective it remained difficult to fully integrate France.[71]

Regarding the future of German export control policy, clearly the emphasis has shifted from East-West issues to so-called new security threats with a stronger North-South dimension. In the aforementioned speech to the German foreign policy society, Genscher argued that the Conference on Security and Cooperation in Europe (CSCE) had to be transformed into a pillar and forum for a new cooperative European

> . . . stability system which fully includes the Soviet Union as an equal and responsible partner.
>
> Such a system could . . . include: The creation of a permanent and partially institutionalized disarmament, arms control and verification process which addresses all militarily relevant security issues, including

> crisis prevention, arms budgets, arms exports to third countries, the conversion of the arms industry, the nonproliferation of specified weapons technologies, as well as preventive technological arms control, in short all militarily relevant aspects of cooperative security.[72]

Another likely development in German export control policy is that German officials will increasingly attempt to reach an EC-wide consensus on export controls. Certainly, the German business community will push for that as it becomes more and more concerned with unilateral German controls. Efforts to formulate a common EC policy on this issue did not bear fruit in the past, but there have recently been signs that this may change. EC commissioners Bangemann, Andriessen, and Scrivener have launched an initiative to establish a common EC list for dual-use goods and to harmonize the export control practices of member countries.[73] Within the EC, Germany, the Netherlands, and Italy have argued for a relatively broad common export control policy which would cover nuclear, chemical, biological, and ballistic missile technologies as well as conventional arms exports, while France and the United Kingdom have favored a more narrow approach.[74]

Conclusion

The most significant characteristic of German export control policy in the early 1990s has been the rapidity of change. To the extent that Germany has begun to pursue a much stricter policy than in the past, we may also begin to see interesting parallels between domestic political controversies in the United States and in Germany. In the 1980s representatives of the U.S. business community became much more outspoken than before in their criticisms of unilateral U.S. controls. Now, German industry associations are beginning to voice similar concerns about unilateral German controls, licensing delays, the unpredictability of licensing decisions, and the negative effect of these developments on the competitiveness of German exporters. To anybody who followed the debate on these issues in the United States, such complaints sound rather familiar.

NOTES

1. Russell Baker and Robert Bohlig, "The Control of Exports: A Comparison of the Laws of the United States, Canada, Japan, and the Federal Republic of Germany," *International Lawyer* 1 (January 1967): 166–67. Stefan Oerter has provided a more recent evaluation of changes in German export control laws and compared German practices to the situation in France, the United States, and some smaller European

nations. See Stefan Oerter, "Neute Wege der Exportkontrolle im Bereich der Rüstungsgüter," *Zeitschrift für Rechtspolitik* 25 (February, 1992): 49–55.

2. Angela E. Stent, *Technology Transfer to the Soviet Union: A Challenge for the Cohesiveness of the Western Alliance,* Arbeitspapiere zur International Politik, no. 24 (Bonn: Europa Union Verlag, 1983), 33.

3. Country group H included Egypt, Ethiopia, Afghanistan, Albania, Algeria, Angola, Argentina, Bahrain, Brazil, Bulgaria, Chile, China, Djibouti, Guyana, India, Iraq, Iran, Israel, Jordan, Cambodia, Quatar, Comoro Islands, North and South Korea, Cuba, Kuwait, Laos, Lebanon, Libya, Morocco, Mauritania, Monaco, Mongolia, Mozambique, Myanmar (Burma), Namibia, Niger, Oman, Pakistan, Romania, Zambia, Zimbabwe, Singapore, Somalia, South Africa, Syria, Taiwan, Tanzania, United Arab Emirates, Vanuatu, Vietnam, Saudi Arabia, and the Republic of Yemen. Some of these countries were put in group H only because they had not signed the NPT. Therefore, restrictions applied only for goods listed in section I B of the *Ausfuhrliste*.

4. "GUS-Staaten ausgespart," *Handelsblatt,* January 23, 1992, 8.

5. For more detailed discussions of the statutory basis of German arms export controls up to 1989, see Michael Brzoska, "Bundesdeutsche Rüstungsexporte in die Dritte Welt: Daten-Verfahren-Zusammenhänge," in *Militarismus und Rüstung: Beiträge zur ökumenischen Diskussion,* edited by Bernard Moltmann (Heidelberg: Forschungsstätte der evangelischen Studiengemeinschaft, 1981), 175–182; Michael Brzoska, "Neue Richtlinien für den Waffenexport aus der Bundesrepublik Deutschland in die Dritte Welt," in *Jahrbuch Dritte Welt: Daten, Übersichten, Analysen* (Munich: Verlag C.H. Beck, 1983), 88–89; Eckehart Ehrenberg, *Der deutsche Rüstungsexport: Beurteilung und Perspektiven* (Munich: Bernard & Graefe Verlag, 1981), 66–67; Frederic S. Pearson, "'Necessary Evil': Perspectives on West German Arms Transfer Policies," *Armed Forces & Society* 12 (Summer 1986): 531–34. A more recent analysis is provided by Herbert Wulf, "The Federal Republic of Germany," in *Arms Export Regulations,* edited by Ian Anthony (New York: Oxford University Press, 1991), 72–85.

6. For a more extended legal analysis, which does not cover the most recent changes, however, see Gerhard Meyer-Wöbse, *Rechtsfragen des Exports von Kernanlagen in Nichtkernwaffenstaaten,* Studien zum International Wirtschaftsrecht und Atomenergierecht, vol. 62 (Cologne: Carl Heymanns Verlag KG, 1979).

7. West Germany, Deutscher Bundestag, *Drucksache* 11/2120, 1.

8. West Germany, Deutscher Bundestag, *Drucksache* 11/3726, 3.

9. Ibid.

10. Germany, Deutscher Bundestag, *Drucksache* 12/487, 2.

11. Erwin Häckel, *Die Bundesrepublik Deutschland und der Atomwaffensperrvertrag: Rückblick und Ausblick,* Arbeitspapiere zur Internationalen Politik, no. 53 (Bonn: Europa Union Verlag, 1989), 1.

12. West Germany, *Bulletin der Bundesregierung,* no. 36 (April 15, 1977), 331.

13. William Walker and Måns Lönnroth, *Nuclear Power Struggles: Industrial Competition and Proliferation Control* (London: George Allen & Unwin, 1983), 141–42.

14. Edward Wonder, "Nuclear Commerce and Nuclear Proliferation: Germany and Brazil, 1975," *Orbis* 21 (Summer 1977): 304.

15. Leonard S. Spector, *The New Nuclear Nations* (New York: Vintage Books, 1985), 246–47.

16. Lothar Wilker, "Nuklearexport—und Nichtverbreitungspolitik—ein Prioritätenkonflikt für die Bundesrepublik?" in *Nuklearpolitik im Zielkonflikt: Verbreitung der Kernenergie zwischen nationalem Interesse und internationaler Kontrolle*, edited by Lothar Wilker (Cologne: Verlag Wissenschaft und Politik, 1980), 96–98.

17. John Markoff, "3 Western Allies Seek End to a High-Tech Export Ban," *New York Times*, February 7, 1992, C1.

18. Peter Rudolf, "Non-Proliferation and International Export Control," *Aussenpolitik* 42 (1991): 395.

19. Germany, Deutscher Bundestag, *Drucksache* 11/8512, 5.

20. Michael Brzoska, *Rüstungsexportpolitik: Lenkung, Kontrolle und Einschränkung bundesdeutscher Rüstungsexporte in die Dritte Welt* (Frankfurt: Haag & Herchen, 1986), 121.

21. Harald Müller, *Nach den Skandalen: Deutsche Nichtverbreitungspolitik*, HSFK-Report 5/1989 (Frankfurt: Hessische Stiftung Friedens und Konfliktforschung, 1989), 31–32.

22. Brzoska, *Rüstungsexportpolitik*, 121.

23. Klaus Spychalski, "Der Bundessicherheitsrat," *Wehrtechnik* (November 1982), 27.

24. Interview, June 21, 1990.

25. Arnold Brecht and Comstock Glaser, *The Art and Technique of Administration in German Ministries* (Cambridge, Mass.: Harvard University Press, 1940; Westport, Conn.: Greenwood Press, 1971), 6–12.

26. Bundesamt für gewerbliche Wirtschaft, *BAW: Bundesamt für gewerbliche Wirtschaft*, 4th ed. (Eschborn: Bundesamt für gewerbliche Wirtschaft, 1984), 4–19.

27. Germany, Deutscher Bundestag, *Drucksache* 11/8510, 3.

28. Germany, Deutscher Bundestag, *Drucksache* 11/7800, 750– 51.

29. Ibid., 717.

30. Ibid., 718.

31. "Standort für Exportamt bleibt offen," *Frankfurter Allgemeine Zeitung*, August 15, 1991, 9.

32. "Der Bundestag beschließt Verschärfung der Exportkontrollen," *Frankfurter Allgemeine Zeitung*, January 24, 1992, 1.

33. Germany, Deutscher Bundestag, *Drucksache* 12/1461.

34. "Spezialisten haben bei der Ausfuhrkontrolle jetzt mehr zu sagen," *Frankfurter Allgemeine Zeitung*, June 11, 1992, 16.

35. "Exportkontrollgesetz wird abermals beraten," *Frankfurter Allgemeine Zeitung*, June 27, 1991, 17.

36. Germany, Deutscher Bundestag, *Drucksache* 12/400.

37. German Information Center, *Focus on Export Controls* (New York: German Information Center, 1992), 4–5.

38. Uwe Thaysen, Roger H. Davidson, and Robert G. Livingston, "US-Kongress und Deutscher Bundestag im Vergleich. Ein Ergänzendes Resümee," in *US-Kongress und Deutscher Bundestag: Bestandsaufnahmen im Vergleich,* edited by Uwe Thaysen, Roger H. Davidson, and Robert G. Livingston (Opladen: Westdeutscher Verlag, 1988), 517–68.

39. Baker and Bohlig, "The Control of Exports," 168.

40. Kurt Tudyka, "Gesellschaftliche Interessen und Auswärtige Beziehungen: Das Röhrenembargo," *Politische Vierteljahresschrift* 10, no. 1 (1969), 210–11.

41. Angela E. Stent, *From Embargo to Ostpolitik: The Political Economy of West German–Soviet Relations 1955–1980* (Cambridge: Cambridge University Press, 1980).

42. Christian Loeck, "Die Politik des Transfers konventioneller Rüstung: Strukturen und Einflussfaktoren im Entscheidungsprozess," in *Verwaltete Aussenpolitik: Sicherheitsund entspannungspolitische Entscheidungsprozesse in Bonn,* edited by Helga Haftendorn, Wolf-Dieter Karl, Joachim Krause, and Lothar Wilker (Cologne: Verlag Wissenschaft und Politik, 1978), 215, 218.

43. Helga Haftendorn, *Militärhilfe und Rüstungsexporte der BRD* (Dusseldorf: Bertelsmann Universitätsverlag, 1971), 68.

44. West Germany, *Verhandlungen des Deutschen Bundestages,* 11th Wahlperiode, Stenographische Berichte 11/153; West Germany, Deutscher Bundestag, *Drucksache* 11/3995; West Germany, *Verhandlungen des Deutschen Bundestages,* 11th Wahlperiode, Stenographische Berichte 11/215; interviews, June 25 and July 9, 1990.

45. West Germany, Deutscher Bundestag, *Drucksache* 11/4609.

46. West Germany, *Verhandlungen des Deutschen Bundestages,* 11th Wahlperiode, Stenographische Berichte 11/215.

47. West Germany, Deutscher Bundesrat, *Stenographischer Bericht* 615.

48. West Germany, Deutscher Bundesrat, *Drucksache* 396/90.

49. Thomas Ellwein, *Das Regierungssystem der Bundesrepublik Deutschland,* 5th ed. (Opladen: Westdeutscher Verlag, 1983), 290.

50. "Waffenexprot-Gesetz scheitert im Vermittlungsausschuss," *Frankfurter Allgemeine Zeitung,* June 4, 1991, 1.

51. "Exportkontrollgesetz wird abermals beraten," *Frankfurter Allgemeine Zeitung,* June 27, 1991, 17.

52. Stephen Kinzer, "Germany Acts to Curb Arms Exports," *New York Times,* January 24, 1992, A3.

53. West Germany, Deutscher Bundestag, *Drucksache* 11/6141; Holger Koppe and Egmont R. Koch, *Bombengeschäfte: Tödliche Waffen für die Dritte Welt* (Munich: Knesebeck & Schuler, 1990).

54. Germany, Deutscher Bundestag, *Drucksache* 11/7800.

55. Wolfgang Hoffmann, "Relikt des Kalten Krieges," *Die Zeit* (Canadian edition), April 6, 1990, 13.

56. West Germany, Deutscher Bundestag, Ausschuss für Wirtschaft, *Stenographisches Protokoll* 11/56.

57. Wolfgang Hoffmann, "Quittung für Bombengeschäfte," *Die Zeit* (Canadian edition), November 29, 1991, 10.

58. For statements summarizing the positions of arms export opponents, see Thomas Nielebock, ed., *Rüstungsexport: Analysen, Daten, Stellungnahman* (Tübingen: Verein für Friedenspädagogik, 1984); West Germany, Deutscher Bundestag, Ausschuss für wirtschaftliche Zusammenarbeit, *Stenographisches Protokoll* 10/18.

59. Christian Wellmann, "Gewerkschaftliche Alternativplanstrategie," in *Das Geschäft mit dem Tod: Fakten & Hintergründe der Rüstungsindustrie,* edited by Michael Brzoska et al. (Frankfurt: Eichborn Verlag, 1982), 123 61.

60. West Germany, Deutscher Bundestag, Ausschuss für Wirtschaft, *Ausschuss Drucksache* 467/11.

61. Hanns-Dieter Jacobsen, "East-West Trade and Export Controls: The West German Perspective," in *Controlling East-West Trade and Technology Transfer,* edited by Gary K. Bertsch (Durham, N.C.: Duke University Press, 1988), 159.

62. Bundesverband der Deutschen Industrie, *Bericht 1986–88 des Bundesverbandes der Deutschen Industrie e. V.* (Cologne: BDI, 1988), 287.

63. Germany, Deutscher Bundestag, *Drucksache* 11/7800, 712.

64. Ibid.

65. "Klagen über Wettbewerbsnachteile durch resttriktive Ausfuhrkontrollen," *Handelsblatt,* August 23, 1991, 6; "Streit um Exportkontrollen verschärft sich," *Frankfurter Allgemeine Zeitung,* August 24, 1991, 11.

66. Michael Brzoska, "The Erosion of Restraint in West German Arms Transfer Policy," *Journal of Peace Research* 26 (May 1989): 165.

67. Ibid., 166.

68. Lothar Wilker, "Bundestag und Aussenpolitik," in *US-Kongress und Deutscher Bundestag: Bestandsaufnahmen im Vergleich,* edited by Uwe Thaysen, Roger H. Davidson, and Robert G. Livingston (Opladen: Westdeutscher Verlag, 1988), 394.

69. *Europa-Archiv* 45 (August 10, 1990): 474.

70. Robert Mark Spaulding, Jr., "German Trade Policy in Eastern Europe 1890–1990: Preconditions for Applying International Trade Leverage," *International Organization* 45 (Summer 1991): 343.

71. Interview, July 10, 1990.

72. *Europa-Archiv* 45 (August 10, 1990): 476.

73. "EG-Initiative zur Regelung von Dual-Use Exporten," *Handelsblatt,* January 23, 1992, 8.

74. Wolfgang H. Reinicke, "Arms Sales Abroad: European Community Export Controls Beyond 1992," *Brookings Review* 10 (Summer 1992): 23.

CHAPTER 9

French Export Control Policy

Marie-Hélène Labbé

Introduction

In France, arms sales and their control are clearly distinguished from the control of dual-use goods and technology. Generally speaking, we can consider that in arms sales, what prevails are economic considerations helped by the military-industrial lobby, whereas with dual-use goods, where the industrial lobbies are less present and less structured and where the economic stakes may be less important, it is easier to grant a greater place to considerations of security.

Controlling Arms Sales

Like the export of dual-use items and technology, arms sales are controlled by a list of articles, the exportation of which is subject to approval whatever the destination. This list, known as the list of war material and assimilated material, published in the form of a ministerial order (adopted on April 2, 1971, with subsequent modifications), is a more extensive national list than COCOM's list of war material. It includes certain articles in COCOM's international civil list, in particular lasers and computers with high calculating capacities.

Applications for export approval are submitted to the Commission Interministérielle pour l'Etude des Exportations de Matériel de Guerre (CIEEMG), set up in 1949, and approval must be requested at every stage of commercialization: canvassing, negotiating, sales, and so on.

Presided over by the general secretary for national defense, the commission includes representatives from the Ministries of Foreign Affairs, Defense, and Economy and Finance. If the participating ministers agree, the exporter is notified of the authorization and obtains an authorization to export war materiel (AEMG), which allows the material to leave French territory. If the participating ministers do not agree, the matter is submitted to the prime minister for a decision.

If the request concerns war material that is specified in an article of COCOM's list and destined for a country targeted by COCOM's controls, the commission, if it agrees, passes the matter over to the French delegation at COCOM so that the delegation can submit it to the committee.[1] This system is specifically French, and there is no equivalent in France's trade competitors. Since 1989, there has been some talk of simplifying this process and of doing away with the first step. Each month, the CIEEMG examines about 600 authorizations, half of which are applications for approval to canvass, the rest concerning the other two steps of commercialization. A ministerial order is presently being studied with the aim of eliminating the prerequisite step of applying for approval to canvass, while of course maintaining the obligation to respect the constraints of any embargo that may be decreed.[2] Jean-Luc Lagardère, president of Matra, a French armaments company, declared that he was very much in favor of the order.[3] However, as of October, 1993, the order had still not been signed.

Controlling Dual-Use Goods and Technologies

COCOM's Controls

The HLMs of June, 1990, and May, 1991, ratified the upheavals that have taken place in Eastern Europe since the 1989 revolution. On May 23 and 24, 1991, COCOM member countries adopted a revised and very much reduced list of controlled products, which went into effect on September 1, 1991. It has indeed been applied by all COCOM member countries, including France. The actual list was published in the United States in the *Federal Register,* and France published it on January 24, 1992.

The new list is organized into nine spheres of sensitive technology: highly developed materials, material processing, telecommunications and computer security, calculators, electronics, captors and lasers, marine, navigation and aeroelectronics, and propulsion. In this new structure, divided into technical fields, the materials, software, technologies, components, production equipment, and finished products that could be considered strategic in their field are controlled in each sector.

As far as the targeted countries are concerned, a distinction is made between Poland, Hungary, and Czechoslovakia, which have set up COCOM-like domestic controls, and the other Eastern bloc countries. Exports to these three countries have the benefit of preferential regulations. In May, 1992, Hungary was dropped from the list of nations subject to export controls because of its adoption of an export control law similar to those of Western countries. A similar decision has not been made for Czechoslovakia because of concerns about arms exports to Middle East countries; Poland's internal political squabbles have delayed a decision like that for Hungary.

Furthermore, France has become involved, with the other EC countries who are members of COCOM, in establishing an intra-COCOM free trade zone. Incidentally, we should keep in mind that more than 55 percent of exchanges of products subject to COCOM controls are carried out between member countries, called group 1 countries in French regulations. Just as the British created an Open General License in May, 1989, the French, in February, 1991, instituted the G1 general license, which covers most of the exports bound for COCOM countries and Ireland, which is a member of the EC but not of COCOM.

Each EC country has its own export control system. After 1993, this diversity will no longer be compatible with the single market. But if internal controls have to be removed, member countries will have to set up strong export controls; otherwise, there will be leakages through the more lax countries. The EC commission is actively working on this problem and identifying the weaknesses and strengths of each EC member. This step has been completed. The second step is to determine whether controls have to be harmonized, the lists published at the same time, etc.

The New Control Mechanisms

France participates in all of the new mechanisms to control the proliferation of weapons of mass destruction: it is a member of the AG and has been a member of the MTCR since 1987; and although it did not sign the NPT in 1968, which in its view symbolized the American-Soviet condominium, which it denounced, it has applied the NSG guidelines since 1975. In June, 1991, France announced that it would sign the NPT and apply the full-scope safeguards (see below). France joined the NPT in August, 1992.

Participation in International Export Control Mechanisms

France is a member of all the international control mechanisms, including the NPT, which it signed in 1992. What form does this participation take?

France has been a member of the MTCR since its inception in 1987. However, it did not publish specific MTCR lists until 1990. Why? Because potential exporters were already subjected to two types of controls (COCOM and CIEEMG), a combination that in fact covered MTCR controls. Only after the COCOM list was considerably reduced following the meeting of June, 1990, were articles that fell within the scope of the MTCR controls no longer controlled by COCOM's core list, hence France's promptness to publish an

MTCR list on November 10, 1990, a few days before publishing the French COCOM list on November 29.

French policy became more assertive in 1990, and economic priorities yielded to security concerns. In an unprecedented statement before an international assembly of armaments engineers on June 27, 1990, General Marcel Benichou warned of "a new form of proliferation just as dangerous as nuclear proliferation: the proliferation to the Third World of missile guidance systems." These technologies, he said, "should be closely watched."[4] France has already refused to sell additional rocket engine technology and cooperated during the Persian Gulf War in coalition efforts to defeat and destroy the equipment it provided to Iraq.[5] But, according to a researcher at the Stockholm International Peace Research Institute (SIPRI), "several of the seven original members—especially France, Germany and Italy—continued to conduct policy as before the MTCR came into effect."[6] However, the French have accepted a part-time secretariat duty for the MTCR.

France has also been a member of the AG since its inception in 1985, although its attitude has evolved a great deal since then. For a long time, it was very reserved, but since early 1991, it has become more assertive, because of certain internal reflections.

These reflections seem to be the fruit of a double realization: first, that even if the convention on chemical weapons came into force in three years, there would be three years not covered by controls, while revelations concerning the Iraqi potential were multiplying and, second, that unilateral controls must be established.

How is this change expressed? France continues to oppose any attempt to institutionalize the AG: "not a new COCOM!" someone confided to me. "Not a chemical MTCR!" said another official. Accordingly, France does not want there to be a secretariat nor, above all, a system of joint decision making. Controls should be national with national sanctions. However, the change in attitude can be seen many ways: (1) France's cooperation within the AG has changed. Whereas, up until 1990, France used to say no to everything, it has now agreed to control the fifty products that the Americans wanted to control, and even proposed controlling five more! There is a bureaucratic reason to be found behind these changes: the Ministry of Industry, which tended to slow down movement, has lost its influence to the Ministry of Foreign Affairs, which also wanted to draw lessons from the Gulf War. (2) France has retroactively accepted cross-notification mechanisms (still not codecisions). (3) To avoid the "chemical MTCR," the French have been open to pedagogical actions such as technical cooperation between customs officers. France published the lists of products and the lists of equipment on October 26, 1991.

French policy concerning nonproliferation considerably evolved after the 1974 explosion in India. The realization of the absolute necessity of controlling the spread of nuclear technology, without hindering the development of civil nuclear technology, has led France to set up a monitoring system that, even today, is without doubt one of the most efficient for reducing proliferation in the world.

On the international level, France participated in drawing up the NSG guidelines as well as the International Evaluation of the Fuel Cycle and the International Convention on the Physical Protection of Nuclear Matter signed in June, 1980. Moreover, it has systematically signed agreements of guarantee with the countries to which it exports nuclear material so that the material can be submitted to the IAEA's controls.

The most important measures, however, have been taken on the national level. Three fundamental decisions were made in less than two years to evaluate and control foreign nuclear policy. On May 29, 1975, the prime minister set up an interministerial group at the Ministry of Foreign Affairs, entrusting it with the task of examining all projects to export large nuclear units and sensitive materials.

The repercussions of selling South Africa two nuclear plants and supplying Pakistan with a reprocessing plant have led, as a second decision, to the setting up on September 2, 1976, of the Conseil de Politique Nucléaire Extérieure (CPNE). Presided over by the president of the republic, the CPNE defines the different aspects of foreign nuclear policy, particularly regarding the export of sensitive nuclear techniques, equipment, and products. The declaration of October 11, 1976, sets the guidelines for this policy. These guidelines are based on three principles: legitimate access for all countries to civil nuclear technology, independent policy, and international dialogue. The declaration specifies that France "remains prepared to contribute to setting up peaceful applications of nuclear energy which represent a competitive source of energy for a certain number of countries," that it intends to "keep the control of its nuclear export policy while respecting its international commitments," and furthermore that it "will not favor the proliferation of nuclear weapons." From the time it was set up until its last meeting on May 26, 1983, the CPNE held eighteen sessions.

The third decision is the publication in the *Journal Official* (France's equivalent of the *Congressional Record*) on April 25, 1977, of a "notice to exporters," which sets very precisely the procedures for companies to follow before they can export any equipment or sensitive materials concerning nuclear proliferation that appear on the list.[7] This list is regularly updated; it was last updated in August, 1989.

In June, 1991, France announced its intention to join the NPT and did so in August, 1992.[8] This decision does not mean new constraints for exporting nuclear technology, since France was already abiding by the NSG guidelines. Among the advantages, signing the NPT will undoubtedly reinforce France's weight in international organizations, for even if France's partners recognized the strictness of French nonproliferation policy, the fact that they attracted attention to the ambiguity of France's position very often deprived France of the benefits that it could have drawn from its policy. This action will allow France to take part in NPT review conferences. Finally, since France is one of the twelve countries of the European single market, becoming a member of the treaty, after Spain in 1987, will lead to the final consolidation of European cohesion concerning nonproliferation.

As well as joining the NPT, the question also arose whether or not France would apply the full-scope safeguards. As we have seen, since 1976, France has refused to become involved in setting up the rule of full-scope safeguards of the nuclear activities of potential clients. Because of this opposition, the rule, the aim of which was that no nuclear installation could escape from the IAEA's international control, was not retained in the London guidelines. France, at the time, saw in this system the risk of a permanent head-on collision between those countries supplying nuclear equipment and those buying it, which would ultimately lead to a limitation on purchases, and even an embargo. As a repercussion, an embargo could limit exports and in particular develop, as a sort of perverse effect of the system, cooperation between countries of the South, possibly even between China and the South, without any real possibility of control.

At the same time as it announced its membership in the NPT, France announced that it would apply the full-scope safeguards, which it has done since September, 1991.

The Policy-Making Community

For COCOM controls, the French system involves many agencies: Customs, the Ministry of Industry, the Ministry of Defense, and the Ministry of Foreign Affairs. While Customs administers the licensing process, the Ministry of Industry and the Ministry of Defense review and assess the technical aspects of every application. If the application must be referred to COCOM, the Ministry of Foreign Affairs is responsible for presenting it to the committee.[9] The review process (i.e. updating the COCOM lists) involves primarily the Ministry of Industry but also the Ministry of Defense, intelligence services, and the Ministry of Finance; disputes that arise are solved at the subministerial or ministerial level.

The attempt to publish a new hard core list, boosted by the Ministry of Industry and an electronics lobby, is strongly resisted by some at the Defense Ministry, who still argue that the weakness of the former Soviet Union may be more dangerous than its previous strength.[10]

Chemical proliferation controls are under the responsibility of the Strategic Affairs and Disarmament Division (disarmament subdivision) of the Political Affairs Department of the Ministry of Foreign Affairs. The examination procedure is interministerial and involves especially the Ministries of Industry and Defense and the Secretariat Général de la Défense Nationale.

Ballistic proliferation controls are under the responsibility of the General Armament Delegation (Délégation Générale à l'Armement or DGA) of the Ministry of Defense, and within this delegation, they fall within the scope of the international relations delegation, techniques department.

However the administration that represents France at AG, MTCR, NSG, and COCOM conferences is the Foreign Affairs Ministry.

The Political Importance of Export Controls in France

The end of the Gulf War caused a flood of propositions to the effect of "never again": never again should they line up their soldiers to confront others whom they themselves had armed. France, along with the Soviet Union, had been the major supplier of arms to Saddam Hussein. France had in fact sold Fr 25 billion of weapons, including Fr 15 billion that were unpaid for and hence lost. This situation gave rise both to individual indignations with relatively minor implications as well as to official proposals, and it is necessary to see if they have some concrete bureaucratic expression or whether they were simply rhetoric.

Individual Indignations and Proposals

All French politicians from the right to the left wanted to draw lessons from the Gulf War principally in the field of arms sales.

As far as the opposition—the conservatives—is concerned, the most structured proposal was made by the former president of the National Assembly's Defense Commission, François Fillon (Gaullist Party), who introduced a bill on November 21, 1990, to institute parliamentary control of arms sales. For this, a parliamentary delegation for the export of war material would be set up whose task it would be to give a justified opinion on each export application submitted to the CIEEMG. Made up of the two presidents of the Defense Commission and the Foreign Affairs Commission at the Assembly and the president of the Foreign Affairs and Defense Commission at the Senate and called together once a month, this parliamentary delegation would examine all the export applications presented by manufacturing industries to the CIEEMG that were worth more than Fr 20 million,[11] before the prime minister gives the go-ahead. The defense secret cannot be held in their way. But Fillon's proposal, which would have given France a structure of political control similar to the system in force in the United States, was swiftly rejected by the defense minister, Jean-Pierre Chevènement.

As far as the socialist majority is concerned, Laurent Fabius, former socialist prime minister, compared arms to drugs: "the buyers must be helped to break their habit. But the dealers must also be discouraged."[12] The new French Minister of Defense, Pierre Joxe, who took over the position as a result of Chevènement's resignation due to developments during the Gulf War, has pledged to give an annual statement on French arms sales. But the prime minister at the time, Michel Rocard, also socialist but a rival of Joxe, brought up the economic dimension of arms sales.

This is exactly what emerged from the debates in parliament. Numerous representatives, irrespective of their political allegiance, warned against too much otherworldliness: "This matter can only be settled on an international level. If France were the only country to decide on a control, or if it were followed only by one or two countries, it would be a fool's deal" (Daniel Colin, Union for French Democracy, Var). François Hollande (Socialist Party, Corrèze) went even further: "Beware of being too naïve! Just as we are opening this debate, the United States are in the middle of working out a bill aimed at facilitating the export of their arms sales."[13]

Official Declarations or Proposals

While representatives are, on the whole, concerned about jeopardizing their seats, especially if an armaments factory is situated in their district, the president of the republic has taken a bolder stand, close in fact to that of President Bush but going further than his regional plan and claiming to encompass the proliferation of weapons of mass destruction throughout the world. Hubert Vedrine, the president's spokesman at the time, presented a good synthesis of the official French position: the willingness to participate in fighting proliferation, the refusal to accept any policy resembling "technological apartheid," and the intention not to deny third world countries their right to development:

> The fight against all forms of proliferation of non-conventional weapons (atomic, bacteriological, chemical) and against potentially dangerous technologies is an absolute necessity, but it must be conducted in a way so as not to cause the Southern countries to refuse what they would perceive as a "Holy Alliance of developed countries," aimed at prohibiting access to all advanced technology. This would only make them more set on bypassing and fighting any efforts to control proliferation. The Southern countries must therefore see that it is in their interest to

associate themselves with the agreements of autolimitation and prohibition, as the case may be. I have also suggested that control, restriction and prohibition policies be enhanced by giving preferential treatment to those countries who would have implemented reliable safeguards concerning critical technologies. I believe that it is better to concern ourselves with this question early on if we want the controls and bans accepted and respected.

For several years now, France has been at the forefront in many aspects of the fight against proliferation. This is particularly true concerning the Geneva talks for an agreement on the radical elimination of chemical weapons . . . The control of arms sales and the fight against the proliferation of non-conventional weapons and potentially dangerous technologies would be even more effective if we tried to solve the root of the problems and conflicts which sustain the race to acquire arms of all kinds in the Near and Middle East and elsewhere.[14]

A few days after the announcement of the Bush plan for the Middle East, President François Mitterrand made public, on June 3, 1991, his disarmament plan, which claimed to be global:

The multiplication of increasingly costly and destructive systems of weapons is putting the world under growing risks. Inequalities, injustices, imbalances in strength result in a trail of threats, the arms' race and conflicts of all kinds. The proliferation of arms of mass destruction gives a global dimension to this risk. The whole world, the South and North alike, have a vital interest in stopping this race and the dangerous and ruinously expensive proliferation. It is everybody's affair.

Our aims are clear. Chemical weapons must be eliminated. Bacteriological weapons must not be produced. Existing nuclear arsenals must be reduced to the lowest level compatible with maintaining dissuasion. The non-dissemination of nuclear weapons remains a neces esity. On the other hand, recourse to nuclear energy for pacific purposes is justified. The spread of ballistic technology must be strictly controlled in so far as it can be used for aggressive purposes. However, there is no reason to prevent cooperation on space programmes for civil or scientific ends.

As far as conventional arms are concerned, a balance of forces must be maintained or instituted everywhere, region by region, to respect every country's right to security. Arms exports will thus be strictly controlled and carried out so as not to contradict this action. France, which has already adopted these goals, is ready to subscribe to any

> improvement in existing arrangements, any new international or multilateral agreements founded on them. It has already initiated discussions with this end in view with its EC partners.
>
> The global control of armaments and disarmament presupposes action on three levels: according to the category of weapon, the region and on a world-wide scale.[15]

The Mitterrand plan calls for a global approach rather than a Middle East approach and proposes developing a system of restraint region by region, working down toward the lowest levels commensurate with the security of the states in the region. It also pledged that France would join the NPT, and broaden its MTCR controls and bans on chemical and biological weapons.

Signing the NPT was not a difficult decision to make in terms of public opinion or the remnants of Gaullist ideology. The French are aware that they are not far away from North Africa and parts of the Middle East, so up until now, the Mitterrand Plan has been fairly well received in France.

The Bureaucratic Expression

In mid-March, 1991, the minister of defense, Pierre Joxe, entrusted his undersecretary, Gérard Renon, with defining a policy for controlling the export of weapons and fighting against nuclear proliferation. However, when the new government was formed under the leadership of Edith Cresson, Pierre Joxe was kept on in his functions, but Renon disappeared and has not been replaced. After the appointment of a new prime minister, Pierre Bérégovoy, the situation remained the same. So there is no longer an undersecretary specifically responsible for controlling proliferation. I have repeatedly been told that there is no conclusion to be drawn from this new situation. However, I continue to think that to have a deputy secretary in charge of nonproliferation has both a symbolic and an operational value and that the disappearance may convey a negative signal.

Policymakers' Perception of the Effectiveness and Efficiency of National and International Export Control Policies

According to the policymakers I met, French export controls, be they of French origin or of international origin, are fairly effective. "Among the large Western countries, we are one of the countries which have had the fewest problems. Do we have angelic businessmen or excellent customers?"[16] Behind the humor there is a real satisfaction with French implementation of export controls. The only shadow could be cast by the list, seized by the IAEA team in Iraq, of companies that helped Iraq.

Perceived Linkages between Export Controls, Economic Growth, Democracy, and Military Security

If economic growth, democracy, and military security are the goals that every country is striving for, we cannot really refer to them in this context as values. Besides, for each of these objectives, the answer concerning the linkage with export controls is different depending on whether we are interested in the exporting country or the country benefiting from the technologies in question.

Export Controls and Economic Growth

It is obvious that export controls result in a reduction in exports and hence in economic growth, at least in the short term. In the medium and long term, the consequences can be more subtle: one of the fears during the 1970s was that the Eastern bloc countries, benefiting from Western technology and having cheap and obedient labor, would be transformed into NICs and flood West European markets with their production. Export controls, in this perspective, could be considered as a measure of economic protectionism.

For France, respecting COCOM controls has certainly had an economic cost. However, in the opinion of those industrialists questioned, it was less than the cost of lost contracts with their American suppliers and, if they had been put on the blacklist, the cost of the loss of the American market. On the other hand, it is certain that COCOM controls have some responsibility in the limited industrial development in Eastern bloc countries: the infrastructures in the field of computers and telecommunications are in a state of underdevelopment for which the present leaders of these countries hold COCOM directly responsible.[17]

The new export controls are likely to be much more costly for the French economy. As far as controls on arms sales are concerned, they can only be a hard blow for a country that is the third or fourth exporter of weapons to the Third World.[18]

The question of cost for companies has not been taken into consideration by the French authorities. Yet, 90 percent of these companies respect the controls and even refer matters to the administration if an order seems suspicious. This applies to both public and private companies. Why? Because they are afraid that their name will be handed over to the press and because Germany's example of putting company heads in prison has made them cautious.

Export Controls, Technology Transfers, and Democracy

The question that must be considered here is not whether France is a democracy: it has been for 200 years. But a democracy can use export controls as a linkage instrument to encourage more freedom, more respect of human rights, in the benefiting country. It is in this perspective that embargoes have been instituted against South Africa because of its policy of apartheid. It is also possible to consider that transferring goods and technologies eases the spread of ideas and thus initiates democracy. It is because they were aware of this risk that communist leaders refused to equip the civil sector with personal computers. It is certain that being equipped with personal computers and telephone lines can only help to emancipate men and women deprived of freedom and, in time, make them citizens. But that takes time.

Export Controls, Technology Transfers, and Military Security

The perception of a linkage between military security and export controls was particularly strong as far as COCOM controls were concerned, since the military threat posed by the Warsaw Pact was their basis. The perception of this threat has, of course, diminished since the 1989 revolutions in Eastern bloc countries and the failure of the putsch in Moscow in August, 1991. The 1989 revolutions in the Eastern bloc countries led, during the COCOM HLM of June, 1990, to the adoption of a core list and a preferential regime for exports to Hungary, Poland, and Czechoslovakia. As previously stated, Hungary was dropped from the list of targeted countries. Poland and Czechoslovakia are on the waiting list, and the prospects of freeing the Baltic Republics from COCOM controls is a remote one. The former Soviet republics remain targeted by COCOM.

The perception of a linkage between technology transfers and the threat to military security coming from countries of the South was faint until the Gulf crisis. France, like a number of Western countries, participated in the ballistic and nuclear proliferation and in the sales of conventional weapons to the Third World. The Gulf crisis served, in this respect, as a detonator by revealing the extent of French responsibility in building up the Iraqi arsenal and the contradiction in sending soldiers against an enemy that we ourselves had armed. Later revelations concerning the possibility that Algeria was making a nuclear bomb—even if, this time, French companies were not apparently implicated—within firing range of France made people realize the threat that uncontrolled technology transfers constituted. This realization has found expression in France's readiness to take part in new control mechanisms symbolized by the announcement that it would sign the NPT. But

France will not participate—in any case, not with the socialist government—in any measure that resembles a COCOM South (see Hubert Vedrine's statements above).

The Distribution of Power and Export Control Decision Making

In France, when we speak of export controls for military items, we cannot avoid mentioning the military-industrial complex.

This term is bothersome, as it implies that political decisions in the armaments sector are entirely subject to the pressures of a powerful and influential lobby. However, beyond controversy, the military-industrial complex does exist, and it is intrinsically linked to a policy of independence that dates back to General de Gaulle, who did not want France to depend on other countries—especially the United States—for its armament. For this, he needed a powerful administration, industrialists at his disposal, and homogeneity in his staff: high-ranking civil servants educated at the Grandes Ecoles (most prestigious schools) for engineers.

The heart of this complex—which administers a staff of 261,000—is the Ministry of Defense and, within this Ministry, the DGA, which is the architect of defense programs, industrialist, and sales representative all at the same time.

The Research, Study and Techniques Department, which defines the armament programs, is comprised of 24,700 people (including high-ranking military personnel and engineers). After the conceptual phase, the programs are carried out by technical departments (see fig. 9.1).

To the Ministry of Defense, it is necessary to add the armament companies (for example, Thomson CSF, Matra, Aérospatiale) that strongly depend on public funds and where senior armaments engineers go to join the private sector after having served their time in the public service. The subsidies given to these companies now represent only half, if not 40 percent, of the total cost; nevertheless, the DGA provides industrialists with two additional immaterial advantages: the specifications (indicating the requirements of the French army) and a firm order, which enables them to export, since no country in the world will buy material that has not first been sold to the French army. Therefore, the French army, when it bought its Crotale missiles from Thomson, enabled that company to land one of the finest contracts in Saudi Arabia.[19]

What is the role of this military-industrial complex as regards export controls? It is, of course, very hostile to any control that results in a drop in exports. Exports confirm the quality of the material and make up, to a significant degree, the trade deficit by Fr 20 to 30 billion a year. The minister

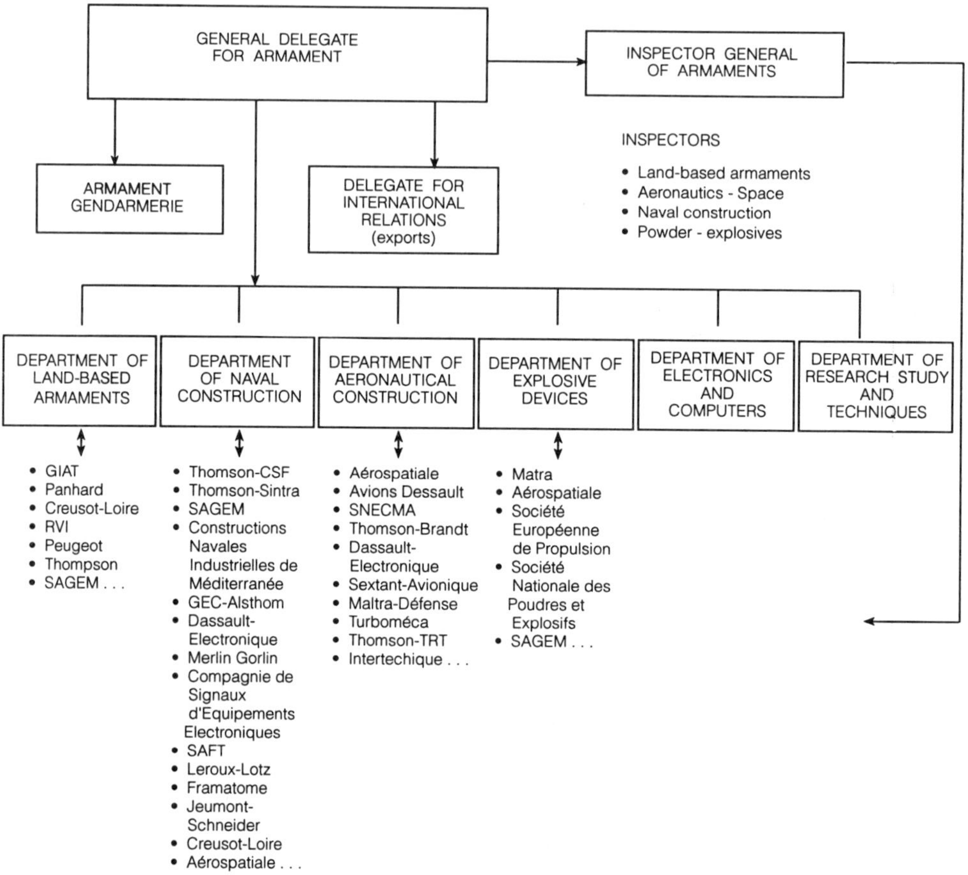

Fig. 9.1. The French military-industrial complex. (Source: Délegation Générale à l'Armement, Ministry of Defense.)

of defense has made himself an advocate for this policy, making a statement to the National Assembly: France must remain an exporting country to "reinforce the lower costs of mass production, to reduce costs per unit, to favor self-financing and therefore limit the budgetary financing in the development of new materials."[20]

The representatives of the military-industrial complex are very skeptical of any new export controls. Henri Martre, then chief executive of Aérospatiale, a French state-run aircraft concern, wrote a long article in the newspaper *Le Monde* in which he pointed out that "some people would like a world consensus to be established to adopt common rules. We can hope for this as far as the proliferation of weapons of mass destruction are concerned. We have doubts concerning conventional technology."[21] Why? In the field of arms sales, hypocrisy prevails, and the United States' attitude, preaching a limitation of arms sales while it massively increases its sales to the Middle East and East Asia, is not likely to facilitate dialogue.

The problem is that French companies are going to suffer from the reduction in military spending due to the alleviation of the Soviet threat. Is it necessary to make their situation worse by limiting sales of conventional arms, missiles, or sensitive technology?

In the Aquitaine region, a major aeronautical and space center, the 27,000 jobs in the defense industry are threatened by layoffs. The Aérospatiale group will have to lay off 400 employees between 1992 and 1994 and the Société Européenne de Propulsion more than 150; the Société Nationale des Poudres et Explosifs, Dassault, and Thomson will also have to reduce their staff. There will certainly be strong resistance to anything that will mean further market losses. The order from Taiwan for Mirage-2000-5s is desperately needed by Dassault Aviation, a privately owned aerospace company, which otherwise may have to shut down a major assembly line. This company has not made a major export sale for five years.

The representatives of the French military-industrial lobby have just won a victory and could win another. The minister of defense had ruled out the possibility of France buying five new Mirage-2000s, which Dassault was asking for to facilitate exporting them. A month later, the general delegate for armament, Yves Sillard, did not exclude the matter. Sillard's project would consist of renovating the Air Force's original Mirage-2000s into as many of the more modern Mirage-2000-5s, which would enable industrialists to tackle foreign markets by pointing out that France had preceded them.[22]

Will the same fate be reserved for the Leclerc tanks (made by GIAT Industries)? This is what its president, Pierre Chiquet, believes, declaring that "whatever the quality of the commercial structures and equipment, it is indispensable that the army equip itself with Leclerc tanks, insofar as it concerns agreements of cooperation between states, which goes beyond the scope of commercial sales."[23]

There are no other forces in France as strongly organized and powerful as the military-industrial complex. For the moment, the only industrial lobby that plays a part in the decision making of COCOM controls is the Federation of Electrical and Electronic Industries. The Commission for the Export of Critical Products (Commission Exportations Produits Sensibles) meets regularly, under the chairmanship of Dominique Lamoureux, who is secretary-general of Thomson International, but its role is limited to that of government adviser. The chemical industrialists have for a long time worked together with the Ministry of Foreign Affairs concerning the Geneva Convention. But the officials at the ministry do not wish to involve them in determining export controls, which does not seem very coherent.

The Probable Future and Preferred Outcome

French officials, in particular in the Ministry of Foreign Affairs, consider that as far as controlling proliferation is concerned, the supply side has received the greatest attention, and it is now necessary to devote time to the demand side. In this respect, they view with interest the agreement that took place between Argentina and Brazil, and between them and the IAEA, or confidence steps occurring in the Korean peninsula. They seem to have two main concerns: (1) how to increase the acceptability of a discriminatory regime (and not to consider the South as a bunch) and (2) how to increase complementarity between the supply side and the demand side.

As far as their own export controls are concerned, they genuinely confess "internal political forces are the key forces. If there is a constituency to satisfy, it will be satisfied, and this has to be taken into account."[24]

Conclusion

French export control policy could be changed if it seemed that the United States was not abiding by the international commitments for which it is so prompt to call.

These commitments apply essentially to arms sales, for which it is clear in 1992 that the shock caused by the Gulf War has subsided and for which competition between American and European, especially French, exporters looks to be merciless. Hence President Bush's announcement in September, 1992, during his election campaign of his approval of the sale of 150 F-16s to Taiwan, despite that the contract seemed to have been taken away by Dassault, seems to dash all hopes for cooperation symbolized by the union of the five permanent members of the UN Security Council, through their meetings on arms transfers.

APPENDIX: PRESIDENT MITTERRAND'S DISARMAMENT PLAN (JUNE 3, 1991)

The objectives concerning specific categories of weapons: each category of weapon calls for specific treatment, by proceeding, if necessary, by steps. To attain clearly defined goals to be imposed on everyone, France, which always makes sure that it adapts its [nonproliferation] regulations, proposes that concrete measures be taken swiftly, sector by sector:

1) Banning and elimination of chemical weapons: The whole international community, which met in Paris in January 1989, recognized the necessity of finalizing the convention on banning chemical weapons as soon as possible. France offered to convene the special chemical weapon committee in Geneva on a ministerial level to conclude negotiations before the end of the year. It is calling for all countries to become members of this convention as soon as it is inaugurated.
2) Prohibition of bacteriological weapons: During the conference to examine the 1972 General Banning Treaty to be held next September, France will propose a protocol for verification.
3) Nuclear disarmament: Nuclear disarmament remains an essential goal. France supports the efforts of the two superpowers to reduce their nuclear arsenals. It confirms that it will participate in the process as soon as the conditions that it set in 1983 are met.

   It is essential during this time to prevent nuclear capability from spreading beyond the five present nuclear powers.

   France, which is already applying all the NPT guidelines, has decided in principle to sign and wants all countries to belong.
4) BMT: The surveillance system for ballistic missile technology (MTCR), which enables those who presently have the expertise to limit the risks of ballistic missile proliferation, should be only a step toward a more general agreement, which will be more extensive geographically, better controlled, and applicable to everyone. It would fix rules favoring cooperation in civil space programs by removing the dangers of the technology being diverted to build up military ballistic missile capabilities. Here again, it would involve reaching a situation where all countries that desire, for their development, to have access to space would cooperate within a framework that would guarantee security.

   Furthermore, France recommends that measures to ensure mutual trust be worked out in the form of a "code of good conduct" applicable to the use of civil and military satellites.
5) Conventional weapons: Exports of conventional weapons must not be at variance with the search, region by region, for an equilibrium of strength at the lowest level respecting each country's right to security.

   The five permanent members of the Security Council—who happen to be the principal producers of conventional weapons—are going to open in the coming weeks in Paris a meeting aimed at defining the rules of restraint. This meeting could then be expanded at the next general meeting to set up an international arms sales register, kept by the Secretary General of the United Nations. During these discussions, the sales of conventional weapons on parallel markets will receive special examination.

   The members of the European Community have already begun talks aimed at making proposals on this subject.

Regional Objectives

The European example is encouraging. The Europeans have gone from the cold war to peaceful coexistence to cooperation within the framework of the CSCE. They have adopted and applied measures to ensure confidence and security. They have signed the first disarmament agreement on conventional weapons. This experience is not directly replicable, but it shows that the arms race is not inevitable. This step could inspire other initiatives in other regions.

We are appealing for regional security arrangements based on the following conditions:

a) Only the beginning of the solution to the conflicts will make it possible to initiate this process and create confidence.
b) Interested parties must adopt regional measures to ensure confidence and security. The first condition of confidence is information. Measures of transparency and confidence, that is to say shared information on the capacities and state of the forces and on the movement of armed forces, reduces the feeling of impending danger and prepares the way for controlling actual disarmament. For this, a framework is necessary, which may be a regional organization, as well as a means of control, both on the spot and by satellite. France would be prepared to convey information in its possession to regional transparency agencies. It would be in favor of transferring to these regional agencies the various means of observation, especially from space, that Europe or the UN may have at their disposal.
c) We must attempt to achieve, by national decisions and by negotiations, a balance of regional forces. Arms export policies should not impede this objective. Once this balance is achieved, its level should gradually be reduced by negotiations to fix the means of control.
d) We must enforce strict regional application of the categorical regimes set down for weapons of mass destruction. It is to this end that Resolution 687 of the United Nations Security Council concerning the cease-fire in the Gulf conflict stated, on France's initiative, that the specific constraints imposed on Iraq concerning nuclear, chemical, and biological weapons as well as ballistic missiles was in keeping with the idea of establishing a zone free of weapons of mass destruction and all missiles, as well as a general ban on chemical weapons. This objective must be pursued in other regions of the world.

The United Nations organization is now in a position to fully exercise the role entrusted to it by the Charter. France believes that it is therefore up to the Security Council to support and eventually to coordinate disarmament and nonproliferation policies. The Council should encourage the signing of categorical, regional, or multilateral agreements on disarmament and nonproliferation. It would issue general rules based on agreements passed and thus perform a function of worldwide vigilance.

This implies that the members of the Security Council, and above all its permanent members, must behave in an exemplary manner.

NOTES

1. Philippe Deslandes, "La réglementation française des contrôles à l'exportation à des fins de sécurité," in *Le contrôle des exportations de Haute Technologie vers les pays de l'Est,* edited by Bernard Chantebout and Bertrand Warusfel (Paris: Masson, 1988).

2. *Le Monde,* April 18, 1991.

3. *Le Monde,* October 30, 1991.

4. "France changes its tune on MTCR," *Mednews,* July 9, 1990, 1–2.

5. Ibid.

6. Aaron Karp, "Controlling Ballistic Missile Proliferation," *Survival,* November–December, 1991, 524.

7. Georges Laury, *Le Seuil Nucléaire* (Geneva: Editions Universitaires, 1991).

8. Marie-Hélène Labbé, *La Prolifération Nucléaire en 50 Questions* (Paris: Editions Jacques Bertoin, 1991).

9. Marie-Hélène Labbé, "Controlling East-West Trade in France," in *Controlling East-West Trade and Technology Transfer,* edited by Gary K. Bertsch (Durham, N.C.: Duke University Press, 1988).

10. Interviews conducted in Paris by the author.

11. *Le Monde,* November 23, 1990.

12. *Libération,* March 21, 1991.

13. *Le Monde,* March 23, 1991.

14. *Le Monde,* March 20, 1991.

15. "President Mitterand's Disarmament Plan," June 3, 1991.

16. Interview with French industrialists, November, 1992.

17. Interview with Hungarian leader, November, 1990.

18. U.S. Office of Technology Assessment, *Global Arms Trade* (Washington, D.C.: U.S. Office of Technology Assessment, 1991).

19. *Le Monde,* March 19, 1991.

20. *Le Monde,* July 2, 1991.

21. *Le Monde,* March 28, 1991.

22. *Le Monde,* December 11, 1991.

23. *Le Monde,* November 27, 1991.

24. Assessment made during a conference organized by the WEU Institute for Security Studies on "The Future of Arms Transfers," Paris, November, 19–20, 1991.

CHAPTER 10

The Technological Imperative: A Brazilian Perspective on Dual-Use Technologies

Clifford P. Graham

Introduction

Prompted by a number of recent political events, the Brazilian government is currently reformulating its policy regarding international attempts to control the flow of dual-use technologies and military hardware. The purpose of this chapter is to discuss the repercussions of this process. Specifically, I address proposed and completed changes to Brazilian policy; changes among the political actors who influence the policy-making process; and the changing perceptions of those actors concerning the relationship between international export controls and the future of democracy, economic growth, and military security for Brazil.

The Technological Imperative

For over twenty years, Brazilian political history was dominated by the armed forces, which staged a coup in 1964 and remained in power until 1985. Subsequently, a transition administration headed by a civilian president, José Sarney, was inaugurated in 1985 following his selection by the members of Brazil's electoral college. In 1989 Brazilians were given the opportunity to directly elect a president for the first time in twenty-nine years. In that election, Fernando Collor de Mello defeated his opponent and assumed the office of president in March, 1990.

At the time President Collor took office, Brazilian policy regarding dual-use technologies had remained essentially unchanged for twenty-six years. Since the 1964 coup, Brazil had avoided participation in any international control regime that could potentially limit the nation's access to dual-use technologies or military hardware. Similarly, Brazil had never implemented a comprehensive domestic policy for controlling the export of these same items. Simply stated, the reason the Brazilian government steadfastly pursued these policies was that it regarded efforts to control the international flow of dual-use technologies as contrary to Brazilian national interests.

National Security Doctrine: Defining the National Interest

During the years of military dictatorship, the Brazilian government defined the national interest in terms of two broadly based and mutually supporting objectives: promoting economic development and guaranteeing the nation's security. In turn, these objectives supported the long-standing aspiration of Brazilian military leaders for Brazil to become an internationally recognized power. This aspiration, and its supporting objectives, were rooted in traditional Brazilian geopolitical literature and in a political philosophy known as National Security Doctrine, which first emerged in Brazil in the 1950s.[1]

National Security Doctrine was developed and taught by the faculty of the Brazilian National War College, known in Portuguese as the Escola Superior de Guerra (ESG). Founded in Rio de Janeiro in 1949, the ESG was one of Brazil's premier educational institutions during the years of military rule (Selcher 1977; Stepan 1971). It served as a training ground for a large number of Brazilian civilians and military officers who later filled prominent executive and advisory positions within the Brazilian government and in the private sector.

At the ESG, students were exposed to an academic year of "lectures and seminars that attempted to determine the basic goals for Brazil, the obstacles to these goals, and specific policies to achieve them" (Stepan 1971, 178). With this background, graduates left the school with a shared understanding of national objectives and a common methodology for pursuing them. As a result, they became a relatively unified and influential force in shaping the efforts of the public and private sectors toward resolving Brazil's security and development problems.[2]

Philosophically, the underpinning to ESG's instruction was the basic premise of National Security Doctrine, which held that "security and development are linked by a relationship of mutual causality" (Selcher 1977, 13). Mutual causality referred to the fact that for the nation to be focused in its efforts to maximize development, Brazil's military leaders had to ensure that those efforts were not fragmented by any internal or external threats to the country's security.

Based on this concept of mutual causality, Brazilian military leaders saw their efforts to suppress the nation's guerrilla insurgency during the decade following the 1964 coup as critical to the process of creating conditions conducive to national development. Similarly, officers also saw a shift in focus by the military away from internal security threats and toward regional and global threats (such as being drawn into a conflict with Argentina, or one between the United States and the Soviet Union), beginning in the early

1970s, as a means of ensuring that the conditions essential to development could be maintained (Hilton 1987, 332).

While the ESG was responsible for developing and teaching national security doctrine, the government agency most closely associated with implementing the policies related to it was the National Security Council. Under the leadership of the Brazilian president, the National Security Council included the chiefs of staff of the army, navy, and air force; the chief of the armed forces general staff; all of the national cabinet ministers; and the chief of the National Intelligence Service (Selcher 1977, 14–15). The National Security Secretariat, responsible for the day-to-day operation of the National Security Council, was headed by a general officer, who also served as head of the Military Household. In turn, his subordinates who headed the council's subdirectorates were normally active duty colonels (Stepan 1988, 141).

While little is known about the actual operation of the National Security Council, it was charged with responsibility for planning, coordinating, and supervising all matters related to national security. These included the right to oversee any area considered essential to national security, establishing permanent national policy objectives, and approving the creation of national security-related industries. This last responsibility is of particular importance to this chapter because Brazil's development of dual-use technologies has been concentrated within the government agencies and private firms most closely associated with the nation's defense industries.

The Need for High Technology

The shift in perspective among Brazilian military leaders during the early 1970s, away from internal security threats and toward those of a regional and global nature, marked a watershed in the nation's drive to acquire high technologies in general, and dual-use technologies in particular. In an attempt to both bolster economic development and meet potential external security challenges, a wide range of initiatives designed to enhance the country's capacity to develop high technologies were implemented by successive Brazilian administrations. These initiatives were propelled by the desire of the nation's leaders to make Brazil more technologically independent, and more like the other great nations of the world.

Within Brazil, concern with the country's technological independence emerged in the early 1970s when research into the innovative capabilities of Brazilian firms revealed that a majority of them depended on foreign sources for critical technologies (Biato, Guimarães, and Figueirdo 1971 and 1973).[3] At the same time, academic literature in Western countries was documenting the negative implications of this form of technological dependence for the long-term development prospects of Third World countries (Stewart 1978, 123–33). The solution to this form of dependence proposed by many Western sources was that countries like Brazil promote indigenous research and development programs capable of generating "appropriate technologies" (Fransman and King 1984, 81–94). To Brazilian military officers aspiring to lead their country to greatness, the most "appropriate technologies" were often the high technologies of the West, which frequently had dual-use applications.

Several reasons can be cited for the special emphasis Brazilian leadership subsequently placed on developing domestic high technologies for Brazil. In terms of economic development, research among the developed countries throughout the 1970s pointed to the fact that the agglomeration of technical and professional workers in the high-technology sector provided a substantial stimulus to regional economic growth (Malecki 1981a, 1981b, and 1984; Nelson 1984; Rushing and Brown 1987; Van Der Knaap and Wever 1987).[4] This growth came in the form of new jobs and the creation of new firms through spin-off. Further, these studies suggested that countries like Brazil would continue to have difficulty competing in the international economy if they failed to enter the product life cycle at its earliest stages (Vernon 1966).[5]

Another reason for the interest of Brazil's leadership in high technology was the nature of the security threat that emerged during the early 1970s. Of particular concern to the Brazilian military was the intensifying verbal warfare between Brazil and and its major antagonist, Argentina. The Argentines held a significant lead over the Brazilians in the nuclear field, a gap that could only be bridged if the Brazilians dedicated considerable resources of their own to this high-technology sector (Gorman 1979; Hilton 1985).

Of similar concern to Brazilian military planners was the speed at which they perceived technological innovation to be changing the modern battlefield (Hilton 1987, 336–38). Studies of the Vietnam and Yom Kippur Wars convinced the Brazilians that the increasing sophistication of weapons systems had become a major obstacle to the long-term viability of their own armed forces. This conclusion was later reinforced by the British defeat of Argentina in the 1982 Falklands War, which the Brazilians attributed to Argentine technological inferiority. To the Brazilians, the most stunning aspect of this defeat was that they considered Argentine military technology to be superior to their own.

This concern with Brazil's ability to successfully counter technologically superior external threats came at the same time the Brazilian military was becoming sensitized to the problems of being dependent on the United States for military hardware. Beginning in 1952, Brazil had been a recipient of American weapons through the U.S. Military Aid Program. During the Vietnam War, however, restrictions on the transfer of military hardware to

Brazil made the Brazilian military aware of the vulnerability of that supply. Further, by the early 1970s, the Brazilians began to recognize that the weapons they did receive were of a vintage that only exacerbated their problems with technologically obsolete systems.

These economic and security concerns, which served as incentives for promoting high-technology development in Brazil, were reinforced by a national leadership strongly committed to the goal of technological independence. The attitude of the former head of Brazil's satellite development program, Aydamo Carlial, typified their conviction when he stated, "We don't want to buy a black box. We want to know how it works" (Rao 1985, 29). Within key economic sectors, leaders like Carlial—whom Adler (1988) has referred to as "antidependency guerrillas"—were convinced that not only could Brazil become technologically independent but also that high-technology programs were contributing to economic development by creating the jobs and spin-off observed in the West. Representative of this belief were comments made by Brigadier General Hugo de Oliveira Piva, former head of Brazil's space launch program:

> Advanced technology programs can pull the rest [of the economy] behind them. For developing countries, this is the way to catch up. The rocket research and development program . . . has already brought great improvements to the country's wealth. A number of sectors have benefited from products and services generated by space activity, and they are quite significant in terms of Brazil's economy and development. (Batista 1984, 37; Condom 1986, 90)

Efforts to Promote High-Technology Development

Given the concern of Brazil's leadership with the country's overall technological dependence, national efforts to develop high technologies became one component of a broader based effort to promote economic development through improvement of the country's technological capabilities. This effort began in the late 1960s when scientific and technological development became a stated national policy objective. In support of that objective, a series of Basic Science and Technology Plans was implemented beginning in 1973 (Brigagão 1984, 95–111). Under these plans, federal funds made available through the National Fund for Scientific and Technological Development were invested in the research and development programs of various government agencies. Particularly important were the military programs discussed below. These plans also attempted to stimulate the development of local technological capabilities by subsidizing the research and development efforts of Brazilian firms and by requiring the federal government to purchase high-technology products from Brazilian manufacturers (Dahlman 1984, 318; Marton 1986, 211–13).

Within this overall policy framework, Brazil's military leaders specifically directed national efforts toward mastering several key high technologies. Some of the most successful of these efforts, in terms of their civilian applications, took place within the aerospace and informatics (computer and data processing) sectors. Through investment in a state-owned aircraft manufacturer known as EMBRAER, Brazil was able to become the sixth largest manufacturer of airplanes in the noncommunist world by 1987 (Hudson 1983; Ramamurti 1987). In a similar manner, Brazil established a microcomputer industry in the late 1970s that was able to meet the burgeoning domestic demand for microcomputers and peripherals that surfaced during late 1970s and early 1980s (Adler 1988; Frischtak 1987).

The Brazilian military targeted several other key high technologies for development, for both their military and civilian applications. In particular, a concerted effort was made to master nuclear and space-related technologies that were considered essential to development and to achieving great power status. As the minister of aeronautics, Octávio Moreira Lima, was once quoted as saying, "any nation that wants to be considered developed must fully master three specific areas: informatics, space and nuclear" (Moreira 1986).

Brazil's attempt to acquire nuclear technologies proceeded along two distinct paths. Within the civilian sector, the Brazilian program centered around a 1975 agreement between Brazil and West Germany. Under the agreement, Brazil was to "purchase the technology to build eight pressurized water reactors" from Germany over a fifteen-year period (Britto de Castro et al. 1989). A conglomerate of German nuclear firms, led by the Siemans affiliate Kraftwerk Union, was to provide the technology and components the Brazilians could not develop on their own as construction on each reactor proceeded. In addition to the reactors, the agreement also called for the Germans to provide Brazil with the know-how to enrich and reprocess uranium, giving them a self-sufficient program and mastery of the nuclear fuel cycle. Brazil further agreed that facilities constructed under this agreement would be subject to inspection by the IAEA.

Within two years after the Brazilian government began working with West Germany on nuclear technology, the Brazilian military implemented a secret nuclear development program not subject to IAEA scrutiny. Based at the Institute for Energy and Nuclear Research (INPEN) near the State University of São Paulo, this parallel program was also designed to master the nuclear fuel cycle. Its existence was only rumored until 1987, when President Sarney officially acknowledged it by announcing that gas centrifuges operating at the INPEN facility had successfully enriched uranium fuel to 1.2

percent uranium 235 (Albright 1989, 18–19; Britto de Castro et al. 1989, 23–24). One year later this program was expanded when Brazil inaugurated a new, more sophisticated uranium enrichment facility known as Aramar, in Iperó, São Paulo.

In a manner similar to the Brazilian nuclear program, the research efforts associated with Brazil's space program were also divided into civilian and military components (Graham 1991). The two principal organizations within this effort were the Institute for Space Research (INPE) and the Institute for Space Activities (IAE). Jointly, INPE and IAE held responsibility for the Complete Brazilian Space Mission, an ambitious program for putting a series of Brazilian manufactured satellites in orbit during the early 1990s.[6] Under the program, the civilian-run organization INPE was responsible for the design and construction of the satellites, while IAE, a division within the Air Force's Center for Aerospace Technology (CTA), was responsible for developing the rocket that would carry the satellites into space.

Concurrent with Brazil's development of nuclear and space technologies, the national government also gave special attention to developing another industrial sector generally regarded as high technology: defense manufacturing. Already sensitized to the vulnerability of their supply of U.S. weapons and of their technological simplicity, the Brazilians set out to develop a domestic defense industry suited to their long-term aspirations. Again Brazilian leaders saw the effort as a vehicle for relieving technological dependence. As Minister of the Army Walter Pires described it, the industry would help "liberate the country from an unacceptable dependence" in the area of technology ("Imbel Poderá Privatizar Tecnologia Bélica" 1982).

Although a variety of small arms manufacturers emerged in Brazil during the 1970s, the main focus of the country's efforts to develop a domestic defense industry centered around three companies: EMBRAER, ENGESA, and AVIBRAS.[7] All three of these companies initially established a niche in the international market by exporting technologically simple products to third world countries.[8] As time progressed, the technological sophistication of these products dramatically improved. One of these companies, EMBRAER, which began as a manufacturer of civilian aircraft, offered a line of light military planes beginning in the late 1970s. ENGESA, which produced a line of wheeled armored vehicles, became one of Brazil's major generators of export earnings during the late 1970s and early 1980s (Graham 1990). Similarly, AVIBRAS became a major exporter of surface-to-surface rockets, which it supplied primarily to the Iraqis during the Iran-Iraq War.

To support development of these dual-use high technologies, the Brazilian government heavily invested in military-run research and development centers that provided a scientific underpinning to the projects identified above. The most important among these were the Air Force's CTA, located in São José dos Campos, São Paulo, and the Army Technological Center (CETEX), located in Guaratiba, Rio de Janeiro (Brigagão 1984, 59–66). Of comparatively less importance was the Naval Institute for Research.

The Center for Aerospace Technology was, and still remains, Brazil's premier technological institution with responsibility for implementing education and research and development programs that support national aerospace policy objectives. In addition to the IAE discussed above, CTA also houses an Aeronautical Technology Institute, responsible for graduate-level engineering programs; a Research and Development Institute (IPD), responsible for developing aeronautical products and manufacturing processes; an Institute for Advanced Studies, responsible for applied research in low-energy nuclear physics, nuclear energy, lasers and radiation-substance interaction, and informatics; and an Institute for Industrial Coordination and Cooperation (IFI), responsible for linking the technologies developed within CTA with potential Brazilian manufacturers ("Centro Tecnico Aeroespacial" n.d.).

CETEX is subdivided into the Development and Research Institute and the Institute for Special Projects. Together with the Military Engineering Institute and the Operational Evaluation Center (a rocket test facility in Restinga da Marambaia near Rio de Janeiro), CETEX supports the Army Science and Technology Secretariat, which has responsibility for "evaluating, preparing and training human resources, and for carrying out research and development in the fields of doctrine, personnel and military materiel" (Motta 1990a).

Both CTA and CETEX were instrumental in encouraging Brazilian industry to participate in the production of components and equipment for the government's various high-technology programs, largely through the transfer of important technologies directly from the centers to Brazilian industry. For example, CTA's IFI was responsible for transferal to the Companhia Vale do Rio Doce and to another company, Electrometal, the production technology for metallic titanium and titanium alloys (Degenar Drumond 1987, 10). CTA also designed and developed technologies for many of the aircraft manufactured by EMBRAER and trained a majority of the firm's engineers (Gouvea Neto 1991, 93; Ramamurti 1987, 184–85). Similarly, the Army's Science and Technology Secretary, General Romero Lepesqueur, noted that at CETEX,

> We do not manufacture these [military] items, we only develop and evaluate them. The Army may even use our projects in IMBEL [the Brazilian War Material Company] products, but our policy is to pass our technology to private companies. (Motta 1990b)

Policy Implications of High-Technology Development

The intense interest of the Brazilian government in developing domestic sources for dual-use high technologies directly shaped the country's policies regarding international efforts to control their flow prior to President Collor's election. These technologies came to represent the barriers that Brazil's leaders felt the country had to overcome to fulfill the dual objectives of security and development defined by National Security Doctrine. Consequently, these leaders viewed any proposal that might limit Brazil's access to these technologies as an attempt by the developed world to thwart Brazil's progress toward great-power status.

During the pre-Collor years, Brazilians were able to identify their nuclear and space programs as just two examples of how the developed world kept them isolated from technologies they considered essential to development. In the first case, Brazil's 1975 nuclear technology agreement with Germany became a technical and financial failure shortly after it was signed. Brazilians placed a large portion of the blame for this failure on objections raised by the United States to Germany's proliferation of enrichment technologies. Likewise, Brazil experienced a dramatic decline in U.S. support for its domestic space program following the 1987 implementation of the MTCR.[9] In fact, the United States stopped providing Brazil with equipment it had supplied prior to the MTCR and temporarily impounded components Brazil had previously purchased from American manufacturers when they were returned to the United States for repairs.[10]

In contrast to these problems, the Brazilians were able to point to the success of their defense industry as an example of the benefits they obtained under conditions where the control of technology into and out of the country was relatively unrestricted. Of particular note was the industry's export success during the late 1970s and early 1980s, when Brazil needed the income to help balance its trade deficit with the Organization of Petroleum Exporting Countries. In fact, between 1980 and 1984, export sales of Brazilian armaments exceeded $200 million annually and reached as high as $298 million in 1983 (Ohlson and Sköns 1987).

The successful development of a domestic arms industry in Brazil and the subsequent success of the industry's exports were based on a document referred to as the "Política Nacional de Exportação de Material de Emprego Militar" ("Survival Depends on Exports" 1983). Approved by President Ernesto Giesel in 1974, this document created a policy framework that linked the establishment of an export-oriented arms industry to the objectives of National Security Doctrine. The policy had a number of specific objectives that included (1) strengthening Brazil's position in international affairs, (2) opening new markets to Brazilian arms manufacturers so they could achieve economies of scale, (3) strengthening the country's military power, and (4) improving the country's balance of payments by decreasing imports of military hardware and increasing exports of Brazilian manufactured military equipment.

Successful formation of Brazil's defense industry was built on the access Brazilians were able to gain to internationally available defense technologies. To acquire the technologies, Brazil created the Empresa Brasileira de Material Bélico [the Brazilian War Material Company (IMBEL)] in 1975 (Brigagão 1984). IMBEL encouraged foreign defense contractors to form joint ventures with Brazilian partners. In seeking these partners, the Brazilians made explicit the terms under which contractors might form a partnership. For any investment proposal to be approved, the Brazilian partner would have to have majority control, the transfer of technology would have to be completed without the payment of royalties, and there could be no obligation on the part of the government to buy anything for the Brazilian armed forces. Despite these restrictions, over sixty representatives of European defense manufacturers visited Brazil in 1974 and 1975 looking for investment opportunities (Rother 1978).

A significant key to the export success of the Brazilian defense industry was the unencumbered access the federal government gave it to foreign markets. Aware that Brazil would be unable to maintain a viable arms industry based on the domestic market alone, the military government encouraged the sale of nationally manufactured weapons overseas. As President João Figueiredo was quoted as saying in 1982, "We sell to whomever wants to buy" (Sieniawski 1982). The only exceptions to this policy ever disclosed were South Africa, because of its racial policies, and Cuba, due to its link with revolutionary activity in Latin America (House 1984).

To further help facilitate these sales, Brazil's government implemented an export approval process that treated weapons exports as largely commercial transactions between buyers and sellers. Brazilian domestic arms manufacturers interested in negotiating with a foreign client were simply required to obtain preliminary approval from the Brazilian government prior to sending the client a proposal. This preliminary approval remained valid for six months and had to be revalidated prior to the initiation of any final negotiations (Goodwin 1986). Once a sale was approved, however, it was regarded as a commercial transaction in which the Brazilian government did not interfere. For that reason, the Brazilian government never required any recipient government to provide an end-use certificate.

The Brazilian government also assisted domestic arms manufacturers in making their enterprises competitive through the implementation of a supportive export policy beginning in 1974. Under this policy, firms exporting defense products were exempted from taxes on their export earnings and on insurance commissions related to services abroad (Evans 1986). The Brazilian government also became involved in providing preexport financing and generous credit terms to customer nations. As an added incentive, barter—particularly oil—was accepted in payment for the purchase of Brazilian arms (Onis 1976).

The success of Brazil's defense industry, compared with the problems the country experienced with nuclear and space technologies, goes a long way in explaining why the Brazilian government stood firmly against the major international efforts to control the spread of dual-use technologies prior to 1990. Brazil never signed the 1968 NPT, denying the IAEA the right to inspect any of the country's parallel nuclear facilities. Despite having signed the 1967 Treaty of Tlateloco, which created a nuclear weapons–free zone in Latin America, Brazil never put the treaty in effect. Further, Brazil never participated in any of the multilateral export control organizations that are the focus of this book, such as the MTCR or the AG.

Redefining the Technological Imperative

The discussion of Brazil's quest for technological independence presented to this point provides a part of the background necessary for understanding the forces that are currently shaping Brazilian dual-use technology policy. The other part of that background comes from understanding a second set of forces that have played an increasingly important role in policy-making since 1990. These forces emerged as a product of three recent political events: the country's transition to democracy, the election of Fernando Collor de Mello as president, and the Persian Gulf War. In turn, these events served as catalysts for reexamining, and in some cases changing, Brazilian policy.

The Transition to Democracy

Brazil's final transition from a military dictatorship to a democracy, which coincided with the 1989 presidential election, created new opportunities for a wide range of organizations to influence policy-making. Whereas the military had largely ignored these organizations, following the election they became legitimate players within the democratic process. In that capacity, they were able to draw attention to several weaknesses in Brazil's dual-use technology programs. This attention played an instrumental role in prompting some of the reforms the Collor administration made discussed below.

One organization that took advantage of this new opportunity was the Brazilian Physics Association (SBF), which during the summer of 1990 forwarded an advisory report to the speaker of Congress, Senator Nelson Carneiro. Under the leadership of Brazilian physicists Luiz Pinguelli Rosa, Odair Dias Goncalves, and Fernando Souza Barros, the SBF noted that the Brazilian Congress had failed to assume its supervisory responsibilities over the military's parallel nuclear program, which had been called for under Brazil's 1988 constitution. Further, the SBF's report noted the organization's concern with the Navy's nuclear enrichment program, which appeared to be leading toward the production of a nuclear bomb ("Study Warns of Near Capability to Make Bomb" 1990).

Concerns the SBF brought to the surface were supported by a similar report to Congress submitted by the Brazilian Society for the Advancement of Science (SPBC), which requested the "formation of a committee of technicians, subordinate to congress and supervised by independent scientists, to continuously oversee the unregulated nuclear installations" ("Previous Plans for Nuclear Bomb Discussed" 1990, 24). Led by physicist Ennio Candotti, the SPBC report further requested that Congress respond to a previous SPBC inquiry regarding a steel-lined concrete borehole discovered in the Serra do Cachimbo region of southern Para State (Sanches 1990). SPBC members suspected the borehole, which was first reported in the Brazilian press in 1986, was being prepared for testing a nuclear explosion.[11]

In their report, SPBC leaders also questioned why administrative responsibility for Brazil's National Nuclear Energy Commission (CNEN, responsible for technical supervision and inspection of Brazil's parallel and civilian nuclear facilities) had remained with the Secretariat for Strategic Affairs (SAE)—the functional descendent of the National Security Council—following President Collor's assumption of office. In drawing attention to the question of administrative responsibility, the report noted that under SAE supervision, "the military-strategic character of control over nuclear energy is being retained" (Sanches 1990). As an alternative, the physicists recommended that complete supervisory responsibility for CNEN be transferred to the Ministry for Science and Technology.

Responding in part to this prompting from the Brazilian scientific community, the Brazilian Congress moved to assume its supervisory responsibilities over the country's parallel nuclear program in the fall of 1990. This process began when the Congressional Investigative Committee on Nuclear Energy held hearings on the program beginning in October of that year. As a part of those hearings, deputies serving on the committee were permitted for the first time to tour the navy's Aramar nuclear facility. It was also through these hearings that investigators first learned that the enriched uranium used by the navy to fuel its experimental nuclear reactor was obtained from the PRC in 1984, through a plan developed by the National Security Council ("Deputies Learn Source of Enriched Uranium" 1990).

The Election of President Collor

While Brazil's transition to democracy created a framework within which Brazilian organizations outside the military could begin playing a role in developing the country's dual-use technology policy, the single most important event associated with changing the direction of that policy was the election of President Ferdnando Collor de Mello. Collor came to office prepared to reject many of the assumptions on which the previous military administrations' policies had been based. Once in office, he implemented a number of initiatives designed to assert civilian control over Brazil's dual-use technology programs while diffusing international concern with the programs' ultimate objectives.

One of President Collor's first initiatives in this regard was to remove military officers from those centers of decision making within the government not directly associated with defense. This action represented a significant change in the character of the Brazilian government, which under previous administrations had relied on military officers to fill a variety of important government posts. Following this action, Collor drastically reduced both the level of staffing and the scope of responsibility of both the National Information Service and the National Security Council.[12] Formerly two of the most powerful organizations within the Brazilian government, both were redesignated by Collor as subdirectorates within the newly created SAE, and placed under the direction of a civilian, businessman Pedro Paulo Leoni Ramos (Costa 1990).

Undoubtedly President Collor's most important initiative regarding Brazil's dual-use technology programs was ordering the armed forces to halt the Solimões project, a previously classified program directed toward the development of a Brazilian nuclear bomb. The existence of this project had been rumored for years, although until President Collor took office, the Brazilian government never admitted it publicly. The president learned of it when he read a transition document prepared by the outgoing Sarney administration in early 1989 (Brooke 1990). This document described four independent efforts to develop a nuclear bomb, each being carried out by a different branch of the armed forces. As a part of the program, the borehole at Serra Cachimbo was intended to be the test site for the explosion.

After learning of Solimões, Collor called the ministers of the army, navy, and air force together and told them he intended to stop the project. On September 17, 1990, the Brazilian press announced that the borehole at Cachimbo had been dug for the purpose of testing a nuclear device and that President Collor had ordered it closed. The following day the president travelled to Cachimbo and symbolically threw the first shovelful of concrete into the hole while the press and the three military ministers stood watching.

Six days later Collor traveled to New York and gave a speech to the General Assembly of the United Nations in which he stated that, "Brazil today rejects the idea of any test that implies nuclear explosions, even for peaceful ends" (Brooke 1990, A1).

In conjunction with these efforts to bring the Brazilian parallel nuclear program under civilian control, President Collor transferred the policy-making responsibilities for all the nation's nuclear programs to the Ministry of Science and Technology in September, 1990. This ministry was headed by José Goldemberg, a former president of the Brazilian Physics Society and longtime critic of the secrecy surrounding Brazil's parallel nuclear program. Following President Collor's speech in New York, Goldemberg announced that "transparency" would be the new policy covering Brazil's parallel and civilian nuclear programs and that he would open the facilities to visits by reporters, scientists, and legislators (Brooke 1990).

Reacting to Goldemberg's policy of transparency, a wave of reports related to Brazil's parallel nuclear program began appearing in the press a few days before and for several weeks after President Collor's decision to close Cachimbo. These reports publicly detailed for for the first time the army's efforts to develop a modulated high-temperature gas-graphic reactor, an air force project to enrich uranium using lasers, and the navy's program to develop a nuclear submarine propulsion plant based on the ultracentrifuge method (Eleuterio 1990; Eustaquio de Freitas 1990; Motta 1990b). Shortly thereafter, the Congressional Investigative Committee on Nuclear Energy began its hearings into the parallel nuclear program. These hearings were followed by the on-site inspection of the navy's Aramar facility by members of the committee and the Brazilian press described above (Eleuterio 1990; Eustaquio de Freitas 1990; Motta 1990b).

President Collor's promise to the United Nations that Brazil would not develop nuclear weapons was followed by a historic meeting between himself and Argentine President Carlos Saul Menem on November 28, 1990. At the Brazilian border town of Foz do Iguaçu, the two presidents signed an agreement in which their two countries renounced the manufacture and testing of nuclear weapons and agreed to comply with the provisions of the Treaty of Tlatelolco. The agreement further stipulated that Argentina and Brazil would call on the IAEA to help establish a independent bilateral organization empowered to inspect the nuclear facilities of both countries. Once established, this organization would then negotiate with the IAEA to permit IAEA inspectors to enter Brazilian and Argentine nuclear facilities (Albright 1990; Christian 1990).

The Persian Gulf War

President Collor's efforts to redirect Brazilian dual-use technology policy during the fall of 1990 were not strictly the product of his initiative or the country's transition to democracy. Equally important to the process were international pressures brought to bear on the Brazilian government following the Iraqi invasion of Kuwait, which had occurred that August. The invasion immediately brought to light Brazil's lack of a coherent technology control policy as an issue within the international community. In particular, concern focused on retired Brazilian Air Force Major General Hugo de Oliveira Piva, whose company, HOP Industries (the name being derived from Piva's initials), had employees in Iraq at the time of the invasion working as consultants for the Iraqi missile program.

The presence of HOP Industries in Iraq generated considerable concern among members of the alliance that had been pulled together by the United States against Saddam Hussain. This concern was based on General Piva's long and close association with the Brazilian space program and the uncertainty of the type of work his company was performing. As the director of CTA's IAE in the early 1980s, Piva had supervised the development and testing of the SONDA III, a two-stage rocket capable of carrying a fifty-kilogram payload to an altitude of 500 kilometers. Later, as CTA's commander, he was responsible for the development and testing of the SONDA III's successor, the SONDA IV, and the initial development of the four-stage VLS, a rocket designed to put a Brazilian-manufactured satellite in space. Piva had also developed contacts with the PRC while at CTA, having negotiated with the Chinese for rocket technologies the Brazilians needed for the VLS.

In addition to his experience with CTA, General Piva had worked for a Brazilian firm known as Orbita following his retirement from the Air Force in 1987. Orbita had been established to manufacture rockets and missiles designed to meet the needs of the Brazilian space program and the country's defense manufacturers. During Piva's tenure with Orbita, the company had tried negotiating with Libya for a financing package to get its line of medium-range missiles started. It was also during Piva's tenure as Orbita's chairman in 1987 that he traveled to Iraq and offered the Iraqis a chance to purchase the company's heat-seeking Piranha air-to-air missile (Godoy 1990; Julio 1991). The Brazilian government had assigned Orbita responsibility for the production of the Piranha, which had been designed and developed by CTA, after controlling interest in the Brazilian firm designated to manufacture it, D.F. Vasconcellos, was sold to a foreign company.

The Iraqis declined Piva's offer of the Piranha, indicating instead their preference for a binational cooperative development plan for a similar missile. Piva returned to Brazil and unsuccessfully attempted to market this alternative with the government and other Orbita executives. After they turned him down, and following an argument with the company's executive vice president, Piva left Orbita and established HOP Industries, a consulting firm for high-technology projects in the space, aeronautics, and material systems technology fields. At the helm of HOP, Piva resurfaced the idea of joint participation in a missile development program with the Iraqis. This time he suggested sending a team of Brazilian technicians to Iraq to serve as consultants to the Iraqi missile program, a suggestion that the Iraqis accepted. Piva subsequently hired twenty-three Brazilian engineers, predominantly from his old employers CTA and Orbita, and sent them to work on Iraqi's Al-Taw' Han missile project beginning in September, 1989 (Godoy 1990).

News that these engineers were working in Iraq began appearing in the Brazilian press in the spring of 1990, but the issue was never seriously scrutinized until the fall of that year following the Iraqi invasion of Kuwait. That scrutiny was triggered when the Brazilian government began negotiating with the Iraqis for the release of a group of Brazilian hostages that included the twenty-three engineers. As negotiations for the hostages proceeded, it became clear that Piva had never received official permission from the Brazilian government to proceed with his project and that his employees had never registered with the Brazilian Embassy as being employed in Iraq. Further, it became apparent that much of the technology that Piva's company was passing to the Iraqis had been developed at CTA at the expense of the Brazilian government, by a group of engineers that had been trained at the expense of Brazilian taxpayers.

The HOP Industries incident could not have come at a more awkward time for the Collor Administration. On the one hand, the president was attempting to accommodate international concern with Brazil's nuclear program while at the same time officially supporting the United Nations–imposed embargo of Iraq. On the other hand, his efforts were being undermined by a renegade Air Force officer who was freely passing sensitive Brazilian technologies to the Iraqis, without the Brazilian government receiving payment or granting its approval. Even more embarrassing to the president was that under Brazilian law, General Piva's actions were perfectly legal. The Brazilian government had no recourse in the matter, other than to appeal to the general's patriotism in supporting the stance taken by his government against Iraq.

The international pressure generated by the presence of HOP Industries in Iraq played a major role in strengthening President Collor's resolve to revamp the country's nuclear program and begin negotiations with Argentina during the fall of 1990. These events also served as a catalyst for his administration to initiate a reexamination of Brazil's export control policies regarding technology and weapons. As a result, the president sent a bill to Congress in February, 1991, proposing government control over the export of dual-use services by Brazilian citizens and private companies (Gasparini-Alves 1992, 22). Congress subsequently approved this bill, known as the Piva Law, closing the legal loophole the general had exploited.

Despite the adoption of the Piva Law, Brazilian policy relative to the government's control over sensitive technologies remained a far cry from the comprehensive legislation the Brazilian government was being pressured to adopt by countries like the United States. In particular, the Americans wanted to see the Brazilians pass legislation mirroring the COCOM restrictions placed over the transfer of technology to Eastern Europe. In response to this pressure, President Collor introduced a new technology control bill in the Brazilian legislature in February, 1992 (Dispoe Sobreas Operaçoes 1992). In its draft form, the bill proposed to "regulate import and export operations regarding items of direct military use, of dual-use, and of nuclear-related use." These items would be "defined on import and export lists, to be regularly updated and published in the Union Federal Register." Further, an "International Import Certificate" would certify that the importer would not export a controlled item without prior governmental authorization.

The Loss of Momentum

While some positive initiatives were taken to control Brazilian dual-use technology during the initial years of the Collor Administration, that progress suffered a reversal when charges of corruption surfaced against the president in the spring of 1992. Within a short period, the real possibility of his impeachment pushed virtually every foreign policy issue to the background of President Collor's agenda. This change in priorities triggered a dramatic decline in the sense of urgency within his administration to pursue changes to Brazilian dual-use technology policy. That sense of urgency suffered an even more dramatic blow in the late summer of 1992 when Congress initiated impeachment proceedings against the president and his vice president, Itamar Franco, was called on to assume the duties of interim president. Since then, President Franco has sent what can be considered, at best, mixed signals regarding the future direction of Brazilian dual-use technology policy.

From one perspective, President Franco has not reversed any of the dual-use technology decisions President Collor made. Among the last of these was to contract with the American firm, U.S. Orbital, to launch Brazil's first nationally manufactured satellite ("Contract Signed for Launching Satellite" 1992). In part, this decision was probably made to help deflect international scrutiny of Brazil's space launch program, although it appears unlikely that the Brazilians would have been able to handle the launch themselves. President Franco has so far also elected not to interfere with a proposal made while President Collor was in office to move the Brazilian space agency from under the supervision of the Armed Forces General Staff to the SAE (Tachinardi 1991). As of this writing, this idea remains a proposal, a form in which it may remain indefinitely.

From a different perspective, at least during the first few weeks of his presidency, Franco has not shown any enthusiasm for carrying forward the dual-use technology initiatives taken by his predecessor. In fact, his appointment of Admiral Mario Cesar Flores as the head of the SAE appears to be a reversal. Flores played an instrumental role in the navy's parallel nuclear program and remains a staunch proponent for a Brazilian-designed and -manufactured nuclear powered submarine (Motta and Monteiro 1992). Flores's appointment may signal a reemerging sense of nationalism in Brazil and a return to some of the military-based pre-Collor objectives of the country's dual-use technology policy.

Conclusion

Unfortunately, international observers of dual-use technology policy in Brazil will have to wait and see. Beyond the nuclear agreement with Argentina, little has changed in terms of actual policy in Brazil, and that occurred in 1990. The legislation introduced in Congress in February, 1992, has yet to be acted on. For at least the short term, the government of the new president will continue struggling to establish itself, while the Brazilian Congress grappled with the issue of redrafting the constitution during 1993. A major concern for Congress will be deciding whether Brazil should abandon its presidential form of democracy in favor of a parliamentary system. Given the priority of this issue and the transitional nature of the current presidency, further changes in dual-use technology policy can be expected to be few and slow in coming.

Clearly the introduction of democracy has had profound implications for policymakers concerned with the control of dual-use technologies and military hardware in Brazil. A curb on the military's influence over the country's nuclear development program and the reexamination of national policies regarding the control of sensitive technologies both represent actions that were taken only after a democratically elected government came to power. Participation in the policy-making process by the electorate, the Congress, the president, and the press have all helped to make that process one of greater accountability and openness. In turn, Brazilian leaders have shown a greater sensitivity to international concerns with the proliferation of weapons and dangerous technologies. Generally speaking, this sensitivity should draw Brazil closer to participation in the international regimes designed to control the flow of these items.

A democratic form of government, however, did not change two of the most fundamental objectives that have driven Brazilian policy since the end of World War II: the ambition of becoming an internationally recognized power and the accompanying need for economic development. While a shift in emphasis between these two objectives has followed Brazilian democratization, in particular away from the military components of international power and toward those of an economic nature, Brazil's destiny as a world leader remains a reoccurring theme among Brazilian government officials. José Francisco Rezek, foreign minister under President Collor, provides just one example of the conviction with which Brazilians believe in this fate. In a 1990 interview, Minister Rezek spoke of his ambitions to see Brazil seated at the table of the First World and to secure for itself a permanent seat on the UN Security Council (Fernandes 1990; "Rezek Wants UNSC Permanent Member Status" 1991). The stance taken by Flores, the new secretary for Strategic Affairs, regarding the construction of a Brazilian nuclear submarine appears to reinforce Rezek's position.

Of course to become an internationally recognized power and to protect the conditions under which a democracy can flourish, the Brazilian government must press ahead with its plans to promote development. Inherent in these plans will be the need to acquire and assimilate technology, especially contemporary high technology. Brazilians have never wavered from their belief in the central role technology will play in furthering their development. President Collor has noted, "The challenges of a worldwide economy are intensified in a system in which science and technology are the basic ingredients of progress" ("President Collor's Speech to the Armed Forces" 1990). Echoing the tone of the president's message, Foreign Minister Rezek has said, "We are going to have high-technology as no other country" ("Rezek Wants UNSC Permanent Member Status" 1991).

In the process of pursuing high technology, Brazilians will invariably seek to acquire some that have potentially dangerous, dual use applications. Brazil retains many high-technology industrial sectors such as informatics, aviation, defense, and space, which are built around such technologies. The country's leaders will expect these same industries to be at the leading edge of economic development. That the technologies they need to assume such a leadership role are potentially dangerous will not prevent Brazilian firms from developing a commercial interest in obtaining them. Nor will the Brazilian government stand in their way. President Collor made it clear that he believed the current international distribution of high technology is inequitable. In a commencement speech to group of graduating Brazilian diplomats, he noted,

> We have heard that our access to those special instruments of highly developed technology, which would be used to confront our structural flaws, as well as opportunities for fruitful cooperation between governments, was conditioned on a good-behavior certificate imposed by a small clique of countries who took it upon themselves to play the role of supreme judges of international ethics. We are tired of promises of being a country of the future. National problems demand urgent solutions. ("Collor Decries Lack of Access to Technology" 1990)

So far, there is no indication President Franco feels any different regarding this subject.

Given this need for urgent solutions, international observers can expect that Brazil will continue to seek dual-use high technologies. As the search for these technologies unfolds, the level of concern it generates among those same observers will be predicated, in part, on the direction Brazil takes with regard to the programs discussed in this chapter. Two that will continue to attract special interest are the navy's uranium enrichment project at Aramar and CTA's development of a satellite launch vehicle. As long as the potential exists for these two programs to be combined and subsequently generate a wave of regional or even global destabilization, they will continue to attract intense international scrutiny.

Even more important to the concern of international observers will be whether or not Brazil becomes a signatory to the international control regimes addressed by this study and whether the country implements a comprehensive set of internal technology control measures. The incident with General Piva clearly demonstrated that Brazil has a legitimate stake in protecting its investment in technology and hence for controlling its export. Unfortunately, Brazilians do not see that same form of legitimacy in other control regimes such as the NPT. Reflecting the perspective of most Brazilians, Minister Goldemberg said, "The treaty is regarded, rightly or wrongly, as a division of the world into the haves and the have-nots. Brazil does not want to be in the position of a frozen situation" (Wines 1990).

The challenge then, is for the international community to demonstrate to the Brazilians that international control regimes are in fact in their best interest. This can be accomplished, at least in part, by linking the transfer of dual-use technologies from the West to Brazil to Brazilian participation in these regimes. Of course this technique has its own set of accompanying problems, not the least of which is that linkage does not always work.

Ultimately, the best approach to solving the problem will be to convince the Brazilians that inherent in the status of a great power, which is a role they are seeking to live up to, is the responsibility to comply with the obligations embodied in the treaties, for the good of the entire community of nations.

NOTES

The views expressed here are entirely the author's. This chapter does not reflect the official views of the Department of the Army, the Department of Defense, or any other U.S. Government Agency. The author would like to think Mr. Lee Peters, U.S. Department of State, and Professor Scott Tollefson, Naval Postgraduate School, for their thoughtful comments regarding his preparation of this chapter.

1. Brazilian geopolitical ideas are strongly reflected in National Security Doctrine. For examples of the geopolitical writings of one of ESG's most influential strategic thinkers, see Couto e Silva (1955 and 1967). An excellent, concise overview of the evolution of Brazilian geopolitical literature can be found in Child 1984.

2. For a discussion of the long-term impact of National Security Doctrine on Brazilian policy-making, see Stepan 1988, 46–48.

3. "Technological dependence arises where the *major source* of a country's technology comes from abroad" (Stewart 1978, 116). See Erber (1981) for a thorough examination of the evolution of technology-related research and policy in Brazil through the late 1970s.

4. An extensive overview of the literature associated with the role of technology in the economic development of regions can be found in Malecki 1983. A representative discussion of the role of science and technology in Brazil's development, as put forward by the president of the Brazilian Financing Agency for Research and Scientific Development, can be found in Deia 1988.

5. For a critique of the product life cycle theory, see Taylor 1987.

6. The Brazilians have a variety of reasons for wanting a domestic space program. Those of a strictly civilian nature include weather forecasting, remote sensing, and satellite communications. See "Space to Meet National Needs" 1985.

7. Though outside the scope of this chapter, several excellent papers document the success of the Brazilian defense industry, particularly in its efforts to export hardware to other third world countries. For a short, comprehensive overview of these efforts from a commercial publication, see Howarth 1985.

8. The exception was EMBRAER, which also found a market for its light aircraft among several developed countries. See Hudson 1983 and Ramamurti 1987 for a further discussion of this market.

9. For an excellent overview of Brazil's ballistic missile program and the impact that the MTCR had on it, see Tollefson 1990, 58–91.

10. Many Brazilians believe that the MTCR was implemented as a means of controlling future competition in the emerging space market. In the opinion of Colonel Roberto Kessel, director of the CTA IPD, "the developed countries are seeking to prevent the entrance of new competitors in the market of services for space technology" ("U.S., France, U.K. Boycotting Space Program" 1990).

11. For detailed press reports concerning the borehole at Cochimba, see Moreira 1986, "Further Reporting of Alleged Nuclear Test Site" 1986, and Falcao 1987.

12. Technically, the National Security Council was abolished in 1988 when the new Brazilian constitution was promulgated. Just prior to the promulgation, however, the Sarney administration had changed the National Security Council into the Advisory Secretariat for National Defense Matters (SADEN). SADEN was actually the organization that President Collor had subordinated to SAE when he assumed office. In this particular description I have referred to SADEN as the National Security Council simply to avoid confusion.

REFERENCES

Adler, Emanuel. 1988. "State Institutions, Ideology and Autonomous Technological Development: Computers and Nuclear Energy in Argentina and Brazil." *Latin American Research Review* 23 (2): 59–90.

Albright, David. 1989. "Bomb Potential for South America." *Bulletin of the Atomic Scientists,* May, 16–20.

———. 1990. "Brazil Comes in from the Cold." *Arms Control Today* 20, no. 10 (December): 13–16.

Batista, Tarlis. 1984. "Sonda III Launch, Economic Benefits of Space Program Viewed." *Manchete,* August 18, 32–39.

Biato, F., E. Guimarães, and M. H. Figueirdo. 1971. "Potencial de Pesquisa Tecnológica no Brasil." *IPEA/IPLAN Relatório de Pesquisas* no. 5.

———. 1973. "A Transferência de Tecnologia no Brasil." *IPEA/IPLAN Estudos para o Planejamento* no. 4.

Brigagão, Clovis. 1984. *O Mercado da Segurança.* Rio de Janeiro: Editora Nova Fronteira.

Britto de Castro, Antonio Rubens, Noberto Majlis, Luiz Pinguelli Rosa, and Fernando de Souza Barros. 1989. "Brazil's Nuclear Shakeup: Military Still in Control." *Bulletin of the Atomic Scientists,* May, 22–25.

Brooke, James. 1990. "Brazil Uncovers Plan by Military to Build Atom Bomb and Stops It." *The New York Times,* October 9, A1.

"Centro Técnico Aeroespacial." N.d. A pamphlet published by the Centro Técnico Aeroespacial, Sãn José dos Campos, São Paulo, Brazil.

Child, Jack. 1984. *Geopolitics and Conflict in South America: Quarrels among Neighbors.* New York: Praeger.

Christian, Shirley. 1990. "Argentina and Brazil Renounce Atomic Weapons." *The New York Times,* November 29, A1.

"Collor Decries Lack of Access to Technology." 1990. *O Globo,* May 26, 3. Reprinted in *FBIS,* May 29, 27.

Condom, Pierre. 1986. "Brazil Aims for Self-Sufficiency in Space." *Interavia* 1:90.

"Contract Signed for Launching Satellite." 1992. *Brasilia Radio Nacional da Amazonia Network,* August 21. Reprinted in *FBIS,* August 21, 19.

Costa, Raymundo. 1990. "Intelligence Sector Has Less Influence." *O Estado de São Paulo,* April 29, 4–5. Reprinted in *FBIS,* June 1, 41.

Couto e Silva, Golbery. 1955. *Planejamento Estatégico.* Rio de Janeiro: Biblioteca do Exército.

———. 1967. *Geopolítica do Brasil.* Rio de Janeiro: Livraria José Olympio.

Dahlman, Carl J. 1984. "Foreign Technology and Indigenous Technological Capability in Brazil." In *Technological Capability in the Third World,* edited by Martin Fransman and Kenneth King. New York: St. Martin's Press.

Degenar Drummond, Cosme. 1987. "CTA Directors Talk to Tecnologia & Defensa." *Tecnologia & Defensa* (English edition), October 3, 10.

Deia, Carmen. 1988. "C&T é essencial para o desenvolvimento do País." *Espacial* 17, no. 70 (September/October): 6–7.

"Deputies Learn Source of Enriched Uranium." 1990. *Rede Globo,* October 24. Reprinted in *FBIS,* October 25, 27–28.

Dispoe Sobre as Operaçoes Relativas à Importacão e exportacão de ens de Emprego Bélico, de Uso Duplo e de Uso Na Area Nuclear e de Servicos Diretamente Vinculados. 1992. *Diario Official,* February 10. (Unofficial English translation.)

Eleuterio, Regina. 1990. "Former Navy Chief on Nuclear Program." *Folha de São Paulo,* September 24, A-5. Reprinted in *FBIS,* September 27, 18–19.

Erber, Fabio Stefano. 1981. "Science and Technology Policy in Brazil: A Review of the Literature." *Latin American Research Review* 16, no. 1: 3–56.

Eustaquio de Freitas, José. 1990. "Air Force Projects Include Reactor, Lasers." *O Globo,* September 16, 39. Reprinted in *FBIS,* September 18, 30.

Evans, Carol. 1986. "Reappraising Third World Arms Production." Survival 28:99–118.

Fernandes, Bob. 1990. "Rezek Views GATT, Tlatelolco, Arms Sales." *Istoe Senhor,* November 14, 4–6. Reprinted in *FBIS,* December 4, 50.

Fransman, Martin, and Kenneth King, eds. 1984. *Technological Capability in the Third World.* New York: St. Martin's Press.

Frischtak, Claudio. 1987. "Brazil." In *National Policies for Developing High Technology Industries: International Comparisons,* edited by Francis W. Rushing and Carole Ganz Brown. Boulder, Colo.: Westview Press.

"Further Reporting of Alleged Nuclear Test Site." 1986. *Folha de São Paulo,* August 8, 6.

Gasparini-Alves, Pericles. 1992. "Missile and Rocket Production and Export: A Survey of the Brazilian Situation." A paper presented at the Sixteenth Conference of the Associação Nacional de Pos-Graduação e Pesquisa em Ciencias Socias, Caxambu, Minas Gerais.

Godoy, Roberto. 1990. "Development of Sparrow-Type Missile in Iraq." *O Estado De São Paulo,* October 3, 13. Reprinted in *FBIS,* October 10, 30.

Goodwin, Jacob. 1986. "Brazil's Success Formula." *Military Logistics Forum* 3 (3): 50.

Gorman, Stephen M. 1979. "Security, Influence and Nuclear Weapons: The Case of Argentina and Brazil." *Parameters* 9 (March): 52–65.

Gouvea Neto, Raul de. 1991. "How Brazil Competes in the Global Defense Industry." *Latin American Research Review* 26 (3): 93.

Graham, Clifford P. 1990. "Technology and Third World Defense Manufacturing: The Brazilian Firm Engesa." *Defense Analysis* 6 (4): 367–83.

———. 1991. "The Brazilian Space Programme—An Overview." *Space Policy* 7 (1): 72–76.

Hilton, Stanley E. 1985. "The Argentine Factor in Twentieth Century Brazilian Foreign Policy Strategy." *Political Science Quarterly* 100 (1): 27–52.

———. 1987. "The Brazilian Military: Changing Strategic Perceptions and the Question of Mission." *Armed Forces & Society* 13 (3): 329–51.

House, Richard. 1984. "Saudi Arabians, Brazilians Agree to Manufacture Weapons Jointly." *Washington Post,* October 12.

Howarth, H. M. F. 1985. "Brazil's Defense Industry: Ambitious and Growing Fast." *International Defense Review* 9: 1413–27.

Hudson, Rexford A. 1983. "The Brazilian Way to Technological Independence: Foreign Joint Ventures and the Aircraft Industry." *Inter-American Economic Affairs* 37 (2): 23–43.

"Imbel Poderá Privatizar Technologia Bélica." 1982. *O Globo*. October 8.

Julio, Ricardo. 1991. "Piva Says Defense Weapons Sold to Iraq." *Folha de São Paulo,* January 19, 5. Reprinted in *FBIS,* March 1, 49.

Malecki, Edward. 1981a. "Product Cycles, Innovation Cycles, and Regional Economic Change." *Technological Forecasting and Social Change* 19:291–306.

———. 1981b. "Science, Technology and Regional Economic Development: Review and Prospects." *Research Policy* 10:312–34.

———. 1983. "Technology and Regional Development: A Survey." *International Regional Science Review* 8 (2): 89–125.

———. 1984. "High Technology and Economic Development Planning." *APA Journal,* Summer, 262–69.

Marton, Katherin. 1986. *Multinationals, Technology and Industrialization*. Lexington, Ky.: Lexington Books.

Moreira, Dalton. 1986. "Minister Comments on Aeronautic, Nuclear R&D." *Folha de São Paulo,* October 19, 8. Reprinted in *JPRS,* November 17, 11.

Motta, Helio, and Joaquim Monteiro. 1992. "Flores on Status of Nuclear Submarine Project." *Correio Brasiliense,* February 9, 10. Reprinted in *FBIS,* March 20, 28–32.

Motta, Paulo. 1990a. "Cetex Studying Chemical, Biological Weapons." *O Globo,* September 20, 21. Reprinted in *FBIS,* September 25, 40.

———. 1990b. "Secretary Discusses Army Nuclear Project Details." *O Globo,* September 16, 38. Reprinted in *FBIS,* September 18, 29–30.

Nelson, Richard R. 1984. *High Technology Policies: A Five Nation Comparison*. Washington, D.C.: American Enterprise Institute.

Ohlson T., and E. Sköns. 1987. "The Trade in Major Conventional Weapons." In *SIPRI Yearbook 1987,* 181–205. Philadelphia: Taylor & Francis.

Onis, Juan de. 1976. "Brazil Is Hopeful Oil Discovery in Iraq Will Turn into Bonanza." *New York Times,* September 27.

"President Collor's Speech to the Armed Forces." 1990. *O Estado de São Paulo,* May 30, 4. Reprinted in *FBIS,* June 1.

"Previous Plans for Nuclear Bomb Discussed." 1990. *Folha de São Paulo,* October 28, B1. Reprinted in *FBIS,* October 31, 23–24.

Ramamurti, R. 1987. *State Owned Industries in High Technology Industries: Studies in India and Brazil.* New York: Praeger.

Rao, Radhakrishna. 1985. "Brazil: Aiming for Self-Sufficiency in Orbit." *Space World,* October, 29.

"Rezek Wants UNSC Permanent Member Status." 1991. *Madrid EFE,* March 19. Reprinted in *FBIS,* March 20, 21.

Rother, L. 1978. "Western Europeans Seek to Join with Brazil in Arms Production." *Washington Post,* May 8.

Rushing, Francis W., and Carole Ganz Brown, eds. 1987. *National Policies for Developing High Technology Industries: International Comparisons.* Boulder, Colo.: Westview Press.

Sanches, Valdir. 1990. "Control of Aramar Nuclear Activities Urged." *Jornal da Tarde,* July 2. Reprinted in *FBIS,* August 1, 34–36.

Selcher, Wayne A. 1977. "The National Security Doctrine and Policies of the Brazilian Government." *Parameters* 7 (1):10–24.

Sieniawski, Michael. 1982. "Brazil Cashes in with Open-Door Policy on Arms Sales." *Christian Science Monitor,* November 12.

"Space to Meet National Needs." 1985. *New Scientist,* July 25, 51.

Stepan, Alfred. 1971. *The Military in Politics: Changing Patterns in Brazil.* Princeton, N.J.: Princeton University Press.

———. 1988. *Rethinking Military Politics: Brazil and the Southern Cone.* Princeton, N.J.: Princeton University Press.

Stewart, Frances. 1978. *Technology and Underdevelopment.* Boulder, Colo.: Westview Press.

"Study Warns of Near Capability to Make Bomb." 1990. *Jornal da Tarde,* July 3. Reprinted in *FBIS,* August 1, 33.

"Survival Depends on Exports." 1983. *Latin American Regional Reports: Brazil,* RB-83-05.

Tachinardi, Helena. 1991. "Motives for Creation of Space Agency Discussed." *Gazeta Mercantil,* December 13, 11. Reprinted in *FBIS,* January 3, 1992, 21–22.

Taylor, M. 1987. "Enterprise and the Product Life Cycle Model: Conceptual Ambiguities." In *New Technology and Regional Development,* edited by Bert Van Der Knapp and Egbert Wever. London: Croom Helm.

Tollefson, Scott D. 1990. *Brazil, the United States, and the Missile Technology Control Regime.* Monterey: Naval Post Graduate School.

"U.S., France, U.K. Boycotting Space Program." 1990. *O Globo,* August 17, 18. Reprinted in *FBIS,* August 24, 27.

Van Der Knapp, Bert, and Egbert Wever, eds. 1987. *New Technology and Regional Development.* London: Croon Helm.

Vernon, R. 1966. "International Investment and International Trade in the Product Life Cycle." *Quarterly Journal of Economics* 80:190–207.

Wines, Michael. 1990. "Brazil Won't Sign Atom Pact but Plans Curbs, Aide Says." *New York Times*, October 17.

CHAPTER 11

South Korea's Export Control Policy

Han S. Park

Introduction

The rapid change in the international and regional political climate surrounding the Korean peninsula has profoundly affected virtually every aspect of South Korean public and foreign policy. One such area is South Korea's export control policy toward countries that pose a threat to its national security. To the extent that it is in South Korea's interest to maintain control over the transfer of dual-use and military technologies, its policy orientation has been consistent with that of the COCOM nations. But the epidemic dissolution of the communist systems and the concurrent development of "northern diplomacy" by South Korea have made export controls unstable and in need of a comprehensive reexamination. South Korea's export control behavior is analyzed in this chapter. I attempt to identify both its facilitating forces and inhibiting factors in the particular context of the country's policy orientations surrounding the current regime's "northern diplomacy." First, we shall attempt to discern the policy goals of the regime to determine the relative significance of the various components of national interest such as economic development, democratization, and national security.[1] Second, we shall examine South Korea's export control policies as evidenced by documents and policy statements by government officials to infer the implications for policy goals. Third, we will examine the actual export behavior exhibited by both the public and private sectors in the area of dual-use and military technology. Finally, we will consider the prospects of export control behavior in the context of the changing world order and especially inter-Korea relations.

Policy Goals: The Domestic Context

Since the creation of South Korea in 1948, and especially since the Korean War (1950–53), national security has been the foremost and overriding policy goal of successive South Korean governments. The goals of democratization and economic growth have, by contrast, been perceived with different degrees of relative significance.

For the First Republic (1948–60) under the leadership of Syngman Rhee and the short-lived Second Republic (1960–61) with Chang Myon as prime minister, democracy was far more important than economic growth. In fact, the two republics had no policy designed to promote economic growth, as evidenced by the absence of any development plans. Both Rhee and Chang had been educated in the United States, favored Western-style democracy, and were being pressured by the United States to democratize. The war-torn South Korean economy heavily depended on American aid. The military junta led by General Park Chung Hee that came to power in the wake of the 1961 coup opened up a new era in which the goal of economic growth took precedence over democratization. The Third and Fourth Republics (1963–79) under Park's leadership initiated a series of government-sponsored plans to promote industrialization and economic growth. As a result, the annual economic growth rate soared to 10 percent or higher during this period. Democracy was placed in obscurity as the military regime found it inherently impossible to claim any legitimate democratic basis. Instead, the regime sought public support by demonstrating its contributions to economic achievement. General Park was known not for his favorable attitudes toward the West but for his adherence to the ideas of self-reliance and national development.[2] The assassination of Park in 1979 was followed by another military coup by General Chun Doo-Hwan, who followed the footsteps of Park and became president of the Fifth Republic. Both the Park and Chun regimes were able to maintain power without direct elections—democracy was virtually suspended—but both regimes were able to generate public support based on economic performance. While democracy never attained supremacy as a national goal, national security became even more salient. In fact, the undermining of democracy was made possible in part by the regimes' successful efforts to use the security issue to justify repressive measures.[3]

However, the unpopular presidency of Chun paved the way for massive student demonstrations and civil strife toward the end of his term (1987). The culmination of the upheaval was the announcement by the chairman of the ruling party, Roh Tae-Woo, who was a close associate of the president, of the government's intention to amend the constitution to allow direct presidential elections. Although Roh became president in the ensuing election, the legislative body, whose members were directly elected, gained substantial power. The popular demand for democracy lent force and substance to labor movements and relatively active party politics. Unlike the previous regimes, the Sixth Republic (1988–93) has attempted to shift the basis of its legitimacy from economic growth to democracy. The highly contested election of Young Sam Kim in 1992 has further solidified the foundation of democracy. In fact, Kim is the first civilian professional and civilian politician to be president since the ill-fated Second Republic of the Chang regime in 1961.

This process of democratization is being reinforced by the demise of communist systems in Europe and the Soviet Union and the continuing need to criticize the paternalistic system of North Korea at a time of Seoul's increasing interaction and competition with the Pyongyang regime. Thus, for the South Korean regime in 1993, democracy as a national goal has been elevated at least to the level of the goal of economic growth, while national security is viewed with a greater sense of proportion as South Korea has established diplomatic relations with most of the former and present socialist countries, including the former Soviet Union. This shift might mean that national security can no longer enjoy the kind of mythical sacredness that the ruling elite has often abused for domestic political expediency.

South Korean export control policy needs to be examined within the domestic context of these changing national priorities.

Export Controls and the International Context

The concept of export controls is relatively new to the South Korean government. It was not until February, 1991, that the government issued a decree in which some export control regulations were specified.[4] There are a variety of explanations for this belated recognition of the concept: (1) the enhancement of South Korea's capability to produce and disseminate dual-use or military technology; (2) changes in Seoul's policy toward the northern countries, including most of the socialist states; and (3) U.S. concern about the possible diffusion of dual-use and military technology by the NICs.

South Korea's one-time desire to join COCOM was denied because COCOM members did not believe that Seoul's level of technological capability posed a threat to COCOM objectives and because they believed that South Korea was simply not inclined to divert advanced technology to communist countries. But the Park government's concerted efforts, especially since the Carter administration's decision to withdraw U.S. troops from South Korea in 1976, to promote indigenous research and development have boosted its defense technology to a level that now warrants COCOM's concern. The government created a centralized institution, the Advanced Institute of Science and Technology, to facilitate effective research and development efforts. The government further encouraged private companies and assisted them through subsidies and joint-programs to expand their research and development activities. Major companies have been allocating large amounts of resources to educate their employees abroad and to hire foreign scientists and engineers to train local personnel. South Korea is now acknowledged to possess enough indigenous technological capabilities to absorb and replicate sophisticated production processes. According to a National Academy of Sciences study, South Korea has both the economic and technological capabilities to produce commodities with technical specifications similar to those of COCOM-controlled items.[5] It is now common knowledge that some private companies such as Samsung, Daewoo, and Hyundai have produced COCOM-controlled commodities such as high-density memory chips and sixteen-bit microcomputers.

Even with the physical capability to produce dual-use technology, South Korean export control policy was not a major concern of COCOM member governments unless Seoul displayed the policy inclinations to export its high technology to those countries that posed security threats to the West. On the contrary, South Korea has been seen as a resolute bulwark against the communist bloc and the last country inclined to divert military technology into communist hands. Perhaps no country in the world has felt a long-term communist threat more intensely than South Korea, and Seoul's policy disposition has been such that its security interests could never fail to coincide with those of the United States and other COCOM countries.

However, the late 1980s witnessed a drastic departure from the conventional trends both in the domestic political climate and the global political milieu. Domestically, the government came under enormous pressure as a result of the popular demand for democratization which, as discussed earlier, was the foundation of the Sixth Republic and the ensuing democratic elections. The renewed emphasis on democracy as a national goal restrains the government from exercising coercive measures against dissidents and other critics of the regime. At the same time, the extent to which the government can exercise control over the private economic sector has also diminished, and many multinational corporations and major South Korean firms have attained significant degrees of autonomy. These developments forced the leadership to assume the role of a more pragmatic actor, rather than a manipulator, not only on the issue of political democracy but also in relation to people's livelihoods. This domestic burden became greater for the government when it faced trade frictions with the United States. The Park and Chun regimes were able to take full advantage of the abundant market that the United States offered, but the Roh administration has been forced to adjust its trade policies to meet the American demands to ease trade barriers. As a result, South Korea has recorded a trade deficit since 1989.

These domestic and international forces have been instrumental in Seoul's pursuing a northern economic policy, exploring new markets in the former Soviet Union, China, and other countries with which it had no diplomatic ties during the cold war era. In establishing economic and diplomatic relations with socialist countries, Seoul has been particularly aggressive not only because it needed additional (alternative) markets but also because it intended to politically isolate North Korea from its traditional allies. The successful 1988 Summer Olympic games were a major turning point in South

Korea's relations with the Soviet Union and Eastern European countries as well as with China. Prior to the Olympics, South Korea was little known to the socialist world; moreover, what they did know about it was largely misinformation provided by North Korea and its sympathizers. Television viewers of the Olympic games in these countries were both amazed and generally impressed at the ultramodern buildings, streets, and industrial constructions throughout South Korea. In fact, some suggest that the Olympic games held in Seoul might have facilitated the pace of liberalization and market development in some socialist systems. Certainly, many people in these countries believed that the establishment of relations with South Korea would bring great economic benefits to their sagging economies. All these countries did not hesitate to establish diplomatic ties with Seoul despite North Korean protests, thus further satisfying the South Korean political objective of isolating Pyongyang from its allies. Virtually all the former Soviet bloc countries as well as China recognized and normalized diplomatic relations with South Korea within four years of the Olympics. Numerous political leaders from these former adversaries, including such dignitaries as Soviet President Gorbachev and Hungarian President Goncz, have visited South Korea in anticipation of hasty economic gains from Seoul. Their expectations exceed what South Korea can deliver, but South Korean determination to live up to their expectations indicates that there will be further strains on the domestic economy. The volume of trade with the former adversaries has soared since 1988 (table 11.1), and Seoul is hard-pressed to sustain the increase.

Thus, while changing national priorities provide the domestic context for an examination of South Korean export control policy, changing diplomatic and foreign economic relations provide the international context.

Influences on South Korean Export Control Policy

Seoul's position and policy behavior concerning export controls are complex, often paradoxical, and highly uncertain. The complexity and uncertainty can be seen in a series of conflicting interests and the structure of cross-pressures under which South Korea has to operate. First, there are incentives for expanding economic relations with the republics of the former Soviet Union, China, and Eastern European countries with which Seoul had no economic interactions in the past, namely, the promise of new market opportunities needed to offset the shrinking market in the United States. By diversifying its economic and trading partners across ideological and political boundaries, Seoul seeks cheaper labor, raw materials, and above all new markets for its goods and services.[6] In this sense, the development and economic prosperity of the northern countries coincide with South Korea's economic and security interests. Second, however, unlike the cold war era when trade and investment activities were largely limited to the United States and Japan, economic interests pose a potential threat and risk that may conflict with security interests. In spite of the two Koreas' simultaneous admission to the United

TABLE 11.1. South Korea's Trade with Selected Countries (in thousands of dollars, percentage change over previous year in parentheses)

Country	1989	1990	1991[a]	1992[b]
China[c]				
Exports	437,355	584,854	1,002,511	1,967,630
	(+17.4)	(+33.7)	(+71.5)	(+149.7)
Imports	1,704,540	2,268,137	3,440,548	3,139,885
	(+22.9)	(+33.0)	(+51.6)	(+11.1)
Total trade	2,141,895	2,852,991	4,443,059	5,107,815
	(+21.7)	(+33.1)	(+55.7)	(+41.3)
USSR				
Exports	207,746	519,147	625,080	374,166
	(+698.3)	(+149.9)	(+20.4)	(+15.6)
Imports	391,700	369,652	557,293	480,415
	(+119.6)	(-5.6)	(+56.1)	(+2.9)
Total trade	599,446	888,799	1,202,373	854,581
	(+193.3)	(+48.3)	(+35.2)	(+8.1)
Eastern Europe				
Exports	270,377	541,396	536,570	273,663
	(+116.3)	(+97.7)	(-0.9)	(-42.2)
Imports	117,762	213,201	267,808	171,345
	(+31.8)	(+81.0)	(+25.6)	(-16.9)
Total trade	388,139	754,597	804,378	445,008
	(+81.1)	(+94.4)	(+6.5)	(-34.5)
Vietnam and Mongolia				
Exports	45,031	117,340	204,254	350,306
	(-27.2)	(+160.5)	(+74.0)	(+115.7)
Imports	42,342	35,571	41,580	49,018
	(+193.5)	(-15.9)	(+16.8)	(+42.0)
Total trade	87,373	152,911	245,834	339,324
	(+14.4)	(+63.5)	(+72.0)	(+108.1)
Total				
Exports	960,509	1,762,737	2,368,415	2,966,065
	(+64.17)	(+83.5)	(+34.4)	(+69.7)
Imports	2,256,344	2,886,561	4,327,229	3,840,663
	(+35.2)	(+27.9)	(+49.9)	(+8.7)
Total trade	3,216,853	4,649,298	6,695,644	6,806,728
	(+42.7)	(+44.2)	(+44.3)	(+28.9)

Source: Pukbang Kyung Jai 1, no. 10 (December 1992): 136.

[a]January–October, 1991.

[b]Statistics for the first ten months of 1992.

[c]Statistics on China exclude indirect trade through Hong Kong and Japan.

Nations (perhaps because of it), they are expected to be even more competitive in protecting the integrity and legitimacy of their respective regimes. North Korea's military capabilities will continue to be the most serious concern for the South Korean government. Any possible diversion of dual-use or military technology from socialist countries to North Korea may well cause an instant cessation of technology exports by Seoul. Third, trade frictions with the United States have profound implications for the South Korean economy and its overall policy postures, including its northern economic policy. Finally, the South Korean government now has less control over the behavior of private exporters, who are extremely aggressive in pursuing their economic interests. We will examine each of these factors more carefully to discern probable directions for South Korean export control policy. Specifically, we will examine the implications of these issues in the context of the national goals discussed earlier.

Northern Economic Policy and Export Controls

For reasons discussed above, previous South Korean governments seldom felt the need for export controls vis-à-vis the communist bloc. But the new opportunities presented to the Sixth Republic have raised the issue of export controls as a real policy concern. On the one hand, South Korea's new economic partners seek to expand trade and joint venture relations with Seoul, especially in the areas of telecommunication and electronics, often involving dual-use technologies. They are attracted to South Korea because it can supply useful technology on more favorable terms than the United States, Japan, and West European countries. Furthermore, they do not feel that South Korea will threaten their economic independence, whereas the more advanced industrial economies might.[7] At the same time, Seoul views most of the former Soviet satellites of Eastern Europe as ideal economic partners. They represent new markets for South Korean products and a source of cheap labor. The South Korean economy has grown to a point that its comparative advantage no longer lies in labor-intensive industries such as textiles. It sees a more promising future in high technology with possible military implications. Thus, from a purely economic perspective, South Korea and its new economic partners seem to share an interest in exploring opportunities for economic cooperation in high-technology areas. It is this mutual interest that makes the issue of export control significant, especially for the United States.

North Korea and Export Controls

One might think that the sweeping changes of the post–cold war world order, the open door policy of South Korea toward the northern countries, and the growing interaction between the two Koreas would give the Seoul government every incentive to reduce its defense capabilities. Considering that both North and South Korea are now members of the United Nations, one might also expect that the two governments should be able to promote peaceful negotiations for the eventual reintegration of the nation. But the stark reality falls far short of these expectations. The perception among South Koreans of the threat from the North is still strong, virtually unaffected by changes in international and domestic policies. In fact, the South Koreans are intensely concerned about the North Korean nuclear weapons programs, and fear and distrust of the North is as high as ever.[8] Despite successive high-level dialogues, the two regimes are not prepared to ease military tensions along the border. Some South Korean analysts seem to believe that pervasive economic problems in North Korea and dwindling popular support for Kim Il Sung's regime may trigger military actions or reactions by the Pyongyang government against the South.[9] Considering that North Korea is most unlikely to follow the precedent of East Germany, this analysis cannot be dismissed. Thus, despite all the rhetoric of cooperation and peaceful resolution, South Korea is not prepared to drop its military guard. The South continues to fear any diversion of dual-use technology that could enhance North Korea's military capabilities, and it is highly unlikely that the Seoul government would compromise national military security interests in the pursuit of economic gain. In this regard, and in view of South Korea's high-technology capabilities and private economic incentives, export controls have become an integral part of the South Korean policy guidelines. Seoul is highly sensitive to Pyongyang's security alliances with Moscow and Beijing and the military assistance that they entail. Furthermore, no country that has established new ties with Seoul has ever denounced or severed its relations with North Korea. On the other hand, as long as there are assurances that strategically critical technologies diverted by (or through) South Korea will not benefit North Korea, Seoul will aggressively pursue economic interests through its northern policy.

Will the new partners provide such assurances? How reliable will the assurances be? What measures might Russia, China, and East European countries need to implement to satisfy South Korea's fears? These questions are the central concerns of South Korean policymakers. Dr. Han Bin Lee, former deputy prime minister and president of the newly instituted International Private Economic Council of Korea, has suggested that no assurances are reliable unless the countries involved are under serious pressure to terminate their relations with North Korea.[10] This condition, however, is unlikely to be met now that North Korea is a legitimate member of the United Nations.

The United States and Seoul's Export Control Policy

Since the initial years of the republic, South Korea has maintained a fraternal relationship with the United States. This relationship has been natural and comprehensive, natural in the sense that the formation of the regime itself was the product of a strong American initiative and that U.S. forces played a critical role in protecting South Korea from the Chinese and North Korean communists during the Korean War (1950–53). It was the United States that poured massive economic and military aid into South Korea and deployed over 40,000 ground troops there. The much-acclaimed economic development might have been impossible without the availability of American market and technical assistance, not to mention the strong military protection. However, the fraternal relationship has suffered from a series of new developments. First, the issue of U.S. troop withdrawal, initially introduced by the Carter administration and recently officially announced by the Bush administration, is a pivotal issue for the South Koreans. President Roh, consistent with his two immediate predecessors, has requested and lobbied Washington to maintain the troop level until South Korea is militarily prepared to deter North Korean aggression. As alluded to earlier, this situation prompted the development of a military industry, including research and development. Furthermore, in an effort to help modernize the Korean military, the United States not only instituted programs to train Korean personnel but relaxed the transfer of technology and sophisticated military equipment and entered into a number of coproduction agreements with South Korea. As a result, South Korea has been able to absorb dual-use and military technology more rapidly, ironically making the U.S. government increasingly uneasy about possible technology transfers by South Korea to potential adversaries.

In 1992, Seoul is presently under great pressure from Washington to comply with COCOM guidelines. The South Korean government's official position is to comply with them but there appears to be little serious effort to implement the necessary controls. First, there does not seem to be any central agency in the government responsible for interpreting or overseeing the implementation of export control guidelines. At least four government agencies are involved but none is charged exclusively with the task of export controls: the Economic Planning Board, the Foreign Ministry, the Ministry of Commerce, and the Office of Science and Technology are all peripherally involved in the task. In addition, the Blue House—South Korea's White House—has its own economic advisory organ with an authority superseding all others. Second, there is the problem of determining the levels and types of technology that should be subjected to control. Even the government agencies seem to have different views at best and are generally uncertain on this issue. As is discussed below, private firms doing business with the northern countries welcome these ambiguities and take advantage of them. Despite U.S. pressure, the South Korean government does not seem to be eager to implement the COCOM guidelines as long as such an action is economically counterproductive. The government seems to be pursuing a dual course. On the one hand, it reaffirms its commitment to fully comply with U.S. demands, but in practice it frequently connives with private firms to circumvent COCOM guidelines until and unless specific complaints are received from the United States. This pattern of South Korean behavior is clearly unconventional and inconsistent with its past, more cooperative position.

One factor that might explain this change is the Roh government's frustrations with the trade frictions with the United States. Under intense pressure from the United States, the largest market for Korean exporters, the government was forced to lift import restrictions on most products, affecting the agricultural sector most severely. By the end of 1991, nearly 85 percent of farm products were liberalized and a completely open market is expected by 1994.[11] Korean farmers have continuously protested against the government's inability to protect them from foreign pressures, and the present government is hard-pressed to alleviate the ever-increasing economic plight of the farmers who still compose a majority of South Korean voters. Many are leaving their farms for Seoul and other cities, thus exacerbating the already serious unemployment and other problems in urban areas. The government insinuates that the United States is unreasonably harsh toward South Korea to find ways to alleviate its own problem of budget deficit. In fact, the anti-American sentiment has recently seeped into the South Korean political culture. It has permeated all segments of society, including the farmers; the government finds it politically expedient to let the people blame Washington for their economic plight. At a time when participatory democracy is being revived, the regime cannot ignore public opinion.

It is in the context of these developments that one should examine the South Korean government's export control policy. On the one hand, Seoul has, willingly or otherwise, been accommodating the American demand for market liberalization with severe economic consequences, including a widening trade deficit with the United States, Japan, and even the northern countries.[12] Trade deficits may be harmful to any country's economy, but its impact on a country such as South Korea, whose economy almost entirely depends on foreign markets, can affect the survival of the regime. At a time when South Korea suffers from a trade deficit for which the United States is greatly (not necessarily fairly, however) blamed, Washington's pressure on Seoul to comply with the COCOM guidelines for its trade with the northern countries has incurred severe South Korean criticism. The ambivalence and perplexity some government officials in Seoul exhibited when asked about their views on export controls should be understood with these circumstances in mind. In other words, South Koreans appear to resent Washington's attempts not only to dictate the terms of Seoul's trade with the United States but also to interfere with its efforts to explore new and alternative markets in the northern countries. There seems to be a great deal of resentment of U.S. pressure, yet the pressure appears to be working at this time. Will the pressure continue to be effective? If so, for how long?

A cursory examination of South Korea's trade behavior indicates that Seoul has been making concerted (and effective) efforts to break into new markets in the EC, Southeast Asia, and the northern countries. In fact, the volumes of trade with these areas are increasing very rapidly, offsetting the declining market in the United States. As South Korea's reliance on the U.S. market declines, Washington's leverage on Seoul will also decline. If the current trends continue, the critical moment may come sooner than expected. Another source of the U.S. leverage concerns Seoul's security interest. The United States not only maintains ground troops on Korean soil but protects the region with nuclear weapons. At a time when North Korea is widely believed to have nuclear capabilities, the South Korean government considers the stationing of troops and especially nuclear weapons essential. But the future of the U.S. military and nuclear presence appears to be fraught with uncertainty.

In the final analysis, South Korea's export controls cannot be externally orchestrated or imposed; only the Koreans themselves can find positive inducement to develop and implement export control policies for their own national interest. Then, in view of the discussion above on South Korean national goals of economic growth, democratization, and national security, what might one conclude about Seoul's export control policy? An answer to this question has to be conjectural and speculative, yet one has to be attempted.

The Prospects: Policy Goals and Export Controls

Based on the discussion in this chapter of national goals and the domestic and international political contexts of export controls in South Korea, we might be able to assess more closely the prospects for South Korean export control practices.

First, export controls become a vitally important policy option when exported technologies are thought to be of assistance to North Korean efforts to enhance its military capabilities. The fact that the northern countries, especially those of the former Soviet Union, will reduce their military spending for economic development might minimize the possibility of their diverting military technology and equipment to North Korea. Such diversion will be especially unlikely if such actions might invite Western and South Korean economic sanctions. On the other hand, however, both the former Soviet republics and China may seek to export their military equipment and technology to countries such as North Korea as their military industry might be most efficient in generating foreign currency earnings. But they will fear that arms sales and military assistance might provoke severe Western retaliation. This fear might be a sufficient deterrent for Beijing and Moscow to aiding North Korea. In the final analysis, Seoul is unlikely to find sufficient security interest in export controls to risk the new economic opportunities offered from the northern countries.

Second, U.S. pressure has been the primary driving force behind South Korea's export control policies. Although Washington's leverage over South Korea has declined due to Seoul's trade diversification policy, South Korea's economy and security still heavily depend on the United States. It is highly improbable that Seoul will assume a policy independent of (or in contradiction to) American desires with respect to export controls. Yet the serious challenge the United States faces of creating a post–cold war world order might cause the issue of export controls to fall into obscurity. In this sense, U.S. pressure on South Korea will become not only unpersuasive but possibly counterproductive, as it will breed anti-Americanism.

Third, South Korea's economy will dictate its export control policy. Depending on the extent to which the northern countries are expected to contribute to the Korean economy, Seoul will be disinclined to control exports. This will especially be true as Seoul's comparative market advantage is found in the high-technology areas. In fact, the rapidly rising labor cost in South Korea has virtually eliminated South Korea from international competition in the labor-intensive manufacturing sector, and many suggest that the key to South Korea's sustained economic growth lies in exploring markets for medium- and high-technology areas, especially in electronics and telecommunications.

Fourth, trade frictions with the United States and their adverse effect on South Korea's economy will discourage Seoul from adhering to export controls. As long as the United States continues to experience a trade deficit and South Korean commodities, especially such conspicuous items as automobiles and electronic equipment, provide ammunition for American politicians critical of South Korean trade practices, trade frictions are not likely to disappear. The same conclusion may be drawn from the South Korean side as well: as Korean consumers appear to be favoring foreign goods, Seoul may feel uneasy about completely liberalizing its market.

Fifth, the degree to which the government is able to control the private sector has immediate implications for export controls. South Korean private businesses have experienced dramatic growth both in trade volumes and independence from government control. Large firms such as Hyundai, Samsung, Daewoo, and Goldstar have their own research capabilities, and they are extremely competitive. They have proven to be aggressive in developing new technologies and commodities with military implications. Even if the government has the desire, it may not have the resources to effectively enforce export control measures before the firms have actually diverted their commodities.

Finally, reforms and stability in the northern countries have a direct bearing on South Korea's export controls. As reforms and demilitarization in those countries continue unabated, Seoul will be confident of the safeguards against the diversion of the exported technologies to North Korea. Needless to say, the political and social stability of these countries will directly influence Seoul's (and many others') trade behavior with them.

These premises seem to clearly indicate that South Korea's export control policy will be moving toward less restrictive export controls. As we have seen, the issue of export controls for South Korea is extremely complicated, defying anyone's prediction. Underlying the complexity are a variety of factors ranging from the more fluid national goals of the present South Korean government to the uncertain dynamics of not only the international community but the northern countries. As a result, Korean government officials seem unable to develop and maintain a consistent policy with respect to export controls. Nevertheless, the issue of export controls is not and cannot be one that the government will be indifferent to because, if nothing else, the issue has intimate implications for its own national goals such as security and economic development.

NOTES

1. See chapter 1.

2. President Park's conception of national security, unlike the one held by President Rhee, included economic strength as an important component. See Han S. Park and Kyung A. Park, "Bases of Regime Legitimacy in North and South Korea," *Korea Observer* 18, no. 3 (Autumn 1987): 321–43.

3. For a further elaboration on this thesis, see Han S. Park, "Democracy in South Korea: Basis of Legitimacy or Prisoner of Security," paper presented at the Annual Meeting of the American Political Science Association, Washington, D.C., August 29–September 1, 1991.

4. Prime Minister's Decree No. 245, effective February 10, 1991.

5. National Academy of Sciences, *Balancing the National Interest: U.S. National Security Export Controls and Global Economic Competition* (Washington, D.C.: National Academy Press 1987), 66, 216.

6. This diversification is also reflected in South Korea's increased trade and investment in the Southeast Asian countries.

7. The deputy foreign minister of Hungary indicated these aspects as being more attractive factors that countries such as South Korea and Taiwan can offer; he also indicated that dealing with Taiwan is politically uncomfortable at this point due to Chinese objections, which Hungary cannot ignore, and that South Korea is a more suitable partner. He accompanied the Hungarian president on a four-day visit to Seoul in the summer of 1990. During the visit, an agreement was reportedly reached for South Korea's Samsung to update the telephone system in Hungary.

8. South Korean defense minister, Lee Chong Kook, even announced on September 27, 1991, that Seoul might be forced to use military force to destroy North Korea's nuclear weapons production capability. *Sae Gae Times,* October 28, 1991.

9. There have been reports on North Korea's mass unrest. A Japanese newspaper, *Sankei Shimbun* (October 27, 1991), reported that there were antigovernment mass demonstrations with an estimated 4,000 people in Shin Ui Ju, a border city just south of the Yalu River.

10. Interview with Dr. Lee, Seoul, April 2, 1991.

11. *Korea News Review,* September 14, 1991, 15.

12. The deficit for 1991 exceeded $9 billion. The U.S. share of Korea's exports was under 30 percent, down from 40 percent in 1986. *Korea Newsreview,* March 30, 1991, 15.

CHAPTER 12

Export Controls and Proliferation: An Indian Perspective

S. Chandrashekar

Background

The Indian viewpoint on the use of export controls as a method for the control of the proliferation of weapons is conditioned to a large extent by India's experience as a victim of such controls. It is also partly determined by a large degree of idealism to see a more equitable and just world order. Over the last twenty years or so, India has been singled out as a special target of concern vis-à-vis proliferation. The "peaceful" nuclear explosion of Pokhran in 1974 was followed by a series of measures directed against India and a tightening of the stranglehold over nuclear technology and nuclear materials exports to India by the developed countries.[1] The launch of the civilian space launcher SLV-3 in 1980 raised similar concerns with regard to missile proliferation and was followed by the MTCR directed primarily against India.[2]

India's close ties with the Soviet Union and the pro-Pakistan and pro-China policy pursued by the United States and its allies as a part of their global strategic doctrine were predominantly responsible for this Indian perception. The legitimate security interests of India, with respect to both China and Pakistan, apparently received little sympathy or consideration in the U.S. strategy. Indian interests were regarded as a minor sideshow to the major problem of East-West confrontation. Indian concerns for a more equitable and just world order and for complete and total disarmament also dictated, to some extent, India's decision not to go nuclear, after Pokhran. India preferred to retain a nuclear option rather than become a full-fledged nuclear power. This position was in keeping with India's nonaligned policy of fighting for a world free of all weapons (especially nuclear weapons) and the perceived linkages India saw between reduced armaments and Third World development.

More than seventeen years have passed since Pokhran without any further testing by India. However, recent developments such as the breakup of the Soviet Union, U.S.-USSR rapprochment, the breakup of the Eastern Bloc, Indian concerns raised by Pakistani interference in Kashmir and Punjab, the increasingly important role of China in world affairs, and India's own regional and domestic problems could alter this position.[3]

Another irritant in the Indian perception of Western intentions has been the Western portrayal of India as a potential irresponsible exporter, because of India's strong economic and political ties with the Soviet Union. As we shall see later in this chapter, the actual position has always been otherwise, and India has always been an extremely responsible exporter, especially of sensitive technology.[4] A lack of understanding of the formal and informal, intentional and unintentional mechanisms that exist within the many departments of the Indian government for the control of critical exports could also have contributed in some measure to this mistaken perception. If India has erred at all, it has been more on the side of exercising controls even when these controls were not warranted. In a world where the export of arms is big business, India has often willingly or unwittingly sacrificed its own economic interest in the interests of a safer world.[5] This portrayal of India as a threat to weapons proliferation is therefore seen by many decision makers in the country as a method of denying India the technology necessary for preserving its own security and to curtail its development in the civilian sector. It is also seen as a method of downgrading India's role in world affairs and in the process eliminating a potential economic competitor.[6]

The direct consequence of this assessment of Western intentions has forced India to significantly enhance its defense forces. It has also forced India to embark on major programs of indigenous development in what India sees as critical sectors. In the core defense sector, new programs such as the integrated missile program, the light advanced combat aircraft, and a main battle tank have been initiated.[7] India is also significantly enhancing its naval capability.[8] Additions include ships, submarines, and frigates. The same policy of self-reliance has been applied across the board in other key high-technology sectors. These sectors include the atomic energy and space programs, in both of which India has been a victim of discriminatory control regimes. The Indian experience of being a victim of control regimes makes it unlikely that in the immediate future India would significantly depart from this policy of self-reliance in key areas.

The extent to which the Indian experience would affect Indian cooperation on export controls to prevent proliferation, however, needs more rigorous analysis before conclusions can be drawn.

Current Global and Regional Determinants of Indian Security Policy and their Implications for Export Control Regimes

Recent international developments are bound to have far-reaching implications on the geopolitical scene. They are also likely to affect Indian policies and decisions. The Gorbachev initiatives, the liberation of Eastern Europe from the shackles of communist socialism, and the altered role of the new loosely linked Soviet-Russian federation are likely to alter Indian perceptions of its national security interests significantly.[9]

The Gulf crisis has also changed superpower and big power relationships. Countries like India have to come to grips with the realities of the major military powers working in tandem in areas that India perceives as strategic to its national interest within the region. The Chinese and French willingness to become parties to the NPT provides an indicator of likely developments. The recent vote of the Soviet Union in the UN General Assembly, in favor of a nuclear free zone in South Asia, a concept that it has always opposed, provides a clear indication of the direction that cooperation between the nuclear haves is likely to take.

The United States no longer depends on Pakistan as a bulwark against the Soviet-Russian threat. Whether this will significantly alter Indo-U.S. relationships in any substantial way is still a matter of speculation. There are some indications of a decrease in the anti-India stance adopted by the United States. The increasing attention being paid to China as a major player in the world arena and China's willingness to become a party to the NPT as a nuclear power are also likely to affect Indian policy significantly.

There are also practical possibilities of closer Sino-Indian cooperation. This could radically alter the existing tripartite relationship between China, India, and Pakistan.[10] Within India, militant activity in Kashmir and Punjab, which enjoys significant support from Pakistan, will be a major contributor to policy.[11] In the northeast, chronic problems have plagued the country for a long time. The unrest in Burma and the possible role of China would be matters of special concern. In the south of India, the Indian Peace Keeping Force mission in Sri Lanka; the Liberation Tigers of Tamil Eelam (LTTE) terrorist action in Tamil Nadu; and the assassination of the former prime minister of India, Shri Rajiv Gandhi, by LTTE militants are also bound to leave their marks.

India is also going through a grave economic crisis, triggered mainly by the Gulf War. As a major exporter of skilled labor, goods, and services to the Middle East, India has been particularly badly hit. Prior to the Gulf

War, over 1.2 million Indians worked in the Middle East. The war-affected zone alone (Saudi Arabia, Kuwait, Syria, Iraq, and Jordan) employed about 500,000 Indians. The Iraqi invasion of Kuwait and the Gulf War forced many Indians to return home. The war and the return of Indian workers resulted in a major decrease in worker foreign exchange remittances to India, resulting in a significant decrease in India's foreign exchange reserves. The foreign exchange crunch was further compounded by the higher prices that India had to pay to ensure the continuity of oil supplies. More than 40 percent of India's crude oil is imported. Saudi Arabia, Kuwait, and Iraq account for a large fraction of these supplies. The disruption in oil supplies from Iraq and Kuwait forced India to buy oil from other sources (Iran, Venezuela, Malaysia, etc.) at higher prices. The third factor contributing to the crisis was a significant decrease in exports to the Gulf brought about by the UN embargo, as well as the effects of the threat of war and the war itself. During the period immediately preceding the war, exports to the Middle East declined by an estimated 87 percent. The combination of these factors created a major economic crisis in the country, affecting all sectors of the economy. In January, 1991, India's foreign exchange reserves had dipped to an all-time low of only 150 crores (approximately $70 million). A significant hike in domestic petrol and diesel prices, drastic cuts in imports, and a credit squeeze to curb inflation were all outcomes of the Gulf War.[12]

The negotiation of an IMF loan to tide India over the foreign exchange crisis has created a furor within India. Many sections in India look on the IMF loan as a first step in the erosion of national sovereignty. The loan could make India the subject of coercive diplomatic action, especially in areas that are perceived as sensitive to Indian security interests.[13] India signing a discriminatory regime like the NPT would clearly come under the category of such coercive diplomacy. Given the nature of the functioning of the current minority Congress government, such pressures would present grave political problems.

The close relationships between Pakistan and some of the countries in the Middle East, especially with regard to Kashmir and the possible development of a joint nuclear capability by some Islamic countries, are also matters of special concern to India. The acquisition of nuclear and missile capability by Pakistan and by countries in the Middle East also have obvious implications for Indian security.[14] The self-restraint excercised by the superpowers, the Western countries, China, and India's other neighbors in the export of arms and critical technologies to this region will play a significant role in Indian policies on export control.

Indian views on export controls will emerge primarily from India's perceptions of its national security interests. These will in turn be dictated by global and regional considerations. Regional considerations will undoubtedly play a more significant role. The extent to which officially stated Indian policy that export controls are discriminatory will change is difficult to predict. The absence of a global plan to eliminate nuclear weapons, the lack of concrete progress toward total disarmament, and the generally irresponsible behavior of the major arms exporters will undoubtedly influence India.[15] Practical implementation of any export controls (as different from officially stated policy) will primarily be dictated by Indian perceptions of responsible behavior by the major arms exporters.

A strong India is considered to be necessary to ensure the survival of India as a nation-state. This is a common sentiment shared by all political parties. Self-reliance in key technology areas (defense, space, atomic energy) and self-sufficiency in core sectors like food, energy, etc., form the cornerstone of this approach. The formal recognition of these legitimate Indian interests, the removal of embargoes against India, and a regional framework for security are possibly key factors that would determine Indian participation in formal and informal export control regimes. In the absence of such developments, the continuation of the voluntary self-restraint that India has put on the export of weapons and weapons-related technology may come under increasing domestic pressure to change. Indian policy will also depend on how other players in the arms market (especially the big exporters) conduct themselves in areas that India thinks are strategic to its national security interests. The need for foreign exchange in the face of a grievous economic crisis may also result in a significant increase in Indian export of military systems and militarily significant technology. (These aspects are touched on in greater detail in the following sections.)

Official Indian Policy on Export Controls

India and the Nuclear Nonproliferation Treaty

The official Indian position on export controls as a method of control over the proliferation of weapons and weapons-related technologies is well known.[16] It has been closely coupled to India's well-known position that control, in the absence of a genuine movement toward total and complete disarmament, especially nuclear disarmament, cannot be acceptable to a country like India.

This position has evolved in a series of steps starting from the late 1940s and early 1950s right down to the present day. The Indian experience with the NPT has, to a large extent, influenced Indian positions in other areas of concern (viz., missile proliferation, chemical and biological weapons, as well as conventional weapons). To understand the Indian viewpoint, it is therefore necessary to look into Indian stands on nuclear weapons proliferation vis-à-vis the formal control mechanism that is supposed to control nuclear proliferation—the NPT.

During the early period of India's existence as a nation-state (the late 1940s and early 1950s), when the Indian atomic energy program under Nehru and Bhabha was still in its infancy, Indian views on disarmament were based on the premise that the primary nuclear powers had an interest in disarming and that the role of countries like India was to mediate and to act as go-betweens to facilitate this process.

However, this is not what happened. On the contrary, more and more countries joined the nuclear bandwagon. The finalization of the Partial Test Ban Treaty (1963), to which India was a party, was followed by negotiations leading to the NPT. Around the same time (1964), China became a nuclear weapons power. The combination of these factors and the possibilities of a Sino-Pakistan anti-India alliance, which India saw as a major threat, forced India into reexamining its nuclear policy options. By this time, India had built up significant indigenous capability in the peaceful uses of atomic energy.

The evolution of official Indian views and positions with regard to proliferation, the NPT, and control are dealt with in great detail in Kapur's book, *India's Nuclear Option.*[17] It is sufficient for our purposes to briefly recapitulate the salient features of Indian perceptions on the NPT, since they are still relevant indicators of the direction that official Indian policy will take. These perceptions can be broadly summarized as follows: (1) the NPT was a discriminatory treaty, allowing the nuclear powers to proliferate without restrictions, while other nonnuclear weapon states could not even pursue peaceful uses of atomic energy without very stringent and restrictive controls, and (2) the NPT ignored the legitimate security interests of many countries that did not want an alliance with either of the two superpowers.

Regional and geopolitical developments forced many countries like India to keep open a nuclear option, which could be excercised at some future date if necessary.[18] In the Indian view, these security considerations could not be satisfied through an alliance with one or the other superpower. Such an alliance would make India subject to coercive controls and prevent it from taking an independent stand. In addition, India saw itself as a leader of the nonaligned movement and the Third World in the struggle for a more equitable and peaceful world. As such a leader, India was duty bound to expose the fallacies inherent in the attitudes of the nuclear powers, who wanted to play the part of nuclear police over the rest of the world, without really trying to create a more peaceful world. The reconciliation of these often conflicting interests has to a large extent shaped Indian policy.

In his statement of May 23, 1967, to the Eighteen Nation Disarmament Committee, Ambassador Trivedi made the following statements on the discriminatory aspects of the NPT:

> A discriminatory treaty which gives a privileged license to the existing nuclear weapons powers to proliferate at will and which heaps ever-increasing prohibitions on non-nuclear powers will in itself be the strongest incentive to a new country to embark on a nuclear weapons program.[19]

The contradictions inherent in the superpowers' case about enhancing security through nonproliferation are further attacked by Ambassador Trivedi:

> These powerful nuclear weapon nations say that the non-nuclear nations would safeguard their security by foreswearing nuclear weapons forever in the midst of mushrooming proliferation by the nuclear weapon powers themselves. This is however not the precept which they have themselves followed and in fact they rejected it for themselves when it was time for them to decide.[20]

Dr. Bhabha also highlighted the need for India to keep open a nuclear option in a radio broadcast over All India Radio on October 25, 1964, immediately after the Chinese nuclear weapons test.[21] Morarji Desai, who was prime minister of India from 1977 to 1979 and strongly against India embarking on a nuclear weapons program,[22] voiced a feeling fairly widespread among decision makers when he is reported to have said,

> I do not believe in nuclear weapons or a nuclear umbrella of any sort. If however I were to make a choice I would rather have my own nuclear weapons than seek the umbrella of any outside power. To ask for such an umbrella would merely make us dependent on others and our independence would be diluted.[23]

The 1971 war with Pakistan, resulting in the creation of Bangladesh, brought home to India the problems faced by a not-so-strong large country, which is subject to coercion by the big powers. The United States dispatched the aircraft carrier *Enterprise* to the Bay of Bengal as a measure to support Pakistan. The Soviet Union remained ambivalent with regard to a possible confrontation with the U.S. over an Indo-Pakistan conflict. These experiences tended to reinforce arguments about the need to be independently strong to retain independence of action.

One of the possible consequences of this experience was the peaceful nuclear explosion at Pokhran in the Rajasthan desert in 1974. The international hue and cry (orchestrated mainly by the Western nuclear powers) that followed this explosion resulted in an international embargo against India. Many of the countries that had helped India with its nuclear program felt betrayed by the Indian explosion.[24] This feeling persisted despite the fact that Indian positions both internationally and domestically on nuclear proliferation and the NPT have always been consistent. India has always rejected the NPT as a discriminatory control regime that was not in keeping with Indian or global interests.

The Indian Response to Controls

Since Pokhran, India has been a special target of embargos. The launch of SLV-3 in 1980 created fears that India would soon possess a delivery system. This launch forced the Western alliance, led by the United States, to formulate the MTCR, directed primarily against India. The development of a Pakistani nuclear and missile capability, with the overt and covert assistance of major nuclear powers during the 1980s, resulted in India embarking on a fairly large program to modernize its armed forces.[25] A significant indigenous program for the development of critical technologies was also initiated.

These embargoes reinforced the basic Indian stand on control regimes. India perceives export controls as discriminatory and as an attempt by powerful nations to impose their will on the not-so-powerful countries. Control mechanisms that do not address larger issues of global disarmament and that do not address Indian regional security interests cannot, in this Indian view, prevent the spread of weapons. During his address to the third special session on disarmament of the UN General Assembly in 1988, the late Rajiv Gandhi, former prime minister of India, proposed an action plan to create "a world free of nuclear weapons."[26] This address was comprehensive in its coverage of Indian views. It can be looked on as a statement of the official Indian position that is valid even today.

While the focus of the plan was on nuclear weapons, issues related to chemical and biological weapons and space weapons as well as conventional weapons were covered in the package that India put to the world. His address articulated rather well Indian views on discriminatory controls and the dangers arising from such controls to countries such as India.

Selective excerpts from Gandhi's address place India's position in its proper perspective.

On the need to broaden discussions on security issues to cover other countries, Gandhi had the following to say:

> There are no technological solutions to the problems of world security. Security can only come from our asserting effective political control over this self-propelled arms race. We cannot accept the logic that a few nations have the right to pursue their security by threatening the survival of humankind.

On controls, he reiterated the Indian position:

> Nor is it acceptable that those who possess nuclear weapons are freed of all controls while those without nuclear weapons are policed against their production. History is full of such prejudices paraded as iron laws that men are superior to women; that the white races are superior to the colored; that colonialism is a civilizing mission; that those who possess nuclear weapons are responsible powers and those who do not are not.

Elsewhere Gandhi made points on chemical weapons and their elimination, the problems associated with the extension of the nuclear arms race into outer space, the possibilities of developments in life sciences endangering the biological weapons convention, and the need to address all means of mass annihilation in a comprehensive way. On conventional weapons, Gandhi made the following observations:

> New technologies have also dramatically expanded the scope and intensity of conventional warfare. Such diabolical technologies generate their own pressures for early use, thus increasing the risk of the outbreak of war. Most of these technologies are at the command of the military blocs. This immensely increases their capacity for interference, interaction and coercive diplomacy.

Gandhi categorically and clearly outlined Indian policy as follows:

> Those of us who do not belong to the military blocs would much rather stay out of the race. We do not want to augment our capacity to kill. But the system, like a whirlpool, sucks us into its vortex. We are compelled to direct resources from development to defense to respond to the arsenals which are constructed as a sideshow to great power rivalries. As the nature and sophistication of threats to our security increase we are forced to incur huge expenditure on raising the threshold of our defenses.
>
> Left to ourselves we would not want to touch nuclear weapons. But when tactical considerations in the passing play of great power rivalries

> are allowed to take precedence over the imperative of nuclear non-proliferation with what leeway are we left?

Gandhi went on to link disarmament and development for all countries.

> A genuine process of disarmament leading to a substantial reduction in military expenditure is bound to promote the prosperity of all nations of the globe. Disarmament accompanied by co-existence will open up opportunities for all countries whatever their socio-economic systems, whatever their levels of development.

Gandhi then proceeded to outline the details of the action plan, which would eliminate all nuclear weapons by 2010 and at the same time ban space weapons. The plan also envisages significant reduction in conventional weapons and provides for control over emerging technologies that have the potential to contribute to the development of new weapon systems.

India and the Missile Technology Control Regime

India's views on the MTCR parallel its views on nuclear proliferation. The behavior of the major powers and arms suppliers have been far from responsible, and many countries possess missiles.[27] The Gulf War and its aftermath clearly indicate that the MTCR has not been effective. Many of the parties to the MTCR have been clearly branded as irresponsible proliferators, a label normally reserved for countries like India.[28] The economic gains from arms exports are significant not only for developed countries but also for big powerful countries like China as well as for smaller countries like South Korea, Singapore, Malaysia, etc. The economic payoff often takes precedence over proliferation concerns. That tends to lend substance to an Indian view that control regimes do have a component of economic self-interest. They are directed primarily at countries with significant export potential, both in the civilian and defense sectors. India is today in a position to build its own missiles totally within the country and is poised to produce them in large numbers.[29] This places India in the category of a potential economic competitor.

Indian Policy after Rajiv Gandhi

Since Gandhi's speech, much has changed internationally and domestically in India. Gandhi's Congress Party lost power in 1989. Since then, the country has witnessed two minority governments and an election in June, 1991. The election of 1991, one of the most violent in India's history, witnessed the tragic assassination of the former prime minister, Rajiv Gandhi. A minority Congress Party (Gandhi's party) holds power in 1993.

The Gulf War created new problems for India. A major evacuation of Indians from the Gulf, a significant hike in oil prices, and a major foreign exchange crisis augmenting an already severe economic crisis have been the direct consequences of this war.

India has been forced by the grave economic crisis to apply to the IMF for financial assistance. The IMF loan has also been linked to a major program of industrial reform that is expected to attract foreign investment into India. Communal problems, an increasingly strident Hindu majority, and problems of militancy in several states with support from India's neighbors pose new challenges to the existence of India as a nation-state. Internationally the realignment of forces with the breaking up of the Soviet Union and the Eastern Europe–USSR alliance, the increasing cooperation between the Western powers and the USSR-Russian federation, the policies of Pakistan and China, and the problems in Sri Lanka are likely to have their impact on Indian actions.

The recently concluded NPT Review Conference shows that the substance of the debate on the NPT has not changed, and opposition to discriminatory NPT provisions continues to be widespread. The need to look for a significant reduction in nuclear arsenals and a time-bound action plan for the elimination of nuclear weapons and general disarmament seems to be a fairly distant dream. The decision by China and France to join the NPT is likely to isolate India. The START treaty has reduced nuclear arsenals by about 30 percent. The Bush-Gorbachev initiatives have cut down on tactical nuclear weapons. The breakup of the Soviet Union will increase the number of countries possessing nuclear weapons. Islamic fundamentalism arising from such a breakup is another factor that India has to contend with. A total action plan for the elimination of nuclear weapons, however, is not in immediate sight. The regional problems and the continued availability of nuclear weapons with some countries may make countries like India stick fairly close to their earlier stated positions on the NPT. In a statement to the Indian Parliament, Narasimha Rao firmly stated that India would not become a party to the NPT.[30]

Many politicians, intellectuals, and others in important positions in India see a linkage between the IMF loan, the NPT, and domestic defense spending. This linkage is not without some basis and enjoys some level of official sanction among the Western powers.

A significant Indian effort in modernizing its armed forces has resulted in India becoming one of the largest importers of weapon systems. The importance India gives to modernization and military strength is shown by the fact that in spite of grave economic crisis, the defense budget has been increased. The lessons from the Gulf War and its aftermath may also force India into going nuclear and investing more heavily in improving its defense capabilities.[31]

India is a party to the biological weapons convention and will abide by its provisions reflected in Article I (the production, stockpiling, and acquisition of biological weapons) and Article III (the transfer of such technology).

India also supports a nondiscriminatory chemical weapons convention with its attendant safeguards and controls on proliferation. The possibilities of the finalization of a universally applicable, nondiscriminatory chemical weapons convention seem to have improved after the Gulf War. If one is instituted, India needs to be able to implement measures to control exports of critical chemicals.

Overall Assessment of Official Policy

One of the main themes of this chapter is that irrespective of India's international posture and the pressures imposed on it, Indian behavior regarding exports of weapon systems and critical technologies has been exemplary. The portrayal of India as a potential irresponsible proliferator has no factual basis. Formal and informal mechanisms, as well as legislation and licensing procedures that exist within the Indian political, governmental, and industrial system, will ensure a continuation of this responsible behavior.

The Indian behavior has been much more mature and pro-peace in comparison to the behavior of some of the major powers, who are parties to both informal and formal mechanisms of export control. This Indian behavior has of course received relatively little mention or praise in either the media or Western assessments of Indian intentions. India, however, will continue to excercise maturity and caution in the export of weapons and sensitive technologies.

In the Indian view, a regional framework that includes China and Pakistan is necessary if areas of major concern (nuclear weapons and missiles) are to be dealt with properly. Without such a framework, India would not be able to subscribe to any regime of controls.

Since missile proliferation in the Middle East is a fact, the involvement of a few of the more important of the Middle East countries may also be necessary in such regional negotiations. This view of course assumes that a chemical weapons convention will soon be finalized and that all major countries of concern to Indian security interests in the region will be parties to this convention. Thus, only nuclear weapons, missiles, and conventional weapons would be the substance of discussions and mutual controls.

This regional framework should be linked to a global plan for total and complete disarmament within a suitable time frame.

Before analyzing in greater detail the likely directions that practical implementation of Indian policy will take, it is necessary to understand existing Indian mechanisms for control over the export of weapons and critical technologies. It is also necessary to understand through available data the Indian record as a potential proliferator of weapons and critical technologies. This is the subject of the next section.

Export Control Practices and Proliferation: The Indian Experience

The Organizational Framework

Unlike many countries, Indian national security policies are not clearly articulated and subjected to political debate and scrutiny. While public involvement and the airing of some aspects have of late become prominent, much of this policy is developed by concerned ministries. The Cabinet Secretariat coordinates aspects related to security (under whom the intelligence wings of the government function), with the appropriate involvement of the Ministries of External Affairs, Defense, and Home; the armed forces; and the intelligence wings. The allocation of business rules formally allots areas of activity to different ministries and departments, who enjoy relative freedom in their day-to-day activities.[32] The defense program, the space program, and the atomic energy program all enjoy great freedom. These ministries and departments are also responsible for international activities in their field. Ministries and departments coordinate policy formulation and decision making on matters related to international cooperation, the export of sensitive technologies, and national security with the Ministry of External Affairs and the Cabinet Secretariat. Policy formulation, especially in sensitive areas, remains with the bureaucracy in the respective ministries and departments.

This method has both advantages and disadvantages. One advantage is that individual ministries responsible for different facets of sensitive programs like defense, atomic energy, space, etc., are able to formulate policy with respect to what they see as advantageous to their individual programs. The absence of a clearly articulated national security policy, and public discussions centered around such a policy, provides a great deal of flexibility to individual departments.

The negative aspect is that outside viewpoints from academia or the public do not directly find any place in decision making. An obsessive concern with security, as perceived by these decision makers, very often results in excessive and restrictive controls. As a consequence, legitimate and lucrative economic and political self-interest is often sacrificed at the altar of what are wrongly perceived as national security interests.[33]

This system of controls is reinforced by direct government ownership over most critical production facilities and technology. The government owns and operates all critical facilities. Security concerns also limit industrial involvement in the production of key weapon systems and the development of critical technologies.[34] Thus there is no military-industrial complex in India. There is only a government-run military complex.

The Indian government has considered setting up a National Security Council to formulate national security strategy.[35] However, it has so far proved to be a nonstarter. There are grave doubts whether such a council could break the bureaucratic control over practical implementation of policy. There are also doubts whether it can function effectively, given the limited resources at its disposal.

The Gulf crisis underlined the need for long-range strategic thinking on likely scenarios affecting Indian interests. The extent to which the yet to be set up National Security Council will be effective in such an environment remains to be seen. The signals so far have not been encouraging. The absence of academic linkages in the formulation of national security policies is also likely to prove an obstacle to the process of creative alternative scenario development, an essential ingredient in the evolution of a national security policy.[36]

The excessive independence given to individual departments; direct government control over critical production facilities and technologies; an obsession with security; and the absence of clearly articulated, well-understood national security policy with clear guidelines have associated with this system both an advantage and a major disadvantage. The advantage has been, of course, that India so far has one of the best records on controls over exports. The disadvantage has been that India has had no appreciable returns on the heavy investments made in the core defense sectors. India has also not used its fairly significant capabilities in defense and other core sectors as a tool for pursuing Indian foreign policy and geopolitical interests.

Government industrial policy in the early 1990s has significantly relaxed licensing procedures as well as export procedures. However, the policy does not significantly depart from existing policies in critical areas. The government has made it clear that critical areas of technology, which are of strategic concern, will continue to be either directly in government hands or in bodies subject to government regulation.

Existing Export Controls in the Areas of Concern

An understanding of the existing rules, regulations, and procedures concerning exports is necessary to assess the Indian contribution to the proliferation of weapons and weapons-related technologies. The major proliferation concerns today relate to (1) nuclear weapons and nuclear materials, (2) missiles, (3) conventional weapons, and (4) chemical and biological weapons.

As mentioned above, the decision and policy-making structure of the Indian government is such that the major responsibilities for formulation and practical implementation of policy are vested with different ministries and departments of the government.

The nodal agency for control over and the regulation of exports has been the Department of Commerce under the Ministry of Commerce.[37] This agency is responsible for import and export trade policy and control over imports and exports. Actual implementation of policy is carried out through the office of the chief controller of exports and imports. The primary emphasis of the Department of Commerce is on the control and regulation of commercially important products, in accordance with the industrial policy and the export-import policies, which the government lays down from time to time. The import-export policy covering 1990–93 is of direct concern for our analysis.[38] Export control is implemented through the maintenance of separate lists, of which there are several categories. Items appearing on each of these lists are covered through separate procedures. These lists are subject to amendments from time to time. These amendments are published through a public gazette notification.

Schedule 1 of the Export (Control) Order lists commodities that are subject to export control. These items are further split into two parts: Part A items and Part B items. Exports of Part A items are totally banned. Exports of Part B items are regulated. Exports of all other items are permitted, provided their exports do not violate any other law of the Government of India.

Even though the Department of Commerce is the nodal agency for export control, a number of other departments play critical roles in the formulation and implementation of export policies.

In the areas of concern to proliferation, the major departments and agencies that are involved are

- the Department of Atomic Energy (DAE) (nuclear technology, nuclear materials),
- the Ministry of Defense (conventional weapons, missiles, military technology),
- the Department of Space (DOS) (space technology),
- the Department of Chemicals (chemical technology), and
- the Department of Biotechnology (biotechnology).

The Ministry of Industry, which is responsible for formulating and implementing industrial policy, is also an important contributor to export-import policy. It is the nodal ministry that decides which areas of industrial activity will be under direct government control and which areas will be in private hands.

Many of these departments and ministries have the responsibility of dealing with international developments in their area, and as a consequence, export issues are also raised by them. These issues are generally discussed by a Committee of Secretaries (chaired by the Cabinet Secretary) and raised to appropriate political levels for final decisions. Implementation is then left to the implementing agency, which, if necessary, seeks appropriate licenses and clearances from other concerned departments or agencies.

We shall, in this section, try to outline in some detail how these different arms of government function in specific areas of concern (atomic energy, missiles, conventional weapons, and chemical weapons) and analyze how effective or ineffective they have been in actual practice.

Nuclear Technology and Materials

The DAE, which functions directly under the prime minister, is the sole agency responsible for all nuclear and nuclear material–related activities.[39] The department's activities cover all activities in the nuclear field, from the mining and production of nuclear ores and materials to the setting up of full-fledged nuclear power plants. The export of nuclear materials is separately covered by the Control of Production and Use of Atomic Energy Act of 1962, which is also the implementing authority for the DAE.[40]

The department exercises total control over prospecting, drilling, and mining of all materials and minerals listed under the act. A number of public sector undertakings solely owned and run by the DAE carry out the production of uranium, thorium, heavy water, and other nuclear critical materials such as zirconia and beryllia, including rare earths. Many of the other research facilities are run as regular government undertakings.

The DAE subcontracts many items to industry, especially in the area of fabrication. However, all critical technologies are directly with and under the control of the department.

This DAE control is supplemented through a secondary system of controls governing export. These controls are exercised by the Department of Commerce. The export of critical nuclear materials and ores is banned under Part A of Schedule 1 of Export Control Order 1988. The items banned include a number of nuclear important metals and their compounds as well as a number of nuclear important ores and minerals.

The nuclear important metals and their compounds, whose export is banned, include beryllium, lithium, neptunium, plutonium, radium, thorium, uranium, zirconium, iridium, iridosmine, osmiridium, selenium, and deuterium compounds. Nuclear important minerals, ores, and concentrates, whose export is banned, include radium ores and concentrates, uranium ores and concentrates, and uranium bearing tailings left over from ores after the extraction of copper or gold. While the export of thorium metal and compounds is banned, the export of thorium ores and concentrates is not completely banned. However, these exports must be canalized through the canalizing agency, which, in this case, is Indian Rare Earths Ltd., a fully owned subsidiary of the DAE.

Since the production of all nuclear materials and ores is only through government-owned and government-run companies, control over the export of these materials is guaranteed. Export is not possible unless it is in consonance with national policy.

The export of minerals that contain columbite, monazite, samerskite, and uraniferrous allamite also have to be canalized through the canalizing agency. All ores and materials containing uranium, thorium, and zircon ores as subsidiary or secondary materials also have to be canalized through the canalizing agency, which is always in the public sector and fully government-owned and controlled. Thus, through a system of ownership, direct control over the production of ores and materials, and the control of exports by banning and canalizing, complete control over the export of nuclear materials and ores is ensured.

With regard to nuclear technology, the DAE is the sole repository of the technology through its numerous agencies. While industry is involved in providing components and subsystems for various elements of the program, critical technologies have always remained directly under government control. This control has been reinforced even in the latest industrial policy of the government. Keeping in mind the strategic and proliferation dangers posed by nuclear technology, atomic energy is one area of industrial activity where government ownership and control will continue. Technology exports in this area will therefore be only at a government-to-government level and will need government clearances from the highest political levels.

These export controls have so far worked very successfully. No country can point its finger at India and say that nuclear materials and nuclear technology of relevance to weapons production have leaked out of India. The same statement cannot be made about most of the nuclear powers. This applies not only to countries that form a part of informal and formal technology cartels like the NSG and the NPT but also to countries like China, which are outside these cartels.[41]

There has been much speculation in the press in the early 1990s about the Indian export of a nuclear research reactor to Iran and its possible impact on proliferation. The United States has expressed special concern, and the subject came up for discussion during the recent visit of U.S. Under Secretary of State for National Security Affairs Bartholomew. Iran is a signatory to the NPT and already possesses research reactors supplied by the Soviet Union. India is not unaware of the implications of an Iranian-Pakistani link with respect to nuclear weapons. However, India views the sale of a reactor to Iran in the same light as sales that other countries have made to parties subject to NPT and IAEA safeguards. Whatever the Indian decision, one can be sure that it will be reasoned and well thought out and take into account all factors affecting Indian interests.[42]

The actual situation is that India has behaved and will continue to behave responsibly with regard to the export of nuclear technologies and materials.

Missiles

The responsibility for the development of missiles vests with the Defense Research and Development Laboratory (DRDL) of the DRDO. The production of missiles in large numbers for deployment is the responsibility of the Department of Defense Production and Supplies. All these organizations function under the Ministry of Defense.

Under the integrated missile development program, the DRDO is developing four missiles: (1) Trishul, an antitank missile (9-kilometer range); (2) Akash, an antiaircraft missile (27-kilometer range); (3) Prithvi, a surface-to-surface missile (250-kilometer range); and (4) Agni, an intermediate-range ballistic missile (2500-kilometer range).

This missile program is completely indigenous. After development is complete, responsibility for production will be transferred from the DRDO to Bharath Dynamics Ltd., which is a public-sector company fully owned and operated by the Department of Defense Production and Supplies.

In the development of its missiles, DRDO is reported to have received assistance and help from the DOS, which is responsibile for the development of civilian capabilities in the area of space.[43] The DOS responsibilities include both the development of satellites and launchers and the promotion of the applications of space for national development tasks. It is also responsible for projects and industries concerned with the utilization of outer space as well as international matters related to space. In 1980, India became the sixth country to launch a satellite with an indigenously developed launcher—an event that heralded the creation of a new technology control regime, the MTCR. When the first development missiles under the integrated missile program were launched, there was much speculation that technology acquired for civilian space uses had been diverted into the successful development of missiles. The first stage of the two-stage Agni rocket is reported to be derived from the first stage of DOS's civilian launcher SLV-3.

There is no doubt that throughout the 1960s and early 1970s, India received significant international help (from the United States, the Soviet Union, and France) in setting up facilities for launching sounding rockets. The French also assisted India in setting up production facilities for the small Centaur sounding rocket. While these did help to a limited extent in creating Indian capabilities in rocket technology, it is incorrect to conclude that Indian developments in rocket technology critically depended on technology from abroad.[44] A strong indigenous program formed the core of the space program's strategy for the development of civilian launcher capability right from the early days.

The DRDO also had an independent program for the development of liquid rockets. The series of missiles that are currently under development are a direct result of these DRDO efforts, all of which are indigenous.

Coming down to basic issues of exports, vis-à-vis missile technologies, the technology for the development and production of missiles and launchers rests with two government agencies: the DOS and the DRDO. Most of the critical technologies—propellant production, control and guidance, and integration and test facilities—are directly under these departments or with other fully government-owned and -controlled production units. Issues concerning the export of critical materials and technologies, therefore, have to follow the standard procedure of departmental review and scrutiny, discussions by a Committee of Secretaries, and final political decisions at the highest levels.

Like its atomic energy program, the Indian record on the export of missile critical technologies is excellent. There are indications that in view of the foreign exchange crisis and the need to reduce heavy government expenditure on defense, the export of some high-technology defense systems including missiles may be considered.[45] The official policy of the Ministry of Defense so far has been that while India has no problems with the export of nonsensitive defense items, certain categories of weapons and defense systems can only be exported country to country.[46]

Therefore, while India does not rule out exports in the missile area, it is clear that such exports must be cleared at the highest political level and fall in line with Indian sensitivities with regard to its perceived security interests. The export behavior of countries like China, Pakistan, and the Western alliance, as well as countries like Korea, Singapore, etc., will also influence Indian practice on exports. There is, however, little doubt that the process India will follow will be mature and well considered in keeping with its national interests.

The recent industrial policy of the government reinforces this commitment. The production of arms, ammunition, and allied items of defense equipment, defense aircraft, and warships will continue to be directly under government ownership. All other key industrial activities related to defense, such as electronics, aerospace, explosives, explosive materials, etc., need an industrial license. Thus, even though in the civilian space sector, there is a likelihood that private industry will get more involved with actual production and development tasks, the existing system provides a strong base for export controls. It is therefore unlikely that India would export missiles or missile technologies without going through a fairly complex decision-making process involving a critical analysis of its security interests. India will therefore continue to behave as a responsible exporter in this area.

Conventional Weapons

The major responsibility on all matters related to conventional weapons is vested with the Indian Ministry of Defense. Three departments function under the ambit of the Ministry of Defense. These are the Department of Defense, the Department of Defense Production and Supplies, and the DRDO.

The Department of Defense Production and Supplies is responsible for the production of various arms, weapon systems, and other necessary support systems for use by the armed forces. It is also responsible for the indigenization program for all items of defense equipment that are manufactured under license.[47]

The Department of Defense Production and Supplies has under its direct control thirty-five ordnance factories producing a variety of weapon systems. Eight public sector (fully government-owned companies) also operate under the department. These produce a number of critical items, including fighter aircraft, radars, defense control equipment, frigates, ships, missiles, and special materials.[48] The Department of Defense Production and Supplies in 1989–90 produced equipment worth 5,000 crores (approximately $2–2.5 billion).

The involvement of private industry in the defense production program has, at best, been marginal. The total value of subcontracts with industry was only about 700 crores ($300 million). This is only a relatively small 14 percent of the total value of defense production of about 5,000 crores. In spite of repeated protests from industry and in spite of increased liberalization, this policy is likely to continue.

The DRDO is the agency responsible for assessing and advising the Ministry of Defense on national security aspects of emerging developments in science and technology. In addition, the DRDO advises and assists the Ministry of Defense in the acquisition and evaluation of all weapon systems and related technologies. The DRDO is also responsible for research and development in all fields related to defense and national security. It is the nodal agency for control over technologies acquired from foreign countries, which are subject to export control by India.[49]

The DRDO carries on its research and development activities through a string of laboratories and facilities distributed all over the country. It is currently responsible for three major programs: (1) integrated missile development program, (2) the development of an advanced light-combat aircraft, and (3) the development of a mainfield battle tank.

Its research activities encompass a spectrum of technology areas and include the development of integrated circuits, robotics, artificial intelligence, and the production of application-specific integrated circuits, materials, etc.

As mentioned above, the Indian record in controlling exports of weapons and weapons-related technologies has been exemplary. This control has been achieved because of the virtual stranglehold that the government has over the production of critical defense equipment and through procedures of ensuring direct control over exports on grounds of national security. India can in principle export arms and technologies. However, the control procedures are such that it can do so only on a government-to-government basis. Much of Indian defense production is also carried out under license. Exports may require permissions from the country or company granting the license. This permission is not always granted. The absence of a clearly articulated, well-understood national security policy also facilitates the control process exercised by the bureaucracy.

Indian exports of defense items totalled 64 crores ($30 million) in 1989, one of the lowest figures in the world. This is only 1.3 percent of the total value of defense production of about 5,000 crores. According to one source, India ranked thirty-eighth in the export of arms. In 1989, India was ranked as the biggest importer.[50] In comparison, China is the fifth largest exporter of weapons. The Pakistani record of export is also far superior.[51] Even countries like Singapore, Malaysia, Indonesia, etc., rank far above India in export of weapons and defense equipment.[52] There is within the Indian decision-making structure an excessive concern with security, very often at the expense of business. The general view is that business cannot be carried out without compromising so-called security interests. This obsession can be seen even in other non-defense-related areas like the supply of satellite imagery.[53]

The latest industrial policy makes it clear that all critical defense production and development will continue to be with the government. The privatization of defense production will also not take place on any substantial scale.[54] The export control policy also lays down controls for the export of small arms and ammunition by companies. Anyway, those exports are subject to control by Ministry of Defense since it produces all the weapons, including small arms.

In view of the major economic crisis the country is facing, there may be increasing pressure for the defense establishments to export. There has been much talk about setting up a separate company to promote defense exports. Air defense radars, missiles, etc., are some of the items being considered for export.[55] Nothing concrete has emerged so far. The arms market today is characterized by a plethora of suppliers and is highly competitive. Indian companies in the defense business are all government-owned and -run and subsidized to a great extent. They have always been able to sell to a captive domestic market and have had very little experience in trying to sell goods and services in the highly competitive international arms market.

In the absence of a national security council and a clear national security policy, the existing systems are likely to continue. This is particularly true since exports require a major thrust and initiative. Any export-oriented drive is likely to face significant resistance from the bureaucracy and the armed forces.

However, economic pressures may make India wake up to the fact that it is a significant possessor of technological and defense capabilities and that these capabilities can be used as an instrument of policy for enhancing security as well as for economic and political purposes. Initiatives announced by the defense minister in 1990 speak of a significant increase in the export of defense products and services. How much will actually fructify is a matter for speculation.[56]

Chemical Weapons

The Department of Chemicals in the Ministry of Petroleum and Chemicals is the nodal agency that is responsible for all organic and inorganic chemicals. It is concerned with

- drugs and pharmaceuticals,
- insecticides,
- dyestuffs and dye intermediates,
- all organic and inorganic chemicals not allotted to any other department or ministry,
- petrochemicals,
- industries relating to noncellulosic synthetic fibers,
- synthetic rubber, and
- plastics.

Most chemicals that are of interest to chemical weapons are covered by this list.[57]

Unlike atomic energy, missiles, and defense technologies, the chemical industry is not completely dominated by government-owned and government-run industries, though there are some big companies in the government-owned public sector.

The distribution of production responsibilities in the chemical area between public and private sector is normally outlined in the industrial policy of the government. Exports of chemicals are covered by the export-import policy of the Department of Commerce. As mentioned earlier, the Export Control Order contains different lists that either ban or regulate items appearing on the list. None of the chemicals identified as chemical intermediates for chemical weapons by the AG find a place in this Indian list.

Companies are thus free to export these without any controls. The chemical industry in India is fairly large, and technology is distributed between large, medium, and small industries. As of the time of this writing, India has not paid much attention to controlling the export of chemicals considered critical for weapons production. One reason for this has been the slow progress on a universal chemical weapons convention. The Geneva Conference on Disarmament negotiations have been bogged down mainly by U.S. concerns, which have prevented the finalization of such a convention.

Recent events in the Gulf and the UN–U.S.-led war against Iraq have brought home to the international community the need to control and even eliminate chemical weapons. This experience is likely to influence the multilateral negotiations in Geneva and may soon result in the finalization of a chemical weapons convention. India had, before the embargo, exported chemicals that could be used for weapons to Iraq.[58] Both in volume and money terms, this in no way compares to significant exports of technology made by many developed countries. West German exports for example apparently had a major role to play in Iraq's development of chemical weapons.[59] Even in the case of Indian exports, almost all the companies involved have been established as joint ventures with German collaboration.

India is of the view that in the absence of a chemical weapons convention, a prohibition on the exports of chemicals (which, apart from being used for weapons, can also be used for civilian purposes) by Indian industry makes no sense. This was particularly so when some of the most vociferous adherents of export controls were major exporters of such material. India participated in the Paris Conference on Prohibition of Chemical Weapons as well as in the International Government-Industry Conference against chemical weapons held in Canberra in 1989. At both conferences, India stressed the need to finalize a universal nondiscriminatory convention to eliminate chemical weapons.

The regulation of exports of chemicals from India is closely linked with the finalization of a universally applicable chemical weapons convention. If such a convention comes into effect, would India be in position to implement its international obligations arising from a chemical weapons convention? That is a question that needs to be answered.

The Ministry of Environment in India has recently enacted an act regulating hazardous chemicals and wastes in India. A comprehensive list of hazardous chemicals has been drawn up.[60] Most chemicals identified by the AG as potential precursors of chemical weapons in some form or variant find a place in this list. Their production and use would therefore be subject to governmental regulation of some kind. In the recent industrial policy statement of the Indian government, hazardous chemicals have been identified as industries subject to compulsory licensing.[61] Government regulation and control over chemicals which are deemed critical can therefore be implemented without much difficulty, should the need arise.

The Indian chemical industry would be obliged to abide by any controls government might impose to prevent exports of critical technologies. These controls could be implemented both by amending or modifying the export control list or by controlling the granting of licenses to industries capable of producing critical chemicals. Chemicals are an industrial growth area. Controls have to be selective not to hamper normal commercial growth. The support of Indian industry is also required for effective implementation. The general consensus within India is that India would not be found wanting in the implementation of a universal nondiscriminatory chemical weapons convention.

Biological Weapons

In the area of biological weapons, India is party to the biological weapons convention and is obliged to abide by the provisions of this convention. The Indian biotechnology industry is still at a very nascent stage, and the focus is predominantly commercial. Unlike other areas such as missiles, conventional weapons, and atomic energy, comparatively little public money is spent on biotechnology. The obligations under the convention prevent India from developing biological weapons. It is unlikely that in the near or medium term, Indian biotechnological firms would develop capabilities in this area. India would be even more unlikely to be an exporter of such technologies.

The Impact of Recent International Developments on Indian Policy

As I mentioned above, recent international developments are likely to have a significant impact on Indian views on the theory and practice of using export controls as a method for controlling proliferation.

To recapitulate, these developments are

1. the breakup of the Soviet Union and the emergence of Russia as the strongest of the erstwhile Soviet republics;
2. the breakup of the WTO;
3. the aftermath of the war against Iraq following the Iraqi invasion of Kuwait;
4. the reduction in the role of Russia or the former Soviet Union as a military and economic power;
5. the ascendancy of the United States as the singlemost significant power;
6. closer cooperation between the nuclear weapon states on issues related to arms control and proliferation, especially China and France joining the NPT;
7. the emergence of Japan as a major economic power and the increasingly important role of China as an economic military power;
8. problems associated with Pakistani nuclear capabilities and their impact on India, especially on Kashmir and Punjab;
9. problems of separatism in India and associated problems in Sri Lanka and LTTE terrorism in India;
10. the developments in the Gulf region and in the former Soviet Muslim republics and their side effects on the large Muslim population of India and the potential for nuclear blackmail posed by erstwhile Soviet Muslim republics in collaboration with other Islamic states; and
11. the economic crisis in India.

Some clear and some not-so-clear trends seem to emerge out of these developments.

The first trend appears to be that to cope with the breakup and marginalization of the Soviet Union as a military power, India needs to become militarily stronger. This strength is needed to safeguard legitimate Indian national interests in the region from a position of reasonable strength.

The second trend is that in view of Pakistan's development of nuclear weapons, India needs to reassess its stated intentions of not developing and deploying nuclear weapons. There is a school of thought in India that says that strategic concerns leave India with no choice but to exercise the nuclear option. To substantiate this view, proponents point to the results of the Gulf War. The outcome of this war, in their view, would have been totally different if Iraq had had a nuclear capability.[62]

The third trend that emerges is the need for India to create strong indigenous capabilities in militarily significant technologies. India has always articulated the need for self-reliance. This is now likely to become a more important goal with or without foreign assistance. The modernization of defense forces to cope with both China and Pakistan in a conventional war could be the driving force behind Indian actions.[63] The problems of Punjab, Kashmir, the northeastern states, and the LTTE in southern India would also contribute in some measure to this view.

The Gulf War has emphasized the need to promote regional arms control and security arrangements with the participation of all relevant parties. It has also resulted in a move to convene an Arab-Israeli peace conference to promote such an arrangement. Whether this conference will address issues of arms control in the region is not clear, especially because of Israeli nuclear capability. Similar proposals have been mooted in the past for the Indian region. While India may not oppose the Arab-Israeli peace talks to solve the Palestinian issue, it may consider itself an affected party in any regional security arrangement. Pakistan's Islamic connections in the Middle East are well known. To protect domestic Indian interests in Kashmir and Punjab, Indian involvement is essential in any peace process and regional security arrangements. India also has one of the largest populations of Muslims in the world, and Islamic linkages of this population with the Middle East are matters of legitimate concern to India.[64] There is a possibility that India and Israel may also work closer together to break the Pakistan–Middle East nexus. This cooperation would call for a significant shift in India's pro-Arab policy but cannot be ruled out.

Any regional initiative in the Indian region should also necessarily involve both China and Pakistan. In the absence of either of these two countries and in the absence of clear linkages that these countries may have with the Middle East, India would find it difficult to participate in any regional security arrangement. Hence any informal or formal Indian commitments on export controls would depend on the feasibility of realizing such an arrangement. From the way things are shaping up in the Middle East, an Arab-Israeli peace conference may take place because of U.S. pressure on Israel. While there has been a lot of talk on regional security arrangements in the Middle East, there have not been any tangible moves toward this end. Meanwhile, the major arms exporters are having a field day in the aftermath of the Gulf War.[65] The Middle East with its oil-based economic power will continue to be an arena for the collection of more and more sophisticated weapons.

China has always remained aloof from any regional security arrangements covering the subcontinent, whereas Pakistani intentions on such arrangements do not appear to be sincere according to India. A regional security arrangement acceptable to India therefore appears unlikely at this stage. China's willingness to sign the NPT and the possibilities of countries like Brazil and Argentina yielding to U.S. pressure may isolate India as the lone voice opposing the NPT. During the visit in 1991 of U.S. Under Secretary of State for National Security Affairs Bartholomew to India and Pakistan, the issue of a regional security arrangement with regard to nuclear weapons was apparently discussed.[66]

The other trend that emerges is a closer link between the United States and India, with Pakistan becoming less important to U.S. strategic interests in the absence of a Soviet threat. There is some improvement in Indo-U.S. relations. The United States has also cooperated with India in supplying high-technology equipment in some areas.[67] This cooperation may continue. The extent to which India formally or informally accedes to any controls will depend to a large extent on a regional security arrangement involving China. However, even in the absence of such an arrangement (China has always been cool to such an idea), it is possible that cooperation between India and the United States will improve and even expand.

Apart from these trends, two other factors are likely to influence Indian policy. First, investment in defense and in the development of high-technology weapons is likely to increase. India is faced with a major economic crisis, which dictates that India reduce the impact of high defense expenditure through an increase in exports. And second, Indian export of defense items has been low partly because of the absence of clearly articulated national security policy and close and excessive control by the bureaucracy. This may change soon, and if the proposed National Security Council is set up, the export of defense items and technology may find an increasing role in the formulation and protection of Indian foreign and security policy.

Conclusions

The following conclusions seem warranted:

First, it appears unlikely that India will become a party to the NPT or any variant of the NPT in the near future. Formally, therefore, India will not accept or subscribe to any controls over nuclear materials and nuclear technology that it develops.

Second, this decision on the NPT is linked directly to the possibility that India may exercise an option to go nuclear. This is critically dependent on the demonstration of Pakistani nuclear capability. It is possible that if Pakistan does not go nuclear and the nuclear genie remains in the bottle, the status quo on the NPT may continue. A Pakistani explosion will trigger a definite Indian reaction to go nuclear. Indian infrastructure in this field is adequate to protect it against any punitive actions by the nuclear powers. In either of the two scenarios, India will continue to be a responsible nuclear exporter.

Third, India would not be against regional agreements on arms control, arms regulation, and attendant obligations to control proliferation. Crucial to this agreement would be the involvement of China and Pakistan. A linkage with arms control and proliferation control measures in the Middle East would also be necessary for India's agreement. It appears unlikely that this will emerge in the near future. The recent Chinese indication that China will sign the NPT is bound to raise Indian suspicions that this is an orchestrated, well-planned move to isolate India.

Fourth, in the area of missiles, India considers the MTCR discriminatory and directed against it. India has established significant capabilities in the development of missiles, and it will continue to go ahead with their deployment. It is unlikely that India would formally become a party to the MTCR, even if countries who are parties to it want India to join. India, however, will continue to exercise restraint in the export of sensitive weapon systems and technologies. The removal of India as a subject of MTCR regulations may facilitate a process of dialogue on the export of missile technologies.

Fifth, the economic crisis in India is also likely to increase pressure on the Indian defense establishment to export weapons and earn foreign exchange. However, that is not expected to alter the current role of India as a responsible exporter. The creation of a National Security Council and the articulation of a national security policy is likely to help the export drive of the Indian defense establishment.

Sixth, the Indian defense budget is also likely to increase. The easing of rules and regulations governing industry in India will promote joint ventures in India especially in high-technology fields. Existing Indian controls over exports with some strengthening are adequate, in case India needs to exercise controls over sensitive technology.

Seventh, if a nondiscriminatory chemical weapons convention is finalized, India will become a party to it. India would also abide by any export control obligations arising from such a convention. Existing control mechanisms within India (with some modifications) could take care of any export control obligations arising out of such a convention. The regulation of the hazardous chemicals industry and international obligations arising out of the transnational transportation of hazardous chemicals could provide a basis for future regulation.

Eighth, as far as biological weapons are concerned, India is a party to the biological weapons convention and will abide by the provisions of this treaty.

Ninth, the export of critical weapons and technologies will be primarily dictated by Indian interests. This policy will be somewhat of a shift from the past Indian policy of overwhelming export restrictions. The export of weapons and critical technologies by India is also likely to become a more important component in the conduct of India's foreign policy.

Tenth, India has behaved as a responsible exporter and will continue to be one. While India may not formally adhere and become a party to regimes like the NPT or the MTCR, in practice India will follow policies that will not result in proliferation. This is in sharp contradiction to the general image that India has in Western policy-making circles as a potential proliferator and as a country that has to be subject to special controls for receiving sensitive technology. In practice the Indian record on controls has been far better than most countries party to export control regimes.

Finally, there are areas of mutual interest where India can work in tandem with other countries with regard to export control. This cooperation can happen if there is an understanding of Indian security interests and some common perceptions on regional and global security interests. This process can be facilitated by the formal recognition of India as a regional power with legitimate security interests in the region and by removing India from the blacklist of potential proliferators under both the NPT and the MTCR.

NOTES

I would like to thank Shri Raghavendra Rao and the staff of the Indian Space Research Organization (ISRO) headquarters library for their help in collecting the material used in this chapter. Dr. V. Siddhartha of the Defense Research and Development Organization (DRDO); Mr. Y. S. Rajan, adviser, Department of Science and Technology; and Mr. A. Chandran, associate director, Launch Vehicle Programme Office of ISRO helped me with critical inputs and reviews of this article. Special thanks are due to my secretary, K. R. Ambrose, for the patient typing of the numerous drafts of this article. I would also like to place on record my special thanks to Professor U. R. Rao, chairman of ISRO, without whose support this research would not have been possible. The views expressed in this chapter are my own and do not reflect in any way the views of ISRO.

1. For details of the world reaction after Pokhran, see K. K. Pathak, *Nuclear Policy of India* (New Delhi: Geetanjali Prakashan, 1980), 121–89.

2. There is no doubt that the United States and many other countries saw the launch of SLV-3 in 1980 as a major contributor to the proliferation threat. See, for example, chapter 2.

3. See C. Rajamohan, "Non-Proliferation: New Perceptions," *The Hindu,* July 18, 1991, for a scenario of close Indo-U.S. cooperation on nuclear and weapons proliferation issues.

4. India's name does not figure at all in the SIPRI list of major exporters. See "The Trade in Major Conventional Weapons," in *SIPRI Yearbook 1990* (Oxford: Oxford University Press, 1990), 220–21.

5. The United States issues over 3,500 licences per year for the export of sensitive dual-use technology items to India as a result of an Indo-U.S. agreement on technology transfer. There have been no reported instances of any technology diversion. See Hamish McDonald, "Technically Friends," *Far Eastern Economic Review,* January 31, 1991, 13–14.

6. There is no doubt that U.S. commercial concerns play a role in the implementation of, say, the MTCR. In spite of Soviet-U.S. cooperation, U.S. satellites still cannot fly on Soviet rockets. The United States also raised several objections to U.S.-built satellites being launched on Chinese rockets. It finally agreed to only a limited number of launches by China. The MTCR also restricts, for example, exports of cryogenic technology. As everybody knows, cryogenics cannot be used for operational missiles due to problems of loading cryogenic fluids and the complexities associated with launch pad checks. This restriction raises the doubt that U.S. motives are not purely military but also stem from commercial concerns.

7. For a more detailed list, see the special report, "Agni: Chariot of Fire," *India Today,* June 15, 1989, 31.

8. Ministry of Defense, Government of India, *Annual Report 1989–90* (New Delhi: Ministry of Defense, 1990), 17–18. See also "Command of the Seas," *Far Eastern Economic Review,* July 27, 1989, 16–17.

9. For an official view of Indian national security environment as seen by the Ministry of Defense, see Ministry of Defense, *Annual Report.*

10. Rajiv Gandhi visited China in December, 1989, apparently in pursuit of such a possibility. It does appear that it may be a while before the past irritants are forgotten. China and Pakistan are perceived as the combination that India may have to fight. See, for example, an interview with former chief of Army staff, General Sundarji, "I Had to Aim for the Moon," *India Today,* May 15, 1988, 83.

11. "Will Words Lead to War," *Far Eastern Economic Review,* April 26, 1990, 10–11.

12. "Gulf War: How It Will Hit Us," *Business India,* January 21–February 3, 1991, 62–72; "The Foreign Exchange Squeeze," *Business India,* April 1–14, 1991, 46–52.

13. Exchanges between opposition members in the Indian Parliament and the ruling Congress (I) government in June–July, 1991, indicate fears that the granting of an IMF loan may be linked with India signing the NPT. The linking of U.S. aid with good behavior is well known. There are many references in Western literature where such a linkage is suggested for proliferation control. For one recent example, see

"Wish Them Luck," *Economist,* July 6, 1991, 17–18. Also see editorial, "NPT and China," *Economic Times,* August 17, 1991, which refers to World Bank and IMF loans being linked to the NPT.

14. For an overview of the missile problem, see Janne E. Nolan and Albert D. Wheelon, "Third World Ballistic Missiles," *Scientific American,* August, 1990, 16–22, and "Breaking the Ballistic Missile Export Barrier," *Interavia Aerospace Review* 11 (1990): 994–97. For an Indian view on the Pakistani bomb effort and its linkages with the rest of the world, see Sreedhar, *Pakistan's Bomb, a Documentary Study* (New Delhi: ABC Publishing House, 1987). Also see Aaron Karp, "Space Technology in the Third World," *Space Policy,* May, 1986, 157–68.

15. There are reports of major arms exports by several countries to the Middle East. F. J. Khergamkvalla, "Arms Control in West Asia Turning into a Race," *The Hindu,* June 28, 1991.

16. For a detailed discussion on the evolution of Indian policy during the NPT discussions, see Ashok Kapur, *India's Nuclear Option: Atomic Diplomacy and Decision-Making* (New York: Praeger Publishers, 1976).

17. Ibid.

18. Pakistan has also expressed such a view. See Sreedhar, *Pakistan's Bomb,* 248–53. Other countries like Brazil and Argentina would also have similar views. Chinese policy is also driven by such an approach.

19. Kapur, *India's Nuclear Option,* 139.

20. Ibid.

21. Ibid., 166.

22. Pathak, *Nuclear Policy of India,* 194–98. A change in policy apparently took place when Desai was prime minister.

23. B. Chatterjee, *The Mind of Morarji Desai* (Bombay: Orient Longmans, 1969), 90–91, quoted in Kapur, *India's Nuclear Option,* 166.

24. See Pathak, *Nuclear Policy of India,* 161–64.

25. The Indian defense budget more than tripled since 1981 from 4,200 crores ($2.5 billion) to 13,200 crores in 1988 ($7.5 billion). The budget for 1990–91 was estimated at 16,350 crores. See "India's Modernization Program Worries Neighbors: Builds up Backlash," *Far Eastern Economic Review,* July 27, 1988, 18–19. Also see the text of the budget speech of the Indian finance minister, Manmohan Singh, in *The Hindu,* July 25, 1991, 6.

26. Rajiv Gandhi, "A World Free of Nuclear Weapons: An Action Plan," address to the Third Special Session on Disarmament of the UN General Assembly, June 9, 1988.

27. See "China: Major Supplier of Nuclear Technology to the Third World," *The Hindu,* July 2, 1991. Quoting a survey conducted by the *International Herald Tribune,* this article shows that Pakistan has been an important purchaser of Chinese weapons and nuclear technology. Chinese M-11 missiles are reported to have been sold to Pakistan. CSS-2 missiles with a 2,400-kilometer range have also apparently been sold to Saudi Arabia. Also see "China and North Korea Pass Arms to West Asia through Cyprus," *The Hindu,* July 4, 1991, quoting the *Washington Post* and Bush administration officials.

28. The role Western countries played in developing Iraq's missile capabilities is well known. For a typical connection, see "Iraqi Scuds Improved through Western Sales," *Space Business News,* February 4, 1991, 8–9. The role of German, U.S., British, and French firms is mentioned.

29. In a speech at the Administrative Staff College of India, A. P. J. Kalam, director, Defense Research and Development Laboratory, is reported to have said that the surface-to-surface missile, Prithvi, and the antitank missile, Trishul, will enter service in 1992 while Nag, an antitank missile, and Akash, an antiaircraft missile, will enter service in 1994.

30. The Indian prime minister, Shri Narasimha Rao, has clarified that there has been no pressure on India to sign the NPT because of the IMF loan. He said India's opposition to the NPT remains as firm as ever. Also see Rajamohan, "Non-Proliferation."

31. See former chief of Army staff, General K. Sundarji, "Myopic Strategy," *India Today,* September 30, 1990, 147. Also see C. Rajamohan, "India's Agenda for Arms Control," *The Hindu,* June 20, 1991.

32. The allocation of business rules lays down areas of responsibility of the different departments of the government. Government of India, "Allocation of Business Rules 1961," issued by the Cabinet Secretariat (1986).

33. See the feature article, "Defense Forces: Heading for a Crisis," *India Today,* February 28, 1989, 90–98, in which these aspects are analyzed in some detail. In an interview quoted in this chapter, K. C. Pant, former minister of defense, did not rule out the possibility of setting up a company to promote exports. A number of people interviewed indicated that India may not be very successful. Short-sighted views on arms exports by the armed forces and the bureaucracy with no review from outside have been cited as one of the problems.

34. Private industry receives very little money from Indian defense spending. See ibid. and Ministry of Defense, *Annual Report,* 28, where for a three-year period, total procurement from industry is reported to be about 2,088 crores or an average of 700 crores per year.

35. The V. P. Singh government indicated that a National Security Council would be established. However, before anything could happen, the government fell.

36. See Sundarji, "Myopic Strategy."

37. See Government of India, "Allocation of Business Rules 1961," 9–10.

38. Government of India, Ministry of Commerce, "Import and Export Policy," 1 and 2 (April–March, 1990).

39. See Government of India, "Allocation of Business Rules 1961," 66–67.

40. "Government of India, Atomic Energy Act 1962 and Some of the Rules under the Act and Notifications," publication of the Atomic Energy Regulatory Board.

41. See "China: Major Supplier of Nuclear Technology." Also see "Power Politics," *Far Eastern Economic Review,* March 8, 1990, 17, in which French plans for selling a nuclear power plant to Pakistan are revealed. Also see "Bending the Rules," *Far Eastern Economic Review,* May 16, 1991, in which Chinese exports of nuclear technology to several countries are cited.

42. The issues dealing with the Indian sale of a research reactor to Iran and U.S.

concerns with it have been extensively reported and commented on in the Indian press. See, for example C. Rajamohan, "Nuclear Fundamentalism Must Go," *The Hindu,* January 21, 1991. Also see Editorial, "A Matter of Principle," *The Hindu,* November 25, 1991.

43. See "Agni." Dr. Kalam, the architect of the Indian missile program, was also responsible for the first civilian launcher, SLV-3.

44. The technology and even the propellants used in the missile program are different from those acquired from France. The Viking engine acquired by ISRO from France will only be used in the civilian launcher PSLV (Polar Satellite Launch Vehicle). For an account of the international cooperation aspects of the Indian Space Program, see the Indian National Paper for the UNISPACE 82 Conference, UN Document "National Paper of India" UNA/CONF.101/NP/6, May 8, 1981.

45. See "Agni" and "Defense Forces," in which export possibilities are discussed. Also "Missile Launch Likely to Affect Defense Strategy: Testing Reactions," *Far Eastern Economic Review,* June 8, 1989, 38, in which export of Indian missiles is again discussed.

46. Official policy guidelines of the Ministry of Defense make it clear that missile exports can only be country to country. See Ministry of Defense, *Annual Report,* 40.

47. See Government of India, "Allocations of Business Rules 1961," 12.

48. See Ministry of Defense, *Annual Report,* 35–40, which lists products made by ordnance factories and their value.

49. See Government of India, "Allocations of Business Rules 1961," 13.

50. "The Trade in Major Conventional Weapons," *SIPRI Yearbook 1989* (New York: Oxford University Press, 1989), 228–29. India is ranked as the number one importer of arms. "Defense Forces," 96. *India Today,* quoting the U.S. State Department's Arms Control and Disarmament Agency, ranked India as number thirty-eight in arms export. Also see "Power Amid Poverty," *Far Eastern Economic Review,* June 7, 1990, 47–51. The problems in exporting from India are dealt with in some detail.

51. See "Pakistan's Defense Industry Competes to Win Orders: Off-the-Shelf Arsenals," *Far Eastern Economic Review,* November 15, 1990, 72–73. According to this article, Pakistan exports are reported to have exceeded $170 million, with peak exports in some years going up to $300 million.

52. "Asian Defense Industries Go Separate Ways: Breaking Ranks," *Far Eastern Economic Review,* August 30, 1990, 50–53.

53. There have been reports and statements about the nonavailability of even nonsensitive weather data from the INSAT satellites.

54. "Peripheral Vision," *India Today,* February 28, 1989, 96–97. Also see "Power Amid Poverty." A very small percentage of the defense budget is spent in Indian industry.

55. See the interview with Shri K. C. Pant, "These Are Difficult Times," *India Today,* February 28, 1989, 92–93. Also see "Agni," 28–32.

56. For some details of India's exports, see "Arms and the Man," *Indian Weekly Sunday,* August 25–31, 1989, 8–10. The problems related to the export of arms are detailed.

57. See Government of India, "Allocation of Business Rules 1961," 38–39.

58. Indian export of chemicals that are possible precursors to chemical weapons has been widely reported. See, for example, "Chemical Reaction," *Far Eastern Economic Review,* September 6, 1990, 10–11. The Indian firms involved are also reported to have had West Germany ties.

59. See, for example, "Germany and Iraq: A Blind Eye," *The Economist,* February 16, 1991, 84.

60. See "The Regulation of Hazardous Chemicals Act," Ministry of Environment and Forests, Department of Forests and Wild Life, "Manufacture, storage and import of hazardous chemical rules, 1989," published in *Gazette of India,* November 27, 1989, pt. 2, §.3(i).

61. See the latest statement of Indian industrial policy reported in all leading newspapers in India. For example, see *The Hindu,* July 25, 1991.

62. See Shri K. C. Pant, "Minimum Deterrence Mooted," *The Hindu,* June 25, 1991. Also see C. Rajamohan, "India's Agenda for Arms Control," *The Hindu,* June 20, 1991, and "Non-Proliferation: New Perceptions," *The Hindu,* July 18, 1991. Also "Myopic Strategy," which makes the same point.

63. "I Had to Aim for the Moon," 82–83.

64. See F. J. Khergamvalla, "OIC Secretary General Slams India," *The Hindu,* August 7, 1991, and F. J. Khergamvalla, "OIC Meet Takes Pro-Pakistan Stand," *The Hindu,* August 8, 1991.

65. See Khergamvalla, "Arms Control in West Asia."

66. K. K. Katyal, "Nuclear Talks: India to Study U.S. Suggestion," *The Hindu,* November 24, 1991.

67. McDonald, "Technically Friends."

Part 3
Conclusion

CHAPTER 13

Synthesis and Implications: Export Controls for the 1990s and Beyond

Richard T. Cupitt

From Containment to Counterproliferation

The focus of Western export control policies has moved from containment to counterproliferation. In the 1980s, the MTCR and the AG emerged to address proliferation concerns. In 1992, members of the NSG agreed to adopt controls on dual-use items. Finally, COCOM members not only agreed to a procedure that could lead to the eventual deproscription of the emerging democracies in Eastern Europe and the former Soviet Union, they even created the CCF and invited in many of the former targets of COCOM to discuss export control cooperation in the interests of counterproliferation.

Where are these dramatic changes leading? As Long and others in this volume suggest, the most important transformation taking place is the emergence of a new export control typology. As the Cold War, East-West pattern of international relations fades into memory, a new design is emerging. The new typology recognizes that some states have the potential to pose a threat to international peace through their capacity to acquire or produce conventional and nonconventional weapons of mass destruction and the associated delivery systems.

The changes in COCOM as an institution, as well as in the export control policies of France, Germany, and the United States, reflect this dissolution of the old typology. For example, COCOM members grant more favorable consideration to the exports to some of the emerging democracies of Eastern Europe and the former Soviet Union than to other proscribed states, such as the PRC, North Korea, and Vietnam.

The development of a new typology remains incomplete. However, how states associate with the existing multilateral export control arrangements is a criterion especially important for this project. This criterion follows the work of Bueno de Mesquita (1981), who argues that alliance patterns are a good measure of the congruence of foreign policy interests among states. In essence, the pattern of state membership in a set of alliances reveals how it and others view its preferences.

From the discussion of the multilateral export control arrangements, participants in all four export control arrangements hold at least three principles in common:

- The acquisition or development of military or dual-use items by certain proscribed end users poses a military threat against the interests of the participants.
- The export of military or dual-use items is an important source of national wealth, complementing the need to import such items, so technology transfer is a positive sum economic exchange among participants and nonparticipants.
- Multilateral coordination of export controls can be an effective means of managing strategic trade and technology transfer and restricting the acquisition of proscribed items by nonparticipants.

For governments to hold these beliefs in common implies a substantial amount of congruence on both national security and foreign economic policy. It follows that the patterns of interaction between governments and the four multilateral export control arrangements can help build a typology pertaining to the nascent post–cold war world order.

From the discussion of national perspectives, five groups of states form the basis for this typology: coordinating states, collaborating states, sensitive states, threatening states, and peripheral states. What characterizes each group of states and a preliminary classification of states into each group are considered in the following sections.

Coordinating States

One group of countries is working more closely than ever before on export control issues, including those that transcend traditional East-West concerns. Why do these states cooperate on export controls at all, and why are they working in greater harmony than in the past?

The Gulf War sparked the French government to increase its support for multilateral export control arrangements. Labbé acknowledges that the French government opposes the creation of a "COCOM-South" (any denial-based set of counterproliferation export controls focused on the Third World) and has left its leading bureaucratic post vacant. However, the French recently agreed to host the CCF, to become the point of contact (a "part-time secretariat") for MTCR activities, to accept controls on a full list of items in the AG, and to apply full-scope safeguards for nuclear-related exports.

In recent years, German export control efforts have become more strict as well. Often criticized by the United States as lax on the enforcement of its East-West export controls (the "démarche-mellow" syndrome), Germany raised the status of export controls on its political agenda after the Rapta affair and German involvement in Iraqi military programs. As a result, Germany created a new export licensing agency with higher status and with more resources to fulfill its mission. It increased the status of the responsible enforcement office as well.

Even the United States, which has historically been the leading advocate for strong, multilateral export controls, has stepped up its support of counterproliferation controls. As Long notes, the revelations concerning Iraqi chemical, missile, nuclear, and other weapons programs and the somewhat controversial role played by the United States government (and other Western powers) in supporting Saddam Hussein during the 1980s moved counterproliferation export controls further up on the political agenda. Coupled with the disintegration of the former Soviet Union and the WTO and the opportunity to encourage postcommunist governments to apply multilateral guidelines to their export control policies (and to limit the danger of uncontrolled weapons and dual-use technology transfers by those governments as their economies faced hard times), the United States tried to strengthen existing export control arrangements and sought to create new ones.

The impetus of the Single European Act has also driven the policies of all three countries toward ever greater harmonization. As yet, the EC Commission has only developed a framework to resolve the problem of export controls as the EC removes many of the remaining barriers to intra-EC economic activity ("European Export Controls Post 1992" 1992). Nonetheless, the implications are that France, Germany, and the other members of the EC will soon have a harmonized export control policy. The prospect of open borders within the EC was also instrumental in prompting U.S. efforts to increase the harmonization of national export control policies and to open license-free zones among the COCOM states.

The evolving export control policies of France, Germany, and the United States suggest that they be classified as export control *coordinators*, a group of countries that includes all COCOM members, plus Austria, Finland, Ireland, New Zealand, Sweden, and Switzerland.[1] These countries coordinate their export control policies through their participation in (or close concordance with) all four multilateral export control arrangements.

Though France, Germany, and the United States produce most, if not all, of the controlled items on the lists of the four multilateral arrangements, not all the other coordinators produce a wide range of these items. However, because these countries have (or soon will have) few, if any, restrictions on intragroup trade in dual-use items, they are all potential sources of these items. Moreover, most of these states transfer military items with other coordinating countries with few restrictions.

Their rationale for coordination is to make export control policy more effective in response to perceived military threats. These perceived concerns may include direct threats to territorial integrity (such as that once posed by the late Soviet Union) or to key economic and political interests (such as an Iraqi arms buildup). Major changes in the nature and level of a threat, such as the disintegration of the former Soviet Union or the invasion of Kuwait by Iraq, will alter the scope of these policies. Change in the general availability of controlled items to the source of the threat will, at times, affect the extent of controls as well.

Why do the coordinating states agree, in general, on which other states pose a military threat to their common interests? The coordinating states are integrated into the global economy, so behavior that threatens the functioning of the global economy will be seen as a common concern. While not sharing identical economic interests, the closure or collapse of any major market or source of supply would create immediate and widespread harm for each national economy.

These states are also united by their form of government. All these states are democracies, and democracies are much more likely to be threatened by nondemocratic states than by other democracies (Chan 1984; Maoz and Abdolali 1989). On this basis, it is not unreasonable to assume that policymakers in the coordinating states will jointly perceive many of the same nondemocratic states as threats.

From the discussion of all four multilateral arrangements, it also appears that the community of coordinating states are conditioned for policy change well in advance of precipitous, critical events. For example, the preexistence of export licensing systems for containment (the COCOM system) paved the way for the development of export licensing for counterproliferation controls (the NSG, the MTCR, and the AG). The formation of these controls mirrored COCOM classification schemes and licensing procedures in most instances.

While this situation exhibits the institutional determinants identified by Young (1986), Haas (1990), and others, another factor is at work. Each multilateral arrangement began with a set of controls that became less liberal over time. By and large, each came after a crisis or specific threat other than the one that stimulated the formation of the arrangement in the first place. In the case of COCOM, the Soviet threat to Europe may have prompted the formation of COCOM, but the invasion of South Korea turned COCOM members toward a full-scale embargo strategy. The explosion of an Indian nuclear device led to the formation of the NSG, but the revelations about the Iraqi nuclear program pushed NSG members to adopt controls on a broad range of dual-use items. Though Iraqi behavior during the Iran-Iraq conflict contributed to the formation of the MTCR and the AG, its invasion of Kuwait spurred the acceptance of more restrictive export control policies in both arrangements.

Collaborating States

The chapters by Cupitt, Gotchev, Park, Rudka, and Kirichenko describe a second group of countries that collaborate with the coordinating states in some, but not all, of the multilateral export control arrangements. Overall, this group includes the emerging democracies in Eastern Europe, the former Soviet Union, and certain states in Asia and the Pacific, including Singapore, Hong Kong, and South Korea. These states could export or reexport many controlled items but refrain from doing so. However, their export control policies fall short of restricting all the items controlled by the coordinating states.

Soon after the collapse of communism in Czechoslovakia and Poland (and other countries in Central and Eastern Europe not addressed in this volume), the new governments in each country were quick to commit themselves to developing a system of export control safeguards acceptable to COCOM members. They also sought to make the administrative and legal reforms necessary to produce national export control policies consistent with those of the coordinating states, including counterproliferation policies. Here too the harmonization of EC export control policy will have a profound impact, as these governments are most interested in membership in the EC.

Democracy took hold somewhat later in Bulgaria, and its efforts to transform its export control system have been impeded by domestic administrative, economic, and political pressures. Nonetheless, by 1993, Bulgaria was cooperating in the CCF, the AG, and the NSG and was prepared to participate in the MTCR, though it produces little in the way of relevant items.

As the Soviet Union imploded and the newly independent states emerged, the Russian government also committed itself to adopting export control policies similar to those of the coordinating states. It is much less clear how compatible these new Russian export controls will be with those of the coordinating states. For example, the Russian and U.S. interpretation of the MTCR guidelines clearly differed regarding the sale of Russian technology for long-range rockets to the ISRO in 1992–93.

The distinction among the former targets made by COCOM members is not simply an ideological division between communist and postcommunist states. For example, exports to the CSFR and Poland are accorded favorable consideration status, while exports to Russia remain subject to greater control. The distinction between Russia and the other two states stems from concern about the progress toward democracy and economic reform in Russia, the weakness of Russian administrative and legal structures for export controls, the production capacity of the Russian defense industry, and current Russian military capabilities.

As the chapters by Cupitt and Rudka indicate, the vast array of issues facing the CSFR and Poland alone, as well as specific domestic political pressures posed by declining industrial production (overlaid with ethnic differences in the CSFR, now separate republics), derailed rapid harmonization of their export control policies with those of the coordinating states. If anything, political and economic conditions are likely to magnify similar problems in Russia. This implies that many of the postcommunist states are unlikely to be fully integrated into the system of export control arrangements in the immediate future.

The South Korean government has indicated its interest in complying with COCOM guidelines and in joining counterproliferation efforts against North Korea. Both the ratification of the Memorandum of Understanding with the United States on export controls in 1989 and the findings of the fact-finding mission by the National Academy of Sciences (1991) suggest South Korea has at least some interest in developing their export control policies in accordance with those of the coordinating states. However, as Park points out, democratization and economic liberalization have made it more difficult for the South Korean government to control private sector activity. Like in Czechoslovakia, Poland, and Russia, more economic and political freedom in the Republic of Korea means that export controls may no longer be imposed by executive fiat. Instead, the governments of the collaborating states are at the beginning of the process of building a domestic consensus in support of export control policies of any kind. Further, the South Korean concern with proliferation and North Korea masks their relative unconcern regarding proliferation in any other region.

In the near term, access to more advanced technologies may be an insufficient inducement to the Czech and Slovak Republics, Poland, and Russia to become fully integrated with the policies of the coordinating states. These states may not be able to afford or absorb the highest levels of technology available at this time, though the symbolic value of becoming part of the community of coordinating states remains an important factor in building a policy consensus.

Nor is it clear that existing arrangements fully address the critical security issue facing the Republic of Korea—its relationship with North Korea. Unless multilateral arrangements by the coordinating states more explicitly and effectively hinder North Korean weapons programs, South Korea will find export controls more of a burden than a boon.

Sensitive States

A third group of states has the capacity to produce or acquire items currently under control by the coordinating states, and they have projects designed to do so. However, their defense policies and weapons or technology programs are not explicitly threatening to the economic or political interests of the coordinating states.

Of the cases in this book, Brazil and India are sensitive states. Unfortunately, if one includes every country that has, or even allegedly has, a project that concerns the coordinating states, the list of states in this category would be both long and unstable, reducing the utility of this typology.

One criterion that can further delineate the states in this group is that they must have economies wealthy enough (or with enough foreign assistance available) to acquire or develop military or dual-use items sufficient to threaten the interests of the coordinating states. Based on this criterion, one might limit this group to Argentina, Israel, Pakistan, Taiwan, Saudi Arabia, South Africa, Syria, and Vietnam, in addition to Brazil and India.

Generally, these states are emerging industrial powers, or states that can devote significant resources to the acquisition or development of controlled items. Nonetheless, their level of economic development remains significantly below that of the coordinating states.

These states may have the legal and administrative basis for an export control policy, as is the case in India. However, the governments of these states see limited military, economic, or political value in working within the current export control framework. While some of these states have indicated a willingness to abide by some multilateral controls, their commitment remains highly suspect. Typically, states in this group explicitly oppose the current multilateral export control framework.

As democracies, Brazil and India may not be typical of the group as a whole. Unlike the coordinating and collaborating states, this group includes a number of nondemocratic states.

Both the Brazilian and Indian governments express concern that the current multilateral export control arrangements suppress their national economic development and reduce their military security. From their perspectives, current export arrangements have the taint of exploitation by the coordinating states.

As Graham points out, the transition toward civilian rule in Brazil had a major impact on export control issues. The Collor administration sought to increase civilian control over foreign and defense policy in general, and the nuclear program in particular. The revelations concerning the involvement of General Piva in the Iraqi missile program also sparked greater interest in controlling Brazilian military and dual-use exports. However, since President Franco replaced Collor, little has been done to further the export control initiatives of the previous administration. Even though Brazil and its principal military rival, Argentina, have reconciled many of their differences, many powerful actors in Brazil continue to support the security and technology doctrine that impairs the relationship between Brazil and the coordinating states.

The role of India is even more problematic for the coordinating states. As Chandrashekar emphasizes, the emerging regional security and economic environment is likely to push India to increase investment in defense programs, perhaps even to develop nuclear weapons.[2] Indian officials also claim that India is a responsible exporter compared to the United States and other major arms exporters. This leads some Indians to conclude that one purpose of the multilateral export control arrangements is to keep India weak and dependent.

Threatening States

Like the sensitive states, these states explicitly oppose the existing multilateral export control framework. However, these states have also militarized their disputes in a fashion that jeopardizes key economic and political interests of the coordinating states. All these states are producing or acquiring controlled items, and some are exporting these items to projects or countries of concern to the coordinating states as well.

Some of the states are facing a partial embargo and other trade sanctions by the United Nations. Many of the coordinating states operate on the assumption that exports to any end user in these states will eventually enhance the productivity of an inappropriate end user. This group in 1993 included the PRC, Iran, Iraq, Libya, North Korea, and Serbia.

Some of these states may even make a commitment to abide by multilateral guidelines, but, as with the sensitive states, the governments of the coordinating states questioned their overall policies. For example, in November, 1991, officials of the PRC agreed that the PRC would follow the guidelines of the MTCR. However, reports that the PRC may have violated that agreement by transferring M-11 missiles or missile components to Pakistan delayed U.S. approval of the sale of the supercomputer to the PRC in December, 1992. In addition, the scale of arms and technology transfers now underway from Russia to the PRC raises questions not only about Russian behavior but also about the intentions of the PRC.

Peripheral States

These states are all those that neither participate in any multilateral arrangement nor explicitly oppose them. Nor do these states have active projects of concern to the coordinating states.

The bulk of these states have insufficient resources to mount a program designed to acquire or develop military or dual-use items in any significant fashion, if at all. Most of these states face little in the way of direct threats to their external military security, or they have the support of a major power, or both. Even if they did, few of these states have the resources to become a major figure in issues pertinent to export controls. However, given the fluidity of the global political, security, and economic environment in the 1990s, much of that is subject to change.

For example, relations between Algeria and the EC may deteriorate over EC immigration policy and other issues. Continued violence against North Africans living in the EC coupled with the emergence of an anti-Western fundamentalist government in Algiers may lead to a more active Algerian defense posture, including a nuclear weapons program and increased Algerian support for weapons programs in other fundamentalist states.

In Southeast Asia, an incipient regional arms race may soon drive Thailand, Indonesia, the Philippines, and similarly situated states to acquire or develop a panoply of modern weapons systems. The divergence of resources would constrain long-term regional economic development, and a regional military conflict could cut key global trade routes.

How and Why Do States Become Coordinators?

So far, no state has withdrawn its commitment to multilateral cooperation on export controls, once it participates in all the arrangements. At that stage, the dynamic forces seem to be irreversible. True, among the coordinating states tension about export control policies occasionally surfaces. This derives from the need for harmonization and the necessity of controlling new items or proscribing new destinations while liberalizing controls on other items or destinations as security and economic interests dictate. However, the states eventually reach at least a satisfying agreement, a compromise that meets the minimum needs of all states, if not the maximum needs of any individual state.

From our typology, there are other means of improving the effectiveness and efficiency of multilateral export controls. Clearly, turning the sensitive states and the threatening states into coordinators, or at least collaborators, would make a significant contribution to cooperation, also, ensuring that peripheral states may become more central to export control arrangements as coordinators or collaborators rather than as sensitive or threatening states. How can that be done? One guide is to see what distinguishes the coordinating states from the other states.

The most obvious attribute shared by the coordinating states is that all

are ruled by a democratic form of government. Moreover, even though some democracies are classified as collaborating, sensitive, or peripheral states, all the threatening states are nondemocratic. Further, the governments of Brazil, the former CSFR, Poland, and Russia all took steps to harmonize their export control policies more closely with the norms and rules of the multilateral export control arrangements soon after these states became democratic.

Why are democratic states not inclined to acquire or develop proscribed items in a fashion that threatens the coordinating states? One explanation is that democracies are unlikely to use force on one another to settle disputes. Consequently, even if a democratic country acquires proscribed items, it is unlikely to employ them in a fashion that threatens the coordinating states. More generally, Powell (1991) argues that governments are more likely to cooperate when the use of force is not an issue.

Moreover, two means of policy change identified in the case studies—debate and scandal—function more effectively in open societies generally and democracies specifically than in nondemocratic states. In the relatively open polities of the coordinating states, export control policy may be esoteric to many, but it is not impervious to debate in and out of government. In an open society, the domestic and foreign communities can express their satisfaction or discontent with policy. For example, the business communities of France, Germany, and the United States were active proponents of liberalizing COCOM controls even before the collapse of Soviet communism, and the governments in all three countries at least listen to business concerns.

In France, Germany, and the United States, revelations about exports to inappropriate or suspicious end users, each carrying the scent of scandal, provoked increased public commitment by each government toward stricter export controls. In three collaborating states—the postcommunist democracies of the former CSFR, Poland, and Russia—as well as in Brazil—a sensitive state also moving toward civilian democratic rule—scandal prompted at least some symbolic action toward greater cooperation with the coordinating states. In the democratic state most opposed to the current export control framework, it is useful to note that Chandrashekar points out that export control issues and national security policies are rarely subject to meaningful, open debate.

In contrast, nondemocratic states are more inclined to acquire or develop proscribed items for military end use. Classical theories on the relationship between war and nondemocratic governments offer a variety of explanations for this phenomenon, extensively explored elsewhere (Blainey 1973). More recently, Schweller (1992) has demonstrated that nondemocratic states, which may ignore public aversion to the high costs of modern war or can more easily obscure the costs of war, are more likely to respond to shifts in the balance of power by resorting to war. In similar circumstances, demo-

cratic states will focus more on accommodation or building a defensive alliance.

The literature on arms transfers offers another, not incompatible, explanation. In nondemocratic settings, the decision to acquire arms may be more reflective of a domestic political struggle than any determination of national interest (Kolodziej 1979). For example, Saddam Hussein used the military and security capabilities of Iraq against the Kurds and other opponents of his regime as well as external foes. In the PRC, modernizing the military, which requires the acquisition of dual-use items, was a means of keeping the military happy while it underwent substantial restructuring and reform.

Coordinating this sort of internal political-security consideration with multilateral concerns may be seen as an intrusion on national sovereignty and of less relevance to securing internal authority in nondemocratic systems. In more democratic systems, where coercion is a much less important factor in domestic politics, this sort of internal political-security incentive should not be as important (though there may be internal economic incentives for technology acquisition that affect domestic politics).

Unfortunately, creating a democratic security community is not an easy task. Do the coordinating states share other variables that are more amenable to manipulation?

Bureaucratic fragmentation does not appear to impede the development of multilateral cooperation on export controls. Though often a target of critics of U.S. policy, many other countries involve multiple agencies in the licensing process without undue difficulty. Indeed, the Germany case study shows the danger of isolating licensing decisions in a single office, when that is coupled with limited interest in export controls in the political community and little support from exporters.

Among the coordinating states, party identification also appears to have little direct impact on support for multilateral export controls, with the possible exception of Germany. Across states, parties of the left, center, and right appear to support some degree of export control on dual-use items.

In none of the cases did industry appear to dominate decision making on export controls. This does not mean that commercial interests were unimportant in the policy process. Where they have the most influence is in how policymakers balance commercial and military interests in their conception of national security. In the United States, the balance has traditionally favored military security. In other cases, Germany for example, the balance places greater weight on the value of exports to the economy. While multilateral agreement on the balance between military and economic interests is important, complete consensus is not a necessary condition for cooperation. It is much more important that both Germany and the United States, despite differences in their conceptions of security, agree on what is threatening.

Mutual agreement on the balance of military and economic security may make coordination easier. After all, it would allow policymakers to focus on the same set of stakes. Nonetheless, policymakers would still have to agree on the value of specific export control options, when there is substantial room for disagreement.

Other attributes shared by the coordinating states include their high level of economic development and economic interdependence. As Deutsch et al. (1957) argued in their classic work on the North Atlantic security community, strong and mutual economic growth, coupled with a high level of economic interaction, may be crucial to the emergence of a security community among states. Outside of the group of coordinating states, some states, such as South Korea or Taiwan, are experiencing rapid growth and increasing integration with the economies of the coordinating states. However, even if these states become more closely attuned to the export control policies of the coordinating states, the majority of collaborating, sensitive, threatening, and peripheral states do not share these conditions. These too are necessary but not sufficient conditions.

Indeed, *rapid* economic growth can reduce the likelihood of cooperation. For example, as some Middle Eastern governments became wealthy from oil revenue, they emerged from the peripheral category to become sensitive or even threatening states. Currently, the pace of economic growth of some states in Southeast Asia may portend substantially increased concerns regarding proliferation in that region.

If the coordinating states try to deny a wide range of dual-use items to sensitive or peripheral states, their efforts are likely to be counterproductive. Firms in the coordinating states would lose valuable economic opportunities. Such a policy would increase the market access of firms not subject to multilateral export controls. Nor does it seem likely that the potential level of threat posed by sensitive or peripheral states would create and sustain much domestic support for a denial strategy.

On the demand side, states subject to the controls are likely to view an effort to deny commercial technology as a threat to their national security. Firms based in the coordinating states would become likely targets for retaliation. In any case, the target states may obtain many of the items by stealth or import substitution or through foreign sources (though usually at greater cost).

Rather than denial, some coordinating states are emphasizing limits on the end use and end user of controlled items. For example, the COCOM-inspired technical safeguard agreements and safeguard systems permit exports for commercial end purposes while discouraging the export, reexport, or diversion of such items for military purposes. Also, U.S. and German export control policies now include provisions that make businesses and individuals liable if they knowingly export controlled items for an inappropriate end use or end user.

This approach may allay concerns that critical items will be denied the commercial sector (which might impede economic reform and undermine support for the emerging democratic governments) in collaborating, sensitive, or peripheral states. It also inhibits the enhancement of military capabilities of these or threatening states. This approach may help assuage fears that counterproliferation efforts will create a technological apartheid on a global scale.

Of related concern, the neoprotectionist sentiment emerging in the coordinating states may deny or severely limit access to markets or technologies to industries in many nations. If so, some peripheral, sensitive, or even collaborating states would be even less inclined to cooperate with the coordinating states on export controls. Without exports to pay for their imports and without the economic growth that exports stimulate, these states would have little economic incentive to cooperate.

Fostering economic security will not be sufficient either. As Graham, Chandrashekar, and Park clearly show, the acquisition of Western dual-use items is directly related to regional military objectives. While the coordinating states remained relatively neutral in most international conflicts in South America, technological advances by the regional rival of Brazil—Argentina—created a local security imperative not only for the acquisition of dual-use technologies by Brazil but for the capacity to produce those items.

Regional conflicts provided an even greater security imperative for the acquisition of a wide range of dual-use technologies and the capacity to produce those items by India. Unlike the simpler Brazilian case, India found itself in regional military disputes with a threatening state, the PRC, and with another sensitive state, Pakistan. The support rendered Pakistan by a key coordinating state, the United States, jumbled an already complex scenario, so that another threatening state, the Soviet Union, was perceived as an ally. While India developed substantial cooperation with the former Soviet Union, these regional alignments helped motivate India to develop an indigenous arms industry and technological base.

Although South Korea also has a powerful interest in becoming more technologically competitive and faces a dangerous regional opponent, its policies have been less openly divergent from Western interests. There are a number of reasons to explain this relative harmony with the coordinating states. First, the large Western military presence in the country helped to preserve South Korean sovereignty for many years. Second, South Korea is a relatively small nation with few natural resources, unlike Brazil and India. For most small states, antagonizing economic superpowers is not an option if they wish to promote sustained economic development. Finally, North

Korea, which began with more economic resources than the South and also received substantial assistance from the PRC and the former Soviet Union, serves as an object lesson to South Korea on the economic disadvantages of autarchy.

Until the basic determinants of cooperation (democracy, economic interdependence, and regional security) change in the sensitive and threatening states, getting them to participate in a meaningful way within the current framework may be more difficult than evincing strategic cooperation between antagonists like the United States and the former Soviet Union. Unlike the harmonizing of policies within one issue area, at which the existing multilateral arrangements excel, bringing the United States and the Soviet Union together on arms limitations and other issues required bargaining across many issue areas (George, Farley, and Dallin 1988).

Bargaining across arrangements is difficult. For example, it is hard to imagine what promises or threats can be made within the context of the NSG alone that would entice India to participate as a non–nuclear weapons state. Nor is it clear how military (and economic) incentives or disincentives external to an arrangement would be included in its decision-making process.

Managing or resolving regional military disputes is an important factor in building an export control community of states. However, ameliorating enduring ethnic or international rivalries, much like promoting democracy and creating economic interdependence, is often an elusive and frustrating objective. If the critical variables for cooperation are somewhat impervious to manipulation, what is likely to happen and what can be done?

The Incremental Scenario

An institutional approach argues that the most likely prospect is an incremental evolution scenario, in which the multilateral export control framework will remain much as it is today. Each arrangement will maintain a list of controlled dual-use items and proscribed countries. Decisions would reflect a consensus between coordinating states, with the gradual inclusion of the collaborating states.

Building on this framework, the coordinating states would strengthen their cooperative efforts internally. In turn, this would increase the cost of noncooperation to other states, by more effectively denying items crucial to competitiveness in the global economy and victory on the modern battlefield. Over time, more and more states would join the ranks of the coordinating countries.

The existing framework can adjust to the changing military, political, economic, and technological environment. For example, COCOM adapted to the electronic battlefield by adding items to its control list, while eliminating controls or making exceptions for the export of more outmoded items. As political and economic change has taken place in the PRC and in Eastern Europe, COCOM has modified its controls to encourage economic and political reform. By conserving the existing framework, international experience with export control systems would accumulate, which should make each arrangement more administratively effective.

However, our typology raises some questions about the applicability of this view to the future. Relations among coordinating states, though often moving in fits and starts, may follow this path. However, existing export control arrangements have held little appeal outside the West (and now the postcommunist states). To the extent that more and more emerging producers are non-Western, incremental change in the export control framework may not be sufficient to attract these states. This would make the arrangements decidedly less effective in the long run.

More important, the rate of weapons (and technology) proliferation may quickly exceed the pace of bringing these states into the export control arrangements. If so, threats to the security in many regions from weapons of mass destruction, including modern conventional arms, are likely to increase dramatically. The access to technology offered under the current arrangements may not suffice under these conditions of greater military insecurity.

As the productive capabilities of Brazil, the PRC, India, South Korea, and other states increase, the reactive nature of current export control arrangements, which most often form or evolve after a critical event illuminates a deficiency in export control policies, will become even more unsatisfactory. For example, the buildup of Iraqi military capabilities took place over a long period of time, with the consent of most coordinating states, since Iraq was seen as a regional counterweight to Iran. This support permitted the Iraqi acquisition of some potent technologies of mass destruction. Waiting to modify export controls after the fact proved to be an expensive lesson in the need for a broader understanding of the consequences of proliferation.

The Breakdown Scenarios

From a realistic perspective, cooperation will not continue for much longer. If the coordinating states come to see force as more of a factor in settling disputes with other states, then neither group of states is likely to engage in anything more than tactical, short term cooperation with those states. Essentially, that makes one question whether the existing export control arrangements can or need to attract collaborating, sensitive, or threatening states into the arrangements at all. If many of the noncoordinating states become suppliers of controlled items, the arrangements will not effectively delay or prevent proliferation.

The system may also break down if policymakers in the coordinating states begin to see technology transfer as a zero-sum game between the supplier and consumer. In this scenario coordinating export controls will be unnecessary. Instead, each state will jealously administer cross-border transfers of a host of technologies to preserve their comparative advantage.

As few in government express this belief at this time, this scenario seems unlikely. However, if the coordinating states begin to rely on neoprotectionist solutions to trade disputes rather than accommodation and compromise, then this belief may emerge as an important policy rationale. Particularly if the United States becomes more militant in its efforts to prevent the rise of a potential military rival, relations with emerging suppliers will be characterized by confrontation rather than compromise. Moreover, unilateral action by the United States will raise the costs of cooperation for other coordinating states, as well as raise questions about the possibility of metasanctions and threats of force among coordinating states.

A Global Approach

In contrast, from a more rational-functional view, a global export control approach will emerge in the 1990s. For example, a Ministry of International Trade and Industry official reportedly stated that the Japanese wanted to unite the NSG, the AG, and the MTCR into a single body similar to COCOM, and the Japanese would bear most of the costs (Koseki 1992). The discussion of such ideas is conditioned on the political environment for a single multilateral arrangement responsible for coordinating international efforts to monitor and control all transfers of dual-use items covered by the existing framework of multilateral arrangements, as well as a range of new items, including arms transfers. Proposals for centralized national export control policies may also precipitate this view. If this arrangement was formally attached to the Security Council, for example, it might acquire something of a supranational stature and allow member states to impose a broad array of sanctions and metasanctions to enforce decisions. Even without a supranational structure, a global organization has a number of advantages.

A global multilateral export control arrangement would be less redundant than the existing framework, cutting across institutional boundaries. This would also broaden the opportunities to create bargains between countries with divergent (if not contradictory) interests. This system would bring the primary producers together with principal nonproducing consumers, making it easier to integrate incentives to promote the demand for dual-use items for commercial purposes while decreasing demand for military end use into the decision-making process.

A broad arrangement should allow for a freer flow of dual-use technology worldwide, increasing global welfare, by improving the efficiency of export control policies, reducing the administrative costs of controls, and easing global access to a variety of advanced technologies.

Such a comprehensive arrangement seems improbable. Though it reduces the costs of redundant decision making, a less cohesive membership will raise decision-making costs. Decisions will have to balance relative benefits between countries to a much greater extent than happens now, to avoid some countries becoming discontented, long-term losers through their participation (Snidal 1991; Young 1986).

Even though coordinating and harmonizing common policies is detailed and time-consuming work, it does not match the difficulty of reaching acceptable bargains between countries with divergent or contradictory interests. For example, developing the SALT II agreement took years of extensive and intensive negotiation, with less than satisfactory results. Finally, some redundancy may be useful to control certain items more effectively.

The risk of failure is quite high, which makes this a less attractive, and less likely, scenario. One need only look to the generality of numerous UN security resolutions to realize that the specific, technical agreement necessary for a multilateral export control arrangement might well be impossible at the global level. Developing and maintaining technical agreements on a broad range of controlled items one might have in a comprehensive list would be very difficult, even without reaching agreement on the more problematic issue of identifying proscribed countries. Nor are states likely to share the necessary military, technological, and economic intelligence about each other's activities that a global rule-making and enforcement body may require. Finally, at a minimum, one probably would have to discard the rule of unanimity that governs current multilateral arrangements and move to some qualified majority decision-making process, which many states would find objectionable.

Attempting to create a global solution could divert attention from, or postpone the implementation of, desirable regional solutions. Certainly, the lack of global consensus during the Cold War diverted human and material resources away from issues of global economic development, which may be an important ingredient in the incidence and diffusion of militarized disputes throughout the world.

Not only is this approach more intrusive than others, it is more costly. A new level of bureaucracy, monitoring systems, an enforcement mechanism, and information sharing on a large scale all require substantial resources well beyond those now dedicated to export controls. More directly, resources to exploit opportunities to reduce demand for military items and dual-use technology in one region, such as Cambodia, may be immediately available, even when a comprehensive settlement may not.

Combining some features of the existing multilateral export control framework system with those of a more comprehensive system may be more likely. In this scenario, a global body, such as the Security Council, would identify and develop regional security and economic incentives for the nonproliferation (and penalties against the proliferation) of dual-use items and weapons of mass destruction. This body would involve, informally or formally, delegations from each functional multilateral arrangement (the AG, the NSG, and so forth) in its deliberations.

The global body could make suggestions for harmonizing and coordinating controls among the functional groups to reduce some redundancy. The global body could also be at the forefront of a worldwide campaign to monitor the production and spread of dual-use technologies, analogous to that proposed for registering arms transfers and arms production. The multilateral export control arrangements could develop interorganization working groups, at a national and multinational level, as a means of sharing information and coordinating national efforts. That would also encourage close contact within the domestic export control bureaucracies.

The distinction of this system is that the global body would bring together producers and consumers and consider a wide range of policy alternatives, while the functional multilateral arrangements would focus on creating agreement among the primary producers in their particular areas of institutional competence. Most importantly, export control policy would remain under national jurisdiction and direction.

This alternative has its own limitations. The global body could become another layer of ineffective bureaucracy. Without generating serious regional security initiatives and monitoring production, it will remain a reactive, enervating institution, creating more division than consensus. Nor can this alternative, like the others, guarantee that consensus can be reached by the producers in the multilateral arrangements. At the other end of the spectrum, excessive involvement by the global body in either regional security affairs or commercial activity could threaten national sovereignty and individual liberty.

Finally, if the global body has a formal legal stature, such as a UN body, it may be difficult to institutionalize its interaction with the informal multilateral arrangements. Previous efforts to formalize COCOM (in the mid-1980s) were not well received, and the NSG evolved, in part, because France would not sign the NPT. Formalization usually involves strict contractual duties and limitations that governments prefer to avoid under existing arrangements.

Conclusion

National and multilateral export controls will be of considerable consequence in the 1990s and beyond. The lessons of the Persian Gulf War and the collapse of communism indicate that enhancing multilateral cooperation on export control policies necessitates the creation of a new conceptual framework.

The collaborating states and other countries that adopt democratic structures must undertake the difficult task of creating the legal and administrative structures for export controls. To be effective, democratic governments must also create a fundamental consensus in the commercial community that export controls are legitimate. Years of simply denouncing export controls as misbegotten and illegal do not form the basis for a useful dialogue on what specific export control policies the new democracies should adopt.

Western academicians, business leaders, and government officials can contribute valuable information and experience to this dialogue and the building of an export control policy network in newly democratic states.

In addition, the new conceptual framework must make more direct links between export controls and more expansive issues of military, economic, and regional political security. For example, the coordinating states might require a public proliferation impact statement for each exception granted on dual-use export controls or when items are added or deleted to the control lists. Such a statement could focus on how that transfer increases or decreases the effectiveness of existing controls. Indeed, developing similar requirements for significant arms transfers, as well as a report on the overall pattern of arms and arms-related transfers at the national and international level, would help ensure that nonproliferation policies do not become victims of political and military expedience. Subject to public scrutiny, decisions to transfer dual-use or military goods and technologies should reflect a broader range of social interests and policies.

The coordinating states might also produce an economic impact statement of export control policies as well. Among other objectives, this statement could make a rough comparison of the economic costs of export controls possible. Sharing this sort of information should lead to the identification of more efficient control policies; it will likely foster more agreement on what is a fair contribution by each country.

The foundation of any enhanced multinational export control system will require national, international, and transnational dialogues to build consensus in the global community. Recent experimental evidence indicates that communication (jawboning) alone substantially increases the chance that decision makers will choose efficient and fair strategies of cooperation

(Ostrom, Walker, and Gardner 1992). Indeed, absent coercion or side payments, communication even proves more effective than sanctions in inducing efficient and fair cooperative behavior (Ostrom, Walker, and Gardner 1992). The implication is that maintaining a dialogue among the coordinating states and between those states and the collaborating and sensitive states will be more useful than applying sanctions against those states in building a global consensus on export control policies.

By including a wider issue network of policymakers, business leaders, and others in the national policy processes, a better understanding of the many interests in export controls becomes possible. In a number of other issue areas, nongovernmental organizations (NGOs) hold their meetings in conjunction with the major intergovernmental meetings. Nongovernmental conferences on export controls in conjunction with the CCF or other arrangements would permit a freer discussion of ideas and issues than one might find in the more constrained world of multilateral discussions between state representatives.

There is a danger of letting the multilateral export control system stagnate or of simply muddling into the next century without enhancing cooperation on export controls. Such scenarios portend a dramatic increase in the destructive capacity of many states. Under such conditions, defense policies designed to balance the military capacity of others will generate frequent, expensive arms races. The capacity for a state to militarize a conflict by threatening devastating blows will increase, and developing and maintaining this capacity will divert resources from more economically productive enterprises, reducing global welfare.

Which countries can take the lead in initiating the international and transnational dialogues? Which countries can assist in the creation of issue networks in countries where none exist now? The coordinating states have the material capabilities and experience to do so. Though these activities are costly, they are an investment in long-term security. Rich nations with limited military capabilities or interests, such as Japan, are in a position to make meaningful contributions to peace in this area, as a nonviolent approach to military security.

Still, the United States has been the dominant actor in the existing arrangements, a role it will likely continue to play. While the United States should engender export control dialogues worldwide, it must take care not to dictate, or appear to dictate, these dialogues. The coincidence of the collapse of communism and the consequences of the Persian Gulf War gives the United States an unprecedented opportunity to make multilateral export control arrangements more effective and efficient. This can be done by promoting sound and fair multilateral export control arrangements through a politics of inclusion rather than exclusion or unilateral action.

Mastanduno (1992) points out that U.S. efforts to persuade the Soviet Union to change its behavior by tactically changing export controls never had much impact on Soviet policy, in part because U.S. allies did not join in such actions. At the same time, efforts to promote trade, a "structural linkage" approach, might be more successful in building a more democratic, peaceful postcommunist world if the United States engages in more than rhetorical support for the concept (Mastanduno 1992, 317–18). To create this politics of inclusion requires greater awareness of the range of national perspectives and the linkages between export controls and broader issues of democracy, economic prosperity, and military security.

NOTES

1. Though New Zealand does not cooperate with the NSG, its antinuclear policies are even stricter than most of the other coordinating states.

2. Supposedly, the Hindu-nationalist Bharatiya Janata Party, which may unseat Congress as the governing party, supports India signing the NPT, but as a nuclear weapons state.

REFERENCES

Blainey, Geoffrey. 1973. *The Causes of War*. New York: Free Press.

Bueno de Mesquita, Bruce. 1981. *The War Trap*. New Haven: Yale University Press.

Chan, Steve. 1984. "Mirror, Mirror on the Wall . . . Are Freer Countries More Pacific?" *Journal of Conflict Resolution* 28, no. 4: 617–48.

Deutsch, K. W., S. A. Burrell, R. A. Kann, M. Lee, Jr., M. Lichtermann, R. E. Lindgren, F. L. Loewenheim, and R. W. Van Wagenen. 1957. *Political Community and the North Atlantic Area*. Princeton: Princeton University Press.

"European Export Controls Post 1992." 1992. *Export Control News* 6, no. 10 (October 31): 5.

George, Alexander L., Philip J. Farley, and Alexander Dallin. 1988. *U.S.-Soviet Security Cooperation: Achievements, Failures, Lessons*. New York: Oxford University Press.

Haas, Ernst B. 1990. *When Knowledge Is Power: Three Models of Change in International Organizations*. Berkeley: University of California Press.

Kolodziej, Edward A. 1979. "Arms Transfers and International Politics." In *Arms Transfers in the Modern World*, edited by Stephanie G. Neuman and Robert E. Harkavy, 3–26. New York: Praeger.

Koseki, Mari. 1992. "New Regulations Target Arms Trade: MITI Clampdown Comes As COCOM Clout Ebbs." *Japan Times Weekly International Edition* 32, no. 47 (November 23–29): 5.

Maoz, Zeev, and N. Abdolali. 1989. "Regime Types and International Conflict, 1816–1976." *Journal of Conflict Resolution* 33, no. 1: 3–35.

Mastanduno, Michael. 1992. *Economic Containment: COCOM and the Politics of East-West Trade*. Ithaca, N.Y.: Cornell University Press.

Midlarsky, Manus I., ed. 1989. *Handbook of War Studies*. Boston: Unwin Hyman.

National Academy of Sciences. 1991. *Finding Common Ground: U.S. Export Controls in a Changed Global Environment*. Washington, D.C.: National Academy Press.

Ostrom, Elinor, James Walker, and Roy Gardner. 1992. "Covenants with and without a Sword: Self-Governance is Possible." *American Political Science Review* 86, no. 2: 404–17.

Powell, Robert. 1991. "Absolute and Relative Gains in International Relations Theory." *American Political Science Review* 85, no. 4: 1303–20.

Schweller, Randall L. 1992. "Domestic Structure and Preventative War: Are Democracies More Pacific?" *World Politics* 44, no. 2 (January): 235–69.

Snidal, Duncan. 1991. "International Cooperation among Relative Gains Maximizers." *International Studies Quarterly* 35, no. 4: 387–402.

Young, Oran R. 1986. "International Regimes: Toward a New Theory of Institutions." *World Politics* 39, no. 1: 104–22.

Contributors

Gary K. Bertsch is Professor of Political Science and Co-Director of the Center for East-West Trade Policy at the University of Georgia. He is a specialist on export controls and U.S. and Western trade policy toward the CIS and Eastern Europe. His publications include *East-West Strategic Trade, COCOM and the Atlantic Alliance; National Security and Technology Transfer: The Strategic Dimensions of East-West Trade; Controlling East-West Trade and Technology Transfer; After the Revolutions: East-West Trade and Technology Transfer in the 1990s;* and *Export Controls in Transition.*

S. Chandrashekar is a scientist with the Launch Vehicle Programme Office of the Indian Space Research Organisation, and a visiting professor at the Indian Institute of Management. He is an expert on the developmental and disarmament issues related to space and space technology and was a member of the Indian delegation to the UN Committee on the Peaceful Uses of Outer Space between 1976 and 1988. His publications include a chapter in the United Nations Institute of Disarmament Research's *Peaceful and Non-Peaceful Uses of Outer Space;* an article on missile technology control and the Third World; and papers on Pakistan's missile program and India's export of space products and services.

Richard T. Cupitt is Assistant Director of the Center for East-West Trade Policy and Adjunct Professor of Political Science at the University of Georgia. He is the author and coauthor of numerous articles on export controls, trade, and other international issues, including the seminal article "East West Strategic Trade Controls: Crumbling Consensus?" (*Survey* 1980).

Steven J. Elliott-Gower is Director of Foundation Relations and Adjunct Professor of Political Science at the University of Georgia and former Assistant Director of the Center for East-West Trade Policy. He is the author and editor of numerous publications, including *The Impact of Governments on East-West Economic Relations* and *Export Controls in Transition.*

Atanas Gotchev is Associate Professor of International Relations at the University of National and World Economy and Executive Director of the National Academic Foundation in Sofia, Bulgaria. He is the author of numerous articles on East-West economic and technological relations.

Clifford P. Graham is a Major in the U.S. Army. At the time of writing the chapter in this volume, he was Assistant Professor of Geography and Environmental Engineering at West Point. Previous publications include "Technology and Third World Defense Manufacturing" (*Defense Analysis* 1990) and "The Brazilian Space Program" (*Space Policy* 1991).

Claus Hofhansel is Assistant Professor of Political Science at Rhode Island College. His publications in the area of export controls include "Explaining Foreign Economic Policy: A Comparison of U.S. and German Export Controls" (*Journal of Public Policy* 1990) and "Safeguards and Profits: Civilian Nuclear Exports, Neo-Marxism, and the Statist Approach" (*International Studies Quarterly* 1984, with John Kurt Jacobsen). He is currently completing a book manuscript entitled *The Political Economy of Export Controls*.

Elina Kirichenko is a Senior Researcher at the Institute of World Economy and International Relations at the Russian Academy of Sciences. She is a specialist in international economics, foreign trade policy, and export controls and has authored numerous books, monographs, and articles in these areas. Dr. Kirichenko advises the Russian government, foreign trade organizations, and industrial enterprises on export controls and related international trade issues.

Marie-Hélène Labbé is a Senior Research Fellow at the Ecole Polytechnique's Center for Research and Education on Strategy and Technology and Professor of International Relations at the Institute of Political Studies in Paris. She has written numerous articles on weapons proliferation and is currently conducting a two-year project on Western nonproliferation policies.

William J. Long is Associate Professor of International Affairs at the Georgia Institute of Technology. He is the author of *U.S. Export Control Policy: Executive Autonomy versus Congressional Reform* and numerous articles and book chapters on international trade and technology transfer. Prior to entering academia, Dr. Long practiced international law in Washington, D.C.

Han S. Park is Professor of Political Science at the University of Georgia. He is the author of *Human Needs and Political Development* and a wide range of publications on East Asian political, economic, and security affairs, including "NIC Perspectives" in *Export Controls in Transition.*

Andrzej Rudka is Senior Research Fellow at the Institute for East-West Studies in Warsaw. He is a former Research Fellow, Scientific Secretary, and Deputy Director of the Foreign Trade Research Institute in Warsaw, a Fulbright Scholar at Georgetown University's Department of Economics and George Washington University's Department of Economics and the Elliott School of International Affairs, and a Visiting Professor at the College of Saint Rose in Albany, New York. Dr. Rudka has written extensively (in Polish, English, and Russian) on East-West trade and technology transfer, export controls, and U.S.-Polish economic relations.

Index

Advanced materials, 38
Aircraft, 143, 180, 214, 226–28, 262, 279–81
Argentina, 43, 44, 51, 179, 196, 216, 222, 224, 234, 236, 238, 287, 291, 303, 309
  Condor II missile program, 44
Arms Export Control Act (AECA) of 1976, 61
Atomic Energy Act of 1954, 61, 70
Australia Group (AG), 33, 39–42, 79

Baker, James, 75, 119
Ballistic missiles, 44, 61, 218
Barros, Fernando Souza, 232
Bartholomew, Richard, 75, 278, 287
Battle Act. *See* Mutual Defense Assistance Control Act of 1951
Belarus, 75, 173, 176
Benichou, Marcel, 204
Bérégovoy, Pierre, 210
Biological weapons, 40, 60, 70, 78, 131, 156, 167, 180, 189, 210, 218, 265, 268
Biological Weapons Convention (BWC), 33, 91, 269, 272
Brandt, Willy, 183
Brazil, 19, 44, 185, 216, 221–46, 287, 291, 303–4, 306, 309, 311
  Aramar uranium enrichment facility, 227
  Army Technological Center (CETEX), 228
  AVIBRAS, 227
  Basic Science and Technology plans, 225
  Brazilian Physics Association (SBF), 231
  Brazilian War Material Company (IMBEL), 228, 230
  Center for Aerospace Technology (CTA), 227–28
  Companhia Vale do Rio Doce, 228
  Complete Brazilian Space mission, 227, 235
  EMBRAER, 226–28
  ENGESA, 227
  Institute of Energy and Nuclear Research (INPEN), 226
  Institute for Industrial Coordination and Cooperation (IFI), 228
  Institute for Space Activities (IAE), 227
  Institute for Space Research (INPE), 227
  National Security Doctrine, 222, 229
  National War College (ESG), 222–23
  Política National de Exportaçao de Material de Emprego Militar (National Export Policy for Military Goods), 229
  Piranha air-to-air missile, 235–36
  Research and Development Institute (IPD), 228–29
  Satellite development program, 225
  Secretariat for Strategic Affairs (SAE), 232–33, 238
  Society for the Advancement of Science (SPBC), 232
  Sonda III rocket, 235
Bulgaria, 36, 42, 51, 82, 130–60, 196, 301

Bulgaria (*continued*)
  Armtech, 144
  Bulgarian Socialist Party, 145–46
  Decision No. 107 of 1992, 153
  Economic reforms, 149
  Kintex, 143
  Kozloduyi nuclear reactor, 153
  Metalchim Holding Inc., 143
  Ministry of Defense, 150
  Ministry of Foreign Economic Relations, 139, 141–42, 150–51, 153
  Ministry of Health, 150
  Ministry of Industry and Trade, 150
  National Security Council, 153, 159
Bush administration, 76, 79
Bush, George, 63, 71–72, 78, 80

Candotti, Ennio, 232
Carter administration, 249, 255
Carlial, Aydamo, 225
Carneiro, Nelson, 232
Central and East European Investment and Enhancement Act of 1990, 106, 116
CHINCOM, 52
Chang Myon, 248
Chemical and biological weapons, 33, 60, 79, 156, 180, 210, 265, 268, 275
Chemical Weapons Convention (CWC), 33, 91
Chernobyl, 74
Chevènement, Jean Pierre, 208
Chiquet, Pierre, 215
Chun Doo-Hwan, 248, 250
COCOM. *See* Coordinating Committee for Multilateral Export Controls
COCOM Cooperation Forum (CCF), 4, 46, 52, 175, 177, 297–98, 301, 316
Collor de Mello, Fernando, 221, 231, 233–40, 242
Commerce Control List. *See* United States, Commerce Control List (CCL)
Commodity Control List. *See* United States, Commerce Control List (CCL)
Computers, 3, 38, 44, 46, 59, 70, 72–74, 77, 89, 107, 116, 201, 211–12, 226, 250
Conference on Disarmament, 61, 283
Conference on Security and Cooperation in Europe (CSCE), 194, 218
Control lists, 37, 40, 62, 92, 166, 173, 180, 315
Conventional Forces in Europe (CFE) Treaty, 96–97
Conventional weapons, 115, 212, 217–18, 266, 268–70, 272, 275–76, 280, 284, 297
Coordinating Committee for Multilateral Export Controls (COCOM), 3–5, 8, 11, 14, 15–17, 22, 25–26, 33–39, 46–50, 52–55, 59–60, 63–64, 67–69, 71–78, 80, 82, 87–95, 98, 100, 105–10, 113, 115–21, 139–40, 147, 149–50, 152–53, 156–58, 173, 180, 183, 185, 190, 193–94, 201–4, 206–7, 211–13, 215, 237, 247, 249–50, 255–56, 297–302, 306, 308, 310–12, 314
  Controls, 37, 202
  Functions and decision-making structure, 34–35
  High-level meeting (HLM), 35, 75, 116–17, 202, 212
  Science and Technology Export Meeting (STEM), 35
Council for Mutual Economic Assistance (CMEA), 130, 134–35, 137, 139–40, 142, 144, 147–48
Counter-proliferation, 297–302, 308–9
Cresson, Edith, 218
Czech and Slovak Federal Republic (CSFR), 16, 36, 84–99, 105–6, 110, 114, 116–19, 212, 301–2
  Atomic Commission, 92
  Customs Office, 90
  Czech Republic, 94, 302
  Decree, 174/1991, 91

Federal Ministry of Defense, 92
Federal Ministry of Foreign Affairs, 92
Federal Ministry of Foreign Trade, 90–93, 95
Interdepartmental Commission, 91–93
KOVAM, 91
Law, 545/1990, 90
Law, 547/1990, 90
Omnipol, 95–96
SEMTEX, 90
Slovak Republic, 93–94, 302
State Defense Council, 91–93
T-72 tanks, 96–99
VCHZ (East Bohemia Chemical Works) Synthesia-Sentin, 90
ZTS-Martin, 96
Czechoslovakia. *See* Czech and Slovak Federal Republic (CSFR)

Delivery systems, 45, 70, 167, 297
Democracy, 3–5, 14–16, 18–25, 27–29, 87, 97, 114, 132, 140, 193–94, 211–12, 221, 231, 233, 235, 238–39, 248–50, 256, 259, 301–2, 310
Deproscibe, deprosciption, 37, 90, 108, 297
Desai, Morarji, 267
Deterrence, 26
Dienstbier, Jiri, 96
Dimitrov, Philip, 142, 144
Diplomacy, 17, 247, 264, 269
Discriminatory nonproliferation regimes, 151, 184, 216, 262, 265–68, 271–72, 284, 288
Disincentives, 310
Diversion, 16, 46, 73, 76, 90, 92, 108, 115, 119, 142, 254, 248–59, 290, 308
Dlouhy, Vladimir, 97
Dual-use technology, 16, 24, 42, 44, 87–88, 90–93, 131, 140, 142, 144, 147, 149–51, 153, 155, 157, 159, 166–68, 170–73, 199, 201, 237–38, 290, 297–300, 303–5, 307–10

Eastern/Central Europe, 3, 4, 19, 34, 37, 46, 66, 68, 70, 72–73, 88–89, 106, 108, 114–15, 130–34, 136–40, 146–49, 158, 193, 237, 251, 254
Economic growth, 3, 5, 14
Economic warfare, 37, 60
Eighteen Nation Disarmament Committee, 267
Electrometal, 228
Elliot, Richard S., 106, 116
Embargoes, 35, 37–38, 59–60, 65–66, 69, 111, 139, 144, 167, 188, 194, 202, 206, 212, 236, 264–65, 268, 286, 300, 304
Enhanced Proliferation Control Act of 1990, 41
Exocet missiles, 4
Export Adminstration Act (EAA) of 1969, 59–60
Export Adminstration Act (EAA) of 1979, 65
Export Administration Regulations (EAR), 40, 166
Export Control Act of 1949, 59
Export control enforcement, 92
Export controls, 3–5, 7, 9, 11, 13–18, 20, 22–26, 34–35, 37, 39–41, 43, 50, 52, 59–69, 77–78, 87–89, 91, 93–95, 98–99, 103–7, 109–17, 121, 128, 130–31, 137, 138, 146, 148, 150, 151–53, 157–60, 163–64, 166–67, 171–75, 179–81, 183, 185, 187–88, 190–93, 195, 202–3, 207, 210–14, 216, 221, 247, 249, 251, 253–55, 257–58, 261–62, 264–65, 268, 274, 277, 280, 283, 285–86, 297–99, 301–2, 305–9, 311–13, 315–17
Extraterritorial controls, 49, 60

Fabius, Laurent, 208
Favorable consideration, 37–38, 90–91, 95, 107, 109–10, 118–19, 297, 301
Federal Republic of Germany (FRG). *See* Germany

Figueiredo, Joao, 230
Fillon, François, 207
Flores, Admiral Mano Cesar, 238–39
Foreign Assistance Act of 1961, 170
Foreign availability, 35, 63, 77–78
France, 34, 39–40, 42, 44–45, 51, 52, 77, 108–9, 115–16, 170, 184, 194–95, 200–19, 271, 279, 285, 293, 297, 299, 306, 314
  AEMG (Authorization to export war materials), 201
  Aérospatiale, 213–15
  Commission for the Export of Critical Products, 215
  Commission Interministérielle pour l'Etude des Exportations e Matériel de Guerre (CIEEMG), 201–3, 207
  Conseil de Politique Nucléare Extérieure (CPNE), 205
  Crotale missiles, 213
  Dassault, 215
  Federation of Electric and Electronic Industries, 215
  General Armament Delegation (DGA), 207, 213
  GIAT Industries, 215
  Leclerc tanks, 215
  Matra, 202, 213
  Ministry of Defense, 206–17
  Ministry of Foreign Affairs, 204–7, 216
  Mirage-2000 aircraft, 215
  Secretariat Général de la Defense National, 207
  Société Européene de Propulsion, 215
  Société Nationale de Poudres et Explosifs, 215
  Thomson CSF, 213, 215
Franco, Itamar, 237–38, 240, 304

Gaidar, Yegor, 172, 176
Ganev, Stoyan, 146
Gansel, Norbert, 190
General Agreement on Tariffs and Trade (GATT), 19
Germany, 34, 36, 39, 41–45, 51, 52, 68, 74, 77, 89, 115, 130, 145, 170, 179–200, 204, 226, 229, 254, 297, 299, 306–7
  Atomgesetz [Atomic Energy Act], 179–80
  Ausfuhrliste [export list], 180–81
  Aussenwirtschaftgesetz (AWG) [Foreign Trade Act], 179–80, 188
  Aussenwirtschaftsverordnung (AWV) [Foreign Trade Decree], 179–80
  BDI [German Industry Association], 190–92
  Bundesamt für Wirtschaft [Federal Economic Agency], 179, 181
  Bundesausfuhramt (BAA), 187
  Bundesnachrichtendienst, 186
  Bundessicherheitsrat, 186
  Bundestag, 181, 187–90, 192
  Christian Democratic Party, 188–89, 192–93
  DIHT [German Chamber of Commerce], 190, 192
  Foreign Office, 185
  Gesetz über die Kontrolle von Kriegswaffen [War Weapons Control Act], 179, 188
  IG Metall, 191
  Kontrolle bei der Ausfuhr (KOBRA), 179
  Kriegswaffenkontrollegesetz (KWKG), 180
  Ministry of Defense, 185
  Ministry of Economics, 186
  Ministry of Research and Technology, 185
  Social Democratic Party (SDP), 183–85, 188–90, 192–93
  Vermittlangsausschuss, 189
  Weimar Republic, 186
  Zollkriminalamt, 188
  Zollkriminalinstitut (ZKI), 187–88, 190–91

Giesel, Ernesto, 229
Global economy, 14, 16, 89, 98, 300, 310
Goldemberg, José, 234, 240
Goncalves, Odair Dias, 232
Goncz, Arpad, 251
Gorbachev, Mikhail, 68, 89, 139, 168–69, 251, 263, 271
Gulf War, 4, 5, 17, 39, 45, 76, 79, 94, 98, 134, 137, 144, 204, 207–8, 216, 231, 235, 263–64, 270–72, 286–87, 290, 298, 315–16

Han Bin Lee, 254
Havel, Vaclav, 87, 97
Heinz, Senator John, 106, 116
Herzog, Chaim, 96
Hollande, François, 208
Hong Kong, 34, 51, 301
Hussein, Saddam, 207, 235, 299, 307

Implosion system development equipment, 44
Import certificate/delivery verification (IC/DV) system, 108–9, 120, 156, 237
India, 41, 44, 46, 75, 77, 173, 196, 205, 261–96, 300, 303, 304, 309–11
  Agni missile, 278, 290, 293
  Akash missile, 278, 292
  Bharath Dynamics Ltd., 278
  Bharatiya Janata Party (BJP), 317
  Congress Party, 270–71
  Control of Production and Use of Atomic Energy Act of 1962, 276
  Defense Research and Development Laboratory (DRDL), 278
  Defense Research and Development Organization (DRDO), 278–81, 289
  Department of Atomic Energy (DAE), 275–77
  Department of Biotechnology, 275
  Department of Chemicals, 275
  Department of Commerce, 275–76, 283
  Department of Defense Production and Supplies, 278, 280
  Department of Space (DOS), 275, 278–79
  Export Control Order of 1988, 276, 283
  Export (Control) Order list, 275
  Home Ministry, 273
  India Rare Earths Ltd., 277
  Indian Space Research Organization (ISRO), 289, 293, 301
  Indo-U.S. relations, 263, 290
  Ministry of Commerce, 275
  Ministry of Defense, 275, 278–80, 282, 290
  Ministry of Environment, 284
  Ministry of External Affairs, 273
  Ministry of Industry, 275
  Ministry of Petroleum and Chemicals, 282
  National security, 263, 265, 273–74, 278, 280–82, 287–88
  Pokhran nuclear explosion, 261, 268, 289
  Prithvi missile, 278, 292
  Sino-Indian cooperation, 263
  Trishul missile, 278
Industrial List. *See* International List (IL)
Informatics, 226, 228, 239
Intelligence community, 62, 73
Interdependence, 14, 19, 130–32, 145, 148, 308, 310
International Atomic Energy Agency (IAEA), 8, 14, 33, 41–44, 49, 61–62, 111, 115, 156, 174, 205–6, 211, 216, 226, 231, 234, 278
International Government-Industry Conference against chemical weapons, 283
International List (IL), 3, 37–38, 107, 110, 121, 156, 159
International Munitions List (IML), 37
Iran, 39–41, 46, 146, 181, 196, 227, 264, 277–78, 292, 300, 304, 311

Iraq, 4, 17, 19, 39–41, 45–47, 77, 96, 98–99, 111, 115, 144, 179, 181, 190, 196, 204, 211, 212, 218, 227, 235–37, 264, 283, 285–86, 292, 299–300, 303–4, 307, 311
  Al-Taw' Han missile project, 236
  Scud missiles, 45, 292
Israel, 44–45, 51, 55, 77, 96, 196, 286, 303
  Jericho IIb missile, 44
Italy, 34, 39, 42, 45, 51, 52, 68, 195, 204

Japan, 34, 39, 41–42, 44–45, 47, 51, 52, 72, 107, 109, 116, 118, 143, 170, 188, 194, 252, 253, 256, 285, 312, 316
Joxe, Pierre, 208, 210

Kazakhstan, 75, 173, 176
Khizha, Georgi, 172
Klaus, Vaclav, 94
Kloske, Dennis, 105, 116–17
Kohl, Helmut, 189
Kostov, Ivan, 136, 141–42
Kraftwerk Union (KWU), 226

Lagardere, Jean-Luc, 202
Lambsdorff, Count, 192
Lamoreaux, Dominique, 215
Lepesqueur, General Romero, 228
Libya, 40–41, 179, 181, 186–87, 189–90, 192, 196, 235, 304
  Rabta affair, 179, 186–187, 189, 192
Lima, Octávio Moriera, 226
London Club, London Suppliers Group. *See* Nuclear Suppliers Group (NSG)

Machine tools, 73, 89, 107, 116
Marine technology, 38
Martre, Henri, 214
Material processing, 38, 202
Max Planck Society, 190
Meciar, Vladimir, 94–95
Menem, Carlos Saul, 234
Militarily Critical Technologies List (MCTL), 38, 62
Military-industrial complex, 46, 142–44, 147, 152, 159, 167, 170, 175, 213, 215, 274
Military security, 5, 14–15, 17–23, 25, 67, 96, 114–15, 193, 211–12, 221, 254, 303, 305, 307, 316–17
Missile Techology Control Regime (MTCR), 33, 44–48, 60–61, 75, 77, 88, 111, 153, 157, 159, 170, 175, 177, 185, 203–4, 207, 210, 217, 229, 231, 261, 268, 270, 278, 288–90, 297, 300–301, 304, 312
  Controls, 45
  Functions and decision-making processes, 45
  Origins, 45
Mitterand, François, 209–10, 216
Mosbacher, Robert, 105, 116–17
Multilateral export control arrangements (MXCAs), 15–19, 20–21, 23–24, 33, 88, 99, 297–99, 301, 303–4, 306, 314, 316
Mutual Defense Assistance Control Act of 1951 (Battle Act), 67

National discretion, 38, 110
National security, 20, 59, 63, 68, 70, 74, 81, 131, 137, 145–46, 152, 164, 298, 307–8
National Security Council (NSC), 62, 74, 81, 292
National security export controls, 14, 18, 59–60, 62–63, 68, 71, 77–78, 81–82
Navigation and avionics equipment, 38, 202
Neorealism, 5
North Atlantic Treaty Organization (NATO), 17, 34, 60, 143
North Korea, 36, 169, 249–51, 253–55, 257–60, 291, 297, 302, 304
Norway, 34, 39, 42, 45, 51

Nuclear Nonproliferation Treaty (NPT), 33, 41–43, 52, 156, 170, 176, 180, 183–84, 196, 203, 205–6, 210, 212, 217, 231, 240, 263–68, 271, 277–78, 285, 287–90, 292, 314, 317

Nuclear power, 74, 91, 153, 276, 292

Nuclear Exporters Committee. *See* Zangger Committee

Nuclear Referral List (NRL), 44, 156

Nuclear Suppliers Group (NSG), 33, 41–44, 46–49, 51, 52, 62, 75, 77, 79, 88, 91, 93, 153, 156, 168, 170, 173, 177, 186–84, 203, 205, 277, 297, 300–1, 310, 312, 314, 317
  - Controls, 43
  - Functions and decision-making processes, 42
  - The Bratislava Club, 42

Nuclear weapons, 61, 72, 76, 79, 171, 174
  - Free zones, 231
  - Proliferation of, 42, 62, 184, 205, 209, 234, 254, 257, 260–61, 265–72, 275, 278, 286–87, 291, 304–5, 317
  - States, 42, 44, 170, 172, 310

Olmer, Lionel, 106, 116

On-site inspections, 108–9, 125, 157

Pakistan, 44, 190, 196, 205, 216–64, 266–68, 271–72, 278–79, 281, 285–88, 290, 303–4, 309

Park Chung Hee, 248–50, 259

Partial Test Ban Treaty of 1963, 266

Paul, Rice, Rifkind, Wharton & Garrison, law firm of, 106, 116

People's Republic of China (PRC), 36, 51, 52, 91, 107, 232, 235, 297, 304, 307, 309, 310–11

Pires, Walter, 227

Piva, Brig. Gen. Hugo de Oliviera, 225, 235–37, 240

Plutonium, 276

Poland, 3–4, 16, 36, 42, 51, 73, 87, 90–91, 103–29, 135, 168, 202–3, 212, 301–2, 306
  - Central Board of Customs, 109, 122
  - Committee of Science, 106
  - Council of Ministers, 106–7, 113
  - Economic reforms, 112
  - Ministry of Finance, 106
  - Ministry of Foreign Affairs, 106
  - Ministry of Foreign Economic Relations, 106
  - Ministry of Home Trade and Services, 106
  - Ministry of Industry, 106
  - Ministry of Internal Affairs, 106
  - Ministry of National Defense, 106
  - Solidarity, 103
  - United States–Poland Agreement of 1990 on Mutual Assistance for Customs, 122–28
  - United States–Poland Safeguards System Agreement of 1990, 119–22

Pre-export notification, 38, 204

Propulsion systems, 38

Ramos, Pedro Paolo Leoni, 233

Rao, Narasimha, 271, 289, 292

Rational-functional theory, 6–7, 9

Reagan administration, 17, 35

Reagan, Ronald, 17, 194

Realism, 5

Reexport controls, 4, 16, 60, 67, 92–93, 107–8, 118, 120, 147, 150, 152, 154–57, 174–75, 231, 301, 308

Regional security arrangements, 218, 286–87

Renon, Gerard, 210

Rezek, José Francisco, 239

Rocard, Michel, 288

Roh Tae-Woo, 248, 250, 256

Rosa, Luiz Pinguelli, 232

Roth, Wolfgang, 190

Russia, 3–4, 15, 17–19, 21–22, 34, 36–37, 42, 44–45, 51, 66, 68, 70–76, 89, 91, 94, 98, 114–16, 119, 132–

Russia (*continued*)
35, 144–48, 152–58, 163–77, 181, 185, 191, 193, 206–7, 222, 249–51, 257, 261–63, 267, 271, 278–79, 285, 297, 299, 301–2, 304, 306
ANT Affair, 169
Communist Party of the Soviet Union (CPSU), 169
Council of Ministers, 163–65, 167–69
Export Licensing, 173
Glasnost, 89, 163
Glavkosmos, 75, 173
Gosatomnadzor, 174
Licensintorg, 164
Military Industrial Commission (VPK), 164
Ministry of Atomic Energy (Minatom), 174
Ministry of Economics and Forecasting, 164, 167
Ministry of Foreign Affairs, 75, 167, 172–73, 175
Ministry of Foreign Economic Relations, 165–67, 171–72, 174
Ministry of Foreign Trade, 164
National security, 167–70, 174–77
Office of Export Control (OEC), 164
Order No. 1005, 174
Party Control Commission, 169
Perestroika, 89, 169
Soviet Green Party, 176
Soyuzkhimexport, 167
State Committee for Science and Technology (GKNT), 165
State Foreign Economic Committee (GVK), 166
Strela rockets, 169
Successor states, 4, 36, 70, 76, 82, 163, 173
Union-Republic Monetary Commission, 166
Ryzhkov, Anatoli, 169

Safeguards. *See* Technology safeguards
Saldjiiski, Anton, 143
Sanctions, 4, 7, 45, 49–50, 78, 87, 90, 103, 189, 204, 258, 304, 312, 316
Sarney, José, 221, 226, 233
Scherbakov, Vladimir, 167
Security Council. *See* United Nations
Sementsov, Vladimir, 164
Sensors, 38
Shevarnadze, Eduard, 170
Sillard, Yves, 215
Singapore, 180, 196, 270, 279, 281, 301
South Africa, 190, 196, 205, 212, 230, 303
South Korea, 37, 180, 196, 240–60, 270, 300–302, 308, 311
Daewoo, 250, 259
Economic Planning Board, 255
Export control policy, 247, 249–51, 253, 255, 256–59
Export control regulations, 249
Foreign Ministry, 255
Goldstar, 259
Hyundai, 250, 259
Military industry, 255, 258
Military technologies, 247, 249–50, 253, 255, 258
Ministry of Commerce, 255
National Security, 247–49, 257, 259
"Northern diplomacy," 247, 253
Office of Science and Technology, 255
Samsung, 250, 259–60
Soviet Union. *See* Russia
Strategic Arms Limitation Talks (SALT), 313
Strategic Defense Initiative (SDI), 17, 139
Strategic embargo, 59, 139
Structural linkage, 317
Swiecicki, Marcin, 105, 107, 116–18, 121
Syngman Rhee, 248, 259

Taiwan, 196, 215–16, 260, 303, 308
Technology acquisition, 307

Technology safeguards, 4, 42–44, 61–62, 74, 76, 90, 92, 105, 107–14, 116–19, 121, 167, 172, 174, 184–85, 192, 203, 206, 209, 259, 272, 278, 298, 301
Technology transfer, 12–18, 20, 22–23, 25–26, 35, 46, 49, 62–63, 70, 72–75, 80–82, 88, 103, 114–15, 119, 131, 136, 139, 192, 194, 212, 255, 290, 298–99, 304, 312
Telecommunications, 3, 38, 70–71, 74, 89, 104, 107, 110, 116, 121, 135, 181, 185, 202, 211, 258
Terrorism, 60, 68, 170, 285
Testing of nuclear weapons, 44, 46, 176, 232–33, 235, 261, 267
Third Country Initiative, 50
Toshiba-Konigsberg diversion, 47
Toth, Julius, 95, 98
Transnuklear, 190
Treaty of Tlatelolco, 234
Trigger lists, 41–43, 93
Tserovski, Valentin, 144

Ukraine, 75, 115, 135, 173, 176
United Kingdom, 34, 39, 42, 44–45, 51, 52, 109, 170, 194–95
United Nations, 96, 153, 216–18, 234, 236, 239, 254, 304, 312
  Security Council, 96, 216–18, 239, 312, 314
United States, 14, 21, 22, 34, 39, 40–42, 44–45, 47, 51, 52, 59–63, 67–69, 71–82, 87–88, 96, 99, 105–10, 114, 116–19, 121–29, 139, 145, 150, 153, 170, 172, 179–81, 184–85, 187–89, 191, 193–95, 202, 208, 213, 215–16, 222, 224, 229, 235, 237, 248, 250–53, 255, 256–58, 261, 263, 267–68, 277, 279, 285, 287, 290, 297, 299, 302, 304, 306–7, 309–10, 312, 316–17
  501(k) procedures, 90
  Commerce Control List (CCL), 40, 59, 62
  Customs Service, 122–27
  Department of Commerce, 14, 40, 62, 67, 79, 81, 109–11, 118–19, 170
  Department of Defense, 11, 13, 61, 81, 241
  Department of Energy, 61
  Department of State, 34, 40, 44–45, 52, 61, 110, 119, 129, 241
  Economic security program, 34
  Export control enforcement, 92
  Export control policy, 8–9, 13–14, 18, 21–22, 25, 59–60, 62–67, 69, 71, 75
  Export licensing, 46, 61–63, 110, 119, 156, 300
  General Accounting Office (GAO), 41, 69
  International Traffic in Arms Regulations (ITAR), 40, 61
  Office of Strategic Trade and Technology, 81
  Subgroup on Nuclear Export Controls (SNEC), 61
  US West, 73
Uranium isotope separation equipment, 44, 76, 91, 226–27, 232, 234, 240, 276–77
Urengoi pipeline, 194

Vedrine, Hubert, 208, 213
Volsky, Anatoli, 175–76

Warsaw Pact. *See* Warsaw Treaty Organization (WTO)
Warsaw Treaty Organization (WTO), 60, 94, 98, 105, 116, 119, 130, 137, 144, 212
West Germany. *See* Germany
Wojcik, Andrzej, 106, 117

Yazov, Dmitri, 169
Yeltsin, Boris, 75, 171–73

Zangger Committee, 41, 43, 52, 53, 62, 93, 183
Zhelev, Zhelyu, 143